THE CASE FOR LEGALIZING DRUGS

THE CASE FOR LEGALIZING DRUGS

RICHARD LAWRENCE MILLER

PRAEGER

New York
Westport, Connecticut
London

Library of Congress Cataloging-in-Publication Data

Miller, Richard Lawrence.
    The case for legalizing drugs / Richard Lawrence Miller.
        p.   cm.
    Includes bibliographical references.
    Includes index.
    ISBN 0-275-93459-4
    1. Narcotics, Control of—United States. 2. Drug abuse.
3. Narcotic law—United States. 4. Decriminalization—United
States.   I. Title.
    HV5825.M56   1991
    363.4'5'0973—dc20   90-7379

British Library Cataloguing-in-Publication Data is available.

Library of Congress Catalog Card Number: 90-7379
ISBN: 0-275-93459-4

First published in 1991

Praeger Publishers, One Madison Avenue, New York, NY 10010
An imprint of Greenwood Publishing Group, Inc.

Printed in the United States of America

The paper used in this book complies with the
Permanent Paper Standard issued by the National
Information Standards Organization (Z39.48-1984).

10 9 8 7 6 5 4 3 2 1

When change is offered freely and rationally, it is not permissiveness or defeat of authority but the fulfillment of the highest function of that authority: the common good.

Norman E. Zinberg and John A. Robertson
Drugs and the Public

Contents

Preface

The drug war has consumed so much paper and ink that I hesitate to deplete those resources further. Yet, as a citizen, I cannot idly watch madness gnaw at the soul of my country. From my home in Kansas City, Missouri, I wield no influence in corridors of national power. But at least I can offer facts relevant to public policy debate.

From time to time I get involved in politics. Indeed, this book evolved from a conversation I had with a state legislator. My father was a county patronage man, and I grew up in that world. I see political angles in most public controversies, and the drug war is no exception. Its strategy and tactics are decided by politicians—not by scientists or physicians. That is only appropriate. The core of the drug problem is not a question of chemistry, but a question of values. In that latter realm we all have equal authority. We should ponder reports from pharmacologists and sociologists, but we citizens must decide what to do with that information and then give direction to our agents in government—the politicians—so that their decisions may implement ours.

This book is grounded in reality. I examined classic reports on drug abuse as well as obscure ones. I have read analyses in which experts attack one another with sword and broadax, chopping away errors until the remaining truth is sometimes surprising. In addition, my firsthand experience in politics helps me see pressures faced by politicians, and I have kept those factors in mind. I like to think, also, that I am sensitive to problems faced by law enforcement officers. My father once pursued that line of work. He was threatened by gunmen and beaten by assailants. I know what our police go through. Finally, I have seen what drugs are doing to individuals and to my neighborhood. I have known someone who enjoyed an occasional marijuana cigarette and someone who claimed to have taken LSD hundreds of times. I have known people who used illicit drugs with impunity and others whose careers were probably ruined by arrest and conviction records.

Most of all, I know the great fear. I am a block watch co-captain. I hear what my neighbors say—old folks who see a familiar world disappearing and young parents filled with unease about their children. In two years burglars struck about half the houses on my block. People in the house behind mine were held at gunpoint while robbers helped themselves. A woman across the street installed bars on her home. Kansas City police say most residential burglaries are drug-related. At night the dope fiends roam freely while the law-abiding residents of my block are locked away behind bars.

Something is crazy here. Still, we muddle along as a society thinking about drugs in ways that make our current war against drugs look perfectly sane. There is much hysteria about drugs and drug use in this country and much misinformation. It is time we got rid of both, put drugs and drug abuse in their proper perspective and got on with our lives.

To do that, citizens first need relevant information. Rather little factual data filters through the enormous news media coverage about drugs. This book will present facts long known to researchers but ignored by newscasters and politicians. To ignore relevant facts is to ignore reality. A drug war that disregards reality is likely to produce disaster. Yet drug war strategists call for more of the actions that failed in the past. This book proposes a different strategy.

The first chapter will explain what highly touted illicit drugs really do to users. Like too many other products, drugs fail to live up to their advertising. They are neither as pleasurable nor as powerful nor as perilous as drug warriors would have citizens believe.

The second chapter will address a crucial question that gets little attention, the question of what drug users do to themselves. Much degradation blamed on drugs has little to do with chemicals but instead results from deliberate choices made by self-destructive persons. This chapter will also examine the nature of addiction and argue that it is a psychological process rather than a physical one. The dismal record of treatment programs will be analyzed, and the little known but remarkably successful alternative of self-cure will be discussed. This chapter will argue that drug laws are irrelevant to the behavior of most addicts.

The third chapter will be directed to a topic that receives much attention, what drug users do to other persons. Many citizens have little concern about a drug user's fate. They are more concerned about what a drug-crazed character might do to a citizen's home or skull. This chapter will present scientific findings about the relation of drugs to crime. What scientists have proven is different from what almost everyone else believes. Those findings explain why so many law enforcement efforts fail and suggest that certain changes in public policy would have an enormous impact on crime. Yet those scientific findings and their implications are ignored in drug war debate.

Those opening chapters establish a factual basis for a new strategy designed to reduce drug problems. The fourth chapter tells how the current unsuccessful strategy was devised. Few citizens know that story, and it is important because the origins of current strategy had nothing to do with drug control. Early laws restricted drugs in order to accomplish other social goals, goals that were achieved. Because drug control was not the purpose of the restrictive laws, it is unsurprising that drug use has thrived despite them. Tightening those laws in order to diminish drug use is futile.

The fifth chapter explores the myth of drug abuse. In this context the term "myth" is used in a technical sense relating to emotional forces that drive public policy. This chapter will argue that the drug war is not aimed at drugs, but instead seeks to destroy a different target. The chapter will argue that the target should be preserved rather than destroyed.

The final chapter tells about the experience of drug legalization. We do not have to guess the consequences of legalization. We know them already. We know them because researchers have studied what happens in jursidictions that legalize assorted substances. That knowledge is presented in the final chapter.

It is easy to generate fear about drugs, alarm over users, hatred against dealers. Politicians do that all the time. If the topic were race, the demagoguery of drug war rhetoric would be obvious. Yet despite our leaders' record of inaccuracy on many other subjects, drug war rhetoric is generally accepted without question.

The need in drug-policy debate is just the opposite of what most politicians offer. I disapprove of the conduct of many drug users and dealers, but I feel no need to agitate against them. Hate and fear thrive without my help. It is easy to injure individual citizens and even a whole nation. Healing is harder and takes longer, but that is the task this book seeks to promote. This book explains why I became convinced that legalizing illicit drugs would eliminate most problems associated with them.

THE CASE FOR LEGALIZING DRUGS

1 What Drugs Do to Users

A classic study of drug abuse provided a credo for the present book: "Plausibility is not a satisfying substitute for evidence."[1] Common sense can muddle us through many challenges, but when stuck in a bad situation we should examine assumptions that mired us, no matter how reasonable they seem.

We assume drugs are an enemy that will destroy us, unless we destroy them. Yet even though Americans have declared war on drugs, few citizens know much about the enemy. Attacking an opponent whose capabilities are unknown or misjudged is imprudent. Let us therefore compile an intelligence report.

We consider drugs a monolithic entity. Most citizens make little distinction among heroin, cocaine, marijuana, or LSD; neither does the law. To deal effectively with drugs, however, we must respect their differences. If we attacked "disease" in the way we fight drugs, we would make little distinction among colds, cancer, broken bones, and heart attacks. All would receive the same therapy, differing only in the vigor with which it was applied. Growing numbers of citizens would be crippled or killed. Fear would stalk the land.

Let us avoid that mistake. Let us consider the characteristics of specific drugs. Although this book lacks enough pages to discuss all drugs or even all aspects of the chosen few, four notorious substances can suffice for our purposes.

HEROIN

Heroin is the devil drug, synonymous with addiction and crime. Reporters, movie makers, police, and politicians have shaped the public view of heroin as powerful, a swiftly addictive drug that delivers great pleasure, but at a cost of horrendous physical agony if addicts attempt to stop taking it. That picture, however, is contradicted by medical and sociological investigations.

Heroin is an opiate. Opium poppies produce sap that can be harvested, processed into opium, further refined into morphine, and then converted to heroin. Each step yields a more concentrated opiate. The form makes little difference to the human body. Body chemistry quickly converts heroin back into morphine. Tests confirm that users detect no difference between doses of morphine or heroin.[2] Black market heroin is more common than morphine only because it is more concentrated and therefore easier to smuggle. Its market dominance is a preference of illicit suppliers, not users. All opiates, whether natural products from poppy plants or synthetic opioids from the laboratory, can be substituted for one another. Although their actions do not duplicate one another in every detail, typical opiate effects exist and have been observed repeatedly for years.

If a person injects heroin intravenously, brain tissue begins absorbing the drug 10 to 20 seconds later. Sometimes, but not always, this can produce a euphoria nicknamed the "rush," which lasts 1 or 2 minutes and is described as a bodywide sexual orgasm. Whether or not a rush occurs, a "high" lasting perhaps 4 or 5 hours is likely. The high is total satiation. To a person in a heroin high, nothing matters. Food, sex, jobs, friends, pain, frustrations, and everything else no longer require attention. The high is not a particular sensation but an absence of sensation. Heroin intoxication blots out the world. "That it should be thought of as a 'high' stands as mute testimony to the utter destitution of the life of the addict."[3] Opiates have less appeal than many anti-drug zealots claim. Experimenters who give heroin and morphine injections to subjects report that hardly anyone finds the effects desirable; almost everyone expresses indifference or dislike.[4] The high eases away, and after 6 or 7 hours the intoxication ends, often leaving a residual mental peacefulness.

These typical effects are not inevitable and depend on several factors. One is the heroin's purity. Laboratory tests confirm that consumer supplies of illicit drugs are adulterated.[5] Some impurity is due to poor quality control, but most is probably fraud—in which dealers misbrand a cheap substitute and sell it as the high-priced real thing. Such vitiation means that a heroin user may not receive a strong enough dose to produce the desired effects, or they may be produced by an adulterant. For instance, dealers often mix quinine with heroin, and quinine can produce a rush.[6] The method of administration also shapes effects. Heroin can be sniffed, eaten, smoked, or injected (intravenously, intramuscularly, or subcutaneously). Only intravenous injection, however, is likely to create a rush.

Set and setting are two more factors crucial to a drug's effects. "Set" is a user's general personality and specific expectations about a drug. "Setting" is a person's surroundings, what other people or even background music do to the user. Set and setting guide the direction of a drug experience and can even overcome normal properties of powerful drugs.[7] An experiment demonstrated the guidance.[8] Some subjects who received an epinephrine (adrenalin) injection were told to expect arousal, some were told nothing, and others were misinformed about what to expect. They were then placed in the company of stooges who supposedly had also received injections, and who pretended to be affected in a particular way. Experimental subjects who lacked knowledge about what to expect from the injection imitated the behavior of the stooges, as did subjects who were misinformed. Subjects who had accurate information did not mimic the stooges. Drug users who feel a change in themselves, but who do not understand the reason for change, pick up cues from other users and imitate them. The role of such guidance can be inferred from admission statistics to the Massachusetts Mental Health Center and New York City's Bellevue Hospital. In the latter 6 months of 1967 about 10 percent of patients suffered from bad experiences with psychedelic drugs. In the latter 6 months of 1969 only 3 such patients arrived. Similar trends were noticed by medical personnel at rock music concerts from 1973 to 1977. Researchers doubt that the number of bad psychedelic experiences had declined, but instead believe that users and their friends had achieved a better understanding of what psychedelic drugs do. The new knowledge provided a new set and setting, reducing the power of unpleasant effects; afflicted persons had enough internal strength and external support from friends to be undaunted.[9] Set and setting can even produce effects that conflict with pharmacological actions. After receiving a narcotic antagonist that chemically blocks effects of heroin, a person who then takes heroin can still have autonomic responses associated with the opiate[10]—responses not under voluntary control by most people. Moreover, persons can feel opiate euphoria despite a narcotic antagonist's blockage of pharmacological effect.[11] Experiments produce similar findings for cocaine—"cocaine actions" occurring upon presentation of environmental cues rather than upon presentation of the drug.[12] Set and setting can do more, however, than just affect drug users' interpretation of what is happening. Barbiturates and opiates can be transformed from sedatives to stimulants, cocaine or an amphetamine from a stimulant to a sedative.[13] Similar changes and flip-flops can occur with drugs unassociated with illicit abuse, such as atropine and digitalis.[14]

Effects of heroin and other drugs are predictable. So is the weather. We may have expectations based on probability, but cannot have certainties based on inevitability. Even machines sometimes fail to do what is anticipated, and people are not machines. Drugs do not always do the same things to the same individuals, let alone to different persons. A drug policy based on a contrary assumption will fail.

If someone uses heroin a lot, several times a day for weeks or months, "tolerance" builds up. Higher doses are needed to produce the same level of effects. Tolerance is an oft-cited peril of illicit drugs but happens with many legal substances and causes no alarm about them. With alcohol the process is called "learning to hold your liquor," and is considered admirable. Tolerance, however, does not increase without limit. A heroin user who develops tolerance does not keep raising the dose infinitely; generally a plateau is reached at which the user feels satisfied.[15] Consequently a user does not keep buying larger and larger amounts. The idea that dealers profit from a heroin user's need for limitless quantities is wrong. A user wants a reliable supply, not an infinite one.

Probably the most feared effect of heroin usage is addiction. People view addiction as a consequence of heroin use, a situation in which the addict will do anything to get the drug, a condition that can be broken only by undergoing terrible symptoms of heroin withdrawal. Addiction is viewed as generally permanent, leading to devastating medical problems and to a life of crime and personal degradation. This summary is widely believed but contradicted by scientific research.

If a person takes a lot of heroin frequently and for a long time, the drug may engage in a "physical resonance" with the user's body. In such a development, continued use of heroin is necessary to maintain the body's physical stability, otherwise the user feels sick. Resonance is often called "physical dependence," but that latter term is wrong—and inaccurate terms can mislead our thinking. A diabetic is physically dependent on insulin. Without it, the person gets sicker and sicker. Heroin users do not become physically dependent on their drug. Without it they get sick but soon get better and recover. Heroin users never have an organic need for the substance;[16] that is why some drug abuse treatments can seek abstinence, because heroin users have no physical need for the drug.

To reach a state of resonance, users must work at it hard, for a long time. One obstacle they must overcome is heroin's side effects. After taking an intoxicating dose of heroin the user typically gets nauseated and often vomits. Some heroin users claim to enjoy a queasy stomach. "Yes, it's very warm, good. . . . My stomach would tighten and I would get that warm feeling coming up my esophagus." Another user agreed: "I get a nauseated thing, you know. The nauseating thing is actually, in the subculture, interpreted as being a desirable thing to feel."[17] Learning the joy of nausea takes fortitude. A person unwilling to throw up several times a day will not take enough heroin to create a physical resonance, and will avoid altering the body's stability.

How much heroin would be enough to cause resonance? A classic study of New York City users concluded that resonance cannot develop if someone takes the drug less than once a day.[18] In scientific experiments using 100 percent pure unadulterated heroin, human subjects do not lose physical stability until they have received the drug 3 times a day for 2 weeks.[19] For 15 weeks one subject received higher doses than most addicts get, up to 200 mg daily of pure heroin, and showed no withdrawal symptoms when the drug was cut off.[20] A month may be necessary to establish resonance on pure morphine when given 4 times a day.[21] Those findings mean that resonance can be detected via clinical measurements, not that a user would feel distress if the drug were cut off. People can take injections of pure morphine 1 or 2 times a day for years without developing "appreciable" resonance.[22] People taking injections 4 times a day can stop "without discomfort."[23] Analysis of illicit heroin typically finds it so diluted that the body's physical stability could never be altered; such a consequence is pharmacologically impossible.[24] Such a consequence can occur only if a user of illicit heroin is resourceful enough to find a supply of superior quality and reckless enough to abuse it in the way that alcoholics abuse liquor.[25]

If those two conditions are met, a heroin user will achieve resonance and experience the "withdrawal syndrome" if heroin usage stops. The syndrome is only understood incompletely, but part of the explanation is a rebound effect.[26] For example, heroin promotes constipation and has been used medically to treat loose bowels. A heroin user's body may adjust for the constipating action, resonating with the heroin in an effort to keep bowel movements normal. If the drug then suddenly disappears, compensating efforts still continue awhile and temporary diarrhea may result until body chemistry rebounds to normal.

Heroin and all other opiates have the same withdrawal syndrome. Typical symptoms include sneezing, runny nose, hot and cold flashes, nausea, and diarrhea. Opiate withdrawal symptoms mimic influenza. As with other drug effects, however, set and setting can be all important.[27] Andrew Weil writes, "In a supportive setting, with proper suggestion, a heroin addict can withdraw without medication other than aspirin and have little more discomfort than that of a moderate cold. I saw this in San Francisco in 1968 in men with expensive daily habits."[28] The experience is unpleasant but involves no screaming agonies and requires no medical supervision. One person kept a diary: "Now it's 16 hours since the last injection. Withdrawal symptoms are not bad, merely noticeable. The ever-present feeling of weariness just that much worse. A headache, yawning, shiverings and cold feelings, a nose that feels like a common cold, yawning again, hands a little shaky and poor in grip."[29] A married couple addicted to heroin decided to stop. They were staying with relatives from whom they had hidden their addiction, and explained they had caught influenza.[30] Such a charade is not unusual.[31] People can withdraw from heroin in the privacy of their homes on a weekend. They decide heroin is troublesome, go home on Friday and emerge on Monday, cured and feeling fine. This actually happens.[32] Few alcoholics or two-pack-a-day cigarette smokers could duplicate the feat. Breaking a heroin resonance is not only easy but safe. Withdrawal might cause serious problems if a user had an organic problem such as heart disease, but untoward consequences seldom occur. In 1916, a study found no deaths among 12,000 opiate habitués who withdrew in prison over a 12-year period of observation.[33] The unhealthy lifestyle of most convicted criminal users, combined with prison conditions of that era, rigorously tested the safety of opiate withdrawal. (In contrast, withdrawal from substances such as alcohol or barbiturates can be fatal, regardless of medical assistance.)

Physical resonance is different from heroin addiction. Resonance is only one part of the latter condition. Addiction will be discussed in detail later, but for now we can say that ending addiction is much harder than ending resonance. The ease of withdrawing from resonance is important, however, because some people believe that heroin users take the drug and accept a life of crime and debasement simply to avoid the withdrawal syndrome. People who continually use heroin will want to avoid the syndrome, but no one is likely to run the risks of illicit use simply to avoid a few days with a drippy nose and a touch of the runs. Addicts take heroin for other reasons.

Users who achieve resonance may avoid withdrawal by routinely taking a small "maintenance" dose. A maintenance dose is not strong enough to produce intoxication. No rush or high occurs. The user feels and acts normal; behavior is indistinguishable from someone who uses no opiates.[34] Only a body fluid work-up can determine if a person is on a maintenance dose.

Job performance is normal.[35] That fact has been documented for years. In a 1962 book Lawrence Kolb wrote,

> According to a 1919 survey, 75 per cent of addicts were gainfully employed, and there were many cases where victims were people of the highest qualities, morally and intellectually, and of great value to their communities. . . . I have observed a number of professional and clerical workers as well as laborers who worked regularly for years despite their use of as much as 40 grains of morphine daily.[36]

In a 1964 book Isidor Chein and associates reported, "There are many addicts we studied who continued at their jobs, with sufficient industry and deportment to satisfy their employers."[37] Chein and associates also noted, "Work habits of the few carefully observed patients who were readdicted in the research wards at the United States Public Health Service Hospital in Lexington, were not sufficiently different from those of the other, abstinent patients to provoke comment."[38] Around 1900, a New York Central railroad engineer was famed for making every run assigned to him during a 20-year period of morphine use.[39] A more recent example comes from former District of Columbia police department general counsel Gerald M. Caplan, who says that around 1971 "more than 100 officers were taking heroin. How did we learn about them? Not because their performance was poor. . . . We took urine specimens."[40] A study of college student grade-point averages found no significant difference between users and non-users of opiates.[41] Physician opiate users typically have their work unimpaired.[42] British physician addicts have been allowed to continue their medical practices and treat patients.[43] In the United States there is the famous case of Doctor X, addicted to morphine for 62 years without noticeable impairment of physical or mental abilities.[44] (The even more famous case of Dr. William Stewart Halsted is less relevant. Halsted was a pioneer at the Johns Hopkins medical school and a top surgeon despite his morphine addiction. His case is less relevant because a brilliant person's capabilities may not be shared by the rest of us. Moreover, his teaching ability declined after he started opiates, and he occasionally disappeared for days and even weeks[45]—behavior that few employers would tolerate from ordinary mortals.)

"Normal" job productivity does not mean that a worker is unaffected by a maintenance dose of heroin or other opiates,[46] but that such a worker performs as well as the average employee. Some experts deny that opiate users can work normally at their jobs while on maintenance doses.[47] These denials, however, are contrary to a consensus that spans a century of observations.

Friends and even close family members may notice nothing unusual and be unaware that someone uses an opiate.[48] "Only a few days ago I met a gentleman on Carroll avenue who has taken morphine thirteen years, in doses of from two to fifty grains daily. He was well dressed, had a healthy color, and was in every respect as respectable looking as the majority I saw on the street."[49] That meeting occurred around 1880, when addicts could buy morphine legally. "I never knew how many individuals of this type there are until after the law made it necessary to report them to this bureau. Almost invariably they are people of importance in their communities, some of them executives in banking, business or industry."[50] That observation was made in 1919, soon after morphine sales were forbidden. Similar observations were made in the 1960s and 1970s and 1980s, of American heroin addicts leading outwardly ordinary lives while steadily employed at middle class jobs for years.[51]

Heroin and other opiates apparently cause no ill effects of consequence.[52] Organic afflictions attributed to heroin[53] more likely reflect adulterants and the users' lifestyles—including poor hygiene, such as sharing dirty hypodermic needles and using public toilet water to prepare solutions for injection.[54] That type of behavior is particularly self-destructive, however, and (as we shall see later) has little to do with heroin.

As with job performance, some experts dissent from the consensus of opiate safety.[55] From 1908 to 1938, opium smokers over the age of 40 in Japanese-controlled Formosa had a higher death rate than the general population.[56] Apparently the actuarial experience of life insurance companies was consistent with the Formosa experience; around 1931 a League of Nations survey found that life insurers charged higher rates to Far Eastern opium smokers,[57] although earlier the New York Life Insurance Company gladly issued policies to opium users because their risk was no higher than non-users.[58] A study revealed that about 85 percent of Formosan opium smokers used the drug as self-medication for asthma, coughs, bloody sputum, gastrointestional illness, and gonorrhea—factors that could well affect mortality.[59] Also, Japanese-controlled Formosa restricted opium and prosecuted tens of thousands of users; Japanese police methods may have affected mortality.[60] A critic of heroin safety cited a finding that addicts under medical supervision in Great Britain had a higher death rate than unsupervised addicts in the United States,[61] but the cited finding emphasized that opiates themselves appeared safe; mortality was increased by other factors such as neglect of health and nutrition.[62] Another study noted the British addict death rate is raised by suicides.[63] Instantaneous deaths have been observed among street users after they inject heroin intravenously, but the drug's role in such fatalities is questionable.[64]

Despite controversy over "heroin overdose," the physical safety of opiates is widely recognized. Morphine and methadone are widely used in U.S. medical practice, with some patients taking methadone every day for years without noticeable ill effect. The same has long been observed with persons who use opiates outside medical contexts.

Various studies reveal no psychosis caused by opiates.[65] One study examined 200 addicts without finding a single schizophrenic.[66] Another traced 100 addicts over a 12-year span and found just 1 schizophrenic.[67] These are studies of people brought to the attention of authorities, through run-ins with the law or institutionalization for detoxification. If researchers cannot find heroin psychosis in that population, it probably does not exist.

Someone can be on heroin 24 hours a day, year after year, yet feel and act the same as anyone else. Methadone is an opiate, and the fact that opiate addicts can live and work normally is the basis of methadone "drug treatment" programs advocated by many government officials. Methadone patients are not cured of opiate addiction, but are merely switched from heroin (which no U.S. physician can prescribe) to the prescription drug methadone. Opiates have "cross tolerance," meaning that methadone, heroin, morphine, and all the rest can be substituted for one another and will give a person the same effects. A maintenance dose allows addicts to function normally in society.[68] What works with methadone will work with any opiate.

From a public health standpoint, we have no reason to fear heroin. It is far less harmful than alcohol or tobacco.

COCAINE

At first glance cocaine seems to be a chameleon drug, changing its attributes as years go by. In the early twentieth century widespread cocaine use was reported among impoverished African-Americans. By mid-century the drug was dismissed as a historical curiosity, used by hardly anyone. In the 1970s it was proclaimed the outrageously expensive drug of choice among chic rich folk, and in the 1980s it was termed a cheap "fast food drug" of urban ghettos. For decades numerous authorities insisted that cocaine was nonaddictive. In 1989, a physician told me that cocaine is the most addictive substance known. Yet, in all these years, the chemistry of cocaine never changed.

What has changed is attitudes about the drug. Such flip-flops are not unique to cocaine. Heroin was once "known" to be nonaddictive[69] and used as a "cure" for opiate addiction.[70] In the 1930s marijuana was feared as a drug that caused hyperactivity and violent crime. Fifty years later the weed was decried for making users lethargic and passive. The message here is not that drug actions are an impenetrable mystery—researchers know very well what they do. The message is that we can face cocaine with steadiness; Americans once had no fear of it, and its properties have not changed since then. Experience shows that, from time to time, some persons choose to promote dread about a particular drug; whenever those persons disappear from the scene, so does the panic. (A later chapter will talk about specific individuals and their motives.)

Leaves of the coca plant can be processed to yield cocaine. It normally acts as a stimulant. Thus its work is just the opposite of opiates, which are soothing sedatives. A person on a heroin high wants to leave other people alone. In contrast, someone on cocaine is ready for action. Violence by cocaine users, even by hard-core criminal users, is nonetheless uncommon.[71] Cocaine increases endurance and muscle power, gives users the impression of increased intellectual prowess,[72] can increase a user's zest for life, and embolden a person to take risks. Such effects are documented by a century of study.

Crack, a refined derivative of cocaine, has a shorter history. Crack research only began in the 1980s, and when this book was written scientists knew little about the substance. In addition to normal cocaine effects, however, inhaling crack smoke can sometimes produce a two-minute "rush" likened to a total body sexual orgasm, followed by an afterglow of 10 or 20 minutes. As with heroin, however, the mode of administration helps determine effects—persons who sniff crack, instead of smoking it, do not report euphoria.[73] Horror stories about "instant" crack addiction are unconfirmed by scientific research. In the early 1980s, researchers at a California clinic gave the drug to 200 volunteers. None became addicts or even turned into abusers. A study of 175 illicit crack users in Los Angeles found none with a compulsive habit; all used the drug in moderation.[74] Monkeys allowed to smoke crack will limit their intake.[75] Compulsive use of a drug need not grow as preparations grow in potency. A cocaine user can achieve certain effects with a particular amount of cocaine hydrochloride salt or a smaller amount of the free base of cocaine liberated from the salt. Format, admittedly, is not irrelevant; with a high potency preparation a user can achieve intense effects more easily. Yet, not all users of high potency preparations seek intense effects. Persons who use crack in moderation typically sniff it, a mode of administration that produces a low level of effects for a long time.[76] In contrast, hedonists who desire intense experiences will smoke crack, producing strong effects for a brief time. Because those hedonists want to experience the intensity for a long time, they smoke crack again whenever the effects weaken. Amount of use depends on the person, not the drug. Research on freebase cocaine is probably relevant to crack; despite different manufacturing processes the two products are similar. Freebase research shows compulsive users to have prior histories of polydrug abuse, especially amphetamines and other stimulants.[77] Drug abusers who seek ever more powerful stimulant experiences can be expected to find crack appealing; their compulsive use of crack may be due less to the drug than to well-established personalities. A 1987 survey of Canadian crack users supports that view; they used other drugs as well (marijuana, heroin, barbiturates, LSD, PCP) and in large quantities (5 or more drinks of alcohol at a time, every day).[78] People who use a lot of crack are people who use all sorts of drugs to excess.

The pharmacological basis of cocaine's appeal is unclear. Experienced users cannot tell the difference between cocaine and a nasal anesthetic,[79] nor can they reliably differentiate the effects of amphetamine and cocaine.[80] At small dosage levels people feel no difference between cocaine and a placebo; effects after receiving a placebo can mimic (though not absolutely duplicate) 40 mg of cocaine; street users of cocaine have proclaimed marijuana (an active placebo) to be a satisfying substitute.[81] A person who used cocaine daily for 55 years switched to aspirin whenever her supply ran short.[82] Cocaine does have effects but their power may be exaggerated. Persons can sniff or smoke crack without becoming addicted and without losing social productivity.[83] Set and setting may be more important than chemistry and may explain cocaine's fluctuating popularity. When the drug was publicized as a symbol of debonair opulence in the 1970s, it rocketed from obscurity. When it was publicized as a symbol of rebellious violence in the 1980s, it became popular in urban ghettos. Cocaine use may have as much to do with social statements as with pharmacology.

Numerous afflictions have been associated with cocaine,[84] but ailments seem related to astonishing levels of abuse, levels at which even innocuous substances such as coffee could turn nasty. Paranoia and hallucinations can occur, but they clear up quickly if cocaine usage stops.[85] Organic brain damage is unproven.[86] Examination of a person who used 2 grams a week for decades found no organic, mental, or social deterioration.[87] People can *daily* use 1 gram of *crack* "without severe dysfunction."[88] No harm has been proven among South American Indians whose blood levels of cocaine are as high as those found among users in the United States.[89]

Some "cocaine-related" afflictions are due to a user's method of administration, not due to pharmacological effects. For instance, respiratory problems attributed to chronic cocaine smoking are found just as readily among heavy smokers of nicotine; in either case a different method of administration would avoid the lung trouble. If a user chooses to sniff cocaine powder, nasal difficulties can occur: rhinitis, nosebleeds, and in extreme cases nasal ulcers or even a perforated septum cartilage. Those difficulties can be avoided by using another means to take the drug. Another problem is the size of a lethal dose, which can change unexpectedly depending on the user's condition—a person can drop dead from a dose that gave pleasure the previous day. That seldom happens,[90] but "seldom" also means "sometimes," and a user always takes a risk.

The above hazards are real, but in practice the damage is less than in these worst-case scenarios.[91] Research supporting that comforting thought appears in a book endorsed by the Reagan White House and published by a legitimate scientific press, a book that can in no way be read as minimizing cocaine problems. In a passage referring to addiction, not just occasional use 2 or 3 times a year, one authority writes, "It is not uncommon for young persons to have been on cocaine for up to a year before it was noticed by their parents. In my experience a person may have snorted cocaine for up to two years or more before deterioration occurred."[92] One could read that passage as a frightening warning, that a child might be a cocaine addict for years without a parent realizing it. Or one could read that passage as saying a person has to abuse cocaine severely, for a long time, before anything bad happens. A 1989 study found that adults need to abuse cocaine for an average of 6.6 years before experiencing a single problem.[93]

Cocaine was studied for a century without anyone detecting resonance or physical dependence among users of the drug. Only after politicians decried cocaine in the 1980s did a handful of scientists claim that dependence develops. The claim became widely believed and merits consideration here.

Proponents of the dependence concept used innovative terminology to change attitudes toward long-observed effects of cocaine. For example, not until 1986 was a three-stage "cocaine abstinence syndrome" proclaimed.[94] The first stage was called the "crash," likened to an alcohol hangover,[95] in which a person who stops a cocaine binge feels exhausted and depressed. Cocaine and other stimulants work by using up energy stored in the body. At the end of a binge a person will feel like someone who has done hard physical labor for days without food or sleep. Those symptoms do not mean a person has a metabolic need for such punishment. Nor are they evidence that physical resonance has been established with cocaine, any more than a hangover is evidence of physical resonance with alcohol. If cocaine resonance existed, a user could quickly resume normal functioning by taking another dose of cocaine. But such a dose would worsen the user's condition, not restore it to normal; a maintenance dose is impossible because cocaine resonance does not exist. Although the second stage in "cocaine abstinence syndrome" was called "withdrawal," proponents of the concept admitted that "this does not mean that a classic drug abstinence syndrome formally occurs"[96] and admitted that the second stage was "dissimilar [to] 'withdrawal' in alcohol, barbiturate, or opiate abuse."[97] Indeed, these proponents declared, "Withdrawal has . . . assumed a clinical meaning, independent of its pharmacological definition, that derives from the postdrug syndromes for which drug users seek treatment. . . . Strict pharmacological use of the term can cause clinical treatment errors."[98] In other words, "cocaine withdrawal" has no pharmacological component. That is, it is not caused by the drug. The third and final "abstinence syndrome" stage was called "extinction," and describes the process by which drug-seeking behavior learned by psychological conditioning is extinguished. Once again, a pharmacological component is absent from the "cocaine abstinence syndrome."

As will be noted in a later chapter, such claims of "cocaine dependence" met immediate skepticism from scientists who research drug actions, and no consensus accepted the claims as the 1980s ended.[99] Proponents, however, achieved a victory in 1987 when the American Psychiatric Association invented a new disease called "cocaine dependence" that did not require resonance or physical dependence for the diagnosis.[100] An "epidemic" of "cocaine dependence" appeared overnight because the symptoms had never been classified as disease until then. Even the APA admitted this, albeit with hedging: "*Because of the broadened criteria* for Dependence included in this manual, and because of the definite increase in use in recent years, the prevalence of Cocaine Dependence is believed to be far higher" than formerly (emphasis added).[101] The APA's action gave the term official medical and governmental recognition even though the APA itself conceded, "Continuing use of cocaine appears to be driven by persistent craving and urges for the substance rather than attempts to avoid or alleviate withdrawal symptoms."[102] Even a prominent "cocaine dependence" proponent concurred, "This craving . . . can be understood as a memory of the stimulant euphoria."[103] Lacking a physical condition to treat, psychiatrists attempt to change a user's attitude toward cocaine.

Criteria that describe "cocaine dependence" are psychological and not pharmacological. The clinical condition termed "cocaine dependence" may be real, even devastating, but it is caused by a psychological process instead of a pharmacological one. Two consequences follow. First, diagnosing someone as "psychologically dependent" on cocaine is the same as saying the person likes to use cocaine a lot. Such a "diagnosis" may provide a psychiatrist with a patient but provides no insight for treatment. Second, if a pharmacological component is absent from the disease, the drug is irrelevant. Psychiatric personnel freely admit as much: "Cocaine abusers do not require a treatment program that is distinct from programs for other substance abusers."[104] That is, despite extreme differences among opiates, cocaine, alcohol, and nicotine, the drug of abuse does not affect the disease of psychological dependence. If a drug is irrelevant to the disease, if the disease is a mental attitude about a drug, then harsh laws against the drug itself have no medical justification.

It is probably not coincidental that medical and governmental acceptance of "cocaine dependence" was followed by efforts to demonstrate a physical component that might justify harsh laws. As with "cocaine dependence," however, scientific research played a lesser role than innovative terminology. The innovative terminology, in turn, was used in a complex chain of reasoning leading to a hypothesis that a physical component exists. Proponents of the hypothesis have yet to prove its reality. Nonetheless they have affected public policy, so their proposal merits discussion here.

Cocaine, like many other drugs, affects brain chemistry. Animal studies suggest that cocaine may alter human brain tissue, but the extent and duration of such alteration in humans is uncertain. Evidence does exist that cocaine increases the dopamine level in the brain, accompanied by a decline in the number of dopamine receptors, and that their number returns to normal if cocaine usage stops.[105] Those are facts.

These, too, are facts. Drugs operate by changing body chemistry; that is their function. Such changes, whether in the brain or elsewhere, do not mean a person has established resonance or dependence with a substance. If blood pressure declines after reducing salt intake, that does not mean a hypertensive person is physically dependent on salt. Resonance or dependence is present only if a person *sickens* temporarily or permanently when drug use *ceases*, and *recovers* upon *resuming* drug use. For example, a heroin addict functioning normally on a maintenance dose will take sick if the drug supply ends, and get well if it resumes. In contrast, someone exhausted by cocaine will not recover upon further administration of cocaine. If a drug itself sickens a person, the person is hardly dependent on it—no one has a metabolic need for illness. Nor is resonance or dependence demonstrated by continuation of symptoms after drug use stops. Someone may go blind after one drink of contaminated alcohol, but that blindness does not mean the person is physically dependent on contaminated alcohol.

Given these facts, we can now examine a hypothesis called "neuroadaptation," developed by proponents of "cocaine dependence." According to their reasoning the presence of cocaine alters brain chemistry and may alter tissue, and organic changes in the brain can affect behavior, so behavior of cocaine users demonstrates physical "neuroadaptation" of the brain to cocaine.[106] Supposedly this "neuroadaptation" is "physiological addiction" to cocaine.[107]

At a casual glance those statements seem straightforward, but upon analysis they degenerate into confusion. Cocaine can alter human brain chemistry and may alter tissue, but whether those alterations are damaging is uncertain. The primary example of alteration by cocaine is a decreased number of dopamine receptors as the level of dopamine increases. Rather than causing a person's behavior to change, however, such alterations may limit the amount of behavioral change. Moreover, if the number of receptors returns to normal when dopamine levels become normal, defining the shift in number as "damage" is problematic;[108] the shift may simply be the body's compensation for fluctuations in body chemistry. Even if brain tissue alteration remained permanent, assessing effect on behavior would be difficult. People can suffer outright loss of brain tissue through surgery or cerebral hemorrhage, yet function normally. Possibly, as "neuroadaptation" proponents seem to argue, all behavior is caused by electrochemical activity in the central nervous system. But the cause-effect relationship is largely unknown. No one knows how electrochemical activity creates affection for a friend, hate for an enemy, delight for a Mozart melody, disdain for rock and roll, or even a decision to cross the street. To say that "return of the [dopamine] receptor number to normal" causes "cocaine dependence" and "cocaine withdrawal"[109] is very bold. Still another problem arises by defining tissue change as "physiological addiction." By such definition a diabetes sufferer is addicted to insulin, an asthma sufferer is addicted to theophylline, a headache sufferer is addicted to aspirin. All those persons exhibit changes in body chemistry and tissue, accompanied by a change in behavior, after taking their drugs. Using those criteria to define addiction is a non-standard definition, and bound to cause misconceptions among people who hear the term "physiological addiction" but who are unaware of the special definition.

Although the "neuroadaptation" hypothesis involves undisputed facts, it also involves speculations and assumptions that trail off into nothingness upon scrutiny. Even the foremost proponents of "neuroadaptation" admit that no proof exists: "Neuroadaptive withdrawal state in cocaine abusers remains a not yet proven working hypothesis."[110]

Despite lack of a pharmacological element in "cocaine dependence" and lack of proof for "neuroadaptation," the concepts dovetailed with political needs in the late 1980s and grew in popularity.

Cocaine used to be considered nonaddictive because no physical resonance, let alone dependence, was ever detected. As researchers studied addiction and improved their understanding, they began to realize that addiction can occur without physical resonance. More and more authorities now hold that cocaine can be addictive—a proposition heartily endorsed by some users. Controversy has also arisen about pharmacological tolerance, whether a cocaine user needs larger and larger doses to produce the same effects. A consensus used to exist that no tolerance develops, and indeed evidence was found that sensitizing occurs instead,[111] that is, a person can use smaller and smaller doses to get the same effects. The old consensus is now under challenge, with some researchers claiming that tolerance does develop.[112] These new findings are uncertain, but are consistent with the portrait of tolerance given in a later chapter where the process of addiction is examined.

If cocaine abuse is inevitable, we might be making an artificial distinction by saying ailments rarely occur without reckless usage; but abuse is not inevitable. Indeed researchers find abuse is the exception from the norm.[113] A 1984 study concluded that 10 percent of cocaine users might become abusers,[114] about the same percentage seen among drinkers who become alcoholics. A 1985 investigation found an even lower percentage of cocaine users becoming abusers, 2.5 percent.[115] A 1984 study indicated that people can take cocaine for recreation and continue their moderation.[116] Researchers found that most cocaine users in Canada rarely kept a supply of the drug, normally bought only 1 to 3 grams in a single purchase, made no more than 4 purchases per year, and took a dose less than once a month.[117] A study that tracked specific New York cocaine users from 1971 to 1984 found the typical use to be intermittent rather than compulsive,[118] a finding supported by another study that tracked specific recreational users from 1975 to 1983.[119] A survey asked cocaine users if they had ever tried to give up the drug without success; 3.8 percent said yes.[120] That low percentage should be compared to survey respondents who said they had tried to give up tobacco cigarettes without success, 18 percent.[121] Very few cocaine users have an uncontrollable craving. An 11-year study concluded that most careers and lives are not wrecked if people use cocaine.[122] One researcher summarized the findings: "People who have a stake in conventional life don't throw it all away."[123] Such findings do not mean that cocaine abuse should be disregarded. They do mean the problem is not a fearsome crisis.

Scientific investigators find that most cocaine users do not become addicts, although some do. Reasons for the difference are unclear: "The most we can say is that in all probability whatever conditions are apt to produce amphetamine psychosis and amphetamine abuse are also apt to produce cocaine psychosis and cocaine abuse."[124] Millions of people use amphetamines without difficulties, and we should be unsurprised if the same holds true for cocaine.

Some research does promote the idea that cocaine puts the user and society in grave peril, but close examination can make such findings less frightening. For example, in apparent contrast to the studies noted above, one scientific paper says, "Approximately 70 percent of our patients admit they were addicted after experiencing their first high."[125] That report, however, is limited to a population of patients under medical care for cocaine abuse. One presumes the drug would affect them more than users who function normally in society. Also, the finding is based on anecdotal accounts lacking the validity of immediate clinical examination, let alone a controlled experiment; we do not know if addicts accurately remember the event they "admit." Perhaps more important is the question of whether custodial patients who are seeking release will say what they think authorities want to hear. Even the 70 percent figure is unclear; in another paper for the same symposium the investigator says the "first high of the freebase hit carries a 70-80 percent probability of addiction on the first hit."[126] The fuzzy language disguises whether the figure refers to the first use of freebase or first high achieved, perhaps after numerous uses. Also, the population described by the investigator has changed. In the first paper he spoke of patients under medical care; in the second he applies the 70 percent figure to all freebase users. That is a big difference; hospitalized alcoholics are not the same as people who limit their alcohol use to a few weekend beers. The idea of instant addiction to cocaine is also strange. No other drug seems to have such a property, and cocaine was studied for a century before anyone noticed such a phenomenon in the 1980s. Admittedly crack cocaine is a potent variety, but a variety just the same—not a different drug. In years past "everyone knew" that a single injection of heroin caused addiction; careful scientific research disproved the notion. The same may happen with crack.

In addition to reports that cocaine users face inevitable ruin, some accounts allege grave peril to society. Some claim the drug has caused mounting numbers of car wrecks. A symposium paper reported telephone calls by cocaine users who desired help: "Cocaine related automobile accidents reported by Hotline callers have nearly doubled since 1983. In 1985, nearly one-fifth of all callers said they had had at least one automobile accident . . . while under the influence of cocaine or a combination of cocaine and other drugs."[127] An accompanying chart of statistics is less ominous: in response to questioning by Hotline personnel, the number of callers who admitted car mishaps almost doubled—not the number of accidents. "Cocaine-related" car accidents includes drivers who were simultaneously drunk on alcohol, an inclusion that is bound to inflate the number of incidents.[128] And the population generating these numbers is not a random sample of Americans, nor a random sample of cocaine users, nor even a random sample of addicts, but a population of users so worried about their habit that they seek help. One would expect such persons to have dramatic problems. Despite the study's confident language, its data yields no information allowing conclusions about cocaine and automobile accidents.

Choice of language can promote fear. Hyperbole and colored adjectives are easy enough to spot; less easy are rhetorical constructions that blur reality. For example, a symposium paper that discusses cocaine smoking says, "Potentially irreversible lung damage with impairment of diffusing capacity has also been reported."[129] Another way of phrasing that information would be, "Damage that is at least initially reversible may result, but no confirmation exists." The language in both those sentences is neutral, but the rhetorical impact is different.

Problems in the symposium papers just analyzed are not merely academic. The symposium in question was co-sponsored by the United States government, and the papers were endorsed by the Reagan White House. Such papers coat drug control policy with a scientific veneer, but lack sufficient information to reach any conclusions. In contrast, careful studies that produce reasonable conclusions are typically ignored by government officials. This contrast suggests that drug control policy may have a purpose unrelated to public health. A later chapter will ponder that possibility.

MARIJUANA

Marijuana is another drug that evokes strong feelings among Americans. For now, however, we shall limit our consideration to pharmacological properties. Like opiates and cocaine, marijuana comes in assorted varieties, some more potent than others. They are all the same drug, however, and produce equivalent effects if doses are adjusted for potency.

The late 1960s divided two eras in marijuana research. Although a rich store of work had been compiled by chemists and by observers of marijuana users, only 3 studies had measured effects during the drug session.[130] And those studies, conducted in the 1930s and 1940s, failed to meet later standards of protocol—such as "double blind" administration, in which neither the scientist nor the user knew whether the administered drug was marijuana or a placebo. Almost no valid data existed, a lapse that says less about the quality of research than about general indifference toward the topic. Only in the late 1960s did researchers begin to invite users into laboratories to measure what happened. Prior to that era, marijuana laws had been passed and enforced without benefit of valid scientific data about the drug.

Andrew Weil conducted the first modern marijuana experiments,[131] and his findings have been supported by subsequent researchers.[132] None of the classic reports on marijuana, reviewing findings from researchers around the world, have found any physical peril for users of the drug.[133] Weil characterizes marijuana as an "active placebo,"[134] meaning that it produces trivial physical effects[135] and that users' psychological reactions are created entirely by set and setting rather than by pharmacological action. Earlier we noted an experiment showing that a drug user who feels sensations, but does not understand them, will mimic the behavior of nearby persons who have taken a dose. That happens with marijuana.[136] Smokers worldwide use it for all purposes—to concentrate, stimulate, relax—a "universal drug" producing whatever effects a user wants. If marijuana is publicized as producing violent stimulation, users wanting such effects may feel them.[137] That process may explain "reefer madness" in the 1930s. Fifty years later users sought mellowness and found it. In neither case did pharmacological properties of marijuana produce the mental states. Nor does marijuana cause psychosis.[138]

Marijuana's pharmacological properties are so limited that an experienced user can perform any normal tasks without measurable impairment, whether or not the user is "under the influence."[139] In a controlled experiment heavy marijuana use had no effect on productivity in "fairly demanding manual labor."[140] Even some driving tests show the same number of errors by subjects who received a dose of marijuana and those who took no drug. Said one experimenter, "This result is puzzling because of the elaborate efforts made in this study to maximize marihuana intoxication."[141]

Marijuana's safety can also be measured by its "therapeutic ratio," the difference between the size of dose needed for the desired effect and the size that produces poisoning. Marijuana is so safe that the therapeutic ratio has yet to be found, although it has been estimated in the thousands.[142] Nor has the lethal dose been calculated, though extrapolation from animal experiments suggests that a person might die after eating 24 ounces all at once.[143] Deaths from marijuana overdose are no more common than deaths from drinking too many glasses of water at one sitting.[144] The Drug Abuse Warning Network data system, which collects information on drug-related deaths around the country, indicates marijuana's safety. The 1984 reports mention marijuana in 18 fatalities; the 1986 reports have 12 mentions.[145] And of course a trace of marijuana residue does not mean that the drug even played a role in a particular fatality; aspirin ranked higher than marijuana in the number of mentions. Marijuana does not create physical resonance, so no withdrawal syndrome occurs. None of the major inquiries into marijuana, before or after the 1960s, detected any long-term damage from moderate use. ("Moderate use" is the only meaningful criterion in searching for damage, because "excessive use" of any substance—whether it be marijuana, coffee, or fast food burgers and fries—can cause harm.)

Findings of modern researchers are supported by historical experience. Marijuana has been grown in the United States since colonial times. Marijuana, however, is also called "hemp," and had extensive industrial use in sail-powered maritime vessels. That was the primary market supplied by farmers until the twentieth century. Records from colonial times detail all sorts of drug use, but no mention of marijuana is found. Only in the 1920s did many drug-using Americans turn to marijuana, seeking an affordable substitute for the alcohol outlawed by federal Prohibition. If marijuana had any significant pharmacological action it surely would have been widely used long before then, just as opiates, alcohol, nicotine, caffeine, and cocaine were widely used.

Some people claim that marijuana is a "gateway" drug, that using it leads to more dangerous substances. The weakness of this claim is demonstrated by history, reasoning, and stark experience.

Let us first examine history. In the 1930s civic leaders, government officials, and news stories condemned marijuana as a vicious stimulant, causing users to commit heinous crimes while suffering from "reefer madness." In 1937, at the height of this panic, the federal government outlawed marijuana. In congressional hearings held to establish the need for such action, Congressman John D. Dingell asked Federal Bureau of Narcotics Commissioner Harry J. Anslinger about the gateway theory:

Dingell: I am just wondering whether the marihuana addict graduates into a heroin, an opium, or a cocaine user.

Anslinger: No, sir; I have not heard of a case of that kind. I think it is an entirely
   different class. The marihuana addict does not go in that direction.[146]

Whether or not Harry Anslinger knew what he was talking about, federal
drug enforcement policy denied that marijuana was a gateway drug when it
was outlawed. The drug was banned because supposedly it caused hyperactive
insanity and brutal crime. After Congress took decisive action in response to
public fear of that threat, investigators accumulated evidence that the threat
was imaginary. Only after that evidence became overwhelming, after the need
for banning marijuana was disproved, did the gateway claim arise. Here is the
same Commissioner Anslinger in 1955: "Our great concern about the use of
marihuana, that eventually if used over a long period, it does lead to heroin
addiction."[147] The pharmacological properties of marijuana did not change
during the years between Anslinger's two statements. But numerous government officials had staked their reputations, and their jobs, on the premise that
marijuana posed a public health threat. When the "reefer madness" theory
was disproved, those government officials needed a new theory if the
marijuana ban (and the longevity of their jobs) were to be maintained.

Just because they needed a new theory does not mean it was incorrect, but
reasoning and experience disprove it. Traditionally, claims about gateway
drugs rest on a false assumption of causality: if heroin addicts earlier used
marijuana, marijuana must have led to heroin. Such arguments are venerable.
In 1902 a respected scientific publisher brought out a book arguing that coffee
drinking led to opium.[148] Some people have said tobacco leads to
marijuana.[149] Charles B. Towns, a respected narcotics authority of the early
twentieth century, maintained that tobacco smoking led to opiate use.[150]
Those contentions about coffee and tobacco may sound silly today, but they
were based on the same fallacy as the marijuana gateway theory. For example,
persons who say marijuana leads to heroin fail to point out the even higher
correlation of sniffing volatiles (such as gasoline) and later heroin use.[151] Yet
we hear no calls to ban the sale of gasoline. The earlier a criminal becomes
sexually active, the younger the age at which criminal behavior begins,[152] but
that does not mean sex causes crime. Correlations do not demonstrate a
cause/effect relationship.

Even if gateway theory is based on faulty reasoning, it may still be true; the
universe does not operate by Aristotelian logic. Experience demonstrates,
however, that marijuana does not lead to heroin. An observer of African-
American ghetto residents found that 54 percent of the studied group claimed
to use marijuana, but only 3 percent claimed to use heroin.[153] In a group of
drug-using criminals, 75 percent of the heroin addicts had used marijuana, but
so had 68 percent of the non-addicts, a statistically insignificant difference.[154]
No progression from marijuana to other drugs has been found in Jamaica.[155]

Despite wide use of marijuana in Amsterdam, observers have found small interest in heroin.[156] Consider the number of American college students who have used marijuana, and then compare the number of campus heroin addicts.[157] Actually, comparison may be impossible; a 1985 survey computed that almost 62 million Americans had tried marijuana, and 18 million were current users, but heroin usage in the sample population was so minuscule that a statistically valid total could not be generated.[158] The British government's Wootton Report on marijuana found no progression to heroin in any country.[159] If marijuana led to heroin, the phenomenon should be observable.[160]

Having met defeat on the heroin front, in the 1980s gateway theorists proposed that marijuana leads to cocaine.[161] Some even proposed that alcohol leads to cocaine.[162] Such contentions are so recent that no consensus has emerged among researchers. If experience is any guide, however, we can be confident that the gateway theory is wrong here as well.[163]

LSD

Not much was heard of d-lysergic acid diethylamide when this book was written in mid-1989, but the general public still feared and loathed LSD. Reasons for those emotions will be explored in a later chapter; for now we shall concentrate on what the chemical does to users.

In a way, LSD might be viewed as a stimulant, an extremely powerful stimulant. It can be used as an antidote to barbiturate poisoning. Long ago Kenneth Godfrey, a Veterans Administration psychotherapist who ran one of the last legal LSD research programs in the 1970s, told me that LSD strikes down barriers. That is the most apt summary I have found of LSD's effects. It strikes down barriers between senses, for example, allowing sounds to be seen as a shifting kaleidoscope of colors. Barriers between the conscious and unconscious mind may fall, bringing forth deep psychological concerns. Vivid hallucinations may appear—perhaps mythological in essence, or images of ancient cultures. The hallucinations can be so vivid as to raise questions about the nature of reality, questions that go beyond the scope of this book.

As with other drugs, set and setting are important. A user who seeks self-insight may achieve it and be satisfied with a single LSD dose. A hedonist who wants to see a light show may take the drug hundreds of times. A depressed and fearful person may have a bad LSD experience, experiencing panic that deepens if nearby people become afraid as well. Several curiosity seekers with no particular expectations about the drug told me that little happened when they took it. LSD is no placebo; it is a drug of power, meriting deep respect. As powerful as it is, however, set and setting shape its effects.

Paradoxically, the powerful drug is also "exceptionally safe."[164] The size of a lethal dose has yet to be found because no one has died from LSD.[165] Babies have emerged unscathed from enormous doses.[166] Massive abuse apparently causes no organic brain damage.[167] Highly publicized reports of chromosome damage were later disproved,[168] and infants born to LSD users show no more chomosome damage or birth defects than the general population.[169] Psychosis lasting longer than 48 hours is rare—twice in a thousand cases for psychiatric patients, less often for normal volunteers.[170] Results from 75,000 clinically supervised LSD, psilocybin, and mescaline experiences among nearly 10,000 persons found no subsequent suicides among normal subjects, and no more than 5 among psychiatric patients—the latter figure consistent with the rate among members of that population who did not receive a psychedelic.[171]

Flashback is particularly feared, at least by non-users. LSD "flashback" is an unexpected repetition of a mental state achieved in an LSD session, a repetition when no psychedelic is being used. Flashback, however, is a normal experience[172] in which a prior emotional experience is suddenly felt once again with intensity. Perhaps a song not heard for years evokes an experience associated with it; or perhaps no trigger is apparent, but memories and emotions flood over a person's consciousness and temporarily supersede present reality. Such a happenstance is a sign of normality, not mental illness. Given the occasional high emotion of some LSD experiences, an absence of flashbacks would be surprising. Someone having a flashback can normally snap out of it at will. A person is not trapped. A survey of 247 LSD users yielded only 1 report of a flashback that remained persistent while the person tried to abandon it.[173] LSD flashbacks tend to be overreported, perhaps because the drug users are less precise about the term than clinicians are. Typical reports include remembering a psychedelic experience upon hearing music that was played at the time, or becoming drunk on alcohol and suddenly feeling afraid to die.[174] Those are not LSD flashbacks, but such reports can inflate the statistics.

A different phenomenon is also called "flashback," but to avoid confusion let us call it "adept skill." In this situation, without using a drug someone enters an altered state of consciousness previously achieved while using a drug. An analogy would be riding a bicycle without assistance from training wheels that were formerly needed; the unassisted ride is a new one, not a replay of a past one. The phenomenon is observed with marijuana; an experienced user can slip into the desired state without help from the drug.[175] With LSD, too, the phenomenon grows in frequency with the amount of experience an individual has with the drug.[176] The implication is that achieving altered states of consciousness is a learned skill, an ability inherent in everyone, and that drugs simply help teach people how to do it. Once they have learned, they no longer need the drugs. From this viewpoint "adept skill" is a desirable consequence of LSD, not a hazard. Indeed, one study found that most users welcome "adept skill."[177]

Those of us around LSD users need fear no harm from them. They cause no more traffic accidents than anyone else.[178] Careful study fails to reveal significant psychological difference between LSD users and everyone else.[179] LSD may be part of the lifestyle chosen by hippies and flower children, but LSD did not cause them to choose that lifestyle. Despite intense publicity, the drug has never been popular; most regular users take it in moderation; and most quit after a while (a process called "maturing out"). LSD has never raised problems of public health or social cost.

The substances mentioned in this chapter cover the range in illicit drugs of abuse—sedatives, stimulants, and hallucinogens. There are none worse. Yet our examination shows them to be far less powerful and dangerous than commonly believed. Scientists who study these drugs are often unable to support claims promoted by drug war zealots; claims of instant addiction, of moral and physical degradation, of massive drug-induced psychosis stalking the land. Abuse of drugs can have bad consequences, as can abuse of anything else. We should respect these chemicals, but we need not fear them.

If illicit drugs do no harm when used in moderation, if they cause harm only when used to excess, we must face the question of why anyone would voluntarily engage in self-destructive behavior. The answer offered in the next chapter will show still more limits to the power of drugs.

2 What Drug Users Do to Themselves

The previous chapter argued that illicit drugs are relatively safe, in the way that power saws are relatively safe. If used responsibly, with due precautions, no harm will come. In contrast, a careless or reckless user may meet disaster. If someone running a table saw wears no goggles, takes no guard against kickback, and stands barefoot in a puddle while reaching for the ungrounded power switch, we would probably not blame the saw for any resultant mishap. This chapter will argue that drugs are wrongly blamed for similar mishaps. Indeed, this chapter will argue that such outcomes are often not accidental but instead result from deliberate self-destructive behavior. That argument has public policy implications: if drugs do not enslave people, if users can be held accountable for their conduct, then laws based on opposite assumptions may be futile.

ADDICTION

Many theories exist about addiction. Most suffer from one or two basic flaws. One is the flaw of "selected population," and the other is the flaw of "invalid variable."

"Selected population" weakens many studies of illicit drug use. Typically the users who are studied, and from whom conclusions are drawn, have brought themselves to the attention of medical or law enforcement authorities. As we shall see, most illicit drug users are never detected by such authorities. Too often, conclusions about drugs are based on the worst possible cases of abuse. By analogy, that is like observing emergency room admissions of injured downhill skiers, without knowing anything about the vast majority who avoid misadventure, and trying to understand why people are drawn to an activity that results in serious disability. A troublesome variant of this flaw comes from the study of drug-using criminals. A decision to arrest someone is political; not partisan, but political in a broad sense. For example, a small-town cop might ignore Rev. Brown when he "roll stops" through a stop sign, but ticket a hippie. Anyone studying criminals is studying people selected by police, and that selection is not a cross-section of population, whether of stop sign violators or drug violators. Moreover, as we shall see in the next chapter, drug-using criminals commonly turn to crime before developing expensive drug habits. Illicit drugs are merely one aspect of a lifestyle that rejects society's values. Values of municipal court thieves, whether expressed in musical tastes or in basic morality, are probably different from yours and mine. We know little about illicit drug use by "normal" citizens, that is, people who live by middle-class values. It is hard to find physicists, bank officers, air traffic controllers, and small-town grade-school teachers who will discuss their use of illicit drugs.[1] Drug use by criminals may have no relevance to usage by citizens who are otherwise law-abiding. Drawing conclusions about drugs from criminals' use of them may be like drawing conclusions about screwdrivers from burglars' use of them.

"Invalid variable" is a flaw in theories of drug addiction. Physics has one basic theory of relativity; biology has one basic theory of evolution. Drug research has many theories of addiction.[2] This multiplicity cannot be due to newness of the research field; drug addiction has been studied as long as relativity and evolution, with great resources devoted to the effort. Yet when a theory about addiction to a specific drug is tested, results may vary from one test to the next. If experimental factors remain steady, but the outcome changes, we have a classic signal that the factors do not control the outcome. Moreover, if no particular process of addiction occurs with a drug, such a result suggests the drug is an invalid variable—that its presence or absence makes no difference in how addiction occurs. In other words, drugs do not cause addiction.

To understand how drug addiction occurs, perhaps we should disregard the drugs. That may sound paradoxical, but such an approach yields practical conclusions, conclusions consistent with psychological knowledge about self-destruction and even consistent with political aspirations expressed by addicts and drug war zealots alike.

Let us first define "addiction." It describes something real but, like a rainbow, it can be hard to reach out and grasp. Part of the difficulty is caused by fuzziness in language normally used to describe the concept. Drug addiction involves resonance, tolerance, and morbid craving. Those symptoms do not make an addict, however. Instead the crucial factor is ⟨...⟩ responds to those symptoms.

Resonance and addiction used to be equated. A person wh⟨...⟩ physical resonance with a drug was called an addict; a pers⟨...⟩ resonance was not an addict. As a rule of thumb, a person with ⟨...⟩nce is probably an addict because massive continual use is required to set up resonance. Nonetheless, such use can occur in legitimate medical settings. Persons who found themselves in such a state were called "medical addicts," but their response showed they were not addicts; they could go through the withdrawal syndrome and feel no inclination to take the drug again.[3] If people do not want a drug, they are not addicted. Another problem in equating resonance and addiction is that resonance is unnecessary for addiction. A person can be addicted even if no withdrawal syndrome occurs upon stoppage. Such a view has become popular among some investigators of cocaine,[4] a drug once labeled as nonaddictive because users acquired no observable physical resonance. Equating resonance with addiction simplifies diagnosis; even though no body fluid work-up can detect resonance, resonance produces definite physical signs of addiction through the withdrawal syndrome. If that syndrome is irrelevant, there is no physical way to detect addiction.[5]

Tolerance is another classic sign of addiction. Tolerance means that higher and higher doses are needed to produce the same effect. No physical explanation has been demonstrated for this phenomenon.[6] It does not typically occur with medicinal drugs; people can take the same dose for weeks, months, or years and still get the effect desired by a physician. Some medical drugs are also drugs of abuse; no chemical difference exists. Patients seeking pain relief can use the same dose of narcotics for years and never seek an increase.[7] The same can happen with cocaine; a patient used 2 grams a week steadily for 55 years without seeking an increase.[8] Tolerance, instead of being governed by a substance, seems related to the purpose for which a drug is taken. Such psychological explanation implies that the phenomenon might be encountered in contexts involving no drugs at all, and indeed such is the case.[9] Anything done for pleasure—credit card spending, wild music, eating, sex—can pale. In response a person addicted to an activity will increase its intensity or frequency in a quest for the original level of sensation. But pleasure does not exist in the external object or activity; pleasure exists only within the mind. If people realize that they themselves create the pleasure, they can avoid tolerance and break addiction. Even regular users of heroin can avoid tolerance,[10] it is a psychological and not a pharmacological phenomenon.[11]

Morbid craving is the key sign of addiction.[12] We all experience ordinary craving for something. What an addict feels is different. First, an addict's functioning—whether physical or mental or social—is impaired until the desired thing is obtained. Second, satisfying the craving is more important than anything else. Without both factors there is no addiction. With those two factors, a person can be addicted to anything. We need to have the cause-effect progression straight here: morbid craving leads to addiction, not vice versa.[13] If a person realizes what is happening, it is possible to restore a sense of balance and prevent addiction. Morbid craving may be continuous or may be intermittent, triggered by stress, years after the last episode.[14] As with tolerance, morbid craving is produced by the person, not from some external source.

Animal experiments are often cited to illustrate morbid craving and other aspects of drug abuse. Typically, however, citations omit information needed to evaluate the experiments. The animal may be caged or strapped down, and be extremely restricted in its activity—allowed only to press or not press a lever. Behavior in such an environment may differ from what occurs when an animal roams freely and chooses from all sorts of optional activities. If a person were tied to a chair in a jail cell 24 hours a day, and allowed to press one lever for food pellets and another for a drug that helped obliterate consciousness of the situation, we might not be too surprised if the person soon preferred the drug to food. Results from that sort of experiment do not mean that drugs warp the mind; experimental conditions are designed to cause warping. Such design does not invalidate the experiment. On the contrary, good investigators restrict an animal's environment and behavior in order to narrow the explanations for its conduct. Scientists recognize inherent limits in results and are usually cautious in interpreting the significance.

Such caution is found less often among drug war zealots. An anti-drug advertisement stated, "In animal studies, monkeys with unlimited access to cocaine self-administer until they die. One monkey pressed a bar 12,800 times to obtain a single dose of cocaine."[15] The ad does not say whether the cited monkey was typical or an extreme case. Animals are individuals, just as humans are, and behavior by one cannot be extrapolated to all. The ad does not reveal that in psychological conditioning the strength of response (number of bar pressings) can be increased by withholding the reward (cocaine),[16] the exact technique used in the cited experiment. Nor does the ad reveal how often the bar was pressed before rewards started (the "base line"), how often it was pressed per unit of time, how often it was pressed for other rewards, or what total period of time the experiment covered. Animals typically press a bar for cocaine several hours after it is no longer delivered, and then quit.[17] Such behavior is no more alarming than humans who insert money in a vending machine and keep yanking the lever when nothing is delivered. Humans have even died after pulling tightfisted vending machines onto themselves, but that tells little about the dangers of candy bars or soda pop. Likewise, experiments normally do not test whether an animal will press a bar many times: conditioning principles of Pavlov and Skinner can train animals to do remarkable things, even water can produce the same compulsive behavior as cocaine.[18] Instead, experiments examine how that behavior alters in the presence of variables. But the ad does not tell what the cited experiments studied, nor reveal methods or environments. The ad simply prints a meaningless number of bar pressings that may shock persons unfamiliar with animal tests. And despite the ad's implication that monkeys died of self-administered cocaine overdose, fatalities may have had another cause. The ad also says monkeys will starve to death because they prefer cocaine to food, "Like monkey, like man." Yet we never hear of cocaine addicts starving to death because, unlike experimenters who withhold food from an animal needing it, malnourished people are given assistance. Moreover, scientists who reported one such monkey experiment warned, "Human beings do not use cocaine in this way."[19] The ad presents information in a misleading context. Wide dissemination of such propaganda, presented as objective truth, promotes an ill-informed public.[20]

Whenever we hear about animal experiments we should ask if they force choices upon the animals. When allowed to move around in natural-seeming habitats, when allowed to choose among many options, animals do not use drugs to excess.[21] Even in some laboratory settings monkeys limit their cocaine intake.[22] Bizarre conduct provoked by experimental manipulation does not occur just because drugs are freely available. This is true even though many kinds of animals like to use drugs that humans abuse.[23]

The power of experimental setting, and the danger of attributing odd conduct to spurious qualities in substances, is illustrated by conditions in Europe right after World War II. Cigarettes were scarce. To get them, nicotine addicts reduced themselves to depravity. They became liars and thieves, bartered treasured possessions, and traded away food even though they were already underfed.[24] Some reports say women smokers resorted to prostitution.[25]

As noted previously, setting exerts powerful influence on drug effects. Effects of addiction are also influenced by setting, as demonstrated among smokers in Europe after World War II and among animals in laboratories today. Too often, effects of setting are misattributed to a drug. From the European experience one might argue that nicotine causes malnutrition and prostitution, but the argument confuses nicotine with its setting. The same mistake occurs with cocaine and heroin, blamed for wickedness elicited by their setting (which includes laws).

Realization that set and setting influence drug effects, and that addiction can occur without resonance, has led to the concept of "psychological addiction." Some workers in the field resist the idea, calling it "a contradiction in medical terminology—a nonsense term."[26] The danger they see is that "psychological addiction" disregards pharmacology. If a drug's chemistry is irrelevant to addiction, then addiction has nothing to do with the drug. Any scientific foundation for drug addiction legislation begins to crumble.

As we shall see later, an addict's choice of drug can have a basis in chemistry. But that basis is irrelevant to addiction. No drug is universally addictive; only certain persons with particular desires will become addicted, while most persons will use the drug in moderation or abandon it. Factors leading to addiction are within the person, not the drug. The distinction between physical and psychological addiction became blurred many years ago,[27] but only recently have investigators realized the distinction is meaningless.[28]

A nonpharmacological basis for addiction means that attempted cures will fail if aimed at the substance. Futility of mere detoxification has been demonstrated in numerous treatment programs directed against alcohol, tobacco, and narcotics. At least 90 percent of patients resume using the substance.[29] Detoxification confuses "a relatively minor symptom with the disease."[30] Successful treatment must attack *motives* for addiction, not the *drugs*.

Psychological, rather than chemical, basis of addiction is demonstrated by a person addicted to a placebo, exhibiting craving, tolerance, and a withdrawal syndrome.[31] Evidence for psychological mechanism is also found in the substitution phenomenon, by which an addict changes drugs and remains satisfied. Opiate addicts can turn to alcohol, Valium, or marijuana.[32] "Marijuana saved me," said one heroin addict.[33] If an active placebo like marijuana can suffice the desire of an opiate addict, chemistry has no role. Not all addicts can switch comfortably, and alternatives such as alcohol and Valium certainly have pharmacological actions. Nonetheless, substitution illustrates the psychological origin of addiction.

Addiction longevity also demonstrates the dominance of psychology and triviality of chemistry. Fond memories of soothing heroin or nicotine crop up whenever a person faces pressure they once eased. The old answer to the same problem can be hard to resist. As far back as the 1930s addicts referred to "cures" that had no effect on longing for their drug.[34] Abstinence does not cure addiction.[35] If strong craving persists years after a drug and its by-products are no longer present in the body,[36] addiction is not physical. In other words, drugs do not cause addiction.

If a drug is used to meet a need, craving may persist as long as the need does. Researchers find that a typical drug user satisfies needs with the substance; using it is not a sign of craziness but is a rational response to problems that otherwise fester without relief.[37] A response can be rational without being wise, but for some persons drugs are the only available answer—the best of a bad lot. Some users see drugs as solving problems rather than creating them. If people feel drugs improve their lives, the appeal will be strong and persistent. The "improvement" may surprise someone outside the drug culture. For example, an outsider may pity a heroin addict who spends hours every day scrounging for drug money and searching for dealers. An addict, however, who was previously unable or unwilling to hold a normal job, might feel the day was filled with purposeful activity leading to personal fulfillment.[38] Hustling for drugs advertises energy and shrewdness, making the user a role model of industriousness and success rather than a derelict to be shunned. Drug addiction can give a person self-esteem where none existed before. Such a person may feel liberated rather than enslaved. It all depends on what an individual's values are. Everyone engages in conduct that causes both harm and happiness; in principle drug abusers behave no differently from anyone else.[39]

Some users of illicit drugs may have a special need. Many people have an imbalance or lack of chemicals needed for normal functioning; physicians prescribe drugs to correct such conditions. Investigators suspect that certain illicit drugs may correct conditions unrecognized by medical science, that some users are medicating themselves.[40] More and more conditions, such as alcoholism and schizophrenia, previously thought to originate in mental processes are now thought to have genetic and physiological components. Perhaps physical explanations will also be demonstrated for some types of illicit drug use; if so, needs of those users can probably be met in no other way.

Still another explanation for longevity of addiction can be found in psychological conditioning.[41] There is nothing sinister about psychological conditioning—it occurred for centuries before researchers exposed its processes. In the type relevant here, behavior precedes a reinforcement, such as someone injecting heroin (behavior) to feel soothed (reinforcement). If reinforcement only occurs now and then, rather than every time, the behavior will occur more often in hopes of evoking the reinforcement. Thus, because street heroin is adulterated and unreliable, an addict will use it more often than if effects were dependable. Indeed the behavior will persist even when followed by undesirable consequences, such as getting beaten up or arrested. Once established, such conditioning will be maintained even if the desired reinforcement rarely appears. The behavior will stop only if it fails to produce the desired reinforcement many, many times in a row. And, of course, that is not the case with heroin or any other illicit drug. Drug addiction that results from psychological conditioning may be strengthened by anti-drug laws that guarantee intermittent reinforcement.[42]

If drugs do not cause addiction, if people addict themselves, we should find many persons using heroin and cocaine without becoming addicted. Such persons exist. They are called "chippers," and authorities say that chippers outnumber addicts.[43] People can use heroin in moderation for years without becoming addicted, and they can stop without distress.[44] Such users get along well in society; except for heroin use they seem like anyone else.[45] The same goes for cocaine.[46] Such research findings support everyday observation; most users of the addictive drug alcohol are chippers. We should not be surprised if chippers predominate among users of any drug.

The cause of drug use and the cause of addiction are different. If we understand the difference we can see why many drug control efforts fail.

Today many investigators ask why people abuse drugs. In former times similar energy was devoted to discovering the so-called criminal personality. The outcome of that latter effort provides a clue about drug abuse. Crime is socially defined. Example: In Missouri a grocer who legally sells a bottle of whiskey on Saturday would violate the law by selling on Sunday. Nothing about the seller, the commodity, or the buyer changes; yet on one day the act is legal and on the next it is illegal. The grocer's personality stays the same; an upstanding businessman on Saturday changes into a criminal on Sunday only because of a piece of paper with a printed statute. Even with acts that remain legal or illegal all the time, definition of criminality is arbitrary—this can be demonstrated by comparing laws of the United States, Britain, Iran, and the Soviet Union. The same behavior can leave a person unmolested or imprisoned, depending on where it occurs. In other words, the cause of crime is human behavior.

None of this denies that dangerous psychopaths exist and must be prevented from preying upon everyone else. But whether psychopathic behavior is labeled "criminal" is a result of when and where a particular act occurs. Nothing is inherently a crime. Crime is socially defined. A psychopath may be different from you and me, but a criminal is not. That is the outcome of the search for the "criminal personality."

Drugs, like crime, are socially defined. Lives ruined by cigarettes far outnumber those harmed by heroin, yet nicotine sellers openly urge more Americans to take up the habit; indeed, by compulsory taxation the federal government forces citizens to aid tobacco growers. Nicotine's physical danger and addictive potential are so well demonstrated that the federal drug control law of 1970 specifically exempted tobacco because otherwise it fit the scientific criteria used to describe banned drugs. Regardless of scientific evidence, most Americans do not consider tobacco users to be drug users. Alcohol has generated far more violence than cocaine, but alcohol inebriation is considered so innocuous that in Missouri a drunk driver who endangers innocent people may repeat such conduct and still retain a driver's license. Regardless of scientific evidence, most Americans do not consider alcohol a drug.

Drug abuse, like drugs themselves, is socially defined. A good citizen can use prescribed amphetamines purchased from a pharmacist; a user who avoids physicians and turns to the black market is considered a sick criminal. Yet the substance and the motive for consuming are the same. One person might buy a round of beers for friends and join in their merriment, while another might buy marijuana for friends and smoke it with them. The first person may be praised as a swell fellow, while the second is sent to prison for years. The issue here is not whether people should get intoxicated with drugs; the issue is which drugs should be used—a matter of taste rather than a moral decision about intoxication. Different cultures may use the same drug for different purposes; Andrew Weil found Indians of the Amazon taking drugs associated with rebellion and self-destruction in the United States, but Indian usage lacked such associations.[47] The chemicals were the same, but attitudes toward them were different; those social attitudes led to abuse in one society but not in the other. The same phenomenon has been observed with alcohol; drinking problems prevalent in the United States are less common in Italy, leading Stanton Peele to conclude that perceptions of a drug are more important than its chemistry: "If the drug is seen as mysterious and uncontrollable, or if it stands for escape and oblivion, then it will be widely misused. . . . Where people can readily accept a drug, then dramatic personal deterioration and social disruption will not result."[48] Richard H. Blum and Eva M. Blum even find that if drinking problems are recognized they still may not be considered abuse: "In rural Greece there are illnesses that villagers say the doctors do not recognize; alcoholism is one that *no one* recognizes."[49] Because the villager considers "wine as one of the most important elements in his life, as well as valuing himself and the honor of his country as blameless, he will be appalled at any suggestion that his nation could be afflicted with a disease—when it is so clear to him that it is, to the contrary, much blest by the grape."[50]

Two cultures may use the same drug for different purposes, as in the Amazon and the United States. Or a culture may use different drugs (alcohol and marijuana) for the same purpose. A culture may accept a drug, but distinguish harshly between methods used to obtain it (as with prescription or black market amphetamines). The same behavior (drinking problems) may occur in two cultures, with one treating it as disease and the other denying the disease exists. Drug use may be seen as deviance by the law, or as social conformity by members of a peaceful commune or a violent gang.[51] All these different attitudes are socially determined, forcing drug abuse to be defined socially.

Drug laws deal more with social control than with drugs. There is nothing wrong with such control—what else are laws for? The social control element in drug legislation is seldom recognized, however, and blindness to that factor limits effectiveness of drug laws. Essentially, drug abuse laws give a medical definition to nonmedical problems. We shall deal further with this issue later.

Certain behaviors may exist everywhere, but labeling the conduct as "crime" or "drug abuse" is arbitrary.[52] That does not make the label meaningless or undesirable. But it does mean that just as there is no "criminal personality," there is no "drug abuser personality." The cause of drug abuse, like crime, is human behavior. That explanation sounds stupid, but is important because if a portrait of the general population excludes drug habits but includes other personal characteristics (even self-destructiveness), there is no way to tell who is a drug abuser and who is not. In other words, drug abusers are the same as everyone else.[53]

That notion can be hard to accept. Drug abusers are such vile outcasts that it may scarcely seem possible that they are as normal as the rest of the population. Nonetheless, researchers have demonstrated this fact. Indeed, some have even found drug *addicts*, not just users, to be no different from the general population.[54] Andrew Weil recalls heroin addicts he knew:

> Most were working-class whites who held steady jobs, bought their drugs with money from their salaries, and led unobtrusive lives in suburbs far removed from what most of us think of as the world of the addict. Some of these people would take one injection of heroin in the morning before going to work and no further doses; others would fix in the morning and evening. Most had kept up these patterns for years.[55]

Middle class and wealthy addicts may get opiates from physicians on plausible excuses.[56] In 1950, an expensive private sanitarium (as opposed to a public clinic for the indigent) had no difficulty finding narcotics addicts able to pay its fee—businessmen, teachers, clergymen, housewives, and others of social standing inconsistent with the dope fiend stereotype.[57] In the 1960s, similar addicts emerged from about 30 percent of case reports found in records of the Federal Bureau of Narcotics.[58] That finding is particularly significant in a law enforcement data base; police burglary division records would not show 30 percent of the offenders as teachers and clergymen. To be apprehended in great numbers, middle and upper class narcotics users must be numerous.[59] Drug addicts are stereotyped as impoverished, but drug use does not match the level of poverty; the poorest people are not the highest users.[60] Addicts are also stereotyped as persons whose criminal violations go beyond drug laws, but some authorities question that belief as well.[61]

The reason that no difference can be found between user and non-user populations is because the desire to alter one's state of consciousness is normal.[62] Normality of drug use is illustrated by free-roaming animals who gladly intoxicate themselves when opportunity arises: cats with catnip, cattle with locoweed, squirrels with pine cone seeds, bees with fermented sap.[63] Dim evidence exists that chimpanzees may alter their consciousness through ritual dancing;[64] humans are well known for such conduct. Performing artists can go into transported states, as can their audiences. Religious traditions are filled with accounts of altered states. Drug users simply choose a particular path to goals that most people desire and achieve. In this regard we are all the same.

Drug use, however, and drug addiction have different causes. In that regard we are not all the same. The reasons chippers use drugs differ from reasons of addicts.[65] Typically addicts seek to avoid pain but chippers seek euphoria.[66] Chippers and addicts also use drugs in different ways. Chippers follow rituals; they smoke marijuana only as part of a social occasion or use heroin only to unwind on a weekend.[67] They budget their drug money and avoid slighting their responsibilities.[68] Chippers integrate a drug into their lives in order to enhance other things they do. In contrast, addicts use a drug for its own sake; no time is appropriate or inappropriate, and consequently the drug habit interferes with other activities (such as jobs or family life), activities that may be abandoned as irrelevant to the pursuit of drug sensations.[69] "When I lived and worked in the Haight-Ashbury district of San Francisco," Andrew Weil writes, "the people I met who were in the very worst relationships with drugs (usually with amphetamines, barbiturates, alcohol, and heroin) were always the people who had done away with rules,"[70] people who abandoned ritual. Chippers have assorted interests; drugs are simply one activity among many in a varied life.[71] An addict subordinates or even gives up other interests; everything revolves around the drug.

That decision by the addict is voluntary. Fruitful lives of chippers demonstrate that drugs do not force a dreary outcome on the addict. The addict *desires* a limited life. Therein lies the appeal of addiction.

QUEST FOR ADDICTION

For addicts, or anyone else, illicit drug use normally starts as a casual occurrence involving no more forethought or drama than the first drink of soda pop.[72] Investigators note the "naturalness" of the process: "The transition from knowing about heroin . . . to knowing heroin-users more-or-less casually to personal participation—this transition appears smooth."[73] "It seems that it was not so much if they were going to try it [cocaine] but when the opportunity would present itself."[74] Continued use and overindulgence may relate to personal frustrations, but they have nothing to do with a person's introduction to illicit drugs. "Most contemporary drug users drifted into the choice through mild peer-group pressure and chance."[75]

Although spread of drug use is likened to contagious disease, and with heroin actually follows mathematical models of epidemics,[76] the simile is wrong. People seek to avoid disease and can catch it despite precautions. Unlike disease, drug use is voluntary and deliberate; "victims" desire the experience. Drug users may not consider themselves diseased at all, and many will undergo treatment only if compelled by the judicial system. Spread of heroin use may mimic contagion but is actually a diffusion of information—carried by example and word of mouth rather than by dirty needles and saliva. Rhetoric about a "drug epidemic" causes unjustified fear. Drugs are not out there like bacteria and viruses, are not able to strike anyone at random. Illicit drugs cannot ensnare a person who refuses to take them. We really can "just say no." The only person at risk is someone who decides to use the drugs. They are a sometimes dangerous fad, not a disease.[77]

Much public fear and fury is directed at pushers, drug sellers who recruit novices. Pushers are rare, so rare that not one example emerged during research for this book. A novice's friends, not some lurking stranger, provide introduction to drug use. This has been proven by statements of drug users, field observations of use patterns, and mathematical analysis of the patterns.[78] "Evidence for friendship or peer group spread is now so overwhelming that it is no longer debated among serious researchers, but, in spite of this certitude, there are still many people who believe that new heroin use is the result of some deliberate marketing strategy, in which dealers sell unwary innocents the idea of use as well as the drug itself."[79] Few addicts or dealers try to hook new users; instead novices seek the drug.[80] The abstinent dealer is another rarity; almost all sellers are users.[81]

Drug dealing is a business, albeit an illegal one, and from a business standpoint a seller will not recruit new users. There is no need; drugs are a seller's market, and demand always outstrips the supply. For that reason alone a peddler would never distribute free samples to hook someone; why give away a commodity that can be sold for a high price? Moreover, the amount of use required to establish physical resonance is far higher than most people imagine; to hook someone, a seller would have to give away adulterated doses for months. Rather few legitimate businesses with permanent locations engage in a give away strategy that persists over several months to land a new customer; no street corner drug hustler does. After all, the drug business is illegal. The dealer may have to flee tomorrow, leaving a competitor to profit from the hooked novice. The lack of product quality control (reliable brand names) means that the targeted customer might switch to another source anyway. In addition, a peddler who gave away samples to strangers would quickly be swamped by persistent strangers demanding the same terms, an outcome that would surely deter any other seller from such foolishness. Fear of a police trap may make a seller reluctant to serve a new customer;[82] even a legitimate novice may accidentally led police to the seller,[83] all the more reason to avoid hooking non-users. Pushing would be so reckless that few dealers could try it and survive. Rage directed at pushers is directed at phantoms.

Anyone worried about getting hooked should instead be careful about friends.[84] Anywhere from 20 percent to almost 50 percent of regular marijuana users in the United States sell the substance to friends as a gesture of goodwill.[85] A survey of cocaine users found that almost everyone started while visiting with friends who shared their supply, in a genial atmosphere likened to breaking open a six-pack of beer.[86] Heroin users have recalled their first youthful dose from buddies waiting for a dance to begin.[87]

In addition to fellowship, the decision to use drugs may involve imitation of role models.[88] If we cannot all be virile, good looking, and admired by people we want to impress, at least we can imitate their habits and show that we share their interests. This factor underlies much advertising of alcohol and tobacco, so we may be sure that legal drug dealers regard it as significant. In Hollywood classics, sophisticated characters filled with charm and zest are always filled with alcohol and nicotine. That is subtle advertising, but just as effective as billboards and commercials. People really do take up tobacco smoking if they admire smokers.[89] The admired person need not be upstanding; the individual may be a violent criminal.[90] The point is that role models are important in drug use. The specific model may be a tough gang leader addicted to crack cocaine or a beloved relative who drinks moderately. A person's choice of drug and habit of consumption will vary accordingly. If the esteemed individual is a drug addict, imitation of that conduct may be deliberate rather than an undesired calamity.

In general, becoming addicted to a drug involves hard work. A "wonderful" drug may cause nausea, may have contaminants that cause illness, may be priced outrageously, may require a risk of violence when contacting a dealer. Few persons will put up with such aggravation. Most decline drugs even when available.[91] Only a small minority become addicts; and that outcome is due not to the drug, but to the values and desires of people who become addicted.[92]

Drugs, in the words of Stanton Peele, "are *not* addictive when they serve to fulfill a larger purpose in life."[93] He adds,

> If what a person is engaged in enhances his ability to live—if it enables him to work more effectively, to love more beautifully, to appreciate the things around him more, and finally, if it allows him to grow, to change, and expand—then it is not addictive. If, on the other hand, it diminishes him—if it makes him less attractive, less capable, less sensitive, and if it limits him, stifles him, harms him—then it is addictive.[94]

Such an observation applies to more than drugs, and helps us to understand a key characteristic of addiction: addicts want to escape from freedom.

Peele notes that an addict looks to an outside authority for strength. The addict's

> view of life is not a positive one which anticipates chances for pleasure and ful-
> fillment, but a negative one which fears the world and people as threats to
> himself. When this person is confronted with demands or problems, he seeks
> support from an external source which, since he feels it is stronger than he is,
> he believes can protect him. The addict is not a genuinely rebellious person.
> Rather, he is a fearful one. . . . In giving himself up to these larger [external]
> forces, he is a perpetual invalid.[95]

An addict desires sameness. This helps explain the tolerance phenomenon. An addict wants to repeat the same sensation experienced in a particular drug experience, but the world and its inhabitants are changing all the time. The drug addict uses higher and higher doses in an impossible attempt to repeat the past.

Thirst for sameness can also be seen in the drug hustle that fills an addict's day to the exclusion of most other activity. The hustle is a reassuring steady framework to a life that might otherwise require response to varied oppor-tunities every day.[96] Obtaining drugs may involve creativity and industrious-ness; an addict is not necessarily a slothful dullard,[97] and may play an exciting game all day long. But a game is not life. The addict does not want to face, let alone seek out, other challenges offered by the world.

Addicts also want to avoid accountabilty. By using narcotics a young person afraid of on-coming adult responsibilities can avoid both them and guilt about the cowardice.[98] Such can be the grim result for persons who follow Peter Pan's advice and refuse to grow up.

Addicts want to obey authority. Rather than taking charge of their own lives, they desire orders from some other entity—chemical, medical, or legal. "Treatment communities" are hailed for their rigorous regimentation of residents' lives, but merely provide the same regimentation that drugs did. Looking for an authority to rule their lives, some addicts switch from drugs to religion, following that path with fanaticism incomprehensible to fellow churchgoers.[99] Modern history gives horrifying examples of large populations who believed in charismatic leaders. Uncritical obedience is a sign of addiction.

Society cooperates with the addict's distaste for accountability, agreeing that drugs control behavior. Irresponsibility is thereby not only tolerated from an addict, it is encouraged. Police, courts, newspapers, and the public all agree when an addict claims, "Drugs made me do it." Far from being a rebel, an addict takes the proper pose demanded for the tableau. It is all part of the drug hustle game.

Drugs are no exoneration for behavior. Illicit drugs lack the dark and magical powers that most Americans ascribe to them.[100] Drugs may encourage a person to do something more vigorously or more often, but only if the person already wants to do it;[101] alcohol or cocaine will not change a meek soul into an aggressive monster.[102] Many regular users of heroin avoid degradation; no narcotic is powerful enough to force such a bleak outcome, only personal choice can do it. And to blame marijuana for antisocial conduct is to endow the substance with strength that, by definition, an active placebo lacks. Nonetheless drugs are a splendid scapegoat for an addict's decisions. Not only does such an excuse fulfill the addict's desire, it promotes goals of drug war zealots—serving needs of the righteous and the damned. Uniting such passionate interests produces a powerful political force dependent on the illusion of drug power. Small wonder that scientific reality is pushed aside in public policy debate.

American society promotes addiction by discouraging people from taking charge of their lives. On the most personal level this occurs by thwarting reasonable goals of citizens—a good education relevant to a student's life, prospects that talent will be rewarded by appropriate employment, decent and affordable housing on a block where neighbors help one another and where anyone can stroll without fear of molestation. Those goals are so elementary, so essential to decent life in a democracy, that everyone should expect to achieve them. An appalling percentage of our citizenry never comes close, and not through personal failing. In my town the newspaper routinely carries stories of the disastrous public school system; students cannot be faulted for a lack of textbooks and for schools that are unable to open in the autumn. A diploma does not entitle anyone to a good job, but a bright person shunted into flipping hamburgers will be well aware of talents that go wasted, wasted in a country with problems big enough for all the talent it can produce. As for comfortably priced housing in pleasant neighborhoods—in my town such areas are routinely bulldozed to make way for commercial real estate developments that instead might have healed blighted districts.

When defeated by such a system, year after year, some people give up. Narcotics can be expected to thrive in such a population.[103] Not only do they mask despair that reappears whenever drug effects wear off; the user's sense of futility closes off arguments about hazards. Today we hear much about drug use throughout America, but historically persons from urban racial and ethnic minorities have entered treatment programs in numbers 3 to 9 times higher than if drug addiction was found throughout society equally.[104] This despair is not because people are poor or thwarted in personal goals per se, but because America continually promises a better life if only a person works hard enough. When America continually fails to deliver, or worse yet delivers a fake (such as high-rise public housing), our people's spirit is broken along with the promises. If pain is inescapable, drugs that relieve pain become attractive and even sensible.

Even if drug abuse treatment programs had 100 percent success with clients, drug abuse in American society would continue to thrive. As Robert G. Newman notes,

> tuberculosis was brought under control not by the introduction of chemo-therapeutic agents, but by a substantial improvement in living conditions; in areas where that improvement has not occurred, the disease is widespread . . . even though each individual patient can be readily diagnosed and cured. Similarly, we must recognize that addiction is a social problem which will never be eliminated by measures that are imposed on the addicts themselves.[105]

Addicts are not the cause of addiction. Neither curing them nor killing them can solve the problem.

DRUG-FREE ADDICTION

"Drug addiction" is normally considered in terms of *drugs*, but to grasp the problem we must consider it in terms of *addiction*. The addiction problem in America goes far beyond drugs.

For example, watching television can be an addiction. Sitting in front of the tube diminishes contact with the world and with human beings, yet many persons do it for hours every night. Like the drug hustle, watching television is a retreat from reality, putting structure into the life of a person who is unable to tolerate personal freedom, who prefers to give up freedom's opportunities in exchange for a repetitive sameness to each wasted day. Pre-emption of an expected program may make no difference to the viewing habit; the person simply watches something else. Content of the experience is irrelevant; the important thing is to keep it going. Just as someone on a heroin high wants to be left alone, a television viewer may be annoyed by family members who request attention. Watching television can be characterized by morbid craving, in which viewers forswear any activity that interferes with contemplation of their electronic nirvana, of emptiness.

It is possible to be addicted to people. Stanton Peele tells chilling stories of satisfied couples addicted to each other, who shut themselves off from friends and experiences they enjoyed before they met each other, couples feeling no

pain and no joy, reveling in the same sensation sought by narcotics addicts.[106]
Even America's drug war is an addiction.

Drug war zealots accept drugs as an all-powerful authority: a dark one to be resisted, Satan instead of God, but authority nonetheless. Compulsive behavior is seen throughout the war effort. For example, belief in "drug treatment" programs grows with every reported success—even though almost 100 percent of treated cases are failures. Thus we see the power of intermittent conditioning, with drug war zealots acting no differently from rats that keep pressing a bar even though only one press in thousands brings a reward of cocaine. Retaining and expanding drug treatment programs is compulsive, eating up financial and human resources that could be used productively in other endeavors. The call for more and more anti-drug laws, creating new criminal offenses when officials cannot even keep up with old ones, shows an addict's inability to achieve satiation; anti-drug crusaders never feel they have enough anti-drug laws. If zealots do not get enough sensation of accomplishment through the present level of law enforcement, they call for it to be administered with more power and more frequence—clear evidence that the tolerance phenomenon has taken hold. Morbid craving is seen in the willingness to ignore more important community needs in order to fulfill the desire to fight drugs. Self-destructiveness is seen in efforts that promote the very abuses (such as disease, crime, and corruption) that drug war zealots claim to fight, while curtailing civil liberties that Americans claim to cherish. Crusaders declare their goal is a drug-free America, a goal guaranteed to perpetuate their addictive game because no country has ever become free of drugs or addicts. Abstinence does not cure addiction, but zealots propose abstinence as a simple answer. Belief in a simple answer is, in itself, a sign of addiction.[107]

There is aimlessness in the lives of people who choose addiction.[108] Addicts in methadone programs, who are generally considered more motivated to change their lot than addicts who do not seek help, show "low self-esteem, poor impulse control, low frustration tolerance, . . . pervasive feelings of boredom and emptiness."[109] One heroin abuser resumed after quitting and gave this explanation: "I started shooting up again. I don't know why."[110] In 1973 a study tried to follow the whereabouts of "street users" in Detroit, Los Angeles, and Washington, D.C., but 33 percent of them disappeared within 6 months.[111] Another study found that, contrary to popular belief, street addicts are not on welfare—they do not bother to apply.[112]

Having divided the term "drug addiction," having pulled away the drugs, we begin to see that addiction permeates American society. "Young people who suddenly repudiate convention and seek solace in drugs . . . are only expressing tendencies that were always present in acceptable guises in their home and school lives."[113] The irrelevance of drugs to addiction explains the failure to find a psychological difference between drug addicts and the general population. So many members of the general population are involved with other addictions that their personalities will match members who have selected drugs as their addiction of choice. Drugs are an invalid variable in addiction.

Tendencies toward addiction are normal and reside within each of us. Unfortunately, American society today strives to encourage those proclivities. "We are always left looking for the next [academic] degree, the next lover, the next visit to the shrink, the next fix. We are taught . . . that we need school, need marriage, need a steady job, need medicines. What we really need is to be whole in ourselves, to take charge of our own health and education and emotional development."[114]

Today U.S. governmental and social institutions are designed to extinguish that sort of independence. Addiction is the goal of those authorities, because free people run their own lives and reject authorities. Promotion of addiction, the antithesis of democracy, is ominous for the longevity of a democracy.

REWARDS OF DRUG ADDICTION

Having separated "drug" from "addiction," let us restore the term to consider why some people choose drugs from all alternative addictions.

Certain drugs meet certain needs. Someone who is depressed or seeking arousal may turn to a stimulant like cocaine. It produces the desired effect by tapping energy stored in the body, so when the drug wears off the person feels more run down than before. If a person either does not understand or does not care how stimulants work, the outcome may be to take another dose right away to get pepped up again. The mechanics of stimulant addiction are that simple, and relate to stupidity or self-destructiveness in the user rather than anything inherent in the drug.

Someone troubled by anxiety, anger, or frustration may find calming relief in narcotic intoxication. Afterwards, an industrious person might feel rested and refreshed, ready to tackle challenges anew. In contrast, a person who has given up on life may prefer to reenter the narcotic stupor rather than face the same problems again. As someone spends more and more time in narcotic retreat, problems seem ever worse upon regaining normal consciousness. Indeed they really may be worse because the world moves along while the person stands still. So another dose is taken to escape reality awhile longer, to maintain the sameness of narcotic sensation rather than experience the diversity thrust forward by life. A person's relation with the world determines the relation with narcotics. Addiction is created by the person, not by the drug.[115]

Drugs can provide sensations, such as arousal or contentment, that a person desires but does not otherwise receive from life. Many drug users are unaware that such feelings are an internal perception and are available through other means. Therefore, if sensations that come after taking a drug make life seem better, the user can easily be hooked. Such a habit may become a downward spiral because drug-influenced perceptions of the world can be illusory, making the habitual user less and less able to deal with situations that provoked drug use in the first place.

Drugs can also provide nonpharmacological rewards, such as friendship.[116] A user may enter into a circle of associates who have similar, albeit limited, interests. Such friends may provide acceptance, understanding, and fellowship heretofore denied to the user, particularly if the user was already an outcast social deviant. A person rejected by society may well use outlawed drugs as a political statement of contempt for solid citizens.[117] Social attitudes toward a substance, rather than pharmacological properties, can be the basis of use.

A person's needs, not the drugs, determine the possibility and power of addiction.[118] The more needs a drug meets, the stronger the addiction.[119] Those needs, not the drugs, must be addressed in order to reduce the amount of drug use and addiction.

SELF-DESTRUCTION

Drug addiction is self-destructive behavior. Why some people choose self-destruction is beyond the scope of this book, but the work of Paul Blachly identifies typical self-destructive characteristics in drug addiction:

1. Active participation by the victim in his own victimization.
2. Negativism (knowing the usual adverse consequences of one's actions, but doing it anyway).
3. Short-term gain.
4. Long-term punishment.[120]

Probably everyone has done something that fits those 4 criteria. Such behavior is normal. It becomes abnormal when repeated over and over. That sort of conduct is self-destruction.

The element of negativism is particularly important. Many people hope that education will deter drug use, and researchers have found support for that hope.[121] Researchers, however, have also found that many drug abusers knew of risks before starting, but discounted them as applying only to other persons.[122] If facts are irrelevant to some drug abusers, education will not change their conduct, and appeals to self-interest will not work .

The characteristics identified by Paul Blachly fit drug abuse well but also fit other types of conduct: truancy, gambling, overeating, sexual promiscuity, driving over the speed limit, parole violations, terrible marriages and divorces, suicide.[123] By implication these apparently different behaviors all meet the same need and are interchangeable for that purpose. We should expect self-destructive people to exhibit more than one harmful behavior, to have a multiproblem lifestyle. Researchers find that to be the case.[124]

For example, not all automobile wrecks are accidents. Investigators find a high correlation between the way people run their lives and the way they run their cars:

> Subject received a citation for negligent collision and for driving without a valid operator's license. He was divorced from his wife and had not seen either his wife or his two children for six months prior to being interviewed. He had recently lost his job as a laborer after he had broken his ankle while drunk, and since that time had been unemployed. His vehicle was found to have defective brakes, defective steering, a defective suspension system, and slick tires which resulted in poor friction on the wet pavement, plus inoperative windshield wipers which had helped to obstruct his vision. When he was asked why he had allowed his vehicle to get into such a state, he said, "I thought I could adjust to it."[125]

A study comparing alcohol abuse and forms of violent death, using worldwide statistics from the World Health Organization, found positive correlation for fatal traffic "accidents."[126] A study of 28 consecutive automobile deaths in Houston, Texas, found that the drivers at fault in 25 cases comprised a group of "intoxicated, depressed, angry and impulsive persons."[127] Another study of 34 drivers who crashed found that 22 were "psychiatrically abnormal." Ten of the abnormal drivers operated cars with mechanical problems that caused the wrecks; only one of the "normal" drivers had such a defective car. Seventeen of the disturbed drivers were held at fault in the crashes, as opposed to two of the normal drivers. Conclusion: "Abnormal personality leads to poor vehicle maintenance and to poor driving."[128]

Fears are misplaced about drugs impairing a driver's ability. People who take their responsibilities seriously do not drive while intoxicated; heroin chippers are careful to avoid driving while under the influence.[129] Irresponsible driving is merely one aspect of a drug addict's multiproblem lifestyle. Drug abuse does not cause trouble on the road; instead the two behaviors go together.

Overeating fits the same pattern of self-destruction: willing participation by the victim despite knowledge of danger, short-term gain, long-term penalty. Physicians have noted that patients addicted to drugs and those addicted to food behave in the same basic ways; they are dishonest, uncooperative, prone to skip appointments, and to abandon the medical regimen.[130] One 5-foot 7-inch tall narcotics addict switched from dope to food, weighing in at nearly 260 pounds. This case was cited as a successful cure of addiction.[131]

Multiple problems of drug abusers are seen in their simultaneous abuse of multiple drugs. A typical heroin addict does not just use heroin, but also cocaine, marijuana, tobacco, alcohol, barbiturates, amphetamines, or glue.[132] Case studies reveal astonishing levels of consumption. On a typical day one subject drank up to $15 worth of alcohol. In that person's neighborhood $15 could buy over a half gallon of hard liquor or almost 4 gallons of beer. On the same day, the subject also used tranquilizers, heroin, and cocaine.[133] When we read of a crime committed by someone who has taken cocaine, we should ask how much whiskey the person drank before the act as well.[134] The worst abusers of drugs have so many substances sloshing in them simultaneously, with so many interactions, that it is impossible to determine how a particular substance is influencing behavior. Moreover, even though a user may claim to have taken a particular drug, the misbranding of illicit supplies means that the person may not be using the substance that was paid for. An act may be blamed on a substance that was not even in the person's system. Avid willingness to stuff unknown chemicals into one's body is itself a mark of self-destruction.[135]

On top of all that is the recklessness of some addicts. Some cheat drug dealers who are violent and heavily armed.[136] Some use public toilet water to mix solutions for intravenous injection.[137] Taking drugs away from such people will not help them. Certain individuals are simply doomed.

TREATMENT

Many people consider "disease" a scientific concept that can be measured apart from cultural context. A person either has a heart problem or does not, has a liver infection or does not. Such thinking confuses description of a condition, which can be scientific, with the decision to label the condition as disease. That decision is cultural.

In the lower Mississippi Valley, some accounts say, malaria was once considered normal—simply part of living in the area, like heat and humidity. A person with malaria was not considered diseased.[138] And just because a condition can be treated medically, that does not make it disease. Human rights activists have been labeled mentally ill in the Soviet Union and confined to psychiatric hospitals for medical treatment. Recreational opium users could expect a similar fate in the United States, even though they would be considered robust and productive citizens in some areas of the old Middle East. Alcoholism is currently considered a disease, but through much of American history it was considered a moral weakness. The condition has not changed, but what happens to the alcoholic depends on whether the person is labeled diseased (thereby receiving help and support) or degenerate (resulting in ostracism and abandonment).

We may all agree that someone has malaria, calls for political change in the U.S.S.R., uses opium, or drinks a lot. We may all agree that each of those conditions can be treated medically. But both history and anthropology disagree about whether these conditions are disease. "Many kinds of people are involved in all types of bizarre, irrational, illogical behavior, and may not necessarily be psychologically or socially sick, given the agreed upon mores and rituals of the time."[139]

In the United States drug addiction was not considered a disease until the mid-twentieth century. In 1921, the Treasury Department, which enforced drug laws, distributed comments by a member of the American Medical Association Committee on Narcotic Drugs condemning "the shallow pretense that drug addiction is a disease which the specialist must be allowed to treat."[140] Only in 1934 did drug addiction receive official sanction as disease, listed as mental illness by the American Psychiatric Association.[141] Later the American Psychiatric Association withdrew its endorsement and no longer considered drug addiction to be mental illness.[142] In 1962 the U.S. Supreme Court ruled otherwise, and declared drug addiction to be illness.[143]

Despite ambivalence about the proper label for drug addiction, many Americans believe that putting addicts under medical control at least ensures efficiency and precision in dealing with them as patients. That attitude is the product of faith rather than rational thought. For instance tonsils are far less challenging than drug abuse. In one study physicians examined tonsils of 389 children. In about half the cases doctors recommended tonsillectomy. The children who received a clean bill of health were then sent away for another examination, with the same results—about half were diagnosed as needing surgery. The children certified as healthy by two physicians were sent away for a third exam; in about half the cases physicians recommended tonsil removal.[144] No matter how healthy a child's tonsils were, chances were fifty/fifty that an examining physician would recommend unnecessary surgery. A medical condition as simple as inflamed tonsils can confound a physician. Many personnel in drug treatment centers have received less training than physicians and would not be trusted with a tonsil exam. Yet those personnel evaluate and supervise patients suffering from complex drug abuse problems.

Methadone clinics are a good example of treatment programs that enjoy wide support from authorities in medicine, law, and politics. These clinics are typical of modern treatment for drug addiction. Let us examine them as representatives of the best that medical practice can offer.

Methadone maintenance clinics started in the 1960s amid controversy. The American Medical Association was leery of them.[145] There is a big difference between maintenance and detoxification. Methadone is an opiate (or, more pedantically, an opioid); thus via pharmacological cross-tolerance it will prevent the withdrawal syndrome in a heroin addict. Methadone effects last longer than heroin, so an opiate addict can be satisfied with fewer doses. Methadone can be used to detoxify an addict, to taper off use of opiates until zero use is reached—abstinence. Maintenance is different. In that therapy a heroin addict simply switches to methadone. In theory the addict will someday become abstinent, but methadone can continue until the proper day arrives, however many years that may take. The clinic supplies enough methadone to prevent withdrawal symptoms but not enough to produce opiate intoxication. A methadone patient can thereby act normal and be integrated into normal society.

The difference between maintenance and pandering is subtle, and methadone clinics came under fire for prolonging an affliction rather than curing it. "Do we provide free whiskey to alcoholics"?[146] Clinic proponents counterargued that medical doctors do not cure afflictions such as diabetes or missing limbs, but are willing to help patients function normally with insulin or prosthetics.[147] Methadone serves that purpose.

Methadone maintenance was also attacked for deliberately satisfying immoral lusts of addicts. Medicine has no answer to the moral issue of whether people have a right to achieve euphoria or any other state, but clinic defenders sidestepped the issue by claiming that methadone blocks heroin's euphoric effects and eliminates desire for heroin.[148] That claim is incorrect. Methadone is an opiate, not an opiate antagonist. Due to cross-tolerance, a person satisfied with the prescribed dosage of methadone will feel no desire to take heroin—nothing would be gained. A dissatisfied person, however, can simply use additional amounts of heroin to get any desired narcotic effect.[149] Methadone itself will produce a narcotic high if someone takes enough,[150] and will produce euphoria if injected intravenously or even subcutaneously.[151] Methadone duplicates effects of morphine,[152] and because body chemistry converts heroin to morphine, methadone also duplicates effects of heroin. Some narcotics addicts declare methadone to be their drug of choice, "sweet but oh so smooth."[153] Methadone has the same withdrawal syndrome as any opiate, although controversy exists about whether symptoms are greater than encountered with heroin.[154]

The similarity of heroin and methadone has led cynics to suggest that the purpose of methadone maintenance is to pacify Hispanic and African-

American populations in neighborhoods where clinics are established, keeping ethnic minorities in a doped stupor so they cannot cause trouble.[155] That view probably credits institutional racism with more foresight than it possesses, but does recognize the futility of substituting one opiate for another rather than dealing with factors that promote narcotics addiction.

The quest for a magic drug to cure addiction is venerable. In the 1800s, some practitioners touted heroin as a non-addicting cure for the morphine habit. Morphine addicts who switched to heroin no longer craved the former drug, and the cure was permanent—as long as patients kept taking heroin.[156] In the 1960s, methadone was touted as a non-addicting[157] cure for the heroin habit.

> Methadone staves off not only the acute effects of withdrawal from heroin . . . but the postaddiction syndrome of anxiety, depression, and craving as well, year after year. On methadone the patient no longer thinks constantly about heroin . . . or shapes his whole life to ensure a continuing supply. He no longer engages compulsively in "drug-seeking behavior." He is, quite soon after going on methadone, freed of the heroin incubus. In this sense, he is "cured."[158]

Cured in the same way that morphine addicts were cured by an uninterrupted supply of heroin. Now there is talk of using even longer acting opiates to get people off methadone.[159]

Here we have persistent belief in the same simple solution—a magic drug—even though it never works. People who succumb to this delusion are willing victims. They know that every previous attempt to implement this "solution" had a bad outcome (otherwise they would not keep abandoning the old efforts), but they think the bad result will not happen this time, to them. Proponents receive short-term gain by imagining that something good is being done about drug abuse, and receive long-term punishment as the feared problem becomes more desperate. Does anything about this behavior sound familiar? Not all the addicts involved with methadone maintenance are patients.

There is a small chance that someone addicted to the methadone treatment can cure someone addicted to the methadone drug. The impractical approach of clinic staff is illustrated by their tendency to define normality by middle class values.[160] In middle class America a person may show maturity by deferring gratification and by saving a portion of wages received. An urban ghetto resident, however, may see wisdom in living for the moment lest a criminal or the police intervene tomorrow, and in spending money right away before anyone can steal it. Such attitudes may prove good adjustment to one's environment. Clinic personnel, however, may insist that treatment continue until such attitudes change. Middle class normality may be maladaptive in an addict's world; either the addict or the middle class behavior may not last long upon the patient's release.

A study identified factors that predicted successful graduation from methadone treatment to a narcotics-free life: middle class upbringing, a high school diploma, being self-supporting with a stable job record, avoiding criminal behavior, obeying the methadone program rules, and getting along well with clinic staff.[161] In other words, methadone treatment works if a person has no motivation for taking heroin. Most heroin addicts, however, have some reason for getting into their situation. For almost all heroin addicts, methadone treatment fails.

Proponents argue otherwise, but analysts find no support for the arguments. One program reported 100 percent of patients stopped regular use of heroin. "Irregular use," however, continued among 15 percent to 45 percent, depending on how one defined the term. Moreover, the reported 100 percent success rate was for patients receiving methadone daily, not for persons no longer getting methadone. And even if all the heroin addicts switched to methadone, that would still leave open the question of what other drugs they continued to abuse.[162] Among patients studied in another methadone program, a minimum of 30 percent continued to use additional opiates,[163] and after months of treatment in another methadone program 92 percent of patients still used heroin.[164]

Supposedly 94 percent of patients in one program stopped committing crimes, with a 98 percent decline in arrests. But patients who continued to commit crimes were expelled from the program and dropped from the statistical base. Of the currently crime-free patients used to calculate program success, 80 percent had never been arrested in the year prior to treatment.[165] Dropping failures from calculation can be legitimate as long as the fact is apparent in the data, but a shrinking sample that becomes ever more biased in a particular direction must yield weak conclusions. Analysts have found, time and again, that methadone program claims of crime reduction, drug abstinence, and improved employment are based on shrinking samples.[166] Unfortunately that quiet fact gets less publicity than the shaky, but bold, conclusions of methadone proponents.

The shrinking sample fallacy is not unique to methadone programs. Another type of program treated 344 parolees from 1956 to 1959. A 1960 follow-up study claimed a success rate of 45 percent; a 1964 study of the same group claimed 65 percent—a result implying the program was so good that more and more participants got better from residual effects as years passed. But determination of drug use was made by looking for needle marks in arms—other possible injection sites were ignored, as were other means of administration. The 65 percent "success rate" was computed on basis of 43 participants who passed arm checks and had been off parole 7 months or more, out of 66 who were in good standing in 1962. Calculations ignored previous failures. Using the 344 original participants, 43 equals a "success rate" of 12.5 percent, not 65 percent. A further study put the number at 30, a "success rate" of 8.7 percent. How many of these "successes" were heroin addicts and how many were chippers is unknown. It is known that parole boards considered them to be good risks for parole, so they were not the toughest antisocial cases.[167]

Ballooning samples also contaminate claims of drug program success. For example, 300 cured drug patients from the California Rehabilitation Center included "a remarkably high proportion" of persons who had never been addicted—they had been ordered into the involuntary program for other reasons.[168] Comparison of heroin treatment records with police records in Phoenix, Arizona, found that 82 percent of patients receiving drug treatment had no police file.[169] Whatever the arrest rate of the entire heroin user population, the subpopulation of *patients* had a low arrest rate to begin with, so any treatment program had a built-in crime-free success rate to advertise.

By ballooning a drug program's statistical base with patients who lack the problems being treated, the success rate can be inflated. If that technique is combined with a shrinking sample that eliminates consideration of patients who do have the treated problems, the success rate can appear extraordinary.

Using a steady sample can give a bleaker perspective. Around 1958 all 247 persons treated in a 1955 program were tracked down. "Only eight remained alive, unaddicted, unimprisoned, and unhospitalized."[170] All 8 claimed they had not been addicts in 1955, and program records verified the claim for 7 of them.[171]

In short, proponents of assorted drug treatment programs may claim brilliant results, but their statements merit the same skepticism as those from sellers of any other merchandise.

Even if some success occurs with methadone programs, it may have nothing to do with pharmacological properties of the drug. For example, reduction in crime may occur because opiate addicts can receive methadone legally and cheaply. Legality means that narcotics offenses will decline, and cheapness means that crimes to generate drug money will decline. Furnishing heroin on the same terms as methadone would do the same thing. Improvement in employment rates may have less to do with methadone than with job counseling.

The criteria for defining "success" keep shifting. In the first decades of the twentieth century, when mere physical withdrawal from resonance was considered a cure,[172] treatment regimens yielded success rates of 90 percent to 99 percent.[173] When skepticism grew about "cures" that ended when treatment did, new definitions of success permitted relapse; for example, success might be measured in "drug-free days"[174] or in holding a job.[175] Some methadone programs have been reduced to defining "success" as lessened heroin use (not elimination of use) and lowered craving for heroin; in other words, a methadone patient who exhibits symptoms caused by methadone is a success.[176]

The biggest question about drug program efficiency is seldom addressed: do patients have a higher cure rate than addicts who receive either different treatment or no treatment? One study found little difference in cure rates among various types of programs, and other investigators have found that program cure rates may even be lower than self-cure rates.[177] A common assumption holds that drug users enter treatment programs to stop using drugs, but in many cases that is incorrect. Voluntary patients may want to take a vacation from the heroin hustle, or detoxify so they can resume heroin and get desired effects with a lower (and less expensive) dose.[178] Other drug patients are involuntary; their goal may be to satisfy a judge, to spend 1 year in treatment rather than 5 years in prison.

The presence of involuntary patients suggests that "drug treatment programs" are agents of social control, enforcing social values through medical means. No other area of medicine uses patients' crime rates to evaluate treatment. No other health practitioners even imply that robbery or auto theft is a medical condition. If the purpose of drug programs is social control, then treatment staffs are political agents enforcing decisions of society, rather than healers attempting to cure afflictions. That in itself explains the low success rate of drug programs; they serve society rather than patients. Any success with patients is coincidental. Indeed the definition of drug clinic activity as "therapy" becomes problematical; criminal trials of physicians, held in Nuremberg during the late 1940s, established principles that might apply.

If treatment programs respond to desires of society, rather than desires of patients, we can better understand why the programs remain popular despite their lack of impact on drug abuse. For example, methadone clinics are cheaper than some alternatives,[179] so the cheaper method is chosen because it satisfies society as much as more expensive alternatives would. The public demands that drug clinics have patients, and opiate addicts are much more likely to stick with a program that provides them with opiates,[180] so methadone clinics meet the need for treatment that will attract patients. Sending criminals and psychotic individuals to methadone programs saves the cost of contested trials, new prisons, and psychiatric care.[181] Generally patients are kept in or returned to the environment that promoted their drug addiction, as if a patient's addiction were irrelevant to the treatment program's purpose. (In former times, drug treatment dogma held that a cure was impossible without changing the patient's environment.[182] Animal experiments show that a rat will resume drugs faster when it is returned to the environment where use began, leading one skeptic to facetiously suggest that treatment programs "might be viewed as a clear plot of the drug pushers to increase habit strength."[183]) Methadone clinics seem intended to reduce problems caused by addicts, rather than problems that cause addicts. A revolving door is set up, with patients going into treatment, getting readdicted, and becoming eligible for another session of treatment.[184] Programs that offer continual treatment, rather than cure, will attract patients who want what is offered.

SELF-CURE

Many drug addicts, perhaps most, cure themselves. Such persons might benefit from assistance, but their success stories demonstrate that the key factor is a desire to give up addiction.

Some people simply fall into one or more varieties of addiction, easy enough when American society promotes so many. If addiction was accidental, the person may feel dissatisfied with that way of life. Even a person who deliberately chose addiction may rescind the decision if circumstances change. Reasons for the original decision may no longer exist, or reasons for abandoning addiction may develop. In the case of drugs, Sigmund Freud easily quit cocaine after using it 3 years.

> When he [Freud] found other ways of being strong and effective—as a person and as a therapist—he gave up this particular method of coping with stress. The answer to whether a person finds it easy or difficult to give up a drug habit thus lies not in the drug, but in the use to which the person who takes it puts it, and in the substitutes for it that he can or wants to employ."[185]

Years of research into drug abuse led Rufus King to agree, "When most users become strongly motivated to give up on drugs or bring their habits under control it is not much of a strain for them to do so."[186] Lawrence Kolb, one of the foremost students of drug addiction, concurred: "I have known many addicts, who, without assistance, suddenly terminated the use of narcotics and thereafter permanently abstained."[187]

When reasons for drug addiction end, pharmacological effects that were once attractive can become repulsive, reducing inclination to use the substance. An active heroin addict explained the drug's appeal: "I got real sleepy. I went in to lay on the bed. . . . I thought, this is for me! And I never missed a day since."[188] A *former* heroin addict gave it a try again and reported: "It was just so uncomfortable. I came home and laid on the bed and I said, 'Never again.' It was a drag. It was horrible. I puked. I just went, 'I ever liked this?' I couldn't imagine that I had liked it."[189] Another former addict made a similar report after trying heroin again: "I just didn't like it. Rather than complaining like I used to complain, 'I'm not high enough.' I was complaining, 'I'm too high, I don't like this.' I was too loaded. I couldn't keep my eyes open. I couldn't do anything. I just sat there on the couch and couldn't do anything. I couldn't talk. I really didn't like it. I didn't like it at all. I didn't do it again."[190] A person who used heroin daily as a medical experiment declared afterward, "It's been wonderful to feel fit and to relish life again."[191] Because addicts give up the chemical when the reason for use ends, drug use should decline if causes of despair leading to drug use are attacked.

Researchers have found chronological age to be a prevalent reason for drug abuse. Abuse is typically a young person's habit, given up as the individual matures.[192] Most opiate addicts relinquish their drug within 10 years.[193] A decade can be a long time, but is hardly a lifetime; one study found that barely 7 percent of addicts use opiates for as long as 15 years.[194] Another study found the "average duration of [narcotics] abuse is 8½ years."[195] Still another found 78 addicts, in a group of 101, whose addiction careers spanned 6 years or less,[196] and that finding is particularly important because the time was measured from first use of heroin to the last use—the addiction careers included periods of abstinence, so the 78 addicts did not necessarily even use heroin throughout the entire 6 years. In that group of 101, only 9 had addiction careers spanning 15 years or more. Still another study followed high school students from 1971 through young adulthood in the 1980s. Of persons who had ever tried heroin, 73 percent had stopped by 1980 and another 8 percent stopped by 1983. Of psychedelics users, 78 percent had stopped by 1980 and another 13 percent stopped by 1983. Of cocaine users, 30 percent had stopped by 1980 and another 22 percent by 1983. Even marijuana use declined—35 percent of users stopped by 1980 and another 14 percent by 1983.[197] Addiction is not forever; persistent addicts are a small minority of addicts, who in turn are a minority of users. The lack of older addicts is not due to deaths, but due to quitting. The "maturing out" process is one reason why statistics about drug use among young people can be viewed without panic. Young folks will continue to outgrow the habit as they always have in the past.

People also leave addiction if they develop reasons to avoid it.[198] A former addict finds interests to pursue and goals to accomplish, and the old pattern of life loses out in comparison. New jobs, new friends, new loves, and other positive changes can develop as addiction recedes. These are investments in life, investments that an addict does not bother to make but which become valuable when someone finds meaning in life. A user spoke of "getting into a security type trip. Building a family, building a home, working for a living."[199] Stanton Peele observes that ending addiction involves "development of internal capacities—interests, joys, competencies—to counteract the desire for escape and self-obliteration. It means wanting, and having, something to offer another person."[200] As David Bellis notes, "While . . . factors—like love—may be related to treatment outcome, they are often difficult to measure and are therefore frequently omitted from research designs."[201] Accounts by people who broke addiction, however, repeatedly emphasize the crucial role of a loving relationship with another person.[202] No treatment program provides that.

Vietnam veterans proved that drug addicts can cure themselves. Widespread heroin addiction among military personnel in Vietnam was reported—10 percent or 15 percent or 25 percent of enlisted men—and reports carried official or semiofficial cachets of authority from government committees or major newspapers.[203] Alarm spread about thousands of combat-trained junkies who would menace American neighborhoods upon their return. Military authorities searched the ranks and found essentially every heroin user;[204] that is important because authorities normally encounter only the worst cases, both in level of abuse and level of social deviance. The Vietnam findings allow us to track heroin in a population of overall normality (despite transient stress), so we can confidently extrapolate results to the general American population.

First, heroin use turned out to be much lower than feared, about 4 percent.[205] That is still a lot, but "use" is not addiction; even the Nixon White House admitted that many service personnel were chippers.[206] Although one study found almost 50 percent of the troops tried opiates at some time, and 20 percent claimed to use them regularly,[207] no one ever noticed a bad impact on combat performance of units.[208] Fighting personnel explained that opiates allowed them to function effectively by relaxing them off duty when they would otherwise be crippled by fear.[209]

That is a second important finding of the Vietnam experience: heroin users turned to the drug for clearly defined reasons relevant to their life situation in Vietnam. U.S. military personnel in Thailand, where cheap heroin was also plentiful, had a much lower rate of use.[210] When Vietnam personnel returned to the United States, their reason for consumption no longer existed, and almost all of them stopped.[211] Their behavior illustrated that use ends when the reason for use ends. Moreover, the veterans were able to resume all sorts of interests and relationships from which they had been cut off in Vietnam, activities that would have been impaired by heroin. Therefore reasons for *not* using the drug existed in America, reasons which also promoted self-cures. Even though the high purity of heroin in Vietnam created a resonance much stronger than most American street addicts are ever able to achieve,[212] Vietnam addicts stopped. Drugs do not cause addiction. Addiction is something that users do to themselves.

Researchers have studied the process of self cure. Most addicts who cure themselves make a conscious decision to do so, based on careful evaluation of continued drug use. One heroin addict faced the financial drain:

> The only way I was going to be able to manage it was to start dealing, and I didn't want to take the chance on dealing, of getting busted. And . . . I couldn't have people call me up at work to score. . . . So I sat down and thought to myself: "Would I be willing to trade the rest of my life for dope?" and the answer was, "Yes, I would if I could insure myself of a regular, steady supply." But in that sort of game you usually get busted sooner or later. So, I say, I envisioned the future as trading my life for dope and then winding up, also, out of dope. And I could see it wasn't going to work. . . . It was kind of a rational decision.[213]

A smaller percentage comes to the decision through a traumatic crisis. And a still smaller percentage simply drifts out of addiction without any decision, accidentally, the way some people drift into addiction.[214]

Methods of self-cure vary. Some addicts gradually taper down consumption;[215] others cut themselves off instantly, cold turkey. Some reduce temptation by avoiding old haunts and associates, perhaps by moving to another town. A new environment can also avoid the drug stigma by which a former addict is held to impossible standards of conduct, ostracism which can lead to despair and resumption of the habit.[216] Relapse, however, can benefit the self-cure effort.[217] Occasional use can help someone get through trying moments, conserving the person's strength to face normal challenges. Indeed, addicts can evolve into chippers.[218] In those cases continued drug use is not failure, but rather a sign of acquired maturity—a successful cure. (After all, abstinence does not cure addiction.) In the self-cure process, abandonment of one bad habit tends to help extinguish others.[219] The process snowballs, and improves the former addict's life in many ways.

At some point, after enough changes in conduct and in life situation, the drug user is no longer an addict. It is important for the person to realize that. Self-image affects behavior. Certain behaviors are expected from an addict, and those expectations encourage an addict's inclinations. A person who fails to give up the self-identity of "addict" is unlikely to be cured. This is contrary to the dogma of groups such as Alcoholics Anonymous, who not only insist on people retaining the addict identity but insist on addicts continuing to associate with one another. Methadone programs, too, encourage patients to congregate at clinics, supporting the addict identity.[220] Such an approach offers continual treatment instead of cure. Research has demonstrated that addicts who cure themselves also abandon their identity as addicts, either resuming a pre-addiction identity or finding a new one.[221]

Self-cures have one ironic drawback. Because part of the process is to avoid old associates, and because the social stigma of drug addiction normally impels former addicts to keep their stories secret, role models for self-cure are unavailable to addicts.[222] Addicts do not realize that most can cure themselves. Instead, as one would expect with addicts, they accept the word of authorities who push a simple answer such as methadone. When such a simple solution fails, addicts regard that as proof that the authorities are right about the near-impossibility of resisting the power of drugs. If only addicts knew that those authorities are wrong, that most addicts achieve cures, and that most do so without a treatment program. Then more addicts might find the hope and strength to cure themselves sooner.

Like the cause of addiction, the cure is not to be found in an outside agency. Not every addict has what it takes. Plenty of hopeless cases exist. But far more can achieve cure. Living proof of the possibility exists in every city throughout America. If those role models could reveal their stories without fear, perhaps addicts, public poilcy makers, and citizens would all be better served.

3 What Drug Users Do to Others

We should not be surprised if people who choose to harm themselves also choose to harm others. Any number of legal ways exist to hurt others, especially family members, but generally we think of drug users causing trouble through crime. Criminals certainly generate the fear that citizens feel about drugs.

To understand the potential impact of legalizing drugs, we must understand the relation of drugs to crime. News accounts of drug-related crime make the relationship seem clear-cut, but the stories promote misunderstanding. Drugs play a role in crime, but the role is different from what is commonly believed.

PHARMACOLOGY AND CRIME

In general, drugs do not make people do things. Instead, people who already want to do things may use drugs to facilitate those desires. A robber may drink whiskey to loosen inhibitions, but the alcohol does not cause the robbery; the same can be said of illicit drugs. Normal people are not made violent by drugs.[1] Researchers have found that even a substance such as PCP (phencyclidine or "angel dust"), notorious for supposedly turning meek individuals into uncontrollable killing machines, does not live up to its reputation. PCP rarely promotes aggressiveness, and users who become violent already have a history of violence without PCP.[2] Few users of any illicit drug are arrested for violence. In the 1970s, a nationwide survey made for the U.S. Bureau of Narcotics and Dangerous Drugs found that burglary accounted for about 20 percent of offenses charged against drug users, robbery accounted for about 20 percent, automobile theft about 5 percent, and drug law violations accounted for the rest.[3] Murders, rapes, and assaults were so uncommon that they did not appear in the nearly 2,000 cases examined. Analysis of all 414 murders committed in 17 New York City police precincts from March to October 1988 found only a half dozen in which pharmacological properties of an illicit drug were to blame.[4] In 1958, the director of the Federal Bureau of Prisons stated, "The drug user does not commit serious crimes of violence— aggravated assault, bank robbery, kidnapping."[5] The lack of violence had been noticed since the 1920s.[6]

Sure, a particular incident may be influenced by a drug's impact on body chemistry. Someone drunk on beer may get into a fight, or a psychopathic robber made irritable by an early stage of the opiate withdrawal syndrome may become brutal. Drugs do affect a criminal's behavior, but they seldom influence a burglar's decision to break into a house or a mugger's decision to search for victims. Pharmacological properties have little impact on the crime rate.[7]

And the crime rate is what concerns most citizens. We are accustomed to stories of robberies and beatings; such can be found even in ancient history. Alarm rises, however, when incidents grow in frequency and occur closer to home. Let us, therefore, consider the nature of drug-related crime.

"DRUG-RELATED" CRIME

Here are examples of "drug-related" crime: a clash between a drug courier and a peace officer,[8] people beaten or killed because they owed money to a drug dealer,[9] 70 percent of burglaries in Kansas City, Missouri.[10]

Although these crimes are called "drug-related," they have little to do with drugs. The first example occurred when the courier was stopped for a vehicular offense. The ensuing fight broke out because the vehicle contained contraband; untaxed cigarettes could have produced the same result. Because the confrontation erupted after a vehicular violation, why not list this as "traffic-related" crime? In the second example, the key factor was debt. People get beaten up for illegal debt (gambling, loan sharking) all the time. Why not list the incident as "debt-related"? In the third example, crooks sought to generate income. Why not call the break-ins "income-related"? Sometimes male burglars share loot with female companions, "girlfriend-related" crime.

The decision of what label to give a crime is political. If pressure existed for a crackdown on tax evasion, the incidents cited above could be called "tax evasion-related" (sales, income, excise), and cries would be heard for expanded police and prosecutor budgets to meet the explosion of tax evasion.

Calling a crime "drug-related" is arbitrary. The label is not meaningless, but reveals information about the labeler rather than the crime. Drug-related crime could be called "money-related," but we hear no calls to ban money. The very idea of a money-free America is absurd, both because Americans want money and because there is no way to eliminate it. The same can be said of drugs, of course.

WHAT POLICE STATISTICS REVEAL ABOUT CRIME

Police statistics measure police activity, not criminal activity. Whether an offense becomes a statistic is determined not only by whether witnesses or victims report a crime but also by political demands. Political demands are important. When Iowa City, Iowa, hired a new police chief in the 1970s, he announced a change in law enforcement policy. Resources devoted to parking violations would be reassigned to fight rape. Young women in that college town rejoiced, but after the chief met with city officials he recanted. The old policy continued. The chief did not give a reason, but his decision clearly reflected political judgement, allocating resources to police work that generated municipal revenue (parking tickets) instead of work that consumed revenue (rape investigations). Politics of law enforcement are rarely so public, but every police chief soon gets a sense of which crimes to investigate and which to ignore. A political decision related to drugs was apparent in Kansas City, Missouri, in 1989. Facing a lack of landfill space, the city experimented with trash recycling in some neighborhoods. Residents received special bins for curbside pick-up of glass, aluminum, and newspaper. Scavengers stole so many bins and recyclables that the economics of the pilot program became shaky. Thefts were made a municipal offense, but no cases appeared in court. A prosecutor declared that judges would be offended by spending time on stolen trash when the city was threatened by drugs.[11] A political decision determined that the recycling, with its impact on environmental safety, was less important than pursuing drug violations. Police resources were directed accordingly. Whether crimes seem major or minor, police statistics on them are shaped as much by political activity as by criminal activity.

Political pressure forces police to demonstrate vigorous enforcement against drug offenses. Because no impact can be detected in the robust illicit drug trade, police must instead demonstrate effectiveness with statistics. One result is the "drug-related" label, analogous to the ballooning sample in methadone programs; arrests having little to do with drugs are nonetheless placed in that category, inflating the success rate. In 1960, Chicago police raised their narcotics arrest record by simply changing some classes of offenses to the narcotics category.[12] Arresting users and street level dealers can boost enforcement statistics without having to reduce illicit use or sales. Arresting the usual suspects can be especially effective in that regard. In 1960, previous narcotics offenders comprised 96 percent of drug arrests by Chicago police.[13] Users can even decline in number while arrests increase. Arrests can make the size of a problem, and police response, look enormous; but we seldom see a breakdown of how many different suspects are involved. Arresting someone 5 or 6 times a year can do wonders for enforcement statistics, even if arrests lead to no convictions—convictions that would not reduce the illicit trade anyway.

The process outlined above feeds upon itself. As drug-related arrests rise, so does public concern, producing political pressure to increase drug-related arrests. Such a situation is excellent for law enforcement agencies that receive more money and staff to produce more arrests, and excellent for politicians who can point to expanded agencies as proof that something is being done about drugs. But any public gain is questionable.

Although police statistics mean little by themselves, they can nonetheless yield worthwhile information when combined with results of anthropological field expeditions.

WHAT ANTHROPOLOGISTS SAY ABOUT CRIME

Rather than penetrating a tropical jungle to study a culture, some anthropologists explore urban jungles to examine those cultures. Crime is one aspect of those cultures. Police try to control that aspect; scientists devote their energies to describing it. Therefore crime data from police and from anthropologists will have different slants. Reports from anthropologists are particularly important because they observe criminal conduct that is never reported to police, and the forces that skew police statistics leave scientific data unaffected. In short, anthropologists study criminal activity rather than police activity. Understanding a phenomenon improves the chance of controlling it, and to understand urban crime, we should pay attention to what scientists discover.

Popular notions turn out to be wrong, such as the idea that people become addicts and then resort to crime to finance their addiction. Anthropologists find the opposite sequence to be true. Drug-using criminals typically become burglars or prostitutes or other types of offenders before drug use begins.[14] Many criminals use heroin, but that only says that many are social deviants—hardly a revelation. Typically a heroin user's first arrest occurs 18 months before heroin use begins.[15] A study of New York City and Miami drug-using prostitutes showed them criminally active for 12 months before starting illicit drugs.[16] Most criminals are generalists—the robber also burglarizes, the prostitute also shoplifts. Crime is a lifestyle, and illicit drugs are merely one part. Their use does not lead to criminality but is just a new variation on an established pattern of deviancy. That fact is obscured by statistical correlations of crime and drug use, just as similar correlations obscure that marijuana does not lead to heroin; correlations do not demonstrate causality. One group of researchers even concluded that "crime was a better explanation of opioid use variance than opioid use was of crime.,"[17] If drug use does not cause crime, the failure of much drug control policy becomes inevitable because it is based on a mistaken premise.

Lawrence Kolb, who was a pioneering drug control expert for the U.S. government, saw no connection between drug addiction rates and crime rates, whether the crimes be murder or misdemeanor larceny. He found that some cities with low addiction rates had higher crime rates than New York, the nation's addiction capital.[18] In 1959, when juvenile drug addicts were blamed for crime across the nation, the Federal Bureau of Narcotics reported a total of 130 addicts under the age of 17, a total of 1,743 under the age of 21. FBI figures dovetailed.[19] Work by later researchers showed that drug use by chippers had no connection with crime rates; the amount used by a chipper did not affect the amount of crime committed.[20] In the 1950s Ohio showed an 80 percent decline in the number of drug addicts, without overall change in numbers of robbery, burglary, or larceny.[21] In cities with comparable heroin prices and addiction rates, the percentage of heroin addict criminals (measured by arrests) can differ greatly.[22] Higher price for heroin does not necessarily boost the crime rate; increase in price can be followed by a decrease in property crime.[23] Sometimes mass arrest campaigns against heroin users reduce crime in a city, sometimes not;[24] such differing outcomes suggest that heroin use is an invalid variable in crime production. (A criminal who uses heroin may exhibit an increase in criminality as use increases, but—except for drug law violations—many users are not criminals.)

Crime attributed to addicts tends to be exaggerated. A book endorsed by the Reagan administration stated, "Hundreds of thousands of dollars a year might be spent on crack by one person. . . . A new wave of theft and bur[g]laries in many cities is being attributed to the growing use of crack."[25] Burglars cannot sell loot at full retail prices. Burglars must steal millions of dollars in merchandise to get hundreds of thousands of dollars in cash.[26] Multiply by the number of crack-using thieves, and the result is billions of dollars in burglary losses for each large city, a trillion dollars or more for the whole country every year from crack users alone. That is not happening.[27] Studies of cocaine use fail to support allegations of cocaine-induced crime waves. In the 1980s, half the users in a Canadian survey claimed to spend no more than $50 a month on cocaine. Another quarter said they spent over $100, and only a minuscule percentage reported exceeding $300 in a month.

"We had little indication that our sample members resorted to criminal activities to obtain money for cocaine."[28] Moreover, the lower the quantity used, the lower the likelihood that a user will resort to crime if funds for purchase are lacking.[29] That finding implies that "cocaine-related" thievery is limited to the financially strapped fraction of the already minuscule percentage of heavy users.

Politicians seem especially prone to exaggerating "drug-related" crime. When the Nixon presidency began, Attorney General John Mitchell publicized a figure of $2 billion for narcotics addict theft in New York City.[30] At about the same time, Governor Nelson Rockefeller of New York put the annual statewide total at $6.5 billion.[31] The Federal Bureau of Investigation, however, totaled nationwide theft losses (whether related to drugs or not) at $1.3 billion.[32] Addicts, too, exaggerate their criminality. A Miami heroin user claimed to have done thousands of burglaries in a year. An anthropologist helped reconstruct the burglar's activities over that time and found the number to be closer to 45.[33] Exaggeration also occurs with users' claims about drug habit size: "When they ask me the size of my habit, they're really asking me whether I'm a real man or a pipsqueak."[34]

Although drugs rarely start someone's criminal career, they can guide that career to income production[35]—selling a stolen automobile instead of joy-riding. A study of teenage boys found no increase in delinquency after drug use began, but the type of crime changed from hell-raising to money-raising.[36]

If criminality already exists, drug addiction can worsen it. Drugs may not increase the number of criminals, but can increase the number of crimes they commit. Observation of California addicts showed that property offenses climbed with habit size.[37] Similar behavior was seen among heroin-using incorrigible criminals in New York City.[38] Study of Baltimore addicts revealed that offenses by heroin-using criminals varied by a factor of 6, depending on whether the criminal was chipping or using heroin daily.[39] Increase in criminality seems related to the expense of heroin rather than its pharmacological properties. Canada has drug laws similar to those of the United States, making heroin illegal and expensive for addicts. When addicts emigrated from Canada to England, where heroin was legal and inexpensive, their arrests and imprisonments declined drastically.[40] Legalizing illicit drugs and making them available cheaply can reduce individual criminality even if a community's overall crime rate remains unaffected.

The more heroin a criminal uses, the higher that person's income will be. Impoverished people cannot afford illicit drugs. A daily heroin user may appear impoverished, measured by physical appearance, clothes, and living quarters; but that is only because so little money is left over from drug purchases. In the early 1970s the mean annual illegal income of California criminals using heroin was $300 for those who took heroin less than once a month, and $10,900 for daily users. Those figures excluded gambling and drug sales—drug dealing alone produced another $6,000 for daily users.[41] A six-city survey of criminal heroin users found a similar trend, an annual illegal income of $2,500 among people who used the drug less than once a week, and $13,000 among daily users.[42] In the early 1980s, New York City criminals had an annual illegal income of $6,000 for irregular heroin users and $18,800 for daily users.[43] Such persons additionally have legal incomes;[44] in the New York study those sources boosted total annual income to $11,400 for irregular heroin users and $23,800 for daily users.[45] Contrary to popular impression, the more heroin someone uses, the more industrious the person becomes. Individuals making five-figure incomes may reject regular jobs but are not lazy or untalented.

Popular notion holds that when drug users finance their habit through crime, the crime is theft. Scientists have shown theft to be a less important income source than is commonly believed. A study of narcotics users nationwide found about 30 percent depended on property crime for their income, 40 percent on consensual crime (drug sales, gambling, prostitution), and 30 percent on lawful occupations.[46] One study found that about 38 percent of a narcotic addict's criminal income is from theft, 25 percent from drug dealing.[47] A study of Chicago addicts found that 38 percent engaged in property crime to pay for drugs; an almost equal number engaged in drug dealing.[48] A California study found that 28 percent of an addict's income derived from drug dealing;[49] a New York study put the total at 50 percent.[50] Still another study found that a sample of daily heroin users made almost twice as much money from drug dealing as from thievery.[51] A careful anthropological project in Miami demonstrated the most prevalent crimes by narcotics users: drug sales (38 percent of their total crimes), prostitution (12 percent), and shoplifting (12 percent).[52] Half that crime was consensual, so-called "victimless" offenses. New York City criminals with a daily heroin habit did almost 10 times as many drug deals as burglaries.[53] Researchers believe that about half the heroin consumed in the United States is bought from proceeds of drug sales.[54] Most drug dealers are small-scale entrepreneurs financing their own habits. The industry operates like a pyramid scam, with people in higher levels profiting from lower levels. No one is indispensable in a pyramid, anyone who drops out can be quickly replaced, and the enterprise remains unperturbed. That is one reason why raids and arrests fail to diminish drug dealing—not because drugs are special, but because pyramid organization confounds a strategy of targeting individuals.

Criminals worry little about being caught, anyway. An anthropological study conducted among narcotics-using criminals in Miami from 1979 to

1981 produced the following ratio of specific crime instances to arrest instances:[55]

Robbery and assault	75:1
Burglary and other theft	219:1
Drug sales	959:1

On average, a Miami burglar on drugs could expect to pull 200 jobs without arrest. And those are ratios merely for arrest, let alone for conviction, let alone for jail time. For citizens who are so inclined, crime is a safe occupation.

THE BLESSINGS OF CRIME

Harm caused by crime is well known. Anthropologists find, however, that crime can also benefit a community. We are unlikely to reduce crime unless we recognize its benefits and understand why crime produces them more efficiently than legal alternatives do. Let us first examine how crime helps individuals and then consider the good that comes to a whole community. We can then see how drugs fit in, allowing us to see what drug legalization would do to crime.

The following explanation of how crime helps various individuals is modeled after findings of anthropologist Bruce Johnson and colleagues in New York City,[56] findings that resonate with work of other researchers.[57]

Suppose a burglar steals a color television for which the owner paid $400 three years ago. Depreciation makes the television's actual cash value $200 at time of loss. In addition to outright loss, the victim must buy a new set for $450—an even exchange of cash for merchandise, but painful to the victim. That one person loses from the crime, but everyone else mentioned in the following paragraphs *benefits* from crime.

The burglar sells the set to an unemployed welfare recipient for $50. Because the merchandise has an actual cash value of $200, the buyer gains $150 on the deal. The purchaser gets $150 for nothing. Crime pays for the stolen goods buyer.

The burglar spends the $50 on drugs and uses them. Crime pays for the burglar. The drug dealer grosses $50 from the burglary. Crime pays for the drug dealer.

A retail television merchant gains $450 of business from the burglary, because otherwise the owner of the old set would not have bought a new one. Crime pays for the legitimate merchant, and even pays a commission to the merchant's salesperson.

The city and state collect a sales tax on the television purchase, and the burglary reduces the demand for welfare payments by $400 (the price of a new set minus the price paid for the stolen one). Crime pays for the government.

Economic ramifications of a single $200 burglary (cash value of the stolen television) can be further extrapolated—to the new television's manufacturer and employees, to delivery companies, to security alarm firms.

In summary, burglary generates economic growth. Superficially this scenario resembles the classic "broken window fallacy" analyzed by economist Frederic Bastiat, in which money spent to repair a window spreads through the economy but fails to benefit a community. In contrast, in New York City "the average heroin abuser's criminality *pays* the legal economy over $6,100 in indirect monetary gains—gains that would not have occurred had heroin abusers not committed these crimes."[58] In addition, the average heroin abuser produces $20,600 annual economic gain for the underground economy, money that can be spent legally.[59] Crime is a major industry promoting jobs, profits, and prosperity in the legitimate economy. Shutting down burglary would have the same financial impact on a community as shutting down any large business.[60] That fact does not mean we should encourage burglary; alternative paths to community prosperity exist, paths with more social benefits and fewer social costs. If we view burglary as a major economic force, however, we see that random arrests of drug-using burglars will have little effect on such crime.

The key element in burglary is not the break-in artist but the purchaser of stolen goods. Burglars do not collect stolen merchandise; they sell it. A middleman may be involved, but the ultimate purchaser is typically a low income person who resides in an ethnic or racial ghetto. In such areas middle class values will hinder survival. To live decently a person needs certain appliances, a certain amount of meat and other commodities. A person who cannot afford them retail may buy from Louis around the block. Louis's customers might not like him (after all, they may be his next victims), and they might feel dirty when dealing with him, but they do what they must in order to survive. Worsening poverty, rather than worsening drug use, may be causing any increase in thefts. We are seeing an illegal transfer of income, stealing from the rich and selling at a discount to the poor. This "self-help" effort makes up for the federally encouraged reduction in legal transfer of income previously provided by social welfare programs.

The stolen goods market produces burglary. Specific thefts may be committed by drug users seeking to generate income for drugs, but thieves are meeting a market demand unrelated to drugs. Thefts would continue even if drug users committed none. As long as a robust stolen goods market exists, someone will do burglaries even if heroin and cocaine are provided free in street corner bins.

A similar picture of economic forces can be sketched for robberies, shoplifting, or any other crime that transfers economic assets. Social deviance may direct individuals toward criminal careers, but such careers take strength from powerful economic forces. Ignoring those forces while jailing criminals is like ignoring the interior fuel supply while spraying water at the burning exterior of a lumber yard.

Here is what it comes to. A burglar may say a crime was committed to generate drug money, but "drug-related" theft occurs only if stolen goods can be converted to cash. If no demand for such merchandise exists, thefts will be limited to items with intrinisic value to the burglar—and there is a limit to how many microwave ovens anyone can use. To reduce "drug-related" theft we must attack the stolen goods market rather than drug use. Victory in such a war would require change in the racial, social, and economic values expressed and enforced by most individuals and institutions in America. Such change may well be feasible, may even promote democracy and prosperity, but is unlikely to occur unless people debate its advisability. Such debate is not encouraged by the drug war.

THE BUSINESS OF ILLICIT DRUGS

Violence is inseparable from the illicit drug trade. Unlike "drug-related" theft, "drug-related" violence can be reduced by simple changes in the law without expensive or disconcerting efforts to implement social justice. To see why, we need to examine illicit drugs from a business standpoint.

The drug war's sound and fury obscure an important fact: the illicit drug trade is a government-protected "closed shop." Only criminals are allowed into the trade. Relieved of the necessity to follow the laws and norms of legitimate business practice, criminal entrepreneurs operate in a pure laissez-faire marketplace unburdened by consumer legislation, tax collectors, or other governmental interference. No agencies restrain unfair business practices. No courts guarantee contracts. Supply, demand, and the invisible hand govern the illicit drug trade, allowing us to see how capitalism operates when freed of governmental meddling.

That fact is ordinarily ignored. Instead citizens are told that government greatly interferes with the illicit drug trade, but that tale is incorrect. An analogy might be a homeowner who puts no herbicides on the lawn and instead occasionally digs out dandelions by hand. Unless apprehended, dandelions thrive on fertilizer and sprinkler water provided by the homeowner, who nourishes them in a protected environment that receives no interference from any outside agency. In a similar way, government may apprehend individual illicit drug dealers, but makes no effort to regulate the trade itself. In contrast, government pays little attention to pharmacists and other individuals who deal in legal drugs, but enforces complex and interlocking regulations directing that commerce. Government is omnipresent in the sales of legal pharmaceuticals, but is absent from the illicit drug industry.

The practical difference is seen in news stories of violence associated with illicit drug sales. Pharmacists and street corner hustlers both sell expensive and dangerous substances. Nothing inherent to their products dictates that one class of businessmen should be prone to gunplay. The difference is nurtured by government attitudes.

For example, penalties limit the illicit drug trade to risk-takers who disregard social norms. Normal people with polite and law-abiding natures will avoid the calling. Therefore dealers tend to be nasty persons looking for trouble. They will exhibit impatience if they think a customer or competitor or neighborhood busybody is causing a moment of inconvenience. The same thing was seen with alcohol during national prohibition. Nothing inherent to alcohol shifted beer dealerships from vicious gangsters in 1932 to kindly grocers in 1933. The change was wrought by reintroducing government regulation of the alcohol trade, creating a business environment in which gangsters could no longer survive.

Gangsters previously flourished because an industry untouched by government regulates itself. If a cocaine dealer grants credit to a customer, and the customer fails to pay, the dealer cannot file a civil lawsuit. Instead the dealer must track down the customer and administer a beating severe enough to cancel the debt. If the dealer's cocaine supply is hijacked by a rival, the theft cannot be reported to police nor can insurance be collected. Before being victimized again, the dealer must shoot the hijacker. A dealer unwilling to administer such sanctions will soon depart the business. Only the most ruthless and violent individuals will remain. That scene changes as soon as government regulation enters. Legitimate businessmen do not personally enforce sanctions; instead they enlist the power of the state through courts and police. Personal violence is unnecessary. With government acting as umpire (and history demonstrates that even the toughest gangster cannot withstand that umpire) success in the business game requires talents and resources possessed by few street bullies. Changing the rules changes the players.

Although legalization would eliminate all institutional violence, an element of "drug-related" pathological violence would remain. That residue would be associated not with dealers but with deviant users—the kind who vandalize a stolen car before abandoning it, or who beat a victim senseless after the wallet is obtained. To ask the law to eliminate such violence is, essentially, to ask for an end to evil. Evil exists.

Fear of the illicit drug trade is promoted by its ability to flourish despite ever-tougher sanctions, but business principles explain that vigor. Harsh penalties work best when gain from crime is independent of the penalty.[61] For example, if someone robs a jewelry store, the loot remains the same regardless of whether the penalty is 90 days on the municipal farm or 90 years at hard labor. The amount of ransom a kidnapper receives is the same regardless of whether the penalty is 20 years or death. Gain does not increase with risk, so deterrence escalates along with the legal sanction. In drug dealing, however, higher penalties yield higher drug prices to compensate for risk, so bigger gain offsets increased peril. That is why illicit drug traders thrive despite harsher laws; if sanctions improve the rewards of criminal behavior, the behavior will persist. Moreover, timid criminals who drop out are replaced by bold ones more willing to take a chance. That does not mean we are helpless to reduce drug trade problems; it just means that criminal sanctions are not the answer.

From a business standpoint, if legalization were accompanied by government policy that discouraged price gouging, the price of illicit drugs should plummet. That should have several good effects. Terrible financial burden would lift from drug users and their families, improving the quality of their lives. Criminals, from neighborhood hustlers to cartel kingpins, would abandon the drug trade because its profit margin would no longer be attractive; an extensive and profitable trade exists in salt but attracts no criminal elements even though many people crave the harmful substance at every mealtime. Money is power, and the loss of drug profits would mean a loss of power among criminals, from street corners to presidential palaces.

Such corrupt power exists not because of sinister criminal genius, but because of anti-drug laws. Eliminating those laws would eliminate corruption in many areas of national life, including areas where corruption pervades so thoroughly that persons unaware of history do not realize that venality has replaced virtue. The threat posed by corruption, and the solution promised by legalizing illicit drugs, will be considered next.

DRUG LAW CRIME

Thus far we have seen that legalizing illicit drugs would have small effect on theft rates but would eliminate violence associated with an illicit trade. That is a real reduction in crime; violent behavior would lessen.

Legalization would also reduce crime by sleight of hand, in that illicit drug offenses would disappear even though the behavior would continue. Real benefits would nonetheless follow.

One benefit would be an end to heavy punishment for trivial conduct. In California while Ronald Reagan was governor, a first offense of selling a marijuana cigarette was punishable by life imprisonment.[62] In the 1970s, an adult-aged college junior who sold marijuana to a minor-aged roommate could be executed in Georgia, Louisiana, and Missouri.[63] During the 1970s, Louisiana's minimum penalty for possessing marijuana was 5 years at hard labor; in Missouri a second possession offense was punishable by life imprisonment without parole.[64] Penalties for other drugs were no lighter, and despite a flurry of reform in the 1970s, in the 1980s the trend was toward harsher laws. In 1982 the U.S. Supreme Court upheld the reasonableness of a 40-year prison term for possessing and distributing 9 ounces of marijuana worth $200.[65] There is a difference between savagery and public welfare. One year in a state penitentiary will harm an individual far more than a bag of marijuana ever will. Our entire society suffers from the loss of talented and productive citizens, ruined by prosecution for conduct that entails no more public danger than an expired parking meter. Legalizing illicit drugs would eliminate that waste.

Another benefit would be an end to corruption caused by anti-drug laws. Some corrupt behaviors are obvious, others less so.

Stories abound of foreign government officials, communist and noncommunist alike, running lucrative illegal drug rings protected by bribes to police and judges. Although corruption financed by drugs would diminish if legalization cut the profits, corrupt individuals are unlikely to reform. They would probably pursue other villainy. Nonetheless, no other illegal avenue is likely to produce so much money; because money is power, corruption should weaken and become easier to attack.

We do not know the extent of such venality in the United States. Public officials chronically complain about being underpaid, and virtue is no more widespread in America than abroad. A member of the California senate was reputed to have made a fortune from illegal drugs.[66] The director of Florida's Department of Natural Resources pleaded guilty to obstruction of justice after being prosecuted for handling a drug smuggler's bribe.[67] Persons who served in the U.S. Congress have been convicted for participation in, and perjury about, drug money laundering.[68] Federal drug agents have long been prone to corruption. In the 1920s, the top U.S. drug enforcement official lost his job when his son and son-in-law were revealed as handling legal affairs for a notorious gangstger.[69] In that era a grand jury found that federal drug agents in New York protected upper level dealers and withheld evidence from prosecutors.[70] Forty years later the situation remained unchanged; in 1969, 70 federal drug agents in New York were exposed in practices ranging from extortion to being enforcers for dealers (the agents would, for a price, arrest a dealer's competitors).[71] Forty Nixon administration drug agents were indicted for such conduct.[72] The dismal record compiled by the U.S. Drug Enforcement Administration, as its top supervisors constantly shifted, was blamed on "pervasive organized corruption."[73] In 1985, an FBI agent was convicted of "massive narcotics trafficking," and the next year a Justice Department Strike Force prosecutor was sentenced to prison for selling information to a drug dealer.[74] Reagan administration officials noted that discovery of corruption among federal drug officers had become routine.[75]

On the local level, in the 1950s police in Washington, D.C., alerted favored dealers about raids and sold drugs from confiscated supplies.[76] In the 1970s, New York City police retained narcotics found in raids, planted narcotics on suspects, committed perjury, financed drug deals, acted as bodyguards for dealers, performed kidnappings, and offered to set up murders.[77] Similar behavior has been seen in other police departments, seen so routinely as to suggest it is standard operating procedure.[78] Around 1975 one prosecutor admitted,

> When you ask for a warrant knowing that it's going to be quashed, when you know it's bad to begin with, you can still get one issued in most counties, make the search and have it thrown out later. You've busted in the guy's house and ransacked the joint, or you've impounded his car and torn the insides out of it. So the warrant is quashed, so what? He's off on the charge which was BS to begin with, but you've really made his life miserable.[79]

If these are the people who protect us from drugs, perhaps we would be better off without such protection.

Someone who dealt with drug cases both as a prosecutor and a judge stated, "Organized crime can never exist to any marked degree in any large community unless one or more of the law enforcement agencies have been corrupted. This is a harsh statement, but I know that close scrutiny of conditions wherever such crime exists will show that it is protected. . . . The narcotics traffic . . . could never be as pervasive and open as it is unless there was connivance between authorities and criminals." Those words were from U.S. Chief Justice Earl Warren.[80]

One of Warren's colleagues on the Supreme Court was Abe Fortas. Around 1962 the American Bar Association chose Fortas, Rufus King, and another attorney to conduct a study on drug laws. Here is what King said in a book 10 years later:

> In illegal gambling . . . it is credibly speculated that something like one-third of the promoters' net goes into bribes and contributions. . . . That kind of money, passing in cash outside channels where it might be traced or taxed, obviously cannot all be absorbed in Cadillacs for commissioners and tuition

payments for police captains' children. I believe the truth is that proceeds from "tolerated" criminal enterprises are helping finance the elective process through practically the whole range of American political life.

There is much to suggest that no aspirant wins a high elective office today without depending, directly or indirectly, knowingly or not, on crime-generated funds. . . . And though dope money is often regarded as dirtier than the proceeds of other kinds of crime, there is so much of it around that it must inevitably have augmented the flow from time to time.[81]

Such sentiments can be found not only among high jurists and distinguished attorneys, but also on the street level where one addict said: "They have never succeeded in knocking off enough of the big peddlers or enough of the syndicate. And they never will because they don't want to, because this is their big source of money and because they look at it as they do gambling. Exactly the same way."[82] Current drug laws are the basis of drug lord wealth and power. Self-interest would cause drug lords to finance candidates pledged to sustain those laws. Unfortunately, the kind of politician chosen by drug lords is unlikely to have sufficient vision and courage to meet problems faced by the world at the turn of the century.

Whatever the extent of political power bought by drug money, investigators have amply demonstrated that drug money operates as an engine driving the legitimate business economy. Banks across the country handle accounts of drug barons, sometimes with full knowledge of how the money is produced.[83] Indeed the flow of cash among drug handlers is so intensive that cocaine has been detected on most currency in southern Florida.[84] Drug money finances legitimate business directly, from sports clothing stores in Boston[85] to a shopping center planned for Kansas City, Missouri.[86]

Corruption in the legitimate drug abuse treatment business has been described as "mind-boggling."[87] Methadone disappears from inventory between time of delivery to clinics and delivery to patients.[88] Assorted frauds boost program income, which is then diverted for personal use of staff. Drug program corruption is even blamed for murders.[89]

Anti-drug laws conflict with laws protecting privacy. To enforce one set of laws, the other must be disregarded. This drives the police crazy. In past decades courts have struck down drug convictions because civil liberties violations could not be tolerated. In recent years courts have limited civil liberties because drugs could not be tolerated. Regardless of the trend, however, the unifying theme is that anti-drug laws conflict with civil liberties. When an important civil liberties question comes to the U.S. Supreme Court, often the question is raised by a drug case.[90]

No other area of criminal law continually clashes with civil liberties. Anti-drug laws are anti-American, violating basic values upon which the United

States is founded. Some citizens may dismiss civil liberties as troublesome, but their practical worth is demonstrated by the consequences of anti-drug laws. As will be noted in a later chapter, prior to those laws neither a drug problem nor its empires of crime and corruption existed in the United States. If anti-drug zealots had not prevailed, if Congress and the courts had respected traditional civil liberties, we would not have anti-drug laws that nurture the evil they ostensibly fight, and the country would be spared the terror it suffers now. Civil liberties do not cause trouble; they prevent it. Consequences of disregarding them should be remembered whenever a zealot of any stripe argues that American freedoms must be limited in order to accomplish something. Possibly the task would best be left undone.

Many employees and job applicants must undergo urine tests to discover if they use an illicit drug. A White House drug adviser declared, "You have a choice: you give up your drugs, or you seek employment elsewhere."[91] The official did not say drugs will harm a worker, but instead said that being exposed as a drug user will harm a worker. Why employers should dictate a worker's off-duty conduct is unclear. No one demands that employees avoid late night movies or dances that impair daytime work. If drugs diminished job performance, the employee could be fired for bad work.

Questions exist about urine test accuracy. Employers generally prefer that labs run cheap commercial tests. Positive results for illicit drugs can be verified via dual column capillary gas chromatography coupled with a mass spectrometry system, but a prominent drug abuse authority instead urged employers to run the same commerical test a second time as verification, a practice that some follow.[92] Such practice is troubling because false positives are common in commercial tests. Eating poppy seed bagels can cause a positive result for opiate use;[93] the pain-reliever Nuprin can cause a positive for marijuana.[94] Laboratory error compounds the problem. In 1972, evidence at congressional hearings put the accuracy rate at about 50 percent to 65 percent for civilian laboratories.[95] In 1973, a formal quality-control study found an overall accuracy of 39 percent in civilian labs.[96] In 1976, a lab rated as outstanding for accuracy by the federal Center for Disease Control reported false positives in 106 samples among 160 submitted in an independent quality control study. The researchers characterized a 66 percent false positive rate as unacceptable, evidence that federal quality standards were inadequate.[97] And not all labs receive "outstanding" ratings from federal inspectors. A decade later little had changed. A 1985 quality control study of 13 labs found false positive rates ranging up to 10 percent for morphine, 66 percent for methadone. Not a single lab had acceptable accuracy for amphetamines, only one had acceptable accuracy for cocaine.[98] Two subsequent studies have been publicized by news media as allegedly showing that urine tests no longer produce false positives,[99] a claim that even test manufacturers do not make.[100] Important details of those two studies received less publicity. The first, in 1987, was funded by the DuPont chemical company at the request of the American Association for Clinical Chemistry (AACC), which wanted to convince the public that labs produce accurate urine analyses.[101] Test samples lacked substances known to produce false positives, thus reducing the likelihood of false positives. Labs knew which samples were for the quality control study. Previous investigators had demonstrated that such knowledge remarkably improves analysis accuracy,[102] but the AACC said their study's purpose was to demonstrate that labs could be accurate, not to demonstrate normal accuracy.[103] Nonetheless, criticism on that point was sufficient to prompt the AACC to do a 1988 study funded by DuPont.[104] The same 47 labs were supposed to be examined again, but the second study was so rushed that 10 were excluded because they were unable to complete the necessary paperwork fast enough. (Another 5 were eliminated because they no longer tested urine for drug abuse, and 1 lab refused to participate again.) Of the 10 different types of urine samples sent to labs, 3 had no illicit substances, 2 had only opiates, 1 had only a cocaine metabolite, 1 had only a marijuana product. Concentrations were well above the minimum sensitivity standards that labs were supposed to meet, exceeding the standards by up to 300 percent. (The first study had even higher concentrations.) Such samples hardly provide the day-to-day challenge presented to labs when they receive urine containing a polydrug mix, including substances that produce false positives. Each lab provided a list of one or more clients willing to ship the AACC samples to the lab. An AACC contractor instructed the chosen client not to let the lab know which samples were the quality control ones. The AACC said this methodology provided a blind study in which labs did not know what samples were the quality control ones. Assuming no breach of security, labs nonetheless knew which samples could not be the AACC ones. Such methodology is not blind. Given the circumstances of the two AACC studies, the meaning of results is uncertain.

In contrast to the AACC studies, less publicized ones continued to reveal false positives. Researchers reported that one commercial test was 50 percent accurate for cocaine use—no better than flipping a coin.[105] The same commercial test yielded false positives in 30 percent of urine samples having no drugs of abuse, and 40 percent when samples had a legal substance known to cause false positives.[106] Another test yielded over 10 percent false positives for opiates, and several could not distinguish between morphine and codeine.[107] One test was so touchy that vibration on the working surface used by technicians could cause false positives for opiates, and polydrug samples caused trouble in another test.[108] Still another study found a false positive rate of 1 percent to 2 percent in popular commercial urine tests,[109] but even that rate means that 100 or 200 persons in every 10,000 will be falsely accused. Moreover, the statistical principle expressed by Bayes' theorem demonstrates that the number of innocent persons falsely accused will soar if actual drug use is low in a random population. If, as a hypothetical example, actual heroin use is 0.5 percent, and a test is 98 percent accurate, in a population of 10,000 there will be 49 true positives and 199 false positives—the vast majority of positive results are false even though the test is 98 percent accurate.

Shoddy lab work helps fuel drug panic. Technicians at one lab used the same microwave oven to dry glassware and to warm tacos; taco grease can cause false positives for marijuana use.[110]

At a 1983 conference of 120 forensic scientists, none was willing to call urine tests dependable.[111] Even a pioneer of basic urine analysis techniques protested that the procedures were misused: "The process was supposed to be for statistical research."[112] If rates of false negatives and positives remain steady, statistical validity is unimpaired. The same cannot be said for careers of individuals who get false positives. But even tests that show negative for illicit drugs may be used to disqualify someone from employment. Although quinine is a legal substance, job applicants at one telephone company were considered heroin users if they showed positive for quinine, because illicit heroin may be adulterated with quinine.[113] Ironically, if body fluid work-ups are required for employment, and reveal internal possession of a banned drug—reveal that a person has committed a crime, then prosecution may violate the Fourth Amendment (search: "the right of the people to be secure in their persons") and Fifth Amendment (coerced self-incrimination). The war on drugs in the work place may provide a criminal immunity bath for every user. No public gain is evident from such tests. Public harm is clear. Yet the practice grows ever wider as the drug war intensifies.

When attending school or seeking a job not only makes a person a suspected criminal, but forces the suspect to produce blood or urine to prove innocence, traditional American values have eroded far indeed.

The Reagan and Bush administrations focused civil liberties questions more tightly with a change in drug war strategy. Until the mid-1980s, despite routine prosecutions of illicit drug users, the ostensible emphasis had been on attacking big dealers, without useful result. Reagan and Bush switched the emphasis to drug users,[114] who are far easier to find. Not only are users to be prosecuted, they are to be denied schooling and employment, even forbidden to drive an automobile.[115] A drug-free America is to be achieved by removing people from society rather than eliminating drugs from society. (By the time Reagan left the presidency, almost 66 percent of persons being sentenced to federal prisons were convicted of drug law violations.[116])

Legal trappings of dictatorship will be accompanied by physical trappings if the desires of Bush administration officials prevail. The Reagan administration authorized the U.S. military to gather intelligence about drug users and to help local police use military equipment to fight drug users. Bush officials proposed a higher profile for the military, urging that troops patrol city streets to watch for drugs.[117] This is not a civil liberties question per se, but does raise the issue of how militarized a society can become before democracy disappears.

Civil commitment for drug "treatment" raises different but urgent questions of civil liberties. Criminal proceedings generally abhor indeterminate punishment and specify an upper limit to prison sentences. In contrast, a person can be locked in a hospital for however long a "treatment program" requires. Moreover, because the ostensible intent is to help the person, civil liberties protections are much weaker even if the incarceration is much longer. For instance, the Sixth Amendment (right to question accusers, right to a lawyer) and the Eighth Amendment (prohibition of cruel and unusual punishment) apply to criminal proceedings, not civil cases. This has not escaped notice from prosecutors who lack enough evidence to convict someone of a crime.

Prosecutors therefore like to promote the notion that drug use is a disease, because people can undergo involuntary civil commitment to a hospital for disease even if they are harming no one. Civil commitment conveniently imprisons people "known" to be guilty of an offense that cannot be proved. California passed a law allowing civil commitment if prosecutors merely demonstrated that a drug user had been convicted of a crime—any crime.[118] A New York law said that a drug user accused of a crime, without proof, could receive lengthy medical incarceration.[119] Mere arrest was accusation enough. Under such practice civil commitment becomes a powerful threat for extorting information at police stations, rather than a therapeutic measure to help a sick person.

Forcing drug users into civil commitment is a sham. With the exception of drug users, hardly anybody undergoes involuntary commitment to a hospital, because almost everyone who feels sick desires cure. If drug users are the only significant element of "ill people" who desire no treatment, a quesiton must arise about whether they are indeed sick, let alone so sick that they cannot rationally refuse treatment. Because drug abuse is socially defined (even though it may have medical symptoms), we should hardly be surprised if many drug users refuse to admit they are sick. A medical sanction (civil commitment) is being used to "treat" a social condition when criminal law (the normal sanction that enforces social values) lacks the power to deal with a specific individual. The sham works because drug use is a crime with medical symptoms—no one would receive civil commitment for the "disease" of burglary.

The sham is further demonstrated by lack of a cure for drug use. If no generally accepted and effective therapy exists, "patients" undergo medical experimentation, not treatment. Civil liberties infringements arise when people are subjected to medical experiments against their will. If someone accepts heart surgery over the alternative of jail, that decision is no more voluntary than a drug user's selection of "therapy" instead of prison. Forcing a choice between mandated alternatives is not consent, and the consent standaard for medical experimentation is much higher than for treatment. In that respect civil commitment is harsher than criminal imprisonment. Felons cannot be used as experimental animals.

From that standpoint it is fortunate that many civil commitment "treatment" programs are fake. Until the 1960s, federal "narcotics farms" were indistinguishable from penitentiaries, and eventually the Public Health Service relinquished them to the Federal Bureau of Prisons. The same is true on the state level; the "California Rehabilitation Center" is a prison. Time spent there is credited to jail sentences.[120] Ditto with civil commitments under federal law.[121] Sometimes civil commitment "patients" are simply locked up in regular prisons with non-addict cell mates, and follow the same routine as any other prisoner.[122]

If "treatment" is deemed unsuccessful, the "patient" can be tried on the criminal charges that prompted civil commitment. Such a trial is still more evidence of sham. To undergo civil commitment, a person must be certified as not responsible for actions leading to commitment, a certification that should remove criminal liability.[123] Failed treatment removes any question that the person was legally incapacitated prior to treatment. Nonetheless somene can be arrested for drug possession, be absolved of responsibility for the offense, and then have that immunity for past behavior revoked if treatment fails (brought to trial because authorities are dissatisfied with prospects for the person's future behavior—a chilling innovation in crimnal proceedings which, unlike treatment, are traditionally directed toward past behavior). None of this would happen if the intent of civil commitment was really therapeutic rather than punitive.

A "successful patient" who is finally released can be recommitted for lawful behavior having nothing to do with drugs, such as losing a job or betting at a racetrack.[124]

Clearly, civil commitment is used to deprive citizens of liberty when no criminal offense can be proved. Toleration of such a scheme is ominous, and the Bush administration urged its expansion with streamlined procedures to reduce delays.[125] The allegation that civil commitment proceedings are too cumbersome is preposterous. The transcript of one civil commitment proceeding (including presentation of facts and subsequent discussion among the judge, the prosecutor, a police matron, the committed person, the person's husband, and the public defender) required just 500 words, including the judge's cursing. The committed person uttered only two sentences: "Jesus Christ, don't I get to say anything?" and "Am I going to jail or what?"[126]

More and more behaviors are being described as "disease," widening the opportunity for civil commitment to remove citizens from society when their conduct offends the community. Zealotry is not unique to anti-drug forces, and zeal may someday focus on other forms of behavior. What about gamblers? What about persons who use certain forms of birth control? Danger escalates as more conduct becomes a target of loathing. A century ago drug users were viewed with compassion and sympathy, cherished as fellow members of a community. If drug users can be persecuted, so can other citizens.

Such are the perils of corrupting civil liberties in the name of drugs.

Corruption extends beyond criminal proceedings to basic civil rights such as freedom of speech. Take the case of Ernest S. Bishop, a respected addiction authority who criticized federal drug laws when they were passed in the World War I era. Investigators targeted him and found a technical drug violation he had made as a practicing physician. The government, however, refused to bring the case to trial. The possibility of conviction simply dangled over him for years to silence his questions about drug laws. The strategy worked; Bishop never spoke out again. And he was never convicted.[127] In the 1930s, Alfred R. Lindesmith became one of the most cogent critics of federal drug laws. The Federal Bureau of Narcotics told his employers, Indiana University, that he was connected with a criminal organization. The basis of that allegation was that Lindesmith had corresponded with the founder of a narcotics research group. The founder was one of several physicians who treated addicts referred to them as public health cases, and all the doctors had been convicted of drug law violations. All were subsequently exonerated, but an error allowed this particular physician's conviction to remain on the books. According to the Federal Bureau of Narcotics, this made the research group a criminal organization, and Lindesmith's correspondence made him part of it. A Narcotics Bureau agent met with Lindesmith for hours and warned him to stop criticizing federal policy if he wanted to retain his job. Soon afterward, a senior Bureau official told Lindesmith that the bureau had a responsibility to stop the spread of bad information. When the university refused to act against Lindesmith, the bureau produced and distributed a 27-page booklet attacking him.[128] Other persons have paid a heavier penalty for challenging drug policy orthodoxy. Professor Leslie Fiedler of the State University of New York at Buffalo says that after he sponsored a student marijuana reform group, police electronically eavesdropped on conversations in his house, convinced a friend of Fiedler's children to hide marijuana in the house, and arrested him for possession.[129] Marijuana arrests of political dissidents[130] may be an excuse to punish them for political activism that is unpopular with governmental authorities, just as a dictatorship finds some criminal charge to use against dissidents. U.S. Congressman Lester Volk declared that drug agents hounded physician Christopher F. J. Laase with politically motivated prosecution and that Laase died from the strain. Volk also suspected the federal government was behind the demise of the journal *Medical Record* after it displeased government officials with a letter it printed on the narcotics situation.[131] In 1961, the Bureau of Narcotics investigated Indiana University for publishing a joint American Bar Association–American Medical Association study that challenged federal drug policies.[132]

For decades the federal government suppressed not only reports of findings but basic research itself. For example, as marijuana research challenged claims by anti-drug zealots, restrictions on the research became ever tighter. The Bureau of Narcotics authorized 87 marijuana studies in 1948, 18 in 1953, 6 in 1958.[133]

Prosecutors seek not only the bodies but the property of drug users, a desire that fosters corruption. Assorted statutes allow the government to seize property when drug charges are proved, filed, or even considered. The ostensible reason is that criminals should not profit from their criminality. The real situation is different. Example: When 52 marijuana plants and 16 ounces of dried plant were discovered in a 208-acre expanse, the federal government encumbered the entire ranch and offered a deal. If the owners made no effort to reclaim their property, the marijuana prosecution (with a 30-year prison term) would be dropped. The ranchers agreed. The federal government acquired agricultural land without proving a crime.[134] Example: In Alaska less than 0.1 ounce of marijuana was discovered in the jacket of a man who was working on his uncle's ocean fishing boat. Although the federal government admitted that the uncle knew nothing about the marijuana, his boat was seized and a $10,000 civil fine imposed—no criminal charges were ever filed. (Even though the uncle eventually got the boat back, and the fine was reduced, he lost his fishing season income.)[135] Example: Federal law assigns drug assets to police and prosecutors. A police chief proudly exhibited a drug dealer's Lincoln Town Car that replaced the chief's old official car. The chief said police now had a strong motive to move against drug dealers, and that a powerful message was delivered when the public saw police driving drug dealer cars. A reporter noted, "The [police] department has directed all district officers to watch for seizure opportunities."[136] In other words, police will most vigorously enforce those laws that produce financial gain for the department, and target violators who have the most useful and easily acquired assets. A person's property rather than a person's acts will determine whether the police attack. When police use robber attitudes to acquire gangster automobiles, a powerful message of corrupt values is delivered.

Seizure of drug assets may sound good in theory, but in practice it leads to extortion, virtual theft, and distortion of law enforcement priorities. Moreover, a basic principle of criminal sanction is corrupted by punishing a person (via property confiscation) before guilt is determined. In civil commitment and property confiscation both, drug authorities need not prove any particular act by the person who receives the sanction. Administering punishment before trial is an invitation to mischief. To save U.S. jurisprudence from such corruption, illicit drugs must be legalized.

Decoys and undercover agents promote corruption. They have a public image of ferreting out gangs of desperados, but that is not how they normally work. More typical is an example related to me with glee by a Missouri law officer. Police decided to arrest a college student for buying marijuana. An undercover agent was given a supply to sell to the student. The student was busy in her dorm room when the agent arrived, so she handed her roommate $20 and told her to take it to the waiting man and bring back the sack. The roommate did not know what was in the bag, but was arrested when she delivered the money. The law officer who told the story thought the outcome was hilarious; police missed the targeted person but caught someone who did not even know she was doing anything illegal. I asked how the public gained by such an operation, and the officer (incredulous at such a question) said the law had been enforced. But the law was not enforced. The police manufactured a crime, providing marijuana and a dealer. Even if the targeted individual had been caught, no crime would have existed had police not created the incident. As it was, a bystander got arrested while the drug dealer went free. Such cases were no laughing matter—about that time, a Missouri high school student received a 7-year penitentiary sentence for selling 0.33 ounce of marijuana to an undercover agent.[137] In my own college days, a fellow student who later turned out to be a police operative suggested that I should vandalize school property and offered to help. I declined, and admonished the agent that such conduct sounded illegal. Inventing a crime opportunity and asking someone to participate may test moral character, but has nothing to do with crime detection. Several of my acquaintances succumbed to the agent's urgings regarding drugs and went to jail on this person's testimony. The law was enforced. A police officer friend once warned me to avoid a particular professor's home; authorities were planning a drug raid, and my friend wanted to be sure I did not get arrested while visiting the professor. I have always appreciated that warning. In one jurisdiction at that time, being a visitor in a house where police found someone using marijuana was punishable by 5 years in prison even if the visitor had refused to use the drug.[138]

Such instances demonstrate official corruption. Officials could not be put on trial for anything they did, but they corrupted law enforcement. They corrupted it by creating crimes instead of detecting them. They corrupted it by putting citizens' morals to a test, guarding a particular definition of morality instead of guarding law-abiding citizens. Officials corrupted law enforcement by arresting people known to be blameless but who could nonetheless be prosecuted, as happened to the roommate and might have happened to me at the professor's house. They corrupted law enforcement by perverting it from promotion of public welfare to promotion of public relations—showing voters that officials are acting with vigor. In short, they corrupted law enforcement by enforcing criminal statutes instead of fighting crime.

Such practices may be corrupt, but they boost drug arrests—a growth that creates more public fear and more public demand for law enforcement. Legalizing illicit drugs would break that circle of corruption.

The drug war also corrupts law itself. One corruption was alluded to earlier, disproportionate penalties that destroy good people instead of bad drugs. When laws are designed to harm large numbers of ordinary citizens, those laws are corrupt. In addition, the definition of illegal conduct becomes corrupt as zeal for ensnaring citizens increases. California made the nature of a substance irrelevant: if a seller claimed to furnish an illegal drug such as heroin but actually delivered a legal product such as quinine, the penalty for selling heroin would apply. No physical evidence was even required for conviction.[139] The federal judiciary has long condemned such laws[140] without effect. The Missouri legislature passed another such law in 1989,[141] as it had in the past.[142] In Ohio a sale of fake "marijuana" (poinsettia) netted the dealer a prison sentence of 20 to 40 years.[143] Illinois declared that needle punctures showed narcotics use;[144] bad news for diabetics who wanted to avoid habitual arrest. Prescription pills outside the original container are presumptive evidence of intent to sell;[145] people with valid prescriptions for a drug have been arrested for having a handful outside the original container.[146] In the 1970s, Massachusetts considered a new death penalty offense: drug possession with intent to sell.[147] Had the proposal been enacted, persons who carried a daily prescribed dose in a pillbox might have been prudent to stay away from Massachusetts. As things stand, such persons still risk arrest anywhere in the country. Law becomes corrupt when, on behalf of the drug war, harmless everyday acts become crimes. Legalizing illicit drugs would help remove corruption from the law itself.

Drug laws also corrupt the judicial system. The Jackson County, Missouri, prosecutor received praise at election time for the number of drug convictions obtained. Less was said about the prosecutor bringing only one drug case to trial in the past year—all other convictions were plea bargains.[148] Normally a plea bargain offers to drop a charge if the accused person will accept punishment for a lesser offense, whether or not the lesser offense occurred. A prosecutor runs an extortion racket, threatening worse punishment if an accused person wants a trial. In such circumstances a right to trial no longer exists—if a person risks harsher treatment by exercising a "right," it is not a right. Do people in a dictatorship have a right to free speech, as long as they are willing to risk punishment? For every person, save one, convicted of a drug offense in Jackson County, Missouri, the United States was a dictatorship.

Fearing the mandatory punishments in some drug laws, defendants in some jurisdictions may agree to plead guilty to lesser crimes that did not happen.[149] When courts convict drug defendants who are known to be innocent of a particular crime, the path is open to convicting other defendants known to be innocent of other crimes. A defendant is no more than an accused person; an accused person is innocent; most readers of this book are innocent. Expediencies required by America's drug war give most readers of this book an expanding opportunity to experience Nazi justice.

One may argue that most drug defendants are scum who merit nothing better than a plea bargain, that worthless persons do not deserve protections of constitutional rights. In other words, constitutional rights are worth no more than the defendants. If people hated by the community can no longer claim protection of the law, citizens are protected only by goodwill of neighbors and authorities. Such an environment is not democracy.

Prosecutors and judges harried by the growing volume of drug cases may protest that plea bargains are the only way to process such enormous numbers of accused persons. Such an attitude corrupts the judicial system, negating its function as a resource available to opposing parties who quest for justice. Instead courts become an administrative processing tool, a means to move defendants quickly through the system rather than a means to seek justice. When more and more citizens are apprehended as criminals, we need to ask whether something is wrong with society or with the law. If behavior that was legal last year is outlawed this year, and police efforts increase, defendants will grow in number regardless of whether the drug situation has changed. Greater quantities of defendants show only that anti-drug laws are becoming more numerous and enforcement more strict. Legalizing illicit drugs would turn off the engine that is clogging courtrooms and jails.

The high volume of cases promotes yet another corruption, a jaded and lackadaisical attitude by lawyers, police, and judges. I have watched assembly-line courtrooms in action.[150] They operate like fast food restaurants. Someone approaches the counter, the judge delivers the order, and everyone moves up one place in line. Prosecutors and court officials have heard all the stories before. For them each case is routine, and they act like it. Even the defendants seem bored. But for a victim, the case is a new experience, involving an incident that may have changed the victim's life forever. I saw no evidence that anyone cared, never a word of sympathy. On the contrary, I saw evidence that victims were regarded as pests—if they filed no complaints, fewer cases would take up the court's time. Such an atmosphere is dangerous because criminal law restrains not criminals but the rest of us, prevents us from going amok with vigilantism. When law-abiding citizens no longer expect justice, they may cease to be law abiding. Admittedly this issue goes beyond drug prosecutions, but if authorities only run plea bargains, if they laugh at the arrest of a blameless person by an undercover agent, then those authorities are more than jaded; they are corrupt.

Still another benefit to legalizing drugs would be a liberation of resources wasted on the drug war. In 1989 President George Bush proposed that the federal government spend nearly $8 billion. Local expenditures are no less astounding. In 1974 each marijuana arrest in California cost almost $1,500, and circa 1977 there were 450,000 marijuana arrests in the United States;[151] marijuana accounted for about 25 percent of all California felony charges as the 1970s began.[152] In 1989 Jackson County, Missouri, officials got a sales tax to finance growing demands from the county drug squad. "I'm excited," the prosecutor said. "It give us an opportunity to do something."[153] Like what? On a federal level this money buys sophisticated aerial radar systems, military transport aircraft, pursuit jets, and attack helicopters.[154] Locally it buys an oak dining table, sofa and love seat, a stereo receiver, 100-watt amplifier, equalizer, and speakers.[155] Such is the equipment needed to fight drugs. When police use stereos to fight a particular conduct, it is time to ask whether that conduct should be called crime.

This chapter has said harsh things about police and courts. Those criticisms give me no pleasure. As a historian I know that the law is the only power that ordinary citizens can turn to for protection against forces that wield money and might. As a block watch captain I know the crucial role that police officers play in neighbors' efforts to protect our homes. As the son of a peace officer, I have socialized with many officers in off-duty contexts and know the good-hearted nature of most cops. But if our friends, the courts and police, are doing bad things, we must say so. Silence is not friendship. We cannot stand idly by if friends are in trouble.

And the trouble is not of their choosing. Drug laws are not passed and enforced in a vacuum. They exist because lawmakers responded to vocal citizens. Other citizens must now speak up, to demand an end. We must stop endangering the lives of police officers over substances that cause no more harm than beer or cigarettes. We must stop illicit profits that corrupt narcotics squads and destroy the morale of honest cops. We must remove the maddening dilemma that confronts police when they enforce one set of laws on drugs that conflicts with another set of laws on civil liberties. We must stop ordering the police to monitor private behavior of people in their homes—a practice that comes very close to establishing a state religion. We must let the police stop enforcing morals and resume detection of crime. We must let the police get back to their rightful job. We must get off their backs about drugs.

By so doing, we would also help prosecutors, judges, and jailers. And most of all we would help ourselves. We are all wounded by the drug war. It is time to declare not surrender, but peace. There are ways to deal with drugs that do not require criminal sanctions. Ways that build upon and strengthen values that founded the republic, ways that allow each citizen to choose a path for pursuit of happiness. If we cherish the ideals of the Enlightenment that inspired eighteenth century Americans, the answers will come. Those ideals are not outdated. The drug disaster is bleak evidence of what happens when we ignore them.

4 Who Is the Drug Problem?

Many persons agree that a drug problem exists, but they often disagree about what the problem is. Those diverse ideas result in a mishmash of solutions that do not work.

Admittedly, human capabilities are inadequate to alter certain forces of nature. It seems odd, however, that a situation of human origin, on which there is wide consensus of concern, and which did not exist a century ago, remains so intransigent to mortal intervention.

This chapter proposes an explanation.

HOW THE DRUG PROBLEM HAPPENED

People seem to have forgotten why anti-drug laws were first passed. Remembrance might help efforts to improve the future.

Opium preparations were well known in colonial America and received extensive medical use. Despite their wide availability, recreational use seems to have been nil.[1] In the 1600s Virginia's colonial government demanded that farmers grow marijuana, imposing sanctions on any who refused.[2] George Washington raised marijuana,[3] and papers of other "Founding Fathers" discuss marijuana crops.[4] Records of that period show no mention of marijuana's pharmaceutical properties; commercial growers served the cloth and rope markets. Mention *is* found of alcohol abuse; early America was awash in beer and liquor, with a per capita consumption far higher than in modern times.[5] Alcohol's effects were noticed among all levels of society.

Although cheap opiates were available to anyone in the nineteenth century, their widest use was for medicine rather than recreation. A typical "addict" developed the habit from medication.[6] Today a "medical addict" can be cured easily, but matters were different a century ago. Often people did not know that medicines contained opiates;. manufacturers did not have to reveal product contents. If people treated themselves with an opiate tonic for diarrhea or influenza, and developed a physical resonance, the symptoms for which the tonic was sold would reappear when doses stopped. So people would resume the nostrum because it kept them healthy. Seeking a "cure" for using the tonic would not have crossed their minds—the *tonic* was viewed as the cure for what ailed them. Such persons may have used opiates continually, but they were not addicts in the modern sense. A different class of "medical addicts" was under professional medical care. In that situation both physician and patient might know that an opiate, typically morphine, was involved. Cures for many afflictions were unknown; symptoms could only be relieved, and opiates dramatically liberated patients from pain and fear. Physical resonance was a negligible price for relief of a chronic condition. Continued use of opiates was more problematic after a temporary condition ceased. If a physician continued to administer them, the most likely reasons were either ignorance or avarice—in the 1880s fees for house calls ranged from 50 cents to 6 dollars, when working class families made 10 dollars a week.[7] The patient's most likely reasons to continue self-administration were either ignorance or undiagnosed chronic needs satisfied by the drug. Such needs may have been psychological; people became just as frustrated 100 years ago as today[8]—anger and anxiety can melt away under opiates. "One apothecary told me of an old lady who formerly came to him as often as four times a week and purchased a fifty-cent bottle of [opiate] 'cough-balsam.' She informed him that it 'quieted her nerves' and afforded rest when everything else had failed."[9] In a time when physicians were considered incompetent and when anyone could purchase opiates legally, absence of a prescription did not label a user as a hedonist. Accounts do exist of individuals who took opiates for pleasure, but medical addicts seemed far more numerous. The typical user is described as a female white Protestant from the middle or upper classes. Men of affairs were also seen as typical users. The custom was more prevalent in the South than in other regions. Opiate consumption mostly occurred in middle age, the years of highest vigor and productivity.[10]

(Not all authorities agree that medical users outnumbered pleasure-seekers; fuzziness surrounds definitions and data. "Opiate addiction" was not defined as a disease or a social malady until the latter nineteenth century, and specialists then groped for a consensus that would permit discussion.[11] An analogy might be rock and roll music. It bothers many people, captivates others, but in the 1980s "authorities" [and who are they?] would have been pressed to determine which listeners were harmed and which were helped, let alone measure [instead of pontificate about] the impact of rock and roll on America. The nebulous understanding of the drug scene in the 1880s mirrors the knowledge of rock and roll in the 1980s. Necessary mental concepts, let alone analytic tools, had yet to be invented.)

Cocaine was widely marketed in the late 1800s. It cost little, and was available straight or as an additive in soft drinks or alcoholic beverages, even in cigars and cigarettes. We find no reports of maddened cocaine smokers. Instead the drug and products containing it were praised by respected and well-known persons: Sigmund Freud, Thomas Edison, Ulysses S. Grant, William McKinley, Jules Verne, Emile Zola, Henrik Ibsen, Sarah Bernhardt, Pope Leo XIII, the Prince of Wales, and the Tsar of Russia.[12]

Marijuana was freely available and was an ingredient in assorted candies, food, and drink.[13]

Throughout the 1800s no link between drug use and crime was observed.[14] Authorities denied any link between opiates and "sexual psychosis."[15] Sales were strong; an Albany, New York, druggist who prepared laudanum in gallon batches during the 1850s mixed it in barrel quantities during the 1880s;[16] and referring to opiates in 1878 an Atlanta druggist said, "We sell enough every week to kill a thousand people."[17] But thousands did not die, and history has answered questions that Americans of the era raised about the effect of widespread drug use on national productivity:[18] the post-Civil War years are remembered as a time of economic and intellectual vigor.

The general attitude toward opiates in the 1880s was similar to the attitude toward cigarettes in the 1980s:

> Employees were not fired for addiction. Wives did not divorce their addicted husbands, or husbands their addicted wives. Children were not taken from their homes and lodged in foster homes or institutions because one or both parents were addicted. Addicts continued to participate fully in the life of the community. Addicted children and young people continued to go to school, Sunday School, and college.[19]

Within that general tolerance two areas of dissent were growing, both calling for restrictions on the drug trade. Eventually they would merge and replace the old benevolence with vicious intolerance. The process would demonstrate how a good idea from one group of persons could be hijacked by persons with different intent, and transformed from a social benefit to a national disaster.

The good idea was product labeling. The late 1800s saw growth of political populism, a term which itself was hijacked in the late 1900s. A century ago populists demanded more power over their lives. They organized, and for a while had enough political strength to push through reforms. One reform was product labeling, giving consumers power to choose or refuse products on the basis of contents rather than advertising. Home remedies now had to list their ingredients. Some concoctions turned out to be laced with opiates, and sales of these products plummeted.[20] When people discovered they had been using opiates in ignorance, many quit. They were not "in love" with the drug.

The other area of dissent was first expressed in the 1870s when western states passed anti-opium laws. The legislation was aimed less at the drug than at the people deemed to be the primary users—Chinese immigrants.[21] Their industriousness and their willingness to accept low pay made them popular among employers in the West. Railroad companies used them as strike breakers, and mining companies used them as a threat against white workers who were disgruntled by pay cuts. Angry white citizens blamed economic hardship on the Chinese, and anti-opium laws harassed them. The laws had no effect on opium use but did provide a framework for lawful attacks on Chinese by white police instead of unlawful attacks by white laborers.[22] The extent of such harassment can be measured by San Francisco police statistics dating from around 1900; crimes against persons or property accounted for 2 percent of arrests of Chinese-Americans, the other 98 percent were crimes against health (including opium) or morals (including gambling).[23] Some years earlier San Francisco authorities declared, "The department of the police, in enforcing the law with regard to this [opium] matter, have found white women and Chinamen side by side under the effects of this drug—a humiliating sight to anyone who has anything left of manhood."[24] In 1902 a committee of the American Pharmaceutical Association said, "If the Chinaman cannot get along without his 'dope,' we can get along without him."[25] Such attitudes "followed the flag." When the United States seized the Philippines, anti-opium laws were introduced, directed against Chinese there.[26]

Powers that controlled the American West's economy also controlled legislation that directed public anger and attention toward the Chinese. Those laws diverted public energies from examination of elites, elites that profited from using the Chinese as a tool to exploit all workers in the West. The anti-drug campaign was a protective smoke screen for wealthy interests. Their victims fought one another while leaving exploiters alone.

Because product labeling protected the public, populist demand for power could easily be misrepresented as a demand for protection. Drug sales restrictions could even be portrayed as an attack on pharmaceutical corporation greed rather than an attack on citizens' rights. Public support for proposals that actually harmed populism was generated by clever rhetoric from racists, opportunists, and elitists who had no sympathy for populism. The most prominent and powerful figure among them was Hamilton Wright. He was a medical man recognized for research on beriberi, which he discovered to be infectious. That discovery turned out to be erroneous, but his professional reputation remained unimpaired, perhaps partly due to his social standing. He was ambitious and had married into a politically prominent family. One of his wife's uncles had been a founder of the Republican Party during the 1850s and governor of Maine during the Civil War. Another uncle was secretary of state under President Ulysses S. Grant. Still another uncle was a lumberman who served as governor of Wisconsin in the 1870s. The wife's father was a U.S. senator; her uncles sat in Congress as well. Wright exploited his political connections and Far East medical research to get diplomatic appointments dealing with the opium trade. He carved a niche of power for himself, eventually becoming the federal government's primary authority on opiates and cocaine, with considerable influence on drug control policy. In addition to Wright, another prominent anti-drug crusader was Ann Harriman Vanderbilt. She used the issue to compete with a high society rival who gained fame as a woman's suffrage advocate. Although Mrs. Vanderbilt had low governmental influence she was credited with considerable power because of her high public profile. Her prominence merits mention because she had a private agenda to score publicity points against a social rival. Vocal power of an anti-drug zealot tells us nothing about the person's concern or motivation.

In regulating opium sales to China, Wright focused the powers of do-gooders and profit-seekers, two groups that normally fought each other. Preachers and missionary aid societies had a long-standing interest in uplifting the heathen Chinese. Rescuing China from opium resonated with that desire. Capitalists saw a chance to improve Chinese productivity and stability, making the country a more lucrative market.[27] Wright promoted an issue that combined selflessness and selfishness, an issue that united voters and power brokers.

Wright, who feared the spread of drug abuse to "higher social ranks,"[28] also enlisted forces of racism with his claim that opium in America increased the number of women living with Chinese males,[29] his claim that almost half the Chinese-American population smoked opium, his claim that up to 150,000 non-Chinese smokers existed, and his implication that America was beset by a spreading Oriental custom that had already ruined China. Later analysts found his figures to be grossly inflated,[30] but they inflamed passion about opium in the United States as well as China, fostering a climate favorable to his proposals of control. (A few years later, Germans would become the scapegoat. During World War I, anti-drug zealots alleged that the kaiser's agents were spreading narcotics addiction in America,[31] and by war's end even the U.S. government described narcotics as "German products."[32] To promote hatred of Germans, drug use was portrayed as un-American. A notion spread that reducing narcotics addiction would help the war effort.[33] Addicts had let their country down, and perhaps they merited hatred as well.)

In a 1910 report submitted to Congress by President William Howard Taft, Wright said "the misuse of cocaine is undoubtedly an American habit"[34] (in contrast to the alien custom of opium). Wright told Congress that a national consensus cried for federal laws to counter "the most threatening of the drug habits that has ever appeared in this country."[35]

This "threat," too, was racial.

Cocaine use began as an upper and middle class practice among whites, but around 1903 reports began to associate cocaine with African-Americans.[36] In that year the American Pharmaceutical Association declared, "The negroes, the lower and criminal classes, are naturally most readily influenced."[37] In 1910 a U.S. House of Representatives committee heard testimony that "the colored people seem to have a weakness for it [cocaine]. . . . They would just as leave rape a woman as anything else and a great many of the southern rape cases have been traced to cocaine."[38] "Jew peddlers" were said to be selling cocaine to African-Americans in the South.[39] Cocaine was believed to embolden African-Americans to challenge fellow citizens who persecuted them.[40] Stories circulated that police bullets could not affect African-Americans who used cocaine.[41] Hamilton Wright said that cocaine turned African-American males into rapists and that cocaine abuse among African-Americans needed more publicity.[42] Indeed he tried to orchestrate hysteria. In 1910 he told the Louisville *Journal Courier* that "a strong editorial from you on the abuse of cocaine in the South would do a great deal of good [but] do not quote me or the Department of State."[43] Wright apparently sought to capitalize on Southern fear of cocaine among African-Americans in order to weaken states' rights arguments against federal anti-drug legislation. If he had merely wanted to promote public education he would have had no concern about keeping his activity secret.[44]

Scientific study of cocaine use by African-Americans demolished claims publicized by the news media and accepted by citizens and government officials. For example, drug abuse tends to increase with general deviancy, but examination of 2,119 African-Americans placed in a Georgia insane asylum between 1909 and 1914 found only 2 who used cocaine.[45] Use among the ordinary population should have been lower yet.

Absence of massive cocaine use by African-Americans is unsurprising. Among them drug use of any type seemed rare in the latter 1800s,[46] and their situation changed little by World War I. At about that time a Jacksonville, Florida, municipal drug clinic found a low rate of addiction among African-Americans.[47] A New York City clinic set up around 1920 as a legal source of drugs for addicts had few calls from anyone for cocaine.[48] Despite a generation of lurid publicity, demand for cocaine was nil. Any use of cocaine among African-Americans may well have been as self-medication rather than abuse.[49] One historian summarized the cocaine scare: "[Hamilton] Wright, the chief authority for the claim of a black cocaine problem, was reporting unsubstantiated gossip, and knowingly misrepresented the evidence before him."[50]

The federal government's response to drug agitation showed a strategy no different from the one used for environmental questions in the 1980s—mollify public opinion while leaving major corporate interests unmolested. The ostensible problem was disregarded. For example, the 1909 congressional action to outlaw import of smoking opium was highly publicized. Less publicized was the fact that the U.S. Food and Drug Administration had long possessed the power to ban such imports, but at election time members of Congress could not take credit for a simple FDA order. Not publicized at all was Secretary of State Robert Bacon's admission that the law was merely intended to make the United States look good at one of Hamilton Wright's international opium conferences and thereby promote a friendlier commercial policy from the government of China.[51] Regarding Bacon's successor, in November 1909 Wright declared, "[Philander] Knox who is a cold blooded little fellow is only now grasping the fact that in this opium business he has the oil to smooth any troubled waters he may meet with at Peking in his aggressive business enterprises there."[52]

Foreign diplomats showed indifference about U.S. drug laws,[53] but Wright falsely claimed otherwise in order to prod more drug restrictions through Congress. Such measures were presented as patriotic acts improving the nation's worldwide prestige and commerce, but in reality the only measures urged by foreign diplomats were laws to ensure that Wright's conferences were not a subterfuge to gain an opiate monopoly for U.S. pharmaceutical corporations.[54]

Following yet another of Wright's international opium meetings, he sought passage of a federal statute that became known as the Harrison Act.[55] Persons dealing in narcotics and cocaine would have to register with the government and pay a small tax, but anyone could engage in the trade. Wright said the law was needed to abide by a 1912 treaty that the United States had just ratified. Congressman Francis Burton Harrison cared little about the measure; he simply introduced it to satisfy Wright, and told Wright to be sure it met the wishes of the drug industry.[56] Promoters said the Harrison Act would gather information to improve understanding of the drug trade but did not claim it would reduce drug consumption. Little concern about a "drug problem" was evident in congressional proceedings, which instead emphasized the treaty obligation. Nor was there much public interest.[57]

The law levied a tax on products and persons in the drug trade, and enforcement duties fell to the Treasury Department. For years existence of federal police power to eliminate drug use had been denied; in 1909 Congressman J. H. Gaines stated the consensus: "It takes plenary power to stamp out such a habit [opium smoking]—if it can be suppressed at all—the full police power. Our Federal Government does not have it."[58] Shortly afterward Wright sputtered, "The Constitution is constantly getting in the way."[59] Wright crafted the Harrison Act to carry out a treaty, thereby (under standard judicial doctrine) creating a federal police power to enforce drug regulations, rather than just collect revenue. Intentions of zealots became clear. Treasury enforcement regulations had the power of law unless successfully challenged in court, and to make such a challenge a person had to be willing to undergo criminal prosecution. A handful of appointed Treasury officials, accountable to neither Congress nor the American people, issued regulations interpreting the Harrison Act in such a way as to severely limit availability of narcotics and cocaine, on pain of fine or imprisonment. After officials adopted this strategy, they orchestrated a propaganda campaign to build public support for drug suppression. That sequence—government decision followed by citizen request—reverses the democratic process.[60]

(The Harrison Act was Wright's biggest accomplishment, and also his last significant one. Secretary of State William Jennings Bryan fired him because Wright smelled so strongly of liquor at drug control meetings.)[61]

Confusion reigned as interested parties tried to reconcile the act's language with draconian Treasury decrees that followed. Even some Treasury officials could scarcely believe what was happening; the Public Health Service was then a Treasury division, and the surgeon general said that addicts were entitled to morphine under the Harrison Act.[62] Internal Revenue disagreed, and announced that the act forbade maintenance doses by physicians.[63] Regulations forbade issuance of narcotics prescriptions in a physician's office; instead the doctor had to make a house call.[64] Many addicts could not obtain regular physician visits, particularly in poor neighborhoods, but regulations declared possession of narcotics without a prescription to be illegal.[65] Thus was a revenue law for suppliers twisted into a prohibitory law for recipients.

The most immediate effect noted after the Harrison Act took effect on March 1, 1915, was the sudden appearance of illicit dealers offering diluted heroin at about 10 times the price that a pure supply had cost at drug stores the previous week.[66]

Neither the medical profession nor the courts viewed Treasury's actions with favor. Judges held that federal intervention in the practice of medicine was unconstitutional,[67] and in 1916 the U.S. Supreme Court ruled that the Harrison Act did not implement a treaty[68]—thereby limiting Treasury's police power In reviewing the Harrison Act's language, Justice Oliver Wendell Holmes said Congress never intended to criminalize a large portion of the public:

> Only words from which there is no escape could warrant the conclusion that Congress meant to strain its powers almost if not quite to the breaking point in order to make the probably very large proportion of citizens who have some preparation of opium in their possession criminal or at least *prima facie* criminal and subject to the serious punishment.[69]

Treasury responded with a new strategy. Law-abiding addicts had to get prescription orders from individual physicians. The impact was analogous to requiring doctor visits for aspirin or condoms or cigarettes. Practitioners were overwhelmed with clients who required no examination or diagnosis but merely needed a slip of paper. Many were bothersome and disrupted office routine. Some physicians responded by writing narcotics prescriptions wholesale. Today that may sound unethical, but doctors of the 1920s came from a background in which these substances were freely available to anyone; if government bureaucrats suddenly said that druggists had to demand a piece of paper from narcotics customers, many physicians saw their duty as simply to help patients get the piece of paper.

The Harrison Act explicitly guaranteed the right of physicians to prescribe narcotics to addicts: "Nothing contained in this section shall apply—(a) To the dispensing or distribution of any of the aforesaid drugs to a patient by a physician, dentist, or veterinary surgeon registered under this Act in the course of his professional practice only."[70] The Treasury Department's new strategy evaded that guarantee by saying that addiction was not a disease, and therefore doctors could not prescribe drugs either to treat addiction or keep addicts comfortable. Treasury then carefully chose prosecutions to establish precedents forbidding physicians to furnish opiates to persons who were not ill. The search for just the right case was painstaking; the government dropped charges in 47,800 cases, lest an unsuitable one set an undesired precedent.[71] Finally Dr. W. S. Webb was allowed to ascend through the judicial system to the U.S. Supreme Court. Webb's behavior stuck out as raw; for 50 cents he would provide a narcotics prescription to anyone, even writing multiple prescriptions with a fictitious patient name on each one, apparently so the customer could receive large quantities without attracting attention from regulatory authorities. The U.S. Attorney General specifically asked the court to determine whether, in the light of Webb's activity, the Harrison Act allowed a physician to maintain an addict on morphine. In 1919 the court ruled that the Act did not permit maintenance.[72] Next Dr. Jin Fuey Moy was prosecuted for selling morphine prescriptions to anybody. In 1920 the Supreme Court held that the Harrison Act forbade physicians to merely gratify the drug appetites of addicts. [73] Finally Dr. Morris Behrman was charged with prescribing quantities large enough to supply an addict recipient for months—the implication being that an addict was likely to sell the excess at black market prices. The indictment, however, did not allege bad faith by Behrman and said the drugs were intended to cure the addict. A conviction, therefore, would establish the illegality of prescribing narcotics or cocaine in good faith as part of a cure regimen.[74] In 1922 the Supreme Court upheld Behrman's conviction.[75]

In the middle of this litigation process, alcohol Prohibition was passed. Early in 1920 the Treasury Department gave Harrison Act enforcement to the Prohibition Unit. There, Harry J. Anslinger would become the key anti-drug activist among Treasury officials. He was a former railroad police agent who worked his way into a U.S. State Department post in the Bahamas, where he fought rum-running during Prohibition in the mid-1920s. His vigor brought him promotion to Washington, to run the Prohibition Bureau's Division of Foreign Control. In 1929 he became assistant commissioner of Prohibition, and the next year he took over narcotics law enforcement. In 1930 that function was removed from the Prohibition Bureau and assigned to a new Federal Bureau of Narcotics in the Treasury Department. President Herbert Hoover put Anslinger in charge as U.S. Commissioner of Narcotics. Prohibition agents continued on the job after Prohibition's end; they merely transferred to Anslinger's Bureau of Narcotics. His visceral hatred of drugs guided decisions in the federal government, the League of Nations, and the United Nations for the next 40 years.

Prohibition agents encouraged a federal crusade to stamp out drug use, rather than regulate it. Motivation was deeper than fanaticism or authoritarianism. The bigger the job that the Prohibition Unit could set out for itself, the bigger its funding and power. The $515,000 appropriated for narcotics work in 1920 was nearly twice the amount authorized in 1919. Thus started the bureaucratic thrust that has propelled drug control policy ever since, providing ever more institutions with a vested interest in supporting that policy.

The Prohibition Bureau's legacy influenced federal drug control policy long after the agency was abolished. Here, for example, is an excerpt from the bureau's regulations of October 19, 1921: "It is well established that the ordinary case of addiction yields to proper treatment and that addicts will remain permanently cured when drug taking is stopped and they are otherwise physically restored to health and strengthened in will power."[76] In the 1950s a National Research Council statement on drug addiction, distributed by the American Medical Association and the Department of Health, Education, and Welfare, quoted government policy on the subject: "It is well established that the ordinary case of addiction yields to proper treatment and that addicts can remain permanently cured when drug taking is stopped and they are otherwise physically restored to health and strengthened in will power."[77] Federal drug policy never changed after it was first dictated by alcohol Prohibition forces.

The difference between "maintenance of a patient" and "gratification of a pervert" is in the eye of the beholder, and the Prohibition Bureau declared that addiction was cured by stopping drug intake. Relying on Supreme Court precedents set in cases of outrageous abuse, in the 1920s federal Prohibition agents around the country descended upon physicians who tried to help individual addicts. In 1922, U.S. Congressman Lester D. Volk, a physician, spoke out.

> There has developed a tendency . . . to substitute for the provisions of the [Harrison] act arbitrary administrative opinions expressed in rules and regulations which amount to practically a repeal and nullification of the law itself. . . . As a substitute for open discussion of known medical facts there has been set up a propaganda for the incarceration of all drug users . . . and complete elimination of the family doctor. An undeniable effort is now being made whereby physicians are to be denied any discretion and power in the prescribing of narcotic drugs and to force all those addicted to the use of these drugs into hospitals exploiting questionable "cures."[78]

Medical organizations and journals joined the protest.[79]

The outrage was heard by the U.S. Supreme Court, and in 1925 it handed down an interpretation of the Harrison Act[80] that stood as definitive until the act was replaced in 1970. Dr. Charles O. Linder was a respected physician in Spokane, Washington. A government informer pretended to be in pain and convinced Linder to prescribe 4 tablets of morphine and cocaine. The agent claimed to have told Linder that she was an addict, making the prescription illegal. The Treasury Department put the doctor on trial, and he was convicted. Linder appealed to the Supreme Court. The tribunal swept away the precedents on which Treasury had relied, narrowing them to situations of reckless professional conduct. The Court held drug addiction to be a disease and declared that doctors could prescribe drugs necessary to prevent withdrawal symptoms. The Court declared that if the Harrison Act had intended otherwise, it "would certainly encounter grave constitutional difficulties."[81]

Treasury's Narcotics Bureau nonetheless continued to rely on the earlier precedents to prosecute physicians for good faith treatment of addicts. In 1932 Narcotics Bureau field supervisor H. T. Nugent admitted "probably the justifiable complaint on the part of some of the professional men [physicians and pharmacists] against the desire of some of our field men to build up a good record at the expense of the professional classes, and made up probably a lot of petty cases.''[82] Although in 1936 a federal judge had invalidated Narcotics Bureau regulations that limited prescriptions to addicts,[83] physicians who wanted to avoid trouble learned that Treasury's word was law regardless of what any court said. By 1938 the Bureau had prosecuted almost 25,000 doctors and convicted 5,000.[84] The Narcotics Bureau's misrepresentation and misuse of law was corrupt, corruption immune from both criminal and impeachment proceedings.

The human cost of such corruption was observed by a Public Health Service official:

> An American woman . . . had been living in Europe where she had been carried on morphine for years for the treatment of a residual pain. . . . The treatment made it possible for her to live an efficient and reasonably comfortable life. . . . Upon returning to this country, she could find no physician who would risk his liberty and right to practice medicine by prescribing the morphine on which she had become dependent. In desperation, she agreed to having a lobotomy performed. This serious operation, which always leaves some undesirable change of personality but often relieves intractable pain, left the woman in worse condition than before and still complaining of pain.[85]

In contrast, U.S. Commissioner of Narcotics Harry Anslinger readily ordered narcotics supplied to individuals who caught his favor. His memoirs tell of aid to a naval officer, a wealthy and beautiful woman, and a powerful member of Congress.[86] (One wonders if Anslinger thereby had a special friend on Capitol Hill.) Narcotics agents routinely furnish drugs to gratify addict informers who are willing to trick physicians into providing narcotics;[87] all the drugs go to the same person, but the agents are left unmolested while the doctors are prosecuted.

Government attacks on individual physicians left addicts without any legal access to drugs. Addicts became victims of criminal suppliers who charged outrageous prices. High profits produced an inexhaustible number of big and little dealers. This was already evident around 1919. Recognizing at that time that such a change in suppliers helped neither addicts nor the community, dozens of cities around the country established clinics to dispense narcotics.

The Shreveport, Louisiana, clinic was a good example. It helped clients find employment and housing, and kept tabs on criminal conduct among clients and tried to discourage such behavior. The police chief declared, "From a police standpoint, the City of Shreveport is greatly benefited by its being here. It has practically eliminated the bootlegger who deals in narcotics, and in this way alone has reduced the number of possible future dope users. . . . The authorities in charge of the Police Department in Shreveport would regard it a calamity should this Clinic be removed."[88]

If municipal clinics provided drug addicts with a legal means of dealing with their habit, the Prohibition Unit could be slimmed down. Anti-drug militants in the Treasury Department focused on problems experienced by some clinics, especially in New York City where the clinic staff was overworked. Difficulties arise in any new public health program, but the Treasury Department's propaganda campaign and legal harassment managed to close all the clinics before they could develop procedures to respond to Treasury's complaints. Now every drug user in the country was the Prohibition Unit's lawful prey.

In 1921, a study of 26 municipal clinics found them serving a total of 1,500 clients, who were typically in early adulthood or middle age. The grand total for all clinics nationwide was about 10,000.[89] Such a small number suggests that most addicts preferred other sources of supply or, more likely, that addiction was uncommon. Nonetheless, magazines routinely carried stories saying that drugs were a major national problem.[90]

Richmond Hobson was a driving force behind drug scare stories. While serving in Congress he declared alcohol to be a narcotic and was a key figure in the passage of alcohol Prohibition. After leaving office he directed his attention toward narcotics. His claims were outlandish. He urged women to have their face powder tested to be sure it contained no heroin, and said that one ounce of heroin yielded 2,000 addicts.[91] These and similar warnings of his were put into the *Congressional Record* and were widely distributed at public expense. He was accepted as a drug expert and received free national network radio time to spread his histrionic messages of doom. American attitudes toward drugs were shaped by such authorities. One element of Hobson's rhetoric is striking because it is found so often in statements of later militants. In 1929 he said, "Ten years ago the narcotic drug addiction problem in America was a minor, medical problem. Today it is a major, national problem, constituting the chief factor menacing the public health, the public morals, the public safety."[92] Yet a 1917 New York legislature report said drug abuse was the number one problem in the state.[93] Zealots claimed a crisis in 1917, but in 1929 they said no significant problem had existed in 1917. Anti-drug crusaders routinely announce that a formerly modest problem has become an emergency, and years later general history books about the era say nothing of a drug problem, let alone crisis. The rhetoric works because current audiences remember no drug problem in the past, but have no experience to challenge militants' allegations about the present. Because a historical perspective shows militants to have a 100 percent inaccuracy rate on the subject, skepticism about their current crisis rhetoric may be prudent.

Government repression dramatically changed the demographics of addiction. The nineteenth century pattern held right up to 1915.[94] Afterwards, when legal availability of opiates became limited, productive persons of middle age no longer turned to them. The age of habit acquisition shifted to adolescence, a stressful time of life in which society's norms are challenged and even disregarded. Illegality may have increased the appeal of drugs to rebellious youth, but use had always been seen among adolescents; previously they were simply outnumbered by older citizens. With that older group eliminated, adolescents became dominant by default. The "maturing out" phenomenon suggests that adolescents use drugs for different reasons than their elders previously did. Youth abandon drugs upon reaching maturity, whereas their elders formerly turned to drugs upon reaching the prime of life. Driving opiates from the routine pharmacopoeia also meant a drastic reduction in medical addicts, the bulk of whom were surely post-adolescents. Moreover, most "respectable people" obey the law even when it is obnoxious, so criminalization of drugs automatically shifted the demographic predominance to users who disregarded laws in general. In short, the demographic shift was not because either the pharmacological properties of drugs or the character of various social classes changed. The shift occurred because formerly accepted behavior became illegal. Mature and productive members of society obeyed the law; rebellious and marginal elements continued drug use as before.

Anti-drug laws also drastically changed the prison population. As the 1920s progressed, the typical federal prisoner was doing drug time.[95] In 1928 the total federal prisoner population was 8,401. Of that total, 2,529 were imprisoned for narcotics violations, another 1,156 for alcohol violations.[96] Narcotics convictions became so numerous that two new penitentiaries were built especially for drug users. A Public Health Service doctor described "a paralyzed, bedridden man who had been sentenced to four years for a narcotic violation. Just how he could be a menace to society was never clear to me."[97] In contrast, major dealers were absent from prison populations.[98]

In 1926 the Treasury Department asked Congress to amend the Harrison Act, strengthening both the act's constitutionality and Treasury's power over drugs. Treasury's concern that the law remain in effect for the department to enforce is an example of bureaucratic thrust. Treasury wanted to maintain and expand its work force, and got Congress to cooperate.

Cheap Mexican labor threatened Anglo jobs during the Great Depression. As concern about Mexican-American labor competition grew in the West and Southwest, so did alarm about a new drug peril—marijuana, then identified as "Mexican opium."[99] "It is fast becoming a terrible menace, particularly in the counties where sugarbeets are grown,"[100] that is, where Mexican farm workers labored. A Colorado newspaper editor wrote, "I wish I could show you what a small marihuana cigaret can do to one of our degenerate Spanish-speaking residents. That's why our problem is so great; the greatest percentage of our population is composed of Spanish-speaking persons."[101] In 1930 the percentage of Spanish-speaking population in the editor's county had yet to reach 6 percent.[102] If such a small fraction could be viewed as overwhelming, Anglo fear of Mexican-American competition must have been high indeed. Despite claims of Mexican lawlessness, the Mexican-American crime rate was low; one study showed it lower than the Anglo rate in the 1920s.[103] Because marijuana use was considered a Mexican custom in the Southwest,[104] state criminalization of the practice was a lawful means to harass Mexican-Americans, forcing them into jail or out of the country. Either way they would no longer compete for Anglo jobs. This was the context of sudden demands for a federal law against marijuana in the late 1930s.

To help pass the 1937 federal ban, Treasury's legal staff asked Anslinger to provide horror stories.[105] Anslinger believed Hispanics caused a marijuana problem[106] but supplemented anti-Mexican agitation with tales about African-Americans. The Bureau of Narcotics revealed "colored students at the Univ. of Minn. partying with female students (white) smoking [marijuana] and getting their sympathy with stories of racial persecution. Result pregnancy." Also "two Negroes took a girl fourteen years old and kept her for two days in a hut under the influence of marihuana. Upon recovery she was found to be *suffering from* syphilis."[107] In 1937 Anslinger also claimed that marijuana should be outlawed because it was a major cause of violent crime, but denied that marijuana users moved on to heroin.[108] In 1955 Anslinger questioned whether marijuana caused violent crime, but said marijuana must remain illegal because its users moved on to heroin.[109] Anslinger basically had a fanatical hatred of drugs, for whatever reasons he could find at a given moment.

In 1937 his marijuana horror stories were questioned by Dr. William C. Woodward, who testified to Congress on behalf of the American Medical Association, which advocated continued legal availability of marijuana.[110] Woodward noted that debate on outlawing marijuana relied on rumor and hearsay; federal agencies with solid facts had not been asked to provide them.[111] If anti-marijuana legislation were to deal with a drug problem, Congress might have taken up Woodward's point. If the legislation's purpose were to harass certain segments of the population, Woodward's objections were irrelevant. Congress treated them as irrelevant and proceeded to outlaw marijuana. (Technically marijuana was not banned outright, but conditions of legal sale were made impossible.)

As the 1950s began, anti-drug forces once again announced that a previously small annoyance had suddenly become a national catastrophe.[112] U.S.

Congressman Hale Boggs argued that a growing drug problem was caused by lenient courts, and in 1951 he persuaded Congress to revoke the power of judges to adjust sentences to individual circumstances. By setting mandatory sentences, the Boggs Act blurred the tradition of having separate legal structures to deal with offense and offender—normally a legislature deals with the former, a court with the latter. (A similar law was passed in 1956 after the Daniel Subcommittee[113] alleged that harsher law enforcement reduced drug use, while judicial leniency increased it. Federal court records fail to support that claim. The "tough" Seventh Circuit showed a rise in narcotics arrests and convictions form 1956 to 1959; the "soft" First Circuit showed a decrease.)[114] Both Boggs and Daniel used anti-drug crusades to fuel their political careers.

The first narcotics offender under the 1956 act was a Mexican-American. He was also an epileptic who scored 69 on an I.Q. test. He was a heroin addict who had nonetheless managed to avoid either a narcotics or a federal criminal record. He was 21 years old and had just spent 14 months in a state insane asylum. Upon his release, Anslinger's Bureau of Narcotics got a 17-year-old heroin addict to purchase small quantities of heroin from him. The law was enforced. The result was a life prison sentence.[115] Severe federal sentences became routine: 50 years without parole for a first marijuana sale offense;[116] 20 years without parole for a first marijuana transportation offense;[117] 40 years for selling marijuana to a police agent.[118] Such federal convictions occurred even when local authorities examined and dismissed the charges, even if it was the person's first arrest (let alone conviction) for any crime. The defendants in these 3 examples were African-Americans. Historically most persons prosecuted for drug offenses have been poor and members of a racial minority.[119] In 1955 a New York judge stated, "In all the years that I have been in practice which is since 1907—and I have been on the bench since 1931—I have not seen a rich user of drugs come before me."[120] A famed student of the subject explained:

> When the addict is a well-to-do professional man . . . and is well spoken and well educated, prosecutors, policemen, and judges alike are especially strongly inclined to regard him as an "unfortunate" or as a "victim" of something like a disease. The harsh penalties of the law, it is felt, were surely not intended for a person like this, and, by an unspoken agreement, arrangements are quietly made to exempt him from such penalties.[121]

Despite highly publicized exceptions to that tradition in the 1980s, the exceptions have not yet confirmed a change.

Because prosecutors have discretion in setting charges against a defendant, "mandatory sentence" laws simply transferred sentencing power from the judicial branch to the executive branch. Prosecutors determined fines and prison terms by fine-tuning indictments. Federal judges eventually rebelled and refused to obey mandatory sentence statutes.[122] When judges defy the law, the law is corrupt.

During the 1950s drug addiction itself was a crime in some states. Given the nature of addiction, a conviction handed police an excuse to continually harass the addict afterwards. And given the demographic characteristics of areas with high drug use, police had a lawful excuse for wide-scale harassment of impoverished African-Americans or Hispanics. Marijuana laws were also useful in this regard. Chicago police practice in the mid-1950s was to arrest any known African-American addict on sight and take the person to a police station, to be pumped for information about dealers.[123] This custom led to many arrests of non-addicts: "Since the age at which drug use started was typically around 16, and since a quarter of those arrested in 1951 were close to this age, the police could not have known who or what these people were when they were arrested—except, of course, that they were black teenagers."[124] A Cook County official frankly admitted that Chicago police arrested people illegally, but explained "you have to go along with a certain amount of that fringe violation, if you see what I mean."[125]

In 1965 Congress gave the U.S. Food and Drug Administration authority over stimulant, depressant, and hallucinogen law enforcement. The scientists were ill-equipped for shoot-outs with underworld characters, so former Narcotics Bureau agents joined the FDA payroll. The FDA commissioner praised them, and said their tough measures had raised the price of illicit drugs so high that the number of dealers had increased also. Therefore the commissioner called for more money to expand FDA police work.[126] This example of bureaucratic thrust demonstrates how a worsening drug problem (number of dealers) is portrayed as success in control.

By the 1960s most drug offenders detected by police were youths and African-Americans. Those were probably the two most persecuted groups in the country. Richard Nixon exploited hatred against those groups to gain the White House, and his demands for harsher anti-drug laws can hardly be co-incidence. His domestic policy chief John Ehrlichman later admitted the political motive: "Narcotics repression is a sexy political issue. Parents are worried about their kids using heroin, and parents are voters. This is why the Nixon White House became involved."[127] Nixon promoted drug panic to get votes. In a June 1970 memorandum one of his advisers noted the political payoff and urged Nixon to hit the drug issue hard.[128] Nixon even personally lobbied producers of television dramas and claimed he got drug peril themes introduced into the plots of popular series.[129] A contemporary observer noted, "Nineteen-seventy may well be remembered as the year of the great drug panic, the year when addiction was a permanent theme in the press and on TV and when government officials and office seekers made instant headlines by pledging a 'massive attack' on the problem."[130] Even such a distinguished journal as *Science* editorialized that drug abuse was moving from Harlem to suburbs,[131] that is, an African-American problem was now harming whites. By 1971 public opinion polls rated the nation's top problems as Vietnam, the economy, and heroin.[132] Nixon said drug abuse was "public enemy number one."[133]

The Nixon administration promised that revamping federal drug laws in 1970 would lead to conviction of the top 10 dealers in every major American city—but to do this, the Bureau of Narcotics and Dangerous Drugs would need to hire more agents. Their numbers increased by 50 percent from 1969 to 1971. At the time a top drug law expert noted, "The new federal drug police force has been given every armament and prerogative that could conceivably be conferred on a peacetime domestic agency."[134] Nonetheless, drug warriors would perennially complain otherwise, and Congress would grant them more and more powers. Nixon also established two special "drug" agencies, the Office of National Narcotics Intelligence (ONNI) and the Office of Drug Abuse Law Enforcement (ODALE). The conduct of those agencies puzzled local law enforcement officials: "The ODALE thing is one of the weirdest things going. . . . It's never been clear to me who the hell these people are responsible to. Supposedly they all work for the U.S. Attorney, but they really didn't work for the U.S. Attorney."[135] A researcher who interviewed local drug prosecutors commented in 1975:

> Although ODALE is allegedly defunct, its function presumably absorbed by the Drug Enforcement Administration, in reality it lingers on. Federal money is still being channeled to ODALE offices, and its personnel continue to operate. The details of the curious history of ODALE have yet to be fully untangled.[136]

A later investigation indicated that ODALE and ONNI camouflaged a secret police operation that kept tabs on Nixon's opponents.[137]

"The heroin addiction crisis has reached threatening proportions," U.S. Congressman Claude Pepper thundered in 1971. "Our cities are besieged. Our suburban areas have become infected. Even our rural areas are now feeling the shocking effect."[138] In 1972 Nixon's reelection campaign portrayed his Democrat opponent George McGovern as the "Triple A" candidate—acid (drugs), abortion, and amnesty (for military draft evaders). After Nixon won reelection he announced that the heroin problem was on the verge of disappearing.[139]

The Jimmy Carter adminstration, like those of his Democrat predecessors Lyndon Johnson and John Kennedy, emphasized medical aspects of drug use and did not advertise law enforcement efforts. Carter even called for decriminalizing possession of small amounts of marijuana.[140] In 1977 the U.S. Labor Department opposed the goal of a "drug-free work place" and one official declared, "Employers who fail to consider qualified alcoholics and drug abusers from [for] employment because of their handicap are clearly violating the law."[141] Rather than ostracize drug abusers, the Carter administration attempted to reunite them with the community.

A new element in drug agitation appeared during the 1980 election campaign when Democrat Governor Hugh Carey of New York denounced the "Russian design to wreck America by flooding the nation with deadly heroin. . . . I am not overstating the case."[142] In 1981, President Reagan ordered the Central Intelligence Agency to assist domestic drug law enforcement.[143] In 1986 he issued a secret National Security Decision Directive that defined the drug trade as endangering national military security. That document increased military and covert operations in the name of drugs.[144] U.S. military personnel and equipment were sent on "drug missions" in Latin American countries.[145] "Former" Central Intelligence Agency operatives appeared on the Drug Enforcement Administraton payroll,[146] and establishment of the CIA's Counter Narcotics Center coincided with a report that the National Security Council was preparing to approve death squad murders of foreign drug traffickers.[147] "Anti-drug" military operations supported by the United States targeted areas and groups once labeled as "communist."[148] Colombia's national police chief commented about the Bush administration's anti-drug aid to that country: "The total package is more suitable for conventional warfare than the kind of struggle we are waging here against narcotics traffickers."[149]

It was as if the drug war disguised other wars that neither Congress nor the people would otherwise tolerate. Selectivity of U.S.-supported military activity was all the more striking as investigators demonstrated that the U.S. government tolerated and encouraged drug trading by groups who supported anticommunist military actions. Apparently American intentions were either to bribe those groups into cooperation or fund some of the military operations. Favored groups included the governments of Nationalist China, Laos, South Vietnam, and Panama, also Corsican crime syndicates, and "freedom fighters" in Afghanistan and Nicaragua.[150]

A thumbnail review of American drug control history suggests that citizens and researchers and policy makers miss the point when they ask, "What is the drug problem?" A more relevant question is, "Who is the drug problem?"[151] Drugs never merited attention until certain users were seen as problems. No one considered middle-aged Southern women or Northern industrialists as hazards to society because they used opiates. Only when Chinese opiate users threatened wage levels and job availability did opium become a target of criminal sanction. "Opium" was a metaphor for "Chinese." Otherwise they could not be attacked without guilt—productive people who worked hard and minded their own business personified the American ideal. Instead of attacking the Chinese for exemplifying American values, something unrelated to those values was found. Cocaine was hailed as a blessing in the nineteenth century. Years later, when the drug was said to be popular among African-Americans, it suddenly became a peril—an inversion of the scapegoating process, whereby the drug acquired the disapprobation already directed against society's victims. Marijuana was first a metaphor for Hispanics, then for African-Americans, still later for youths who challenged social norms.

Thus severe criminal penalties, penalties that are depraved if we only consider pharmaceutical effects, begin to make sense. Penalties are not intended to discourage use. The point is to oppress scapegoats who are metaphors for society's ills, in which case punishment can never be too harsh.

The drug war has continued for so long that people have forgotten its metaphorical origins. Instead, a fundamentalist attitude has evolved in which drugs themselves are viewed as evil, rather than a symbol for evil. Whenever fundamentalists control public policy in a diverse society, terrible turmoil results. The fundamentalists who control American drug policy have now targeted ordinary citizens for destruction—if people can somehow avoid jail they are still to be denied jobs and even permission to drive an automobile. Fundamentalists have expanded attacks on outcasts into a war on everyone. Everyone is the enemy and must repeatedly produce body fluids to be tested for purity until contamination is found. Then punishment can begin. Such is the way of religious inquisitions.

In addition to spiritual energy, a more mundane force also pushes the drug war, a force already mentioned occasionally but which deserves fuller consideration.

BUREAUCRATIC THRUST AS AN ENGINE OF DRUG ABUSE

The drug problem is propelled not by users or suppliers but by a bureaucratic thrust. Certain vested interests depend on the public's perception that a drug problem exists. Without such a public perception, the wealth and power of those vested interests would disappear. They guard their strength first by defining the drug problem in such a way that it cannot be measured, let alone diminished. Concurrently they spread around money they make from the drug problem, giving more and more elements of society a stake in the status quo—the technique worked well for corrupt political machines in big cities and works just as well in the global village.

None of these vested interests cares about drugs. Hamilton Wright and Harry Anslinger wanted power. Ann Harriman Vanderbilt and Richmond Hobson wanted personal fame and citizen righteousness. Richard Nixon and Ronald Reagan wanted votes. Illicit dealers and the legitimate drug abuse industrial complex want jobs and money. In this wide variety of interests, however, there is one unifying theme. None of these vested interests would benefit from a reduction in the drug problem.

One way to perpetuate the problem is to seek an impossible solution. The drug war seeks a drug-free America. No regime has ever eliminated a particular drug,[152] let alone the broad swath targeted in America. Drug warriors promote an impossible goal, assuring they must be given more and more power for as long as citizens accept the goal's feasibility. If one studies leaders who planned and promoted the Vietnam War, one finds the same kind of ignorant zealotry.

Not only is the goal impossible, means to measure progress are absent. For example, criminality of drug use and unreliability of body fluid tests hinder any census of drug users. To get around those limitations, assumptions are extrapolated from limited reliable data. That is, researchers guess at the number of drug users. The broader the statistics on drug use, the broader the underlying assumptions; different assumptions can change the census results drastically. Because the assumptions are not constrained by knowledge of the real world, vested interests can make statistically valid assumptions that produce huge numbers of drug users. Specialists are well aware of the softness in such numbers. Most citizens, however, think the numbers reflect a real situation and accept what vested interests say about the size of the problem.

Moreover, measuring the size of the drug problem by the number of users presumes that use is a problem. Evidence for that proposition is tenuous. We do not know if wide use means that a problem exists. Perhaps drugs can be used both widely and wisely.

Vested interests take care to avoid any link between their own continued importance and the level of drug use. For example, a clinic could cite growing numbers of clients as evidence of success—and as evidence that more funding is needed for treatment. Or a clinic could cite lower numbers of clients as evidence of success—and that more funding is needed to continue services that keep ex-addicts off drugs. Police may say that rising arrests demonstrate effective law enforcement—and that more funding is needed. Or police may declare that fewer arrests show the drug problem is diminishing—and that more funding is needed to maintain police effectiveness as dealers become more cautious. A candidate for elective office may solicit votes with a promise of stronger anti-drug efforts—while noting that their outcome depends on stronger families.

All those tactics are slick evasions of accountability. No matter what happens, every event is seized by vested interests to prove their work is vital and merits more support. Instead, we might argue that if events leave the importance of vested interests unaffected, maybe the interests have no importance.

But of course they do have importance because of their wealth. Money is power. Enormous sums are devoted to law enforcement. Special narcotics squads are heavily funded. A 1968 study found that Los Angeles police officers needed 4 to 8 hours in court appearance time for each marijuana conviction.[153] That is on top of time consumed by investigation and paperwork in *arrests*, and California saw 50,000 marijuana arrests that year.[154] In 1974 each California marijuana arrest cost taxpayers almost $1,500.[155] Take police salaries, add lawyer and court and jail costs, and multiply throughout the country. Those are just local expenditures, just for marijuana enforcement. And none of that money disappears—every penny winds up in some person's pocket, giving each of those persons a financial stake in current drug policies. In addition the federal government earmarks funds for the drug war. In 1969 the total was $65 million. Nixon increased that by a factor of 10. Reagan spent over $1.7 billion in fiscal 1986. In 1989 Bush recommended an expenditure of $7.9 billion. Congress balked, saying that sum was unreasonable—unreasonably low. The Senate raised it to $8.8 billion. Some of that money goes to local governments, giving them a direct stake in federal policies. Some goes to bureaucratic empires, making each employee dependent on current policies. Other public money goes to treatment clinics; nationwide the *Yellow Pages* telephone books listed 6,580 treatment/information businesses in the late 1980s.[156] One specialized directory listed almost 18,000 treatment programs in 1989.[157] Their income goes to employees and landlords and to private contractors, such as companies that sell methadone and laboratories that process millions of urine samples every year. Private employers pay laboratories for millions more. Federal money goes to international agencies and foreign governments, promoting worldwide support for American policies. Universities receive federal grants to study drug abuse. (Necessary research for setting drug policy was completed decades ago, but because the results fail to support current policies, government officials say more research is needed.) At the time this book was written, Congress was considering the issuance of interest-bearing Drug War Bonds linking the government's fiscal solvency to drug control policy.[158] And let us not forget the illicit drug trade profit margins created by control policies, profits that circulate throughout the world.

A goal that cannot be achieved, progress that cannot be measured, results for which no one can be held accountable, and billions of dollars to be gained from the whole thing. Such is the strategy that produces more and more drug warriors. Awesome power is wielded by individuals and institutions who would feel harm if the drug problem diminished, who gain by perpetuating policies that strengthen the illicit drug trade. Policy reform is possible, but reformers face formidable resistance.

This chapter has interpreted the drug war as a metaphor, a struggle against certain people instead of certain drugs. The metaphor, however, encompasses more than one struggle. And the more a symbol encompasses, the greater its power. To understand the drug war's grip on our nation, we must examine more fully what that war represents. Our chances of altering present policies will improve if we understand what those policies are really trying to accomplish. The next chapter attempts to aid that understanding.

5   The Myth of Drug Abuse

Before drug laws existed no drug problem existed. People recognized occasional harm from some drugs, but that was no more considered a social problem than tobacco use was considered a social problem. The previous chapter told how anti-drug laws evolved as a metaphor for anti-people laws. The present chapter will explore the metaphor more deeply.

Myth is a type of metaphor. When passion in public debate runs high, but facts about the topic have no impact, we experience the power of mythology. The symbolism of myth is well understood by politicians, even though they may not be able to articulate it. Politicians know that opposing ineffective or harmful anti-drug legislation will label them as enemies of the people; legislators who desire reelection are trapped by the power of myth. Because myth is an engine pushing the drug war, mere factual arguments may be dismissed as irrelevant by persons who live the myth. To affect the drug war we must address its mythological content. If we paid more attention to mythology our lives might be both richer and less complicated.

THE ENEMY WITHIN

Joseph Campbell, the great student of myth, teaches that myth and dreams come from the same source. In a dream, all the action and all the characters are really the dreamer. What appears to be external is really internal, within the dreamer. If we interpret the drug war in mythological terms, we must seek understanding by examining the warriors rather than the people and substances they fight.

Traditional American values extol democracy. Democracy and freedom are different. Freedom is basically the right to be left alone; it is a passive thing. In contrast democracy requires citizen action, particularly the exercise of authority and responsibility for public policy decisions. Accepting responsibility for what happens in a community, let alone a whole country, can be hard. Many citizens prefer to abdicate their authority to public officials who are only too glad to exercise it and to absolve citizens from responsibility for events. Good citizens then obey officials instead of challenging them to justify their decisions.

That abdication dovetails neatly with the process of addiction. In both cases people surrender their autonomy to outside agencies. Whether criminal conduct is blamed on "drugs" or on "orders" is irrelevant, so long as blame rests elsewhere than on the criminal. When addiction (whether to drugs or television or anything else) is on the rise, it will find political expression. Candidates and officials become more popular as they urge citizens to give up more and more responsibility. Typically that involves giving up more and more freedoms, but many citizens are glad to do so. Freedom is a passive thing, so a citizen does not feel the loss unless a particular freedom concerns something the person wants to do. Many people live such limited lives that they never encounter the walls of their cage; they could feel just as free in a dictatorship as in a democracy.

A drug war is well suited to promote ulterior goals of political opportunists who despise democracy. Their calls for harsh drug legislation offend no political power group; they can look tough without subjecting themselves to risks that real toughness requires. Next they feed terror with statistics on "drug-related" crime, with fact-free alarmist statements, with information-free advertisements for a drug-free America. Then comes the plea for citizens to be "realistic" and abandon more civil liberties in order to save the nation. Portraying the abandonment of democracy as patriotic—it would be hard to find a more alluring strategy to exploit citizens' fears of responsibility.

Because democracy impedes the desires of elitists, the most vigorous drug warriors should have a record of serving the interests of wealthy elites. Indeed such is the case with Nixon, Reagan, and Bush. They promoted the Cold War for the same purpose, as a means of looking tough without risking political damage, while using national security as an excuse for extinguishing ideals that give life to the nation, ideals that impeded consolidation of power by elites. Now that Mikhail Gorbachev has confounded the Cold Warriors they are switching their primary emphasis to drugs, the new excuse for ending American liberties. The warriors' true agenda is revealed by the sameness of the solution they offer when dealing with nuclear weapons in the hands of Russians or marijuana cigarettes in the hands of high school students. The solution is always for citizens to give up more responsibility to leaders who know best. Fears of communism and drugs are used to fight democracy.

That deceitful purpose is why the opportunists hold on to the Cold War with such tenacity. If they are proven wrong on that topic, on which they are acclaimed as the foremost authorities, their word on everything else becomes suspect. Citizens might begin to examine the basis of leaders' decisions on water quality, ozone depletion, greenhouse effect, savings and loan regulation, job safety, affirmative action. Questions might arise about who profits from such decisions, questions that leaders cannot tolerate if they want to retain power in a democracy. The more that democracy is diminished, the less danger that such questions will arise or that any threat to power will occur if such questions do come.

Citizens who fear democracy and opportunists who despise it are united in common cause by the Cold War and the drug war.

From a mythological standpoint, a problem arises because the irresponsibility that many citizens crave also conflicts with traditional values. To live what Joseph Campbell calls an "authentic life" people must consciously choose one of the alternatives—irresponsibility or democracy. Many people refuse to make a conscious choice. They refuse to admit that their addictive lives repudiate democracy. Rather than face reality, they choose to live a lie. The result is mental illness, as guilt grows about betrayal of moral ideals. This personal guilt cannot be faced (otherwise people could make a conscious choice). Yet an outlet for anxiety must be found. Drug addicts become natural scapegoats for wrath; they do freely what their fellow citizens do in shame. Drug addicts personify what Americans hate about themselves.

THE EVIL OTHER

Drug abuse unifies America. Depending on time, place, and social standing, many deviancies can become normal behavior. Drug abuse, however, is universally regarded as deviancy. It is the great equalizer. All social groups agree that it is never acceptable; the very term "abuse" says so. That consensus, however, was forged by the middle class. In modern times middle class values determine society's standards of morality.

Illicit drug use by productive middle class people seems to grow. Such a trend may simply be a return to the pre–1914 traditional middle class dominance in drug use. Persons unfamiliar with the history of drug control, however, may fear that the trend means that middle class users are adopting values of marginal groups. Such users become loathed as traitors to their class, deserving even harsher punishment than is meted out to society's marginals.

That is the origin of calls to ban drug users from middle class employment. They must not get away with their insolence.

Drug tests have nothing to do with protecting the work place. Employers do not need chemical analyses to deal with employees whose performance is impaired by drugs; people get fired every day for poor job performance. Tests are needed only to identify which satisfactory employees use illicit drugs, so those persons can be disciplined or dismissed even though they are good workers. The purpose of drug testing is to create scapegoats for public scorn.

If sophisticated chemical analyses of blood and urine are required to identify who is a deviant, clearly nothing in the "deviant's" observed conduct differs from normal citizens. Conduct is not being punished; the status of being a drug user is punished. (Traditionally, U.S. jurisprudence abhors sanctions against status, but that tradition is yet another casualty in the drug war.) If a chemical test allows the label "drug addict" to be placed on a person, that individual receives a powerful stigma. When someone is introduced as a waitress or pianist or gardener or model railroad enthusiast, normally we are curious to learn more about the person. If someone were introduced as a drug addict, however, we would probably feel there is little more to know. "Drug addict," like "prostitute," is a total identity.[1] Nothing else about the person matters. Social rehabilitation is impossible.

Labeling drug users as evil may be factual nonsense, but serves a strong psychological need. If users are bad, non-users can view themselves as good. That self-concept helps reduce guilt experienced by non-users who fear democracy; the unpatriotic anti-American bums are those pot-smoking peaceniks, not church-goers who relinquish traditional freedoms upon command from government officials. No hard thinking is required to find a moral path; just follow the rules in order to be moral, obedience is goodness. Such a philosophy appeals to people who view the world in black and white contrasts. Everything else may be changing in the world, but at least anti-drug zealots can be certain they are good, and that drug users are bad.

Paradoxically, the Evil Other[2] serves to define goodness. Fanatics look at a drug user and say, "We're not like that." Goodness is the opposite of the Evil Other. In that scheme of values virtue is not its own reward; instead citizens need to be reassured that their conduct is proper. The reassurance comes from witnessing the negative example of scapegoats, who exemplify the consequences of lacking virtue. Without scapegoats, citizens would be unsure of their wholesomeness.

Harsh anti-drug laws seem irrational only if viewed as a response to pharmaceutical properties of drugs. In reality the legislation attacks drug users for daring to question middle class values. That is the real crime. To argue for drug law reform on the basis of drug properties is irrelevant unless that argument is used to draw out citizens' underlying fears. Those must be addressed. Most politicians try to exploit those fears rather than diminish them; if political speeches referred to race rather than drugs, the demagoguery would be obvious. Scapegoats are useful politically. They are a shorthand way of uniting heterogeneous citizens into a common group identity, a cohesion that depends on opposition to the Evil Other. If the Evil Other were to disappear, politicians would be harder pressed to establish their own goodness.

Whether drug control laws actually control drugs is irrelevant to the statutes' purpose. Otherwise they would have been reformed long ago. The point is to punish scapegoats. In that sense drug control statutes are highly successful and would be impeded by reform.

The criminal sanction legitimizes scapegoating. Drug users are shunned not just because they use drugs but because they are criminals. It is hard to refuse a social outing with someone who merely smokes marijuana, but easy if the smoker has spent 5 years in a penitentiary. Attendance at a party where others smoked marijuana may be insufficient grounds to reject a job applicant, but a criminal conviction for attending may be reason enough for rejection. Not only does the law avoid the necessity of any embarrassing explanations, the scapegoater can even feel virtuous for supporting society's values. No rational explanation is needed for ostracizing fellow citizens. Reforming the law would force scapegoaters to justify their discriminatory behavior. Without the law, scapegoats might even cease to exist.

Like the law, therapy chosen to treat drug addicts succeeds in maintaining the supply of scapegoats. That success is rarely articulated explicitly, because such recognition would raise questions about treatment ethics. Nonetheless, the persistence of addiction is a universally recognized outcome of treatment programs, and must be regarded as one of their functions regardless of whether that function is consciously desired.

Evidence of illicit drug use among normal and productive people becomes fearsome because it threatens the existence of the Evil Other. How can normal people be perverts? It is a contradiction in terms. If admirable citizens who promote traditional values can use drugs, the drug war's rationale becomes questionable, and brutality visited upon users becomes immoral. Users have to be portrayed as garbage in order to justify savagery directed against them.

Existence of the Evil Other is determined by society, not by the scapegoats. They are trapped regardless of personal effort to free themselves.

Because one or two black slaves in one hundred escaped to freedom, the success of those few with the underground railroad did not prove that all it takes is individual will power and a strong personality to escape. Those slaves escaped in spite of the system of controls on runaway slaves, and they escaped

as much as by propitious circumstance as by force of personality. The persever-
ance or fortitude of a Dred Scott or any other runaway did not reduce the likelihood of his being caught, beaten, and returned. . . . No matter what his
personality, so long as the society honors a system that catches, supervises,
harasses, and degrades him, only one or two in one hundred will escape.[3]

Drugs are a symbol used to identify scapegoats in the United States during
the 1980s, much as a yellow star or pink triangle was used in Germany 50
years earlier. In both countries blameless victims were sacrificed to protect the
goodness of other citizens.

THE DRUG USER AS CHRIST

We have seen the drug user as the Evil Other. Because scapegoats exist for
the benefit of people who want to project their own guilt upon the blameless,
another motif is suggested. Let us shift the angle of our mythological portrait,
and from the new perspective view the drug user as Christ, a blameless one
who must shoulder the guilt of sinners and save them from punishment that is
rightfully theirs.

The choice of drug scapegoats depends upon what scapegoaters openly fear
and what they secretly hide from. For instance, in nineteenth-century
America the Chinese got along quite well until they were perceived as an
economic threat. That was the open fear. They became an economic threat
because they were willing to work hard for whatever gain the free market
would provide. Laissez-faire ideals threatened the well-being of white
Americans; that insight was what they hid from. Rather than admit the
contradiction of supporting ideals that harmed them, white workers sought to
suppress yellow workers who benefited from the ideals. Because the Chinese
could not be attacked for proving that the ideals worked, opium served as a
pretext of un-Americanism, identifying the Chinese as sinister aliens instead of
patriotic success stories.

The "un-American" theme is one of the most useful ones exploited by anti-
drug zealots.[4] It worked against the Chinese and opium, Africans and cocaine,
Mexicans and marijuana, hippies and psychedelics, youth and the entire
pharmacopoeia. The theme is particularly interesting because the "alien"
drugs have been used in America as soon as they became available, and indeed
have seen wide domestic production. Marijuana seems to grow anywhere.
Opium can thrive wherever corn does; indeed a vigorous domestic opium
industry was assisted by import tariffs during the nineteenth century. Exotic
chemicals pour from private laboratories in forests, farmlands, and urban
neighborhoods. Yet conventional wisdom holds that sealing the country's

borders would cut off supplies. Portraying drugs as an evil foreign influence helps Americans to avoid facing the reality that these substances have always been popular in the United States, that their use is part of the national tradition. Alcohol, nicotine, and caffeine became so widely accepted that few persons even view them as drugs anymore. The current debate is whether other substances should be accepted as well. The question is whose tastes should prevail, not whether drugs should be used. The issue is social power.

The "un-American" theme suggests that the association of drug hysteria with Red Scares is no coincidence—1919, 1950s, 1980s. Communists were blamed for drugs in America each time.[5] Anticommunist and anti-drug zealots are often the same persons, especially among government officials. Blending the two fears helps persuade the public to relinquish more and more freedoms that inconvenience government officials.

Citizens who repudiate democracy in their lives will feel threatened by groups whose members call for more empowerment over *their* lives. In recent years the two groups that have been most vocal are youths and African-Americans. They have been particular targets of drug law enforcement efforts.[6] These efforts seem aimed more at harassing individuals than at reducing drug use. Marijuana charges, for example, are typically filed after a young African-American has been arrested for some other reason. Drug prosecution is used as a club to punish someone whose non-drug activity attracted attention from authorities.[7] Considering the tens of millions of Americans who have used marijuana, the predominantly young and African-American demographics of arrestees cannot represent all users.

African-Americans are superb drug scapegoats. Feared and hated by the rest of society, they are already society's victims. Making the victim bear the oppressor's guilt is scapegoating at its best. In addition, opposition to "drugs" provides a civilized veneer for racist attitudes that have become disreputable.

Let no one doubt that "drug problem" is a code phrase for "African-American problem." We hear that drugs are everywhere, but customers do not cruise streets of wealthy manicured suburbs when looking for drug dealers. Drugs are the contemporary ghetto industry, just as money-lending was in former times. In both cases a product enjoyed high demand, but legal restrictions left the trade to society's dregs. The mere fact that representatives of the ghetto population engaged in the illegal trade was a mark against them, even though they supplied a product desired by the majority population that condemned them for the trade.

Drugs are the one private enterprise niche in which a ghetto resident can expect entrepreneurial success. Small wonder that it is a growth industry in districts where most forms of economic success are choked off by banks and bureaucrats. Yet even as adventure and fortune can be had by trading in gold from Acapulco, steel from Bogotá, and snow from the mountains of Afghanistan, "solid citizens" shake their heads in discouragement, wondering how ghetto dealers can ever be persuaded to return to jobs in domestic service and hamburger flipping. That "solid citizens" can even wonder about such a thing speaks for the depths of racism in this country. The illicit drug trade is capitalism in its purest form. The spirit of the drug dealer is the spirit that made this country. And people wonder why bold ghetto residents are attracted to it?

The illegality allows society to oppress dealers regardless of their financial success, to remind them that no matter how much money they make, they are minority scum that will get the worst. The money is so big that even whites have gotten involved; is hatred directed toward them because of drugs, or because they have betrayed their race by engaging in a business fit only for African-Americans?

Even legalization might be used as a weapon against African-Americans, destroying illicit job opportunities that forestalled urban riots in the 1980s. Merely ending drug crime will not be enough to bring peace and contentment to millions of oppressed citizens.

The situation of youths, the other main drug scapegoat, differs from that of African-Americans. African-Americans are blameless because they ask only for what any other citizen would seek. Youths are blameless in striving for power naturally granted to the next generation as it matures. But youths want to use that power to implement social changes. African-Americans are hated for seeking full partnership in society; youths are hated for seeking to change the partnership's terms.[8]

Fretting about the younger generation's values is perennial, but the level of anger directed toward modern youth is extraordinary. A fashionable explanation is that youths challenge values held deeply by the older generation, such as sexual conduct. But that theory is insufficient. Flaming youths of the 1920s challenged sexual customs, and many others, yet that era left no accounts disowning the younger generation or calling for arrest and imprisonment of its members. The present situation relates to youths' exposure of their elders' addictive behavior. Drug scapegoating is intimately connected with citizens' inability to face their addictive actions that repudiate democracy, so rage will erupt whenever youths confront adults with those feared contradictions. (Those particular contradictions did not exist in the 1920s because addictive behavior did not become a social norm until after World War II.)

The exposure process is simple and familiar. "If you really believe (fill in the blank), then how do you explain your actions?" The question is not always articulated verbally, but it underlies most youthful activities that enrage elders. Elders can handle accusations of mere hypocrisy with equanimity; no generation has a monopoly on that commodity, and accusations can easily be turned back upon the accusers. Ire erupts only when youths probe something that their parents cannot face. "If you believe in democracy at home, why do you support American military defense of a tyrant overseas?" "If our leaders are accountable to the people, why is it unpatriotic to question leaders' decisions?" Youths sense that something has gone awry; the way adults react to such questions confirms the sensation.

Perhaps worse yet, youths try to implement values preached (but abandoned) by the older generation. Youths seek power over their own lives, particularly in decisions regarding their physical bodies. Drug users vividly reject controls over their bodies; for many users drugs are an expression of liberation rather than enslavement. Society's response has been to tighten controls. For example, possession and use of LSD was banned in the late 1960s when political opportunists associated the drug with youthful rebelliousness. Young drug users nonetheless demonstrate the sincerity of their belief in personal freedom by persisting in free choice of drugs even at the risk of arrest and imprisonment. That kind of moral courage contrasts with elders who fear even the right to choose. Youths challenge the validity of orders that other citizens want to obey. Youths who act as though they live in a democracy generate hatred among citizens who fear democracy.[9]

The mere status of being a youth has become grounds for persecution. Conduct that would be intolerable in any other context is blithely accepted in the name of drugs. One day in 1979 almost 3,000 junior and senior high school students in Highland, Indiana, were forced to sit still as dogs sniffed them for drugs. On the basis of canine behavior, school officials forced 4 junior high school girls to strip naked, but no drugs were found on them or any other junior high students. About 16 high schoolers possessed marijuana, "drug paraphernalia," or beer. When a question was raised about whether the humiliating incident, filmed by news media, violated the Fourth Amendment, a federal judge ruled that being a public school student was sufficient justification for such a search. The U.S. Supreme Court let that ruling stand.[10] In 1985 the East Rutherford, New Jersey, school system announced that no student would be allowed to attend classes without first submitting blood and urine for drug tests, and that results would be given to police.[11] A local court forbade that plan, but in 1989 a similar one was welcomed in Parsons, Kansas.[12] In 1984 the Wilmington, Massachusetts, school system decided that any high school student found in possession of aspirin would be suspended. The rule was developed with the help of the federal Drug Enforcement Administration, where a Reagan official explained that an aspirin tablet might have LSD in it.[13]

Drug enforcement helps isolate youths, making its members targets of hatred while cutting off their ties to society. Persons who feel they have done nothing wrong become confused and resentful as formerly protective institutions become persecutory.[14] There is social danger in such confusion. If scapegoats reject the deviant label, they may also reject society's other norms. And as persecution increases, individual scapegoats begin to develop a group cohesion. An outlaw group can evolve from individual citizens who were once as law abiding as everyone else. And when that group comprises the next generation . . .

The drug war's attack on youths is a war against the future. Societies that fight the future are doomed.[15]

Drug warriors did not choose the two primary scapegoats, youths, and African-Americans, at random. They were chosen because each threatened the status quo by demanding that American society live up to its ideals. The scapegoats personify those ideals rather than threaten them. Many citizens do not want to face that they prefer the guilty rewards they receive by rejecting those ideals. Because youths and African-Americans cannot be blamed for cherishing traditional values, they are instead abused for their drug preferences. When they cry out in anguish, society responds by increasing their pain. But their suffering is neither senseless nor in vain, for by their misery scapegoats allow their persecutors to live lives without guilt. Punishing scapegoats saves their tormenters from the punishment merited by traitors to the nation's ideals. Among the most vicious anti-drug fanatics, who call for the cruelest treatment of drug users, are religious devotees who live out a creed that requires a blameless One to shoulder their guilt. Such individuals feel virtuous when they crucify drug users who challenge the social order, who offer new concepts of morality, who challenge the old law. Drug scapegoats perform the function of Christ.

THE DRUG USER AS JEW

Refined and liberal elements of society may disapprove of racist remarks but feel comfortable with their own outpourings of hatred for drug users and dealers, who are termed a threat to the nation. Parallels between America's treatment of drug users in the 1980s and Germany's treatment of Jews in the 1930s are striking.

Public debate is constrained within the same perimeters. In the early 1930s, on one extreme, Nazis wanted to eliminate Jews from German life. On the other extreme, Nazi opponents argued that although Jews might be a problem in some areas of German life, they could be dealt with by specific restrictions. *No one*, however, in mainstream political debate suggested that the "Jewish problem" was imaginary. In order to be a credible participant in German public debate, one had to agree that a Jewish problem existed, even though reasonable persons could differ about the appropriate solution.[16] Participants in that debate were called "good Germans." In mainstream American political debate today, everyone agrees that a "drug problem" exists, even though reasonable persons can differ about the appropriate solution. Upstanding citizens promote policies that conflict with many principles on which their nation was founded, policies that cause misery and terror and death throughout the land, evil that is blamed on drugs but really comes from laws suppressing them. Such persons are praised as "good Americans."

In Nazi Germany the property of Jews was seized even when they had been convicted of no crime, and was either retained by the government or sold at advantageous prices to the Jews' old neighbors. In the United States, property from persons suspected of illicit drug activity is seized even before charges are filed. Drug suspects are punished first, then receive trial. Their property is either retained by the government or sold at auction. In both countries buyers of confiscated property treated the public sales as social occasions to be relished.[17] History has judged the German behavior as vindictive theft. Evaluation of American behavior is still under way.

In the 1930s, German Jews could not stroll on sidewalks without wearing the yellow star. In the 1960s, Indiana narcotics addicts could not appear in public without "positive proof" that a physician was treating the addiction.[18] A murderer or child molester could not be prosecuted for walking along the street. But a narcotics addict could be, even though addiction was legal in Indiana (unlike murder and child molestation). During the 1950s, anyone who had been convicted on a narcotics charge could not legally stay in New Jersey more than 24 hours without completing a lengthy registration process, including photograph and fingerprints. The person had to carry a special identification card and register with local police whenever traveling to a new town for a stay exceeding 24 hours.[19] Ex-cons who had served their time for killing or sexual assault could live and work in New Jersey without harassment. But someone who had paid a fine in California 10 years earlier for possessing a marijuana cigarette (legally defined as a narcotic) could be arrested for not telling New Jersey authorities about an offense for which the lawful penalty had been paid long ago. In the 1970s, Massachusetts law allowed imprisonment for being with someone who had marijuana,[20] just as Nazi Germany imprisoned people who associated too closely with Jews. In both cases the laws intimidated citizens from having contact with targeted groups. In Germany, Nazis marched in the streets chanting slogans warning Jews to beware. Fifty years later in Kansas City, Missouri, anti-drug activists marched through neighborhoods and chanted slogans warning drug dealers to beware.[21] In Germany, shops and homes of Jews were invaded, and their property destroyed. In the United States, businesses and homes of drug users are invaded, and their property vandalized, by agents using invalid search warrants to legalize vindictive harassment of people whom the agents hate.

In New York during the 1970s, loiterers could be arrested if police believed they planned to use narcotics, but conviction for this offense did not require evidence of narcotics use; indeed, using narcotics was legal.[22] New Yorkers could not be jailed for *using* narcotics, but could be jailed for *intending* to use narcotics. Suppose the law targeted some other legal behavior, allowing citizens to be imprisoned for sitting on a park bench with intention of reading the Talmud. The viciousness of such a law and its proponents becomes apparent, yet anti-drug zealots might feel indignant if anyone suggested they suppressed law-abiding citizens. The point, zealots would argue, is that society must be protected from harm caused by a powerful minority; its members must be concentrated in camps where they can no longer defile morality.

In 1966 and again in 1969, the New York state legislature debated setting up concentration camps for drug addicts. A witness testified, "If we can draft our young men who are good and send them to camps in Vietnam, we can draft our addicts and send them to therapeutic communities in health camps for 10 years, 20 years—as long as it takes to cure them."[23] The Bush administration has urged wide-scale use of "boot camps" for drug users; one criminologist said the effort could be described as "a massive program of basically putting young black urban males in concentration camps."[24] No doubt useful labor would be found for inmates, slave labor. In early 1990 officials of Jackson County, Missouri, said that drug defendants were a potential pool of free labor that could be exploited.[25] Under present civil commitment laws, people could even be rounded up if they were not addicts, but were certified as in danger of becoming addicts—just as an Aryan intimately associated with a Jew could be considered in imminent danger of taking on Jewish values, and be locked up. When people can be arrested and sent away because authorities think those citizens might someday engage in legal behavior that authorities find objectionable, democracy ceases to exist. Some may argue that drug users are a special case. In Germany the "special cases" expanded to sweep up more and more groups of citizens; Jews were only the start. Already in the United States more and more ordinary citizens who demonstrate excellent job performance and impeccable community standing are ostracized when their body fluids fail tests that become ever more sophisticated. No one targeted by such measures need believe that the judicial process will afford protection. As the civil case load increases, authorities will resort to the same expediencies used in criminal cases. Participants at a 1985 White House meeting argued that court hearings were too troublesome for civil commitments, that a drug-positive urine test should result in automatic civil commitment.[26] Citizens must be processed; if justice disappears, that is merely the cost of keeping the system functioning smoothly. Already some plea bargains require criminals to confess guilt to crimes they did not commit. That is one step away from making blameless suspects confess, from making victims confess, from making witnesses confess. And someone who is a bystander today may be a participant tomorrow.

Involuntary therapeutic treatment of addicts, when no known treatment is successful, is medical experimentation without consent, no different in principle from what German officials did to concentration camp inmates. Both the addict and camp populations came to the attention of authorities on nonmedical grounds and were held against their will, as captive populations. Consent standards for experimentation are even higher than those required in consent to treatment. Drug addicts, however, lack this basic human right, one retained even by convicted murderers.

Will the parallels continue? In the 1990s will America handle drug users in the same way that Germany handled Jews 50 years earlier?

German mothers with Jewish-tainted blood were once hauled into camps and separated from their infants. In 1989, American mothers with cocaine-tainted blood were hauled into courts and separated from their infants.[27]

In 1979, the U.S. government acknowledged it had encouraged the spraying of paraquat on Mexican marijuana crops to damage them. Paraquat is a poison that would cause severe lung damage to anyone smoking such marijuana,[28] an act decriminalized in some states. Hatred of marijuana users imposed an extra-legal penalty on them, a penalty that surely falls within the definition of "cruel or unusual punishment" banned by the Bill of Rights. People have even advocated adding poison to supplies of illicit drugs and releasing them for illicit sale, in order to kill users. A desire to kill someone is one step away from a willingness to act. If government policy were to authorize such action, if it were declared a social benefit rather than murder, enough activists and sympathizers could probably be found to make such a program feasible. The federal drug control chief has already declared it ethical for citizens to lynch suspected drug dealers;[29] he has expressed satisfaction at the murder of citizens he dislikes;[30] and the National Security Council has reportedly prepared approval for death squads to murder suspected drug traffickers.[31] If the United States orders death squads into action abroad, how long will it be before the nation's borders are characterized as artificial impediments to efficiency? How long before government death squads roam Kansas City?

Wanting to murder fellow citizens because of what they choose to put in their bodies is indistinguishable from wanting to murder them for what they choose to put in their minds. People have already been jailed for what is in their minds—*intent* to use narcotics, *belief* that a legal substance was illicit.

These thought crimes are different from, say, a thwarted theft conspiracy. The thought crimes here involve legal activity or legal substances. Control over one's body is as basic as control over one's beliefs; it is unsurprising that drug suppression has brought thought police to America. Because American jurisprudence now accepts the concept of criminal sanctions against thoughts, raising the penalties should meet no resistance from courts.

Harsh drug penalties are evidence of depravity, yet legislators and police and judges and employers who implement them probably think of themselves as upright moral individuals protecting society—a self-perception shared by Nazis who brutalized people on pretexts just as flimsy. In both cases acts that should have shocked the conscience soothed it instead. The message of the Nazi experience is not what can happen when monsters achieve power, but rather what happens when ordinary people view fellow citizens as subhuman. Plenty of respectable and morally upright people in the United States now proclaim drug users to be subhuman. What happened in Germany in the 1930s happened in the United States 50 years later. Some U.S. government officials now call for a repeat of what happened in Germany during the 1940s. My father was a war crimes investigator in Europe after World War II. I used to wonder how Germans could have let the Holocaust occur. Now I observe my own country, and I understand. All it takes is a morally smug citizenry willing to stand aside while it starts. Bureaucratic thrust will take it from there.

THE POWER OF IMAGINATION

In mythological terms drugs should not be viewed as an external reality but instead as a psychological phenomenon. Drugs are temptation, pleasure, irresponsibility. Drug warriors believe those things disturb the attainment of spiritual perfection. The goal of a drug-free America is a metaphor for achieving spiritual perfection. Laws and guns and jails and taxes are irrelevant to that achievement. Drug warriors are attempting to perfect themselves by perfecting others. But warriors will not know peace and security until they direct their efforts inward, to face and conquer aspects of their personalities that they recognize in drug users. No one else—burglars, robbers, rapists, or murderers—is hated as are drug users. Ordinary citizens do not recognize themselves in burglars, robbers, rapists, and murderers. Only in drug users do citizens confront the reality of their own souls. It is not drugs they fear, but themselves.

This book has considered drugs from various angles: what drugs do to users, what users do to themselves, what users do to other people, what history says about the origin of drug control laws, what mythology says. There is no question that Americans are deeply concerned about drugs. This book argues, however, that the concern is misplaced. To put the matter baldly: The drug problem does not exist.

History tells of crusades that expended treasure and lives to fight an imaginary enemy. Germany's fight against non-Aryans is a recent example. New England colonists once fought witches. In retrospect we can see the hysteria, but it was unapparent to people caught up in it. Learned treatises were produced to document the reality and seriousness of threats that existed only in the minds of people who studied them. No one contests that real and disturbing events agitated New Englanders in the 1600s, Germans in the 1930s, Americans in the 1980s. But problems defined by hunters of witches, Jews, and drugs had no anchor in external reality. It is therefore unsurprising that the strategy and tactics chosen for those crusades failed to produce satisfactory results.

If the drug problem is imaginary, jurisdictions where drugs are legal should not develop a drug crisis. And indeed such is the case. The next chapter will relate that heartening story, and argue that the drug problem will cease if people stop believing in it.

It may sound strange to suggest that the drug problem can end if we admit it does not exist. A Nazi would have been not only bewildered but angered if anyone suggested that the answer to the Jewish problem was to recognize its unreality. How could there be no Jewish problem? Politicians, intellectuals, movies, and the news media spoke of it all the time. Everyone knew that Jews were everywhere. Ruthless government intervention was at last reducing their numbers, and hope was brightening that a final solution had been found. Germans repudiated democracy in pursuit of it. Yet outsiders could plainly see the whole effort was based on delusion. And in the end, the delusion destroyed not only Jews but the nation that persecuted them.

The effort to suppress drugs in America began as a metaphor to suppress minorities. As the struggle grew, the metaphor expanded to encompass more and more people—Chinese, Africans, Mexicans, youths, yuppies, athletes, college students, high school students, job holders, job applicants, automobile drivers. The war on drugs has become a war on American citizens. Today we condemn Germans who did nothing while their friends and neighbors were arrested and brutalized one by one. How long can we watch our friends and neighbors be imprisoned for choosing to exercise control over their physical bodies? Sovereignty over one's physical body is the ultimate human right. When that fundamental right collapses, so will the others. How long can we watch good people lose their liberty, reputations, and careers because zealots demand that everyone worship one image of righteousness? When will we stop this idolatry?

America is not Nazi Germany. But zealots are leading the United States on the same path that Germany followed. Germans at least had the excuse of not knowing what lay ahead. Americans lack that excuse. The ultimate destination is known. It is time to turn back.

6 The Experience of Legalization

Most drug control laws are not aimed at drugs. Yet it is too simple to say the statutes should therefore be repealed. They are, after all, intended to accomplish something even if the purpose is hidden by a haze of drugs. Previously we have considered discriminatory purposes that are inherently unwise. Other purposes may be harmless or even beneficial, such as attempts to promote middle class values. Many citizens worry that moral standards are changing, and see law as a way to protect those standards. The question is whether law is an appropriate vehicle for accomplishing that purpose.

LAW AND MORALITY

In some parts of the world such a question is meaningless. The Islamic heritage, for example, treats law as an expression of morality, and law enforcers are agents of the divine. In many parts of the world touched by the eighteenth-century European Enlightenment, however, church and state are separate. Sometimes their interests are even at odds. The relation of law to morality then becomes problematic.

Contrary to popular belief, it is possible to legislate morality. American colonial governments routinely punished people who belonged to disapproved Christian denominations; the First Amendment to the U.S. Constitution outlawed the practice, and 200 years later citizens regarded such conduct as immoral. Millions of Americans once believed that human slavery was moral, and many gave their lives in defense of that institution. The Thirteenth Amendment forbade slavery, and 100 years later citizens considered slavery immoral. Racial discrimination was once considered a keystone upholding traditional American values; as more and more discriminatory practices are outlawed, a consensus is developing that racism is immoral. Troy Duster tells us that changes in morality come not from the heart but from new conditions affecting social interactions. Therefore outlawing conduct will put a moral stigma on it, even if a statute is viewed with contempt, because the law alters the way citizens can act and creates a "climate for a reinterpretation of the moral issues."[1]

In a society that supports personal freedom—the right to be different—law can be an appropriate vehicle for enforcing certain types of morality. But those types are limited to interactions among citizens, particularly when the interaction is not mutually desired. As the level of interaction declines, so does the rightful role of law. For the most part, drug statutes try to accomplish things beyond the legitimate scope of law. Those things may or may not be worth accomplishing, but should be a matter of indifference to the state. A situation need not be made a legal problem merely because the law can affect it. Other institutions may be more appropriate choices, or perhaps all authorities should stand aside. We can outlaw poverty, but no matter how many poor people we jail, exile, or execute, poverty will not respond to criminal sanction. Nor will cancer or drought. A statute may be an inappropriate response to something citizens dislike, even if the condition is brought about by human behavior. American society turns to lawyers with the same alacrity that former civilizations turned to oracles. Solutions to some problems may lie outside the competence of either.

One such problem is temptation. It is particularly troublesome in a society, such as America's, that bases its existence on temptation; self-control is inconsistent with capitalism, where tempting advertisements urge us to abandon prudence and seek happiness by purchasing material goods. Drugs fit in well with American capitalism as an expensive technological quick fix for psychic troubles. Anti-drug laws run against a basic national trait as they try to protect citizens from temptation.

In former times that task was left to a deity. Now we expect law to lead us not into temptation, and we see the results of forcing a divine role on law—fear and chaos. Anti-drug laws are inconsistent with the Hebraic heritage that teaches people to live with temptation. Perhaps our ancestors were wise to treat it as a problem of the individual rather than society, a challenge to be resisted rather than vanquished.

Richard Blum suggests that it is not the amount of danger in a drug, but the amount of devil in a drug, that underlies prohibition. Citizens hate drugs because they fear the allure.

Sweet melodies singing of love without obligation, of the vision of God beheld by those lacking either inner virtue or outer merit, of the joy of creativity without artistic skill, of aesthetic sensibilities without a sense of taste, of freedom without responsibility or consequence, of self-knowledge without self-criticism, of self-enchantment without increased complexity, of psychotherapy without doubts or anxiety, and, finally, of life itself without struggle. These are the siren songs.[2]

Illicit drugs are considered immoral not because they harm people; plenty of approved substances and activities have that drawback. Illicit drugs are immoral because users feel better than normal or, worse yet, even experience pleasure. Blum calls them "keys to forbidden kingdoms inside ourselves,"[3] forcing us to confront the devil inside us all.

The moral irony in anti-drug laws is that zealots crave them in order to eliminate distress such persons feel when they observe drug use. Both drug users and anti-drug crusaders want to avoid pain. But we have to tolerate a certain amount of pain in life. Passing laws against anything and everything that displeases us is a sign of immaturity. If we want a free society to function, we must permit people to make bad decisions and suffer the consequences. People have a right to ruin their lives. We might even benefit from a little humility when judging people who attempt paths to happiness different from our own; what we regard as ruination may seem quite desirable to someone else.

If millions of citizens indulge in a particular conduct, criminalizing that conduct in a free society is questionable, even undemocratic. Proponents of criminalization are probably pursuing a personal vision of righteousness, trying to reduce sin. That concept is alien to democracy, where the goal is not to vanquish sin, but to give everyone the freedom to choose sin or righteousness. Transforming ordinary productive citizens into criminals, for conduct having less measurable harm than tolerated conduct, is a sign of religious zealotry rather than public welfare.

In that context, drug laws become a metaphor for pretensions of personal virtue, and their repeal a metaphor for confessing the sin of pride. That is one reason anti-drug militants resist legalization; the act would confess error and thereby hinder pride, particularly painful for government officials who have brutalized drug-using citizens for so long. But we are all sinners, and guilt need not be shame unless error persists after it has been recognized.

Criminalizing behavior approved by much of society guarantees social turmoil. Many problems ascribed to drugs actually result from law enforcement. The tougher enforcement gets, the worse trouble will get. The answer is to let go. That is not surrender to drugs; it is recognition that anti-drug laws are inappropriate because they worsen the situation. If we recognize that law is not the answer to every social problem, we should not insist on using criminal sanctions where they do not work. It is possible to deal with serious problems without making them crimes. Indeed, it is even possible to ignore problems by making them crimes, creating the illusion that arrest and conviction statistics measure activity that deals with a problem. Drugs are not the first war where success has been measured by body counts.

Widespread violation of a law changes its purpose. Instead of being directed against a perceived problem, it is enforced merely to assert the power of the state. Punishment is no longer meted out to drug users but to rebels. To relinquish the law would be to relinquish power of the state, to admit that the people reign supreme. Politicians and citizens who loathe democracy will instead urge that the law be made harsher. In eighteenth-century terms, widespread violation of a law is evidence that it violates the social contract. The traditional result when authorities insist on retaining such a law is civil war or revolution. When turmoil in American cities grows to such a level that federal officials urge army patrols of the streets, anyone with a sense of history can sense a great change coming. Whether it will be an end to anti-drug zealotry or an end to American democracy cannot be foreseen, but a choice is approaching.

Some drug law proponents may believe that democracy should encourage freedom of choice, but may nonetheless argue that drug laws promote that goal by protecting people from making a choice that closes off future options. Such protection, however, is paternalism and is inconsistent with democracy. Elites may very well have more wisdom than ordinary folk, but democracy is based on the idea that no citizen has more right to happiness than anyone else—that is why each person has one vote. Some citizens may see future options as irrelevant to happiness. Other citizens may rue a choice that limits their future, but if we respect their autonomy we must give them the right to limit it. That may sound paradoxical, but it happens all the time in other contexts. A person who signs a house mortgage may lose other uses of income for 30 years; someone who marries may lose certain options for a lifetime. The value of preserving options depends on the context; irrevocable commitment can also have value. And of course the preceding discussion assumes that all users of illicit drugs will suffer harm, an assumption disproved by experience.

Drug laws are sometimes defended with a moral argument that users harm other persons, not just themselves. A father whose drug use makes him incapable of working may harm his family's well being. A woman whose drug use leads to a lengthy hospitalization may be unable to meet the expense, hurting other members of society who must pay her bill. But such an argument is treacherous, applying also to a father who ignores medical advice about the link of diet to his cardiac problem, or a woman who is unable to meet expenses after she drives her car into a wreck, or a married police officer who rejects a safe desk job in favor of riskier patrol work. Should we outlaw stubborn fathers, or driving, or police patrols? Our everyday actions risk harm to other persons. Perhaps we can be held accountable for seeking to endanger someone, perhaps even for unintended harm. But risk is inherent to life; we cannot be held criminally accountable for being alive.

In a free society people must have a right to ruin their lives. They must be able to take risks, whether the risks be prudent or reckless. Otherwise citizens are not free. (Whether society is obligated to rescue citizens when their choices go bad is another question.)

When evaluating the wisdom of anti-drug laws, we should consider the wisdom of Herbert L. Packer.

> Crime prevention is not the ultimate aim of the rule of law.
>
> Law, including the criminal law, must in a free society be judged ultimately on the basis of its success in promoting human autonomy and the capacity for individual human growth and development. The prevention of crime is an essential aspect of the environmental protection required if autonomy is to flourish. It is, however, a negative aspect and one which, pursued with single-minded zeal, may end up creating an environment in which all are safe but none is free. . . .
>
> The ultimate goal of law in a free society . . . is to liberate rather than to restrain.[4]

Our credo for invoking criminal sanction must not be mere restraint of behavior by a criminal, but protection—and even enlargement—of opportunity for everyone else. A law that fails to preserve or expand freedom is a bad law. Drug control laws fail the test of freedom.

But dare we abandon them? What would happen to American society? Would use of presently illicit drugs expand? Would economic productivity decline? Would traditional moral values be abandoned? The answers to such questions need not be hypothetical. We can observe experiences of jurisdictions where dangerous drugs have been freely and legally available.

THE VOICE OF EXPERIENCE

A quick scan of foreign countries is heartening. India is a country with a long history of social marijuana and opium use, but drugs attract no blame for that nation's problems. The same can be said of opium in Iran. In the country of China unsatisfactory levels of national productivity in the nineteenth century have been attributed to widespread opium use, but the validity of that attribution is unclear.[5] Another relevant country is the Philippines. After seizing the islands the United States abolished the Spanish opium license system and opened the trade to the free market. Consumption saw a "marked increase,"[6] but U.S. corporations still found their Philippine operations to be profitable. After the country of Hawaii became an American territory it legalized the opium trade in 1903, allowing access to the drug by anyone. Consumption rose somewhat, but the High Sheriff stated that the islands were better served by legalization than by the old restrictions.[7] In the 1950s, cough syrups with heroin were available in the country of Sweden without producing chaos in society or degradation in individuals.[8] In the 1970s and 1980s the country of Holland decided to ignore use and small sales of marijuana although it remained illegal. In those conditions of free availability, a 1983 survey found that 0.5 percent of Dutch youths aged 15 to 24 reported daily marijuana use, compared to 5.5 percent of U.S. high school seniors.[9] The 1983 Dutch rate of use was higher than in 1979, but the rate was no more than in neighboring jurisdictions with stringent anti-marijuana law enforcement.[10] Figures from 1985 showed marijuana use among Netherlands youth declining.[11] Regarding illegal drugs such as heroin and cocaine, a 1989 report stated that the "number of hard-drug users in the Netherlands has been stabilized or is even decreasing."[12]

Harsher laws and more vigorous enforcement may be an American reflex to reports of growing drug abuse, but not all societies see the criminal sanction as appropriate. The country of Italy, for example, had 67 officially reported cases of drug addiction in 1967 but over 1,000 in 1974.[13] The response was to decriminalize possession and use, abolishing criminal sanctions instead of increasing them, attempting to integrate drug users into society instead of banishing them. Such an approach contrasts starkly with that of Great Britain when it faced an increase in drug addiction. The British experience has been misrepresented and is worth examination.

From the 1920s into the 1960s, the language of British drug control statutes was similar to U.S. federal laws, allowing physicians to write prescriptions for opiates and cocaine if the physicians' professional judgment indicated that patients needed such drugs. Enforcement philosophy differed on the two sides of the Atlantic, however, in that British doctors could issue prescriptions to relieve physical or mental symptoms that an addict would suffer if the drug were cut off. Maintenance of addiction was as ethical as elimination of addiction.

That did not mean that anyone in the United Kingdom could lawfully obtain any drug. If a physician did not believe that a supply would serve the patient's best interests, no prescription would be issued. Without a prescription, an addict had to turn to the black market. The same recourse was necessary if an addict wanted more than a doctor would prescribe. Plenty of dealers and users were imprisoned for illegal possession of opiates and cocaine;[14] in one British study 43 percent of the addicts reported drug law convictions.[15] And marijuana was never licit in any circumstance—possession of one cigarette could bring a 10-year prison term.[16] Such drugs were no more "legal" in England than in the United States. British physicians simply worked under less governmental interference, meaning that addicts had a far greater chance of getting prescriptions in England than in the United States.

In the late 1960s Britain experienced an increase in illicit use of stimulants, sedatives, and psychedelics, just as the United States did. News media coverage and official analyses of the situation were similar in both countries, as was the legislative response—tougher anti-drug laws. British physicians suddenly had to obtain special government licenses to prescribe maintenance doses to addicts, and such licenses were basically limited to practitioners in drug abuse clinics. Into the 1980s any doctor could prescribe heroin and cocaine to non-addicts for any reason, and had limited power to prescribe to addicts.[17] But only specially licensed doctors could prescribe for addiction maintenance, and government policy dictated that addicts had to be weaned off the drug promptly.

A consensus of opinion holds that the number of British addicts has risen greatly since the 1960s, approaching the 100,000 mark when this book was written.[18] A consensus also holds that the character of addicts has changed as dramatically as their number. The character change is important because it explains the increase in number. Disadvantaged youths have steadily become more and more predominant in the addict population. They grow up in seedy parts of town, do poorly in school, possess few job skills, may be members of a racial or ethnic minority, live a bored and sorrowful existence without friends and without love, marking off one useless day after another.[19] The addict population explosion of the 1970s and 1980s coincided with worsening conditions for lower classes in Britain, first with declining economic productivity in the 1970s, followed in the 1980s by reduced social justice measures in education, job training, child care, housing, health. Economic and governmental policies nourished conditions known to promote drug addiction. That is the reason for rising numbers of British addicts. Drug laws have nothing to do with it, indeed, statute language and enforcement philosophies have been similar in England and the United States since the 1970s. As despair overwhelms people, who in Britain are often officially termed "redundant," they turn to drugs for a solace unavailable in parish halls or welfare halls. Richard Blum put it this way, "Drugs seem to be the final path of expression for almost any other social problem—poverty, race, families, social class. Drugs, I've come to think, are the chemical tracer that diagnoses the problems of society."[20]

Drug legalization proponents sometimes cite the pre-1960s British experience to prove that "drug legalization works." But addicts, let alone citizens in general, did not have free access to drugs. Opiates could be dispensed only upon presentation of a prescription, and drugs like marijuana were illegal at all times in all circumstances. British law did not hold down the population of addicts, the size of the black market, or the number of robberies committed to get drug money. This can be readily demonstrated by comparing England's situation with that of Hong Kong, which had similar drug laws. The Hong Kong population nonetheless showed a much higher rate of opiate use than Britain's did. Hong Kong also had levels of poverty and squalor unknown in England.[21] As British levels headed in the direction of Hong Kong's in the 1980s, so did the amount of drug use.

Anti-drug militants sometimes cite the growth of drug use in Great Britain to prove that "drug legalization fails." But even in the "golden age" of British policy from the 1920s to the 1960s, England never allowed free access to drugs. A physician always served as gatekeeper. The gatekeeper's prerogatives became more limited in the 1980s, but British addicts have always found their path barred until a physician relented. The rise in number of users was made possible not by prescriptions but by black market supplies. The handful of notorious "scrip doctors" in the late 1960s, who sold narcotics prescriptions to anyone who would pay the fee, did not cause the number of addicts to grow. Mere availability of drugs, or any other products, does not cause people to use them. The scrip doctors responded to a demand normally served by the black market. They merely provided current addicts with a piece of paper that kept police from arresting the addicts. When British authorities put scrip doctors out of business, drug use continued to grow.

And that raises a subtle but important question: Should success of a drug control policy be measured by amount of drug use? Most users experience no difficulties caused by drugs themselves, so maybe the number of users does not measure a nation's drug problem. Perhaps other factors are a better measure—whether users are accepted as members of normal society and allowed to hold jobs, whether the price of drugs harms users and their families, whether drug purity and availability of sterile paraphernalia reduces illness among users, whether a black market is so insignificant that citizens do not fear the power and violence of dealers. If those kinds of factors are important, Britain's experience compares favorably with the United States.

Foreign experiences with drug legalization are encouraging, but the differences between those countries and the United States may be more important than similarities. One clearly relevant jurisdiction does exist, however, one with experience in permitting inexpensive access to opiates, cocaine, and marijuana to adults and children without a doctor's prescription. That jurisdiction is the United States of America, before anti-drug zealots took charge on that subject around 1915. The American experience is often forgotten or ignored. An earlier chapter of this book, however, noted that free access did not hinder national productivity, injure public health, or degrade morality. We do not know how many people used drugs in that era; estimates vary wildly. Perhaps the number was small; if so, free access did not lead to widespread use. Perhaps the number was large; if so, the nation nonetheless prospered and normal family life continued. We do know that no drug houses blighted neighborhoods, no drug gangs had street corner shoot-outs, "drug-related" crime did not exist, and people lived ordinary middle class lives while consuming drugs avidly. We are talking about twentieth-century America, just before World War I, a country with great urban centers suffering from most problems known today and even from some that have since ended. Our own history proves that we have nothing to fear from legalizing drugs, and much to gain.

The United States has had an even more recent experience with drug legalization, when alcohol Prohibition was repealed in the 1930s. Alcohol Prohibition was promoted and enforced by the same people who banned other drugs, and it produced problems similar to those observed in the illicit drug scene during the 1980s. Comparisons and contrasts between the two anti-drug movements may be useful.

Most histories of wars and controversies are written by the winners, and Prohibition is no exception. Proponents of Prohibition are generally portrayed as ignorant and bigoted killjoys whose actions promoted crime and violence without stopping consumption of alcohol. Such a portrayal is a caricature; the distortion communicates truth, but persons unfamiliar with the artist's model may be deceived.

Many prominent Americans were concerned about alcohol consumption and its adverse effects on individuals and society. John Adams prided himself on his efforts to close down bars in Boston.[22] President Thomas Jefferson said,

The habit of using ardent spirits by men in public office has often produced more injury to the public service, and more trouble to me, than any other circumstance that has occurred in the internal concerns of the country during my administration. And were I to commence my administration again, with the knowledge which from experience I have acquired, the first question that I would ask with regard to every candidate for office should be, "Is he addicted to the use of ardent spirits?"[23]

William Lloyd Garrison, Gerrit Smith, Susan B. Anthony, Abraham Lincoln, Walt Whitman, Henry Ward Beecher, Horace Greeley, Henry David Thoreau, Ralph Waldo Emerson, and Henry Wadsworth Longfellow are listed as Prohibition advocates or sympathizers.[24] None of these persons was a single-minded fanatic. Prohibitionists counted many abolitionists among their number: "The precedent of abolition had established that an evil traffic could be destroyed and owners dispossessed of their tainted wealth, all without threatening the legitimate property rights of other economic sectors."[25]

Widespread abuse of alcohol was considered a threat to maintenance of a democratic citizenry, and concern about alcohol fit in with concern about other social ills. After the Civil War, a Prohibition political party was organized; in addition to limiting alcohol consumption it called for full suffrage rights for women and African-Americans and for election of U.S. senators by the people (rather than by state legislatures, as was the law then).[26] Few voters rallied to the party's social reform agenda, but eventually 66 percent of the states enacted Prohibition laws. The Eighteenth Amendment to the U.S. Constitution was an outgrowth of national experience, not a sudden alien innovation.

National Prohibition did not outlaw alcohol, but only its "manufacture, sale, or transportation . . . for beverage purposes."[27] Supplementary statutes and Treasury Department regulations soon established crucial differences between alcohol and Harrison Act enforcement. Throughout the Prohibition era, the purchase, possession, and consumption of beverage alcohol was legal. There were no federal "anti-paraphernalia" laws, and sale of alcohol production equipment was lawful. Even home manufacture for personal consumption was permitted. Users were never persecuted or punished. Moreover, although alcohol could not be sold as a beverage, churches could dispense wine for religious purposes, and alcohol could be sold for medicinal purposes. Pharmacists freely dispensed beer, brandy, wine, and whiskey upon presentation of a doctor's prescription. "Alcohol must be a mighty effective remedy for many of the diseases now going around in Kansas City," one local official grumbled.[28] In a six-month period Chicago physicians wrote over 500,000 prescriptions for whiskey.[29] (All the preceding applies to federal law. Some states had tougher Prohibition statutes, forbidding alcohol possession and public display of paraphernalia such as cocktail shakers.)

Prohibition has been credited with reducing national alcohol consumption by 33 to 50 percent, with most impact on the working class.[30] The change is perhaps more apparent to statisticians than to lay persons who examine the numbers.[31] A highly respected study holds that annual consumption of beverage alcohol was steady from 1890 to 1917 at 1.4 to 1.6 gallons per capita. It declined to 1.13 in 1918, followed by a fantastic drop during the first years of Prohibition: 0.25 gallon consumed in 1920, 0.19 in 1921, and 0.10 in 1922.[32] Measured in terms of alcoholic content, consumption then intermittently rose during Prohibition but only reached a level of 66 percent the pre-World War I level.[33] From those numbers one can argue that Prohibition dented consumption significantly; but if instead of using the years 1911-14 as a base, consumption is compared to the war years, it is generally *higher* during Prohibition.[34] A further twist is that these per capita figures seem based on total population. Another researcher, using only the drinking age population, concluded that the *drinking age* per capita consumption in the four years preceding Prohibition was twice the amount drunk during Prohibition.[35] On the other hand, California vineyard acreage expanded enormously during Prohibition.[36]

Most studies of Prohibition's effects fail to consider that countries without Prohibition registered declines in consumption at the same the United States did.[37] In determining the cause of declining alcohol consumption in those years, Prohibition is an invalid variable.

Other measures have been used to determine Prohibition's effects. One measure is health. Death rates from alcoholism and cirrhosis initially declined but then began to rise; the alcoholism death rate eventually exceeded pre-Prohibition years.[38] A similar dip and rise was seen in alcoholic psychosis.[39] The working class experienced the most improvement in alcohol-related health problems.[40] The meaning here is unclear because such afflictions develop from lengthy abuse; any change caused by Prohibition should not have occurred until years after restrictions began. Later research, covering the years 1920 to 1945, found evidence of declining alcohol disease, suggesting a correlation between Prohibition and a positive effect on health[41] (although a comparison with non-Prohibition jurisdictions is needed). Another measure of Prohibition is alcohol-related family problems. Midway through the Prohibition era one study noted a drop in those problems among people served by welfare agencies.[42] Still another measure is crime. Crime statistics yield ambiguous conclusions. Drunkenness arrests fell when Prohibition began, then rose.[43] The Prohibition era saw some downturn in crime, but not much effect can be attributed to Prohibition. Various studies link murders to alcohol,[44] so a drop would be expected if alcohol consumption declined; instead the murder rate showed a rising trend during Prohibition.[45] Studies indicate, however, that the murder rate rose more slowly than during the twentieth century's first decade.[46] So under Prohibition the crime rate either worsened or improved, and the pace of change may or may not have been a result of alcohol legislation.

One of the most respected students of Prohibition's effects concluded, "National prohibition has failed to reduce the use of alcoholic beverages and has increased the sum spent on them"[47] and "prohibition has not had a measurable effect upon the general health of the nation."[48]

Measurable effects showed distinct harm to the nation. Corruption thrived. Beverage alcohol held in government warehouses leaked away. The Treasury Department's Prohibition agents, who enforced both alcohol and narcotics restrictions, received such low salaries (average $1,500) that bribes had appeal. Moreover, Congress initially exempted Prohibition agents from Civil Service—until 1927 all were patronage appointees. Staff turnover was vigorous; over an 11-year period 17,972 agents hired on and 13,586 departed.[49] The underpaid unprofessional staff swiftly developed a reputation for venality; in 1921, 100 agents were fired in New York alone. Those were the ones who were caught, and would not resign. In addition, most enforcement was left to state and local officials; neither the public nor the federal government was willing to support a massive national alcohol police force. In areas where Prohibition was unpopular, enforcement was lax. Police, prosecutors, and judges who were unfriendly to Prohibition were likely targets of bribery.[50]

The civil liberties record of Prohibition was mixed. Property confiscations were more unusual than in the later drug war; for example an automobile owner could successfully plead ignorance if someone else were arrested while transporting alcohol in the vehicle. That plea, however, did not work against "padlocking"; for example, a hotel could be closed for a year (though not confiscated) if liquor were sold there without the owner's knowledge, and "padlocking" did not require a trial to establish guilt. Federal Prohibition search powers were more limited than normal search powers, just the opposite of drug war procedures. Most proponents of Prohibition were adamant that it not be used as an excuse to intrude on citizens' personal conduct; the target was commerce, not use. Prohibition's purpose was to reduce alcohol problems, not eliminate alcohol or drinkers. When Prohibition began, however, the commissioner of Internal Revenue asked religious clergy in America to set up investigation committees to detect and report alcohol violations,[51] revealing Treasury's zealotry and its insensitivity to separation of church and state. The Prohibition Bureau advocated introduction of poisons into industrial alcohol to make it unfit for human consumption—action that could kill innocent users who made legal purchases from bootleggers.[52] Trigger-happy Prohibition agents killed at least 200 innocent citizens; U.S. Senator Frank L. Greene barely survived wounds he received.[53] Prohibition agents seldom received convictions in such instances, and the federal government provided defense counsel.[54]

Prosecutions against alcohol dealers were pursued with alacrity. By 1930 about 33 percent of the federal penal population was serving alcohol time.[55]

(Another 22 percent was serving narcotics time.)[56] The 5 federal prisons and penitentiaries were so overcrowded that construction was started on 6 more. President Herbert Hoover's stringent law enforcement policy has been credited with creating an unstoppable demand for Prohibition repeal;[57] under state penalties people could, and did, receive life imprisonment for selling 1 quart of alcohol.[58] When ordinary citizens were swept up by the federal dealer dragnet, the public turned against the law rather than their neighbors.

A contemporary critic declared that Prohibition satisfied three popular passions: "The passion of the prohibitionists for law, the passion of the drinking classes for drink, and the passion of the largest and best-organized smuggling trade that has ever existed for money."[59] Prohibition was a modest effort in comparison to the later drug war, and its ill effects had much less impact on the nation, but even proponents eventually reached a glum conclusion:

> The defiance of law that has grown up in the last fourteen years, the hypocrisy, the break-down of governmental machinery, the demoralization in public and private life, is a stain on America that can no longer be tolerated. The American people are definitely aroused in a determination to clean up this source of corruption and to reestablish the integrity and dignity of the law.[60]

When our forebears saw that Prohibition was causing more harm than benefit, they did not wring their hands in bewilderment and wonder if legalization was the "wrong message" or "surrender to alcohol." They simply recognized that a particular tactic did not work, and that something else would have to be tried instead. They abandoned Prohibition. Not in despair, but in determination to try other approaches, for the common good.

THE PROMISE OF THE FUTURE

Historical experience demonstrates benefits in legalizing illicit drugs. Scientific research gives even more reassurance. We should pause, however, to reflect on what is meant by "legalization."

Legalization is different from decriminalization. Basically if a substance is decriminalized, use and possession is permitted, while penalties remain for trafficking and manufacture. During the 1970s, decriminalization of marijuana in various states was hailed as a major reform, which demonstrates just how restrictive marijuana laws were, because the hailed reform gave marijuana roughly the same status that alcohol had during Prohibition. Restoration of alcohol Prohibition conditions is not good enough. We must summon the determination of our forebears and insist on total repeal of anti-drug laws.

Legalization means the entire illicit drug trade would become legal: manufacture, transportation, sale, purchase, possession, use. A legal trade can still be regulated, as any pharmacist or drug company knows. And informal sanctions may well develop, such as higher health and life insurance premiums for drug abusers.[61] But because so many problems associated with illicit drugs are due to legal restrictions, we must be generous about access. For example, requiring prescriptions would merely generate income for Dr. Feel Goods and prescription pad printers. If heroin and cocaine are legalized, they must be available over the counter. And the price must be held down, by government intervention if necessary, to be sure addicts or anyone else can easily afford all they want.

Even some proponents of legalization may gasp at such a prospect. That is because typical arguments for legalization merely recognize that anti-drug laws do not work; many proponents of legalization still fear drugs as evil. Dangerous drugs must, however, be accepted as part of the American heritage. To fear them is to fear ourselves. Drugs need not be embraced, they may even be disliked, users may be forbidden to perform certain tasks while intoxicated; but drugs themselves must be accepted as part of the nation's identity—just as a criminal cousin or in-law must be accepted as a member of the family. Refusal to recognize a dark side in a personality, whether of a single human being or an entire nation, can leave an individual or a population yearning for wholeness. That spiritual discontent cannot be eased until reality is faced.

Anti-drug laws harm spiritual unity of the nation. Respect for law is more than obedience; it involves a feeling of oneness with the community. When the conduct of millions of citizens is criminalized, they are isolated from the community. Its protective institutions no longer shelter them but instead persecute them. Survivors of the Holocaust have told of their bewilderment and horror as one friendly element of the community after another—police, schools, employers, townspeople—turned against them. Victims of such shunning can exhibit the malaise and amotivation often attributed to drugs.[62] A community that casts out ordinary citizens may think it is destroying them, but is only destroying itself. Cutting off parts of one's body does not promote wholeness, and indeed is a symptom of mental illness. The perverse result is that Americans expend enormous resources fighting the behavior of normal and productive people, while tolerating educational and social deprivations that transform independent citizens into welfare cases. Fighting those latter problems, however, first requires acknowledgment of the dark side of American dream, of nightmares. Such acknowledgment does not mean

America is letting anyone down, but is merely the first step in widening the benefits of citizenship, bringing more and more people into full community membership, achieving wholeness.

The effort to eliminate drugs is a misguided effort to achieve national wholeness by eliminating deviancy, to destroy those who are different. A more productive approach would be to lift criminal sanctions against drugs in order to accept users as fellow citizens, to achieve wholeness by assimilating our brothers and sisters instead of expelling them from society. After all, many of their values are shared by non-users: convivial companionship, reflective meditation, enjoyable music, tasty food, humor, peace, love, sex, money, excitement, hard work, free competition, accountability of leaders to the people—all blending into a good life. Before anti-drug zealots achieved power, users and addicts were accepted as fellow citizens, just like coffee drinkers and chess players. Indeed, as we have seen previously, users and non-users are indistinguishable in the population; only drug use sets one apart from the other. To devour users in a drug war is cannibalism.

Neither drugs nor their abuse can be eliminated. To seek the elimination of either is to seek a domestic Vietnam War. Even the harshest oppressions fail to stamp out popular drugs; regimes have executed tobacco smokers and decreed death for coffee drinkers, yet smoking and coffee drinking continued.[63] Drug problems cannot be ended, but they can be reduced by accepting drugs as part of the American heritage, by finding ways to bring them within normal lifestyles rather than converting users into outcasts and outlaws. Rather than urging people to live without drugs, it would be wiser to teach them how to live with drugs. The goal should be to encourage responsible use.

When punishment of conduct disappears, so does the conduct's stigma. Legalization should liberate drug users from the condemnation of "total identity." Look at all the things a user is: a daughter, a citizen concerned about war, a community member without a job, a fellow human being in pain. Real concerns hidden by drug hysteria can then surface and be dealt with: failure as a parent, the relation of military activity to patriotism, the value of work, the expense of social welfare. It is possible to ease many of these concerns, but they will fester as long as drugs are used as metaphors for them. The tragedy is that concentration on the metaphors will only avoid the real issues that disturb citizens. The longer the drug war continues, the more discontent will grow.

Under legalization users could be freed from "total identity," non-users freed from fear of drugs, and energy currently put into using or fighting drugs could be freed for better purposes. Ending the criminal sanction would engage the power of the state to liberate citizens rather than oppress them. And that is the goal of law in a free society.

Ending the drug war would not be surrender to drugs. It would be liberation from them.

Some citizens object that legalization would increase drug abuse. Before examining that concern, let us note what the term "abuse" means. Drug abuse is typically defined as "use without a physician's order," so when officials or researchers talk about drug abuse they do not necessarily refer to conduct that causes harm. This is seldom, if ever, made clear in statements to the public. The term "abuse" has connotations of heroin junkies in a gutter or cocaine-crazed killers, examples useful for promoting anti-drug hysteria but which apply only to a tiny percentage of drug "abusers." In this book "abuse" refers only to conduct that causes harm.

Some citizens worry that legalization would harm persons who are interested in illicit drugs but who are deterred from trying them because of inaccessibility or criminal penalties. The issue of accessibility is moot; substances are already available to anybody who wants them. Current users have small concern about being arrested.[64] One study found less than 2 percent of cocaine users thought they might be apprehended in the next year.[65] Another study found that 100 percent of adult heroin users had no fear of punishment.[66] Sanctions for marijuana possession do not deter convicted users from resuming use.[67] Other studies yield similar results.[68] Such results are hardly surprising; people who live for the moment are undeterred by future consequences; most criminals do not expect to be caught, and indeed most are not. More important is whether non-users are deterred by the possibility of arrest. The use of criminal sanctions for deterrence, however, raises the larger question of temptation and how to respond to it.

If we move from the philosophical issue of temptation to actual behavior of people, the potential impact of legalization becomes reassuring.

Researchers have asked drug users what effect legalization would have on them. Controlled (as opposed to compulsive) users said their consumption would be unaffected; they already had all the drugs they wanted.[69] Compulsive users indicated concern that their consumption might rise—even though they apparently had access already to whatever quantity they wanted.[70] About half the cocaine users in a survey said that increased availability led to increased use,[71] but in a jurisdiction that decriminalized marijuana, less than 4 percent of adult users and only 7 percent of high school users reported a higher intake for that reason.[72] Alcohol research indicates that restricted sale has little effect on consumption but price makes a difference, just as the sales volume of television sets depends less on the number of stores than on price.[73] A strong worldwide correlation exists between higher alcohol prices and lower levels of abuse,[74] although the effect may have more to do with the abuser's income than price per se.[75] A higher price will shift abuser demographics to a wealthier (and therefore smaller) population, just as criminalization shifts use to a deviant population. Some researchers claim that experiments with humans and animals demonstrate that a higher drug price results in less use. Animals, for example, might have to press a lever more times to get the drug; humans might have to ride an exercycle more to get tokens that can be exchanged for drugs. If the work becomes too hard, both animals and humans give up the drug.[76] Measuring how hard experimental subjects are willing to work for drugs, however, is not the same as measuring how much they are willing to pay. It would be more revealing to provide humans with a steady income of tokens that can be exchanged for all sorts of things, then raise the price of the drug.

As we shall see shortly, the experience of drug legalization is not followed by an explosion in consumption even if people can produce their own drugs for free. Most persons have no curiosity about illicit drugs and would not use them even if they became legal.[77] A national survey in 1988 found that 96.2 percent of high school seniors disapproved regular cocaine use, and 89.1 percent opposed even one or two experimental uses. The percentages disapproving heroin were even higher, and attitudes of adults aged 19 to 26 were similar.[78] And even the minority willing to tolerate illicit drugs did not necessarily wish to use the substances personally. There is no reason to expect those attitudes to change suddenly after legalization. A 1990 survey found 1.7 percent of current adult non-users of cocaine interested in trying the drug if it were legalized, 0.9 percent if we count only adults who had never experimented with cocaine previously.[79] If given a free choice, most persons would not even consider using drugs of abuse; most abstainers are repelled by the drugs rather than the law.[80] In a district that decriminalized marijuana, 80 percent of adult and high school non-users said they had no interest in the drug regardless of its legality.[81] In 1988, 69 percent of U.S. high school seniors said they would not use marijuana if it were legal[82]—an impressive number if one considers that marijuana is often viewed as roughly equivalent to beer. A Canadian study found past use of marijuana to be more significant than legal penalties in predicting the impact of legalization.[83]

We can theorize that the appeal of drugs is limited largely to current users; they might buy more if the price declines, but a lower price is unlikely to attract novices.[84] How many people would be more inclined to smoke if cigarettes were a dime a pack? Amount of use may be affected by economics, but the initial decision to use stands aloof from pocketbook factors. The method chosen to measure abuse is also important. For example, experience with alcohol shows that greater accessibility is associated with higher per capita consumption.[85] That does not mean, however, that everyone drinks more. Per capita consumption is computed by taking the total consumption in a geographic area and dividing it by the number of persons residing there. Many persons, such as infants and teetotalers, drink little or no alcohol. Others take in enormous quantities. Abusers tend to nudge the per capita average upwards; one researcher calculated that 41 percent of total alcohol consumption comes from only 6 percent of the population, and 60 percent of consumption from 10 percent of the population.[86] The worst individual abusers may get worse yet, but the number of abusers may not change much. Legalization of other drugs might follow the alcohol pattern; persons who now avoid the drugs might continue to do so, and persons who abuse them might continue to do so.

The number of persons interested in illicit drugs, but who have not tried them, seems relatively small. In 1975, Alaska's supreme court declared that the state constitution's respect for privacy entitled adults to possess and use marijuana at home.[87] No one noticed subsequent loss of productivity or derangement of public morals. We do not know whether marijuana use increased in Alaska. A 1982 survey found that about 4 percent of the state's high school students were daily users, compared to just over 6 percent nation-wide.[88] Oregon decriminalized marijuana in 1973, and several years later 10 percent of the adult population used it—compared to 9 percent when smoking marijuana was a crime.[89] After California decriminalized marijuana in 1976, 14 percent of the population used it, compared to 9 percent when it was a crime.[90] Those increases seem modest enough, and lose all significance when compared to similar jurisdictions that retain criminal sanctions; use rises in decriminalized jurisdictions no more than in criminalized ones. Researchers who study effects of marijuana decriminalization find that it does not produce more users nor does it intensify their use.[91] Indeed, decriminalization of marijuana in several states was followed by a national decrease in the number of users: 25 or 30 million users in 1975,[92] 20 million in the early 1980s.[93] Irrelevance of criminal sanction to the number of users is long demonstrated; a study produced for the American Bar Foundation examined figures from the Federal Bureau of Narcotics in the 1950s and found no relation between severity of penalties and the number of narcotics addicts.[94] A study published by the United Nations in the 1970s found no evidence that anti-drug laws affect illicit consumption, except for temporary blips that disappear once the market adjusts to new suppression efforts.[95]

Legalization may lead to increased use of a substance, but if so, the increase is moderate and its effects on society seem so mild as to be unnoticed.

In addition to price and availability, psychological conditioning affects drug use. For example, a reward having unpredictable strength and occurrence will produce more persistent behavior than a regular reward. The unreliability of adulterated and misbranded illicit drugs sets up just that sort of reinforcement schedule. Legal drugs of guaranteed purity would eliminate such reinforcement. Also, the more work a subject does to get a reward, the stronger the conditioning becomes. The days of some addicts are completely absorbed by the illicit drug hustle, elevating drugs to the sole meaning of life. If drugs were freely and cheaply available, the addict's investment in drug seeking would decline, and so would the strength of that behavior. Even if an addict used the same quantity of drugs, time would open up to develop other interests in life, interests that could eventually eliminate the drug habit. Legalization could help drug addicts quit.

British investigators find that a legal supply of heroin tends to tear addicts away from the drug subculture,[96] a finding that suggests addicts pal around to keep up their drug supply rather than for pleasure of companionship. Legalization would thereby help break social reinforcement of drug use and might help a person lose the "addict identity," an important step in self-cure.

Some researchers hold that entrance into drug marketing results in the entrepreneur using substances that have more hazards.[97] Legalization would wipe out small dealerships and thereby eliminate that incentive to use drugs of greater peril.

In summary, experience suggests that drug use would increase after legalization, but not by much. Moreover, most of the increase would be among current users, particularly among heavy abusers. Few novices would be attracted to drugs if they are freely and cheaply available, and fewer still would experience difficulties unless the novices are already abnormal persons. In terms of drug use, legalization would have no effect on most ordinary non-users.

The law does not restrain people from destroying themselves; intelligence does. There is no reason to anticipate an epidemic of stupidity sweeping the land if illicit drugs are legalized. Although self-destructive people abuse drugs in terrible ways, most persons are not self-destructive. Most will probably avoid harmful drugs or use them with caution. Laws do not make pedestrians look both ways before crossing busy streets or make people be careful with open flames while using flammable liquids. And because so many untoward consequences of illicit drugs arise from their illegality, legalization could allow problems to decline even if the number of users increased. Recall the conclusion of Hawaii's High Sheriff on that very point.

Recall also that social controls develop and reduce problems. Alcohol is an addictive drug causing far more medical harm than heroin and is described as more intoxicating than heroin.[98] In former times most alcohol drinkers were abusers,[99] yet today authorities say that most users avoid untoward consequences.[100] The chemistry of alcohol and the physiology of users have not changed; social attitudes have brought use under control even though it has not been eliminated. Likewise, as LSD users became more familiar with the drug, hospital admissions for bad experiences declined even though consumption went up. Increased use does not mean increased problems, and even can mean just the opposite.[101]

(A more subtle question is the definition of "problem." Opiate users may regard physical resonance as a condition rather than a misery, well worth the drug's soothing effect. "Where drinking is customary or integrated—a matter of acceptable institutional use—there are no problems with drunkenness, no matter how much drinking or drunkenness occurs, for it is approved and part of that larger life pattern which is deemed acceptable."[102] Nicotine addicts are plentiful, yet no one feels they are a problem that threatens the nation. Problems do not occur in nature; they are defined by people.)

Legalizing drugs would promote public health, not harm it. Many untoward consequences of illicit drugs never occur in laboratory settings because labs use pure substances of known potency. Street drugs are adulterated and misbranded. Users never know what they are taking or how strong it is. People have been crippled by contaminants. Admittedly a certain element of our citizenry regards those consequences as just desserts, but such bigotry has no place in public policy. Citizens who choose to use hazardous products (cigarettes, power tools, hang gliders, surfboards) have the same consumer rights as persons who use benign products (apples, vitamins, tricycles, color televisions). Consumers have a right to know that a product is labeled accurately, and whether any special hazards are associated with it. Sellers must be held accountable to those standards. Although government has no responsibility to protect citizens from their own stupidity, government does have a responsibility to protect citizens from deception.

Lower price could reduce the popularity of the most potent varieties of drugs. That sounds unlikely but actually happened when Prohibition ended; the ratio of beer sales grew in comparison to more potent alcoholic beverages such as whiskey.[103] Bootleggers preferred the more concentrated varieties because law officers were less likely to spot a gallon of whiskey than a keg of beer; customers who would have been satisfied with beer might have to buy whiskey or nothing. The same process occurred when opiates were banned; weak smoking opium was more bulky than heroin, so an opiate user might have to buy heroin or nothing. Crack cocaine is yet another example. If artificial price distortions of illegality ended, less harmful drugs might become more available and more popular than the highly refined ones preferred by illicit dealers.

Legalization of drug paraphernalia should also be a boon. Anti-paraphernalia laws are among the most interesting examples of zealotry. The only concern they address is political—the need for officials to look tough. A city council member who tried to end drag racing by banning chrome tail pipes would be ridiculed, but one who fights marijuana by outlawing jeweled roach clips is hailed. Such measures are worse than useless. Limiting sale of hypodermic needles, for example, encourages spread of hepatitis, AIDS, and other afflictions that cause misery and empty the public treasury, while leaving drug use unaffected. (When Dutch authorities gave out 700,000 free needles, the drug-using population failed to grow.)[104] If politics were rational, officials who enact anti-paraphernalia laws would be thrown out of office for harming their communities. Such laws are drug pornography; they are never enacted without a display of paraphernalia, publicly fondled for newspaper and television cameras.

We have yet to address one question frequently posed when legalization is discussed: What about the children?

Cocaine, one of the most deadly and addictive illegal drugs, is available to school kids.[105]

Drug dealers are killing our kids. Is it not the job of the military to protect this country, its future, its kids, for God's sake?[106]

Drugs are alarmingly on the increase in use among our young people. They are destroying the lives of hundreds of thousands of young people all over America, not just of college age or young people in their twenties, but the great tragedy: The uses start even in junior high school, or even in the late grades.[107]

[Grade school children are] swallowing stimulants or sedatives, smoking marijuana, and even injecting heroin.[108]

Addiction and drug abuse has spread to the junior high schools and even the elementary schools.[109]

Even our high school children are beginning to use hard narcotics.[110]

We know all too well that racketeers in this field are making easy victims of many of our finest young people.[111]

Current testimony referring to teen-agers in New York making $500 a week selling narcotics might well be accurate.[112]

Hard pressed to create a market, peddlers have left the slums and invaded middle-class schools.[113]

School children of 44 schools (only a few of these were high schools) were smoking "mootas" [marijuana]. Verifications came in by the hundreds from harassed parents, teachers, neighborhood pastors, priests, welfare workers and club women.[114]

Despite every precaution school children of tender age, have been detected smoking muggles [marijuana].[115]

One of my own cases was a twelve-year-old girl who had used alcohol before she began to experiment with heroin.[116]

Organized efforts are directed at the young. Besides the professional [heroin] peddlers we have a million young recruiting agents in our midst insanely trapping our youth into addiction.[117]

It is not uncommon to find boys and girls sixteen and eighteen years of age who give a history of having taken the drug for two years. We have treated one child, who became a confirmed drug fiend through the mother's milk.[118]

The number of young people addicted is enormous. I have come in contact with individuals sixteen and eighteen years of age, whose history was that they had taken a habit forming drug for at least two years. This includes girls as well as boys.[119]

Inhabitants of Jersey City were startled a while ago to hear that school-children there were buying cocaine from vendors.[120]

Shameful conditions . . . have existed in Memphis . . . [where] children were able to buy for a nickel cocaine, like candy.[121]

There are hundreds, aye thousands, of our American boys and girls who have acquired this deathly [narcotics] habit.[122]

[Narcotics are] widely spread amongst . . . the younger class of boys and girls, many of the latter of the more respected class of families.[123]

In Eureka [Nevada] it has become fashionable among the boys to learn the [narcotics] habit. We noticed, on a recent visit to that locality, half a dozen youths, all the way from 16 to 20 years of age. . . . The boys consider it a great acquisition to their accomplishments, and boast to each other of their capacity in consuming a large amount of the drug.[124]

Concerns expressed in those quotations are all familiar. The quotations, however, are given in reverse chronological order, from the 1980s back to the 1870s. Throughout American history children have used dangerous drugs. From 1900 to 1920 "countless commentators argued that drugs were destroying the next generation."[125] As indicated earlier in this book, youth is the primary time of life for drug use; subsequently the "maturing out" process extinguishes use. Individual casualties may occur, but overall juvenile death rates have declined, life expectancies have risen, and new generations take their place in the normality of life.

Nonetheless, legalization can limit juvenile access to drugs without raising civil liberties difficulties that develop with restrictions on adults. Automobile driving is forbidden to children, bartenders withhold whiskey from children, and retailers do not sell cigarettes to minors. Those restrictions are largely successful. It is possible, of course, for determined juveniles to obtain alcohol or cigarettes from cooperative adults. The same would happen with legalized drugs if age requirements were mandated. Experience suggests, however, that regular use would be limited to children showing other forms of deviancy as well.[126] Ordinary youngsters should be at no risk. Before 1915 all sorts of dangerous drugs were legally available to children. No catastrophe is recorded.

Popular reports of illicit drug use among children tend to be sensationalized.[127] Despite heroin scare stories in the mid-1920s, not one addict was found among 1 million New York City school children.[128] In the 1970s thousands of urine samples were collected from students at a Harlem elementary school. Two samples tested positive.[129] The amount of cocaine use by juveniles can be inferred from autopsies performed on bodies of children who die from all sorts of causes; government drug doctrine holds that cocaine users are far more likely to die than non-users, meaning that cocaine users would be overrepresented in death totals. While the Reagan administration promoted hysteria in 1986, the most recent year for which federal figures were then available (1984) showed 8 instances in which traces of cocaine were found in bodies of children—and that did not even mean it was the fatal agent.[130] When the federal Drug Abuse Warning Network report for 1986 finally became available, it showed cocaine in only 11 corpses of children, out of a total population for that age group of 27.8 million.[131] A reporter received a Pulitzer Prize in 1980 for coverage of heroin addiction among youngsters; the coverage was later exposed as a fabrication. The nation's children, as a whole, seem to navigate their pharmaceutical environment without significant harm.

Surveys repeatedly show illicit drug use declining since 1979, particularly among youths.[132] Use by high school students has been far lower than the news media claim.[133] Press reports of surveys may reveal that some astonishing percentage of students say they have used a particular drug, but fail to note that such "use" is typically a one-time experiment out of curiosity.[134] Defining such "use" as an abuse problem is part of the bureaucratic thrust that sets up an impossible goal requiring more public expenditures.

NEONATAL ABSTINENCE SYNDROME

Stories abound about babies born addicted to crack cocaine, due to the mother's use of the drug during pregnancy. Anti-drug militants often cite the phenomenon as justifying harsh anti-drug laws. The situation merits more careful examination than it commonly receives in speeches and news stories.

Addiction, dependence, and physical resonance are three different things, although all three can occur simultaneously in one person. Because addiction is a psychological phenomenon, it is hard to demonstrate in an infant. In theory a baby might have morbid craving for heroin, desiring the drug more than anything else in the world, but no one has yet shown morbid craving in a baby, nor has anyone shown that a child born of an addicted mother demonstrates a longing for the drug over a period of decades. Someday an experiment may test the existence of neonatal addiction, but such an experiment has yet to be designed, let alone performed. No one knows whether infants can be born addicted to drugs or anything else.

Researchers do know that infants are not born with an illicit drug dependence, as defined in this book. A dependent person deprived of the drug gets sicker and sicker. An infant born of a drug addicted mother may sicken during the detoxification process, but afterwards the child no longer needs the drug to maintain physical normalcy.

Some infants, however, may have a physical resonance with a drug due to interuterine transmission of the drug or its metabolites from the bloodstream outside the uterus. Such a situation is not trivial, but it is neither addiction nor dependence.

Given what is known about pregnancy and about illicit drugs, the existence of neonatal physical resonance is not only theoretically plausible but likely. Numerous investigators have reported the phenomenon. I believe it exists. Nonetheless I am disconcerted by the comment of British drug abuse clinic psychiatrist John Mack, who acknowledged that "the American literature is full of the problem," but noted that when "addicted mothers have their babies, . . . apart from putting the babies into a premature unit just so we could keep a close eye on them, we did nothing. And we observed no withdrawal signs. Not even increased restlessness."[135] Mack's comment was made in the 1970s on the basis of a handful of personal observations. But while researching this book, I found that reports of the phenomenon remained largely, if not entirely, American through the 1980s. The chemistry of a particular illicit drug is the same throughout the world. If neonatal physical resonance is seen mainly in the United States, the explanation may be cultural rather than pharmaceutical. If so, the cultural bias is shared by the author of this book, because I believe the phenomenon exists. Another curiosity is that neonatal opiate withdrawal symptoms may not appear until the fourth week of life and commonly last six to eight weeks, with some symptoms continuing for over four months.[136] If an adult stopped using opiates and exhibited symptoms with such time frames, the symptoms would not be ascribed to withdrawal.

Soon after birth, examination of body fluids and excretions from some infants reveals the presence of certain illicit drugs. In the case of opiates, the baby may show classic signs of the opiate withdrawal syndrome within a day after birth, suggesting that physical resonance exists with the drug. The delay in symptom onset is consistent with opiate deprivation, and symptoms can be swiftly eased by administering an opiate. Those facts are evidence that the observations are based on clinical reality rather than cultural bias. A treatment tool called the Finnegan Scale is widely used to measure severity of withdrawal. The scale is a list of characteristics (such as pitch of cry, nasal flaring, muscle tone) that the tool designers determined, by trial and error, to be typical in infants who are born with opiates in their bodies.[137]

Withdrawing an infant from opiates can be touchier than with an adult. Although opiate withdrawal is safe if a person has no underlying organic difficulty, the infants in question often do have such afflictions. There are two basic reasons. First, many common substances, legal or otherwise, may benefit adults yet devastate a fetus. Even aspirin bottles have labels that warn pregnant women against using the product, and drug addicts typically use products more powerful than aspirin. In addition, many drug abusers, let alone addicts, neglect their bodies. A fetus that takes up harmful substances and is denied vitally needed substances will not develop normally. The resulting infant may be weakened by organic problems that make the opiate withdrawal syndrome risky.

Probably most American medical practitioners would agree with the preceding two paragraphs. Disagreement exists on many other points.

A basic point, on which controversy is far greater than news coverage indicates, is whether any "cocaine babies" or "crack babies" exist. Given the fact that no one has demonstrated either addiction or drug dependence in a newborn, that leaves resonance as the only physical evidence. Claims of cocaine resonance did not appear until the 1980s and were immediately contested. No consensus supported the notion as the decade closed.[138] If cocaine resonance does not exist, neither can cocaine or crack babies.

Investigators who observe a neonate cocaine withdrawal syndrome seem to rely on the Finnegan Scale as an objective measurement. Several difficulties weaken that reliance. The scale was designed to measure opiate withdrawal symptoms.[139] Opiates and cocaine are different. If a physician proclaimed that an adult with opiate abstinence symptoms was in fact exhibiting withdrawal from cocaine, that practitioner would probably be ridiculed. Yet practitioners who make that very declaration about infants are cited as authoritative by news reporters and drug control militants. In addition, populations that generate "cocaine babies" are exclusively abusers and addicts, women with such heavy drug problems that they are under professional care. Such persons are typically polydrug abusers, and their "cocaine babies" frequently have opiates as well. If such newborns have high scores on the Finnegan Scale, should that be attributed to the cocaine or the opiates? Loretta Finnegan, who developed the scale, states, "When cocaine is the primary drug of abuse, most clinicians have not seen symptoms of abstinence significant enough to treat pharmacologically. . . . From a purely physical standpoint the infant need not stay in the nursery longer than the general requirement."[140]

The Finnegan Scale gauges the severity of opiate withdrawal so that care givers know when supportive therapy is needed to help an infant who is known to have opiates in its system. The scale is not a diagnostic tool; other conditions can produce symptoms measured by the scale. The scale merely guides treatment once diagnosis has been made. Investigators who detect "cocaine babies" seem to misuse the scale as a diagnostic tool, believing that if the symptoms measured by the scale exist, the symptoms are caused by "cocaine withdrawal."[141]

Another problem is that much of the Finnegan Scale measures behavior. The behavior is associated with infants undergoing opiate withdrawal, but such a correlation yields no information about cause and effect. Moreover, parts of the scale measure distress. All sorts of things agitate people. Researchers who observe "cocaine babies" say the infants become distressed as the amount of drug decreases. Maybe some are upset by *presence* of the drug; most adults find illicit substances unpleasant. Maybe some babies are afraid of new sensations that they feel; plenty of adults fear change. Maybe "cocaine babies," who may suffer from assorted abnormalities, are just sick in general and are no more protesting cocaine than a cancer patient gasping from pain is protesting an opiate.

"Cocaine babies" are sometimes called "innocent victims" of drug abuse, whose protection merits harsh anti-drug laws. That contention encompasses several points worth examining. The first is the assumption that free availability of banned drugs would lead to much wider use. As noted elsewhere in this book, that assumpton is not supported by experience. Another issue is the definition of "victim." Some research in this area has puzzling terminology, such as "addicted fetuses."[142] Even if we assume that the term refers only to physical resonance, question arises about how such resonance is detected. In a population of pregnant women addicted to a drug, is the drug cut off from the uterine blood supply in some of the women, and the response of the fetus measured? Is the fetus any more resonant than the woman's spleen or thumb? Terms such as "addicted fetus" or "innocent victim" implicitly argue that a fetus possesses civil rights apart from those of the pregnant woman, rights that may conflict with the woman's.

Persons who accept that argument may also advocate that a pregnant woman's activities be limited in order to benefit the fetus. Less common, however, is advocacy of societal intervention to enrich the woman's life in order to benefit the fetus. For example, Reagan and Bush administration officials decried the effect of illicit drugs on fetuses. Those same administrations, however, worked hard to reduce food programs that nourished pregnant women, worked to reduce prenatal care opportunities, to reduce neonatal care availability. If an anti-drug zealot advocates societal intervention to limit a pregnant woman's life in order to benefit a fetus, yet also opposes societal intervention to benefit a fetus by expanding a woman's life, "drugs" and "fetuses" are simply being used as excuses to implement a wider social agenda intended to limit citizens' lives.

Indifference to fetuses is demonstrated by government officials' silence about adverse effects that methadone programs have on fetuses. Harmful fetal effects caused by opiates have been widely documented, yet government officials who bemoan "cocaine babies" raise no objection to pregnant women receiving continual doses of methadone throughout their pregnancy. The silence is all the more remarkable because some researchers have found that government-approved methadone is more harmful to fetuses and newborns than illegal heroin.[143]

A crucial aspect of the "baby addict" controversy is typicaly ignored. All the horror stories, without exception, come from populations of pregnant women who are drug abusers or addicts. "Worst-case" scenarios are no more applicable to general populations in this controversy than in any other debate about illicit drugs. Hardly anyone has examined what happens to the fetuses and newborn of women who are moderate users of drugs. Limited investigation on that broad population has produced results far different than the plentiful headline-grabbing research on pregnant addicts.

Pioneering research into fetal effects of social cocaine use has made two basic discoveries. First, in fetal or subsequent childhood development no difference is detected between groups of women who use cocaine moderately and those who never use cocaine.[144] Second, moderate users stop entirely as soon as they learn they are pregnant,[145] thereby exhibiting the responsible pattern of consumption typically found among chippers. Unlike addicts, for whom drugs are the most important part of their existence, chippers view drugs as simply one aspect of a diverse and rewarding life, a life in which healthy pregnancy and offspring may be more important than drugs.

In summary, fetal and newborn abnormalities are often found in populations of pregnant women who abuse drugs so severely as to merit medical treatment of their addictions. Those addicts are typically polydrug abusers (including tobacco and alcohol), for whom drugs are but one part of a multi-problem lifestyle including poverty, infections, poor nutrition, sexually transmitted disease, two or more elective abortions, and inadequate prenatal care.[146] Researchers repeatedly caution that such factors contaminate efforts to detect the effect of a particular drug,[147] but those warnings are absent from speeches and news stories about "baby addicts." Neither addiction nor illicit drug dependence has been demonstrated in any infant, and resonance is limited to those drugs that produce resonance in adults. Pregnant chippers do not exhibit abnormal fetuses or offspring. Alarm about "baby addicts" is generally used to energize demands to restrict the lives of pregnant women while programs that would enrich their lives are eliminated.

BENEFITS OF DRUG USE

Drug education is often considered an informal sanction; supposedly if people are well informed they will refuse to use drugs. Two assumptions lie within that expectation. One is that the purpose of drug "education" is not to inform, but to elicit a specific response (abstention). The process is not education, nor even propaganda, but rather behavior modification. Students subjected to drug "education" are able to feel what is happening, and resist it. Said one, "I did not take mescaline because I went to Harvard, met Timothy Leary, rebelled against my parents, was amotivated, or sought escape from reality. I took it because I was a normal American teen-ager whose curiosity had survived thirteen years of American education."[148] The other assumption about "drug education" is that facts prove drugs are bad. But they prove no such thing. Benefits to using drugs may be as numerous as drawbacks. This book's argument for legalization is based on democracy and historical experience, but let us briefly think the unthinkable—that benefits of illicit drugs might also justify their legalization.

Most research ignores that proposition; far more attention has been given to harmful effects than to helpful ones. That is a major gap in our understanding of illicit drugs, reflecting cultural bias of investigators rather than pharmaceutical reality. Benefits are normally disregarded in estimates of drug cost to society, and such practice is improper accounting procedure. Alcohol may cost society $X billion in ill health and lost productivity, but may also produce $X billion by relaxing persons who would otherwise take sick from stress or be unable to face another day on the assembly line. Attempts to put a dollar value on such benefits quickly demonstrate the softness in figures that purport to give the dollar losses, losses that often reflect costs of illegality rather than costs of drug use per se.

Some benefits are known. Recreation is one; many persons gain pleasure from illicit drugs, and some users contend the pleasure exacts no price of later misery. A less familiar element of recreational use blends with self-medication, using drugs to unwind from a day's tensions, so that persons may work more efficiently.[149] One college student said of cocaine, "I used just over one gram, sharing it with friends, over the next year. It was great to keep me awake as I studied and wrote papers. . . . My grades were very high. I felt logically that if I used less than a gram of coke a year for studying and social occasions, and I did not experience a compulsion to use it, I should not have a drug problem."[150]

Drugs may benefit productivity in both abnormal and normal persons. The British government has permitted an addict to have drugs if the person cannot function productively without them,[151] recognition that some people need drugs in order to be useful members of the community. For example, opiates may help some addicts avoid schizophrenia.[152] Because opiate addiction lasts a shorter time than schizophrenia, and a person can be far more productive as an addict, such addiction may be a gain for both the individual and society. Heroin can calm rowdy teenagers—reducing aggression, sexual drive, fertility,[153] and teen pregnancy—helping adolescents through that time of life. Another example of productivity through drugs is provided by persons filled with rage, who can calm violent tendencies with opiates.[154] Opiates can also help neurotics hold steady jobs, improve in health and spirits, and get along better with people.[155] This change is especially striking among alcoholics who switch to opiates.[156] Shy people can find courage to pursue social interactions by taking opiates.[157] Soldiers have reported that heroin gave them courage to face combat.[158] Opiates have no monopoly in the pharmacopoeia of beneficial drugs. Cocaine can relieve depression and anxiety.[159] Use of psychedelics among prison inmates may help reduce recidivism.[160] And some alcoholics treated with LSD benefit by subsequent ability to drop drug dependencies.[161]

Helpful effects of illicit drugs can be physical as well as psychological. Marijuana cigarettes were once used to boost stamina of mine workers.[162] Workers doing vigorous labor in India used marijuana for the same purpose,[163] and the same was observed in Costa Rica, Jamaica, and Brazil in the 1970s and 1980s.[164] In the 1800s opium was cited for its ability to aid physical exertion.[165] Around World War I a former laborer at an Alaskan fishery reported that the company administered morphine to make employees endure a harsher pace of work.[166] Cocaine can increase a worker's ability to do familiar and routine tasks requiring attentiveness.[167] In the early 1900s railroad engineers used cocaine to keep up with overtime demands.[168] Louisiana stevedores and cotton pickers used it to improve stamina; stevedores reportedly could work 70 hours straight "without sleep or rest, in rain, in cold, and in heat."[169] Cocaine was also credited for improving the performance of lumberjacks and of workers constructing railroads and levees.[170] Cocaine can restore mobility to persons crippled by arthritis.[171] It can improve athletic performance;[172] soldiers fight more vigorously and on smaller rations after taking the drug.[173] Soldiers and civilian workers have used amphetamines for the same purpose.[174] LSD can ease pain in terminal cancer patients,[175] as can heroin. Heroin can also lower blood sugar levels; users may be less likely to have diabetes mellitus than non-users.[176] Heroin lowers blood pressure[177] and is an excellent cough remedy.[178]

Research about illicit drugs has concentrated on abuse; perhaps it is time to investigate benefits. Any product can be harmful if abused. Dangerous products can be beneficial when used wisely. If researchers assumed that drugs were dangerous, rather than evil, results might be surprising.

THE AMERICAN WAY OF LIFE

Drugs do not threaten the American way of life; they are part of it. Things that citizens fear most about drugs have less to do with pharmaceutical effects than with drug laws, social injustice, and antidemocratic values of political opportunists.

A great complaint against drugs is that they exemplify "permissiveness." What a curious complaint for Americans to voice. The country's traditions call for each citizen to choose a personal path through life. Some paths are more common and more approved than others, but they are supposed to be chosen freely. The nation is founded on permissiveness. Strictures imposed by caste, class, or clergy are abhorred.

When someone inveighs against "permissiveness" the concern is more likely disapproval of choices made by others, and perhaps fear that those choices may someday become elements of a new norm of behavior, a new morality. Morality is not immutable. This chapter began with examples of alterations caused by law; other forces of change are also at work. Change is inherent to life. Only death brings stillness. A person who is pro-life must accept changing morality. To demand that everyone, for all time, accept one person's concept of morality is to call forth the forces of death. It is no coincidence that moral zealots kill people.

Citizens who tightly grasp a particular set of rules and regulations may interpret abandonment of those commandments as society's collapse. American society has nonetheless proven itself sturdy through revolution, civil war, and social turmoil. The national pulse throbs steadily while the country's activities, desires, and directions change. Perhaps our fellow citizens do not follow our path of virtue, but that is good; our tradition demands they choose their own path. Requiring their conduct to conform to a particular concept of righteousness is anti-American. The nation's tradition of personal freedom not only accommodates but promotes different choices. If some citizens reject common standards of sexual conduct, common standards of personal ambition, or common expressions of patriotism, that does not mean the country is falling apart; it means the American way of life is working properly. Political opportunists sense the confusion that many Americans feel about the changing world, and seek to exploit it by falsely portraying the drug war as an anchor holding traditional values steady. Drugs do not threaten America, but drug warriors do. They, and not drug users, urge citizens away from traditional democratic values. The drug war is a smoke screen used by cynical opportunists as they attack the ideals upon which our republic was founded. One by one, elitists pull away the democratic foundation stones that hold up our republic.

Democracy is the framework that must support efforts to reduce drug problems. Addiction is powered by reducing citizen responsibility and leader accountability. The only way to break that cycle is to promote democracy, restoring citizens' power over their communities and their lives. Expanding democracy will have a side effect of reducing drug abuse. "Tuberculosis was brought under control not by the introduction of chemotherapeutic agents, but by a substantial improvement in living conditions; in areas where that improvement has not occurred, the disease is widespread . . . even though each individual patient can be readily diagnosed and cured. Similarly, we must recognize that addiction is a social problem which will never be eliminated by measures that are imposed on the addicts themselves."[179] Just as tuberculosis was greatly reduced by measures not aimed at it, so can drug problems be diminished by an institution normally considered unrelated to health—democracy.

Drug warriors will oppose democracy because it encourages discussion of relevant issues and discourages consideration of irrelevancies (prison furloughs, Pledge of Allegiance, drugs). Drugs provide a smoke screen to hide important issues (profits from hunger, profits from social injustice, profits from polluting air and water). Leaders want those issues ignored, because citizens who examine them call for a change in leadership. Leaders fear drug legalization because the smoke screen would dissipate.

Unfortunately, opposition to democracy extends beyond government officials. A neighborhood group in Kansas City, Missouri, once declared war on real estate developers and city hall bureaucrats who sought to bulldoze thriving residential areas. A series of meetings allowed citizens to identify ways for developers to profit by building upon neighborhood strengths and diminishing weaknesses. A neighborhood economic development plan emerged that expressed the will of the people, but leaders of the neighborhood group refused to adopt it; the plan differed from their notions of what should be done. The goal of neighborhood leaders was not to transfer power from city hall to citizens, but rather from city hall to the neighborhood leaders. A believer in democracy who goes through such an ordeal readily experiences the sense of helplessness that encourages drug use.

Yet those neighborhood meetings, where citizens contributed their knowledge of the neighborhood with enthusiasm and thoughtful reflection, demonstrated that many people thirst for democracy. Addictive lifestyles are still rejected by many of our friends and neighbors. They are willing and anxious to take responsibility for what happens in their block, their neighborhood, their town, their country. All they need is an opportunity, and they will seize it, as they did in one Kansas City neighborhood. And their example can inspire fellow citizens to relinquish addictive behavior and take control over their own lives.

Neighborhood democracy is well suited to attacking drug problems. They are not a national situation requiring a centrally dictated effort. Drug problems are a local situation, best susceptible to local efforts, and renewal of local democracy is an ideal technique to produce solutions tailored to each community. Local democracy would encourage national democracy, seizing political power from elites and restoring America to its own people.

Democracy is a method of dealing with change rather than avoiding it, a celebration of life rather than a call for rigidity and death. Democracy promotes adventure by questioning cherished notions, provides reward by rectifying error. Democracy is a universal antidote to drugs; a single solution but not a simple one, a solution as rich and complex as life itself.

Therefore we must not heed calls to give up democracy in the name of drugs. People in the Bush administration plead for troops to patrol the streets, on the lookout for drugs. The last time troops occupied an American city in peacetime a revolution broke out. The residents of Boston did not revolt in the 1770s because of drugs but because their government refused to leave them alone. That is what the Ninth and Tenth Amendments are all about—the right to be left alone. But drug war zealots will not leave people alone. Militants force passage of electronic eavesdropping laws that invade American homes in search of drugs, eavesdroppng that has no value in detecting murder, rape, robbery, or other major crimes, but zealots diminish the Fourth Amendment in the name of drugs. Americans who simply want to hold jobs are forced to take urine tests, diminishing the Fourth and Fifth Amendments in the name of drugs. Civil commitment evades the Sixth and Eighth Amendments in the name of drugs. The war on drugs is a mask for a war on democracy, a mask for war upon the American people.

Allowing people to mind their own business, one of the greatest national ideals, has accommodated changes that tore apart other societies. Our notions of the good, the true, and the beautiful may bless our lives—yet curse others. Our beliefs may be satisfactory for us, but not for our ancestors or descendants. We all have different desires, different needs. Forcing fellow citizens to adopt our choices is an immoral limitation on their lives, on their potential to contribute to our mutual welfare.

That does not mean anything goes. Civilization cannot exist by the law of the jungle. American civilization can thrive, however, by judging whether conduct liberates people. If conduct sets people free, it promotes the American way of life.

It is unnerving to see the future approach, so different from the present. Great challenges lie ahead, but past challenges seem less daunting only because our country survived them. Citizens of the 1700s were just as uneasy as we are today, and their future was just as uncertain. Our survival, let alone our prosperity, is by no means assured. Nonetheless, if we welcome the future as an opportunity to once again test our nation's ideals of freedom and democracy, once again they will see us through. If we are faithful to them, they will be faithful to us.

Epilogue

Everything known about drug abuse and drug control occurred in the past. Are historians, therefore, the only persons qualified to speak on the subject? I think not. Nor should the presence of a medical component give physicians a monopoly of authority. Nor should a crime component give priority to law enforcers. We and other professionals all have our contributions to make. As do readers of this book.

Paths to knowledge are many. The path I followed in researching this book might not be chosen by everyone. For readers who are interested in such things, I shall describe how I acquired the knowledge I have shared with you.

Essentially I played the role of a detective: "Here is a situation. How did it come about?"

When called into a case, a detective assumes a crime has been committed. That does not mean the investigator is prejudiced and cannot accept innocent explanations, but the assumption of a crime provides a framework in which the investigation can proceed, a framework that determines what is relevant or irrelevant to the question at hand. I began my research by assuming that illicit drugs should be legalized. That does not mean I disregarded drug dangers; rather, I considered them in the context of how they are affected by criminal law. That was the framework determining whether something was relevant to the book. I had thought about the topic before beginning the research, so I began with a working hypothesis. My investigation disproved various aspects of that hypothesis. Certain drugs turned out to be less fearsome than I originally believed, and my research failed to demonstrate the reduction in street crime that I expected from legalization. When I discovered facts that contradicted or even disproved my expectations, I simply changed my thinking.

New thinking provided new angles of investigation. Detectives spend most of their time running down bum leads, doing legwork to develop more bum leads, and sitting at a desk in puzzlement while trying to make sense of research notes. Excitement is minimal. Yet in the end, when the common thread is found in conflicting testimony, when lab reports confirm the suspicion, when the case breaks, detectives know their labor was worth the misery.

So how do we do it? How do detectives determine truth?

Some people but priority on direct experience. To determine the effect of smoking crack, they smoke crack. Some people argue that direct experience is necessary to understand something, but such an argument denies the power of language, denies that communication is possible. The argument rapidly broadens to assert that only persons with direct experience are qualified to speak about it. Only the word of crack smokers can be trusted on the topic. Only a Nazi murderer can be trusted to explain his actions. Eventually, such an argument asserts that you cannot believe what you do not experience. Some people argue that the Holocaust never happened. They did not see it and do not believe it. "What you cannot see cannot hurt you."

Direct experience has value, but detectives do not praise it above other means of gaining knowledge. No human eyes have ever seen an AIDS virus or the planet Pluto, yet we can be confident they exist. Detectives tend to be suspicious of persons who insist upon direct experience, because their demand keeps facts hidden. What are they hiding, and why? Moreover, detectives, by the nature of our work, are normally denied direct experience. We investigate the past. We have only leftover residues, only clues and not the experience. We are not participants in what we investigate. Yet we cannot agree with critics who demand that we abandon our investigation.

Observation of direct experience is another method of obtaining knowledge. Typical observations are performance of an experiment, surveillance of someone's actions, examining an account given by a direct participant, and sometimes even conducting personal interviews of direct participants. Some people argue that personal interviews are the best observations, but detectives use them with caution. Because people's stories must be checked and double-checked, their primary value is for developing leads or verifying what is already known. Detectives investigating historical events can grow exasperated at critics' demands for interviews; because even if witnesses are long dead, good detectives can piece together their stories. For example, today we know far more about the ancient world than its inhabitants did.

Interviews contain a peril. The broader the matter under investigation, the broader the interviews must be. Interviewing illicit drug users may produce entertaining anecdotes, but unless an investigator has the expertise and resources to design and conduct a series of interviews in a properly chosen population, anecdotes may give a misleading picture of reality and therefore be worse than useless. Fortunately an effective solution to that problem is available to a detective engaged in solitary labor.

The solution is to examine reports made by other investigators. People who have never done detective work may think that such an approach yields unoriginal conclusions based on hearsay, but scientists routinely use the same approach to discover truth. Most scientific investigations build upon results of previous ones. Previous ones are accepted if their results remain consistent with new findings. Only when contradictions arise do scientists repeat old investigations. Likewise, a detective accepts research done by previous workers on a case—there is no point to asking the same questions of the same witnesses, running the same lab test on the same sample, making a new print of the same photograph. A detective welcomes a fat file of research, allowing time to be spent on analysis rather than mere fact-gathering. Analysis is what breaks a case.

In my role as detective I relied upon work by previous investigators, just as any scientist would. My reliance was not blind; I asked who the investigators were, whether their findings were accepted by professional colleagues, whether the findings fit smoothly into the emerging structure I was erecting or whether I needed to stop, reconsider, and even disassemble what I had already done. Reports from previous workers comprise the factual foundation of my analysis, and I feel no embarrassment about that. I suspect persons who criticize such reliance probably exhibit such reliance in their own lives. No one criticized Congress for declaring war on December 8, 1941 on the basis of hearsay from President Franklin D. Roosevelt who had not bothered to make a personal inspection tour of the Pacific. Many citizens even accept reports about illicit drug hazards and refuse to sample the products. Reports from other persons form the basis of great decisions by governments and intimate decisions by individuals. People who reject such reports are the kind of people who find books worthless. This book is not directed at such an audience.

To solve a case, a detective picks and chooses among facts. Such selectivity is neither biased nor unethical. For example, a detective may accept part of a story from a witness and discard the rest. If the accepted part is verifiable, and the rejected part contradicts demonstrated facts, such a choice may be wise. Must we believe either everything or nothing a person says? Such a stance rapidly forces us to believe everything or nothing we hear—a ridiculous proposition. Selectivity is not evasion if troublesome facts are addressed rather than ignored. As a picture congeals from the swirling chaos of research data, dropping the inaccurate and irrelevant data allows the picture to clarify into sharpness. Good detectives not only acquire information, they discard it.

My approach to detective work was shaped by my profession, history.

When examining the latest available research, I often traced its origins. I wanted to know its design and structure, to measure them against the edifice I was constructing. Anyone who is fanatic enough to count my cited sources will find a substantial percentage dating from the 1980s, with the bulk coming from 1970 or later. But I have not hesitated to cite earlier scientific research. Antiquity does not invalidate a source, even in science, and surely not in history. Serious research about drug use in America has been conducted for a century; to ignore that work would be similar to writing a U.S. Civil War history that cited modern scholarship but ignored information from the 1860s. In the present book I have, I think rightly, emphasized research from the past 20 years. But I have also cited earlier work. For some topics there is no alternative—research on LSD, for example, virtually ended in the 1970s. Moreover, while older sources remain valid in their own right, they also demonstrate a deep scientific foundation for my conclusions. What I say is supported not only by reputable work from the 1980s, but from the 1970s, 1960s, 1950s, etc. I do not rely upon the oddball finding that contradicts most research. I rely upon a century of reputable investigation. The facts I report have been confirmed again and again and again.

With luck, in the end a detective makes the case. I think I have made the case for legalizing drugs. I think I have shown what happened in the United States, and why, and what must be done about it. The rest is up to this book's readers and their fellow citizens.

Notes

Full citations for abbreviated notes may be found in the Sources Cited section.

CHAPTER 1

1. Chein et al., *Road*, 79.

2. Kaplan, *Hardest*, 7; Rublowsky, *Stoned*, 136; Jaffe, "Drug Addiction and Drug Abuse," in Goodman and Gilman, *Pharmocological* 7th ed., 541-42.

3. Chein et al., *Road*, 231.

4. Lasagna, Felsinger, and Beecher, "Drug," 1115; Oswald, "Personal," 438; Smith and Beecher, "Subjective," 51-52; Alexander and Hadaway, "Opiate," 372, 375; Jaffe and Martin, "Opioid Analgesics and Antagonists," in Goodman and Gilman, *Pharmacological* 7th ed., 498.

5. Louria, *Overcoming*, 101-2; Inciardi, *War*, 39; President's Commission, *Task Force Report: Narcotics*, 3; Krippner, "Drug," 654-55; Cheek, Newell, and Joffe, "Deceptions," 1276.

6. Brecher and Consumer Reports, *Licit*, 13.

7. Blum, "Drugs, Behavior, and Crime," in Blum et al., *Society*, 278-79; Schroeder, *Politics*, 62; Restak, *Mind*, 124-26; Feldman, "PCP Use in Four Cities: An Overview," in Feldman, Agar, and Beschner, *Angel*, 39-40.

8. Schacter and Singer, "Cognitive," 379-99.

9. Zinberg and Robertson, *Drugs*, 57; Weil, *Natural*, 53-54; Jacobson and Zinberg, *Social*, 40; Newmeyer and Johnson, "Drug," 242. A dissenting view is noted without elaboration in Metzner, "Reflections," 139.

10. Griffiths, Bigelow, and Henningfield, "Similarities in Animal and Human Drug-Taking Behavior," in Mello, *Advances*, 54; O'Brien, "Experimental," 533-43. Autonomic responses can occur in abstinent former users when they are exposed to

environmental cues associated with former drug use (Childress, McLellan, O'Brien, "Abstinent," 655-60; Sideroff and Jarvik, "Conditioned," 529-30, 534-35; McAuliffe, "Test," 19; Hinson and Siegel, "Nonpharmacological," 502.

11. O'Brien, "Experimental," 533-43; O'Brien et al., "Conditioning Effects of Narcotics in Humans," in Krasnegor, *Behavioral*, 67-71.

12. Muntaner et al., "Placebo," 282; Bridger et al., "Classical," 213; Barr, "Classical," 1341, 1350; Post, "Drug," 755, 758-59.

13. Zinberg and Robertson, *Drugs*, 58; Jacobson and Zinberg, *Social*, 36; Weil, *Natural*, 29.

14. Zinberg and Robertson, *Drugs*, 95.

15. Duster, *Legislation*, 33; Judson, *Heroin*, 121-22; Schur, *Narcotic*, 161; Weil, *Natural*, 57-58.

16. This fact is obscured by the misleading connotation in the term "physical dependence" used in most works about drugs, in which the term typically stands for—but does not accurately describe—resonance. Time and again, the descriptive narrative accompanying the term demonstrates that so-called "physical dependence" does not involve a metabolic necessity. Alexander and Hadaway ("Opiate," 371) summarize a century of reputable heroin and opiate research by rejecting "the premise that opiate drugs alter the metabolism in some way, making subsequent opiate ingestion physiologically necessary. . . . No metabolic basis for addiction to any single drug has been demonstrated."

17. Users quoted in Biernacki, *Pathways*, 115, 113. See also 109, 120; Laurie, *Drugs*, 22; Jacobson and Zinberg, *Social*, 36.

18. Chein et al., *Road*, 159.

19. Kaplan, *Hardest*, 27.

20. Twycross, "Clinical," 193, 195.

21. Fraser, "Tolerance," 427. A long time frame is also noted by Vogel, Isbell, and Chapman, "Present," 1019.

22. Kolb, *Drug*, 47-48.

23. Zinberg and Robertson, *Drugs*, 42-43. See also Zinberg and Lewis, "Narcotic: Spectrum," 989-93.

24. Bakalar and Grinspoon, *Drug*, 44; Louria, *Overcoming*, 84. Donald Louria, former president of the New York State Council on Drug Addiction, writes that it is "very easy to get most individuals off heroin. Many users are psychologically and not physically addicted" (p. 98). See also Laurie, *Drugs*, 65; President's Commission, *Task Force Report: Narcotics*, 3; Stephen Waldron statement in House Crime Committee, *Improvement*, 287; Alexander and Hadaway, "Opiate," 372.

25. A study of such persons in New York City found they had to take illicit heroin for half a year before resonance developed (Cushman, "Narcotic," 198). If authorities concur that "the first year of heroin use is a crucial one" (Platt and Labate, *Heroin*, 186) in establishing resonance, they recognize the difficulty and drawn-out length of the process.

26. Kaplan, *Hardest*, 15, 21; Jaffe, "Drug Addiction and Drug Abuse," in Good-

man and Gilman, *Pharmacological* 7th ed., 538. Bejerot, *Addiction*, 33, reproduces a table contrasting use and withdrawal symptoms, illustrating the rebound.

27. Chein et al., *Road*, 247; Zinberg and Robertson, *Drugs*, 43. Judson, *Heroin*, 72-73, reports a double blind experiment demonstrating the power of set and setting. One group of users withdrew from methadone over a period of 21 days, another group in 10 days. Both were told the process would take 28 days, and continued receiving fake doses of "methadone" even when the opiate had been stopped days earlier. On a groupwide basis, no difference was observed in the clustering of withdrawal symptoms over the 28 days. Absence of the opiate seemed less important than a person's belief that it was present or absent. Complementary findings are reported in Phillips, Gossop, and Bradley, "Influence," 235-36.

28. Weil, *Natural*, 42. See also Alexander and Hadaway, "Opiate," 372.

29. Oswald, "Personal," 438.

30. Biernacki, *Pathways*, 55.

31. Kolb, *Drug*, 76.

32. Schur, *Narcotic*, 30. This phenomenon has been known for decades, see Crothers, *Morphinism*, 54-55.

33. McGuire and Lichtenstein, "Drug," 185-91.

34. Scores of interviews demonstrate that people have been unable to detect that someone was using drugs (Duster, *Legislation*, 117-28; Hubert S. Howe testimony, Senate Judiciary Committee, *Illicit*, 1339). "Even large doses [of morphine] . . . do not cause slurred speech or significant motor incoordination" (Jaffe and Martin, "Opioid Analgesics and Antagonists," in Goodman and Gilman, *Pharmacological* 7th ed., 498). See also note 68 below.

35. Duster, *Legislation*, 241; Goodman and Gilman, *Pharmacological* 2nd ed., 242-44; Kolb, *Drug*, 46, 57-58, 64, 104-5, 114. This has been demonstrated in foreign countries and cultures as well. See Hutchins, "Two," 129-40; Stimson, *Heroin*, 149, 178.

36. Kolb, *Drug*, 10-11. See also 105.

37. Chein et al., *Road*, 358.

38. Ibid.

39. King, *Drug*, 18.

40. Quoted in Trebach, *Great*, 345.

41. Blum, "Student Characteristics and Major Drugs," in Blum et al., *Students*, 77-78. Brill and Christie found no significant difference in grade point betwen users and non-users of marijuana ("Marihuana," 713). Blum found no difference in grade point between college students who use or abstain from any drug, nor did Mellinger et al. ("Drug Use, Academic Performance, and Career Indecision: Longitudinal Data in Search of a Model," in Kandel, *Longitudinal*, 167-69, 172-73). Few differences of any kind emerge between drug users and non-users in college populations (Pope, Ionescu-Pioggia, and Cole, "Drug," 588-91). The same holds for high schoolers (Johnston, *Drugs*, 193, 218).

42. Peele, *Love*, 35.

43. Schur, *Narcotic*, 151.

44. Cutting, "Morphine," 39-41.

45. Kaplan, *Hardest*, 136.

46. Chein et al. note that pace of labor may slow (*Road*, 358) and that "pupillary constriction may interfere with vision under conditions of poor illumination" (p. 360). Duster notes slowed reaction times (*Legislation*, 36). Smith, Semke, and Beecher note a reduction in speed rather than accuracy on task performance ("Objective," 58) and that, in general, researchers have found little mental impairment (ibid., 53). "Good health and productive work," says Jaffe, are "not incompatible with regular use of opioids" ("Drug Addiction and Drug Abuse," in Goodman and Gilman, *Pharmacological* 7th ed., 542).

47. Kaplan, for example, argues that a heroin user could not drive safely right after receiving an injection (*Hardest*, 176). In contrast, Hubert Howe has stated that someone on a maintenance dose "could drive an automobile just as well as anybody could" (testimony, Senate Judiciary Committee, *Illicit*, 1326). Schur notes potential problems from sporificity and frequency of heroin injections (*Narcotic*, 133), but oral tablets might avoid those difficulties.

48. Biernacki, *Pathways*, 55; Duster, *Legislation*, 9; Morgan, *Yesterday's*, 8; Crothers, *Morphinism*, 31; Rublowsky, *Stoned*, 138, 191; Schur, *Narcotic*, 28; Morgan, *Drugs*, 31; Kolb, *Drug*, 76; Zinberg and Lewis, "Narcotic." 992; Zinberg and Jacobson, "Natural," 38.

49. Earle, "Opium," 445.

50. Blair, "Relation," 288. The "bureau" was Bureau of Drug Control, Pennsylvania Department of Health.

51. Platt and Labate, *Heroin*, 171; Biernacki, *Pathways*, 6, 36; Weil, *Natural*, 57-58.

52. Jaffe, "Drug Addiction and Drug Abuse," in Goodman and Gilman, *Pharmacological* 7th ed., 542; Bellis, *Heroin*, 11-12; Winick, "Narcotics," 13; Eldridge, *Narcotics*, 16-18, 21; Lawrence Kolb quoted in King, *Drug*, 181; Kolb, *Drug*, 104-5, 109, 117; Platt and Labate, *Heroin*, 263; Rublowsky, *Stoned*, 191; Schur, *Narcotic*, 22-23; Trebach, *Great*, 291; Zinberg and Robertson, *Drugs*, 44; Musto and Ramos, "Follow-Up," 1075-76; Wallace, "Rehabilitation," 347; Vogel, Isbell, and Chapman, "Present," 1019.

53. A laundry list of afflictions appears in Platt and Labate, *Heroin*, 80-96.

54. Judson, *Heroin*, 84.

55. Kaplan, *Hardest*, 178; Elmer Gardner comments quoted in Judson, *Heroin*, 148-49.

56. Lindesmith, *Addict*, 206, 210; Tu, "Statistical," 9-11.

57. Lindesmith, *Addict*, 210.

58. N. Macleod interview, Nov. 5, 1903, Senate Doc. 265, *Use*, 79.

59. Described in Kolb, *Drug*, 119. See also Tu, "Statistical," 9-11. Hess (*Chasing*, 67, 93-94) found the same type of usage in modern Hong Kong. Musto and Ramos ("Follow-Up," 1076) demonstrate similar afflictions among clients of the New Haven morphine maintenance clinic.

60. Kolb, *Drug*, 120.

61. Kaplan, *Hardest*, 178, citing Stimson, *Heroin*, 7.

62. Stimson, *Heroin*, 7. "Medical supervision" does not mean that medical advice is followed. Laurie (*Drugs*, 53) reports from Great Britain, "It is part of the daring never to sterilize the needles or to wash out the [hypodermic] barrels." The mere fact that clinic staff stress the importance of sterile technique may be a motivation to avoid it, in expression of contempt for "straight" values. See also Cuskey, Klein, and Krasner, *Drug*, 130; Bejerot, *Addiction*, 154.

63. Glatt et al., *Drug*, 95-96. See also Plant, *Drugtakers*, 48, 232; Glatt et al., *Drug*, 42, 68-69.

64. Expiration occurs so fast that a corpse may still have the needle sticking in its arm. Such deaths are described as "heroin overdose" but the blame may be misplaced. Postmortem exams show normal dose amounts. Moreover, the rapid speed of death is inconsistent with pharmacological properties of heroin. People do not keel over after taking too much heroin; they and their friends have plenty of time to notice something amiss and seek aid. Habituated users can survive doses of fantastic size. During a documented experiment, an addict took 9 times the usual dose of intravenous morphine without problem (Light and Torrance, "Opium," 379, 394). In the same study, in a 2½ hour period an addict received 1,950 mg of clinical quality morphine without ill effect—many times the amount that typical New York City addicts might inject in a 24-hour period (ibid., 379). A Public Health Service doctor wrote about an addict who took almost 3,900 mg of morphine daily, and as much as 1,080 mg of oral heroin over a 5-hour period (Kolb, *Drug*, 98). Autopsy results are inconsistent with opiate action: rapid pulmonary edema, often accompanied by cerebral edema. These deaths did not turn up until dealers began to adulterate heroin supplies with quinine, and until users commonly began to inject heroin while drunk on alcohol (Brecher and Consumer Reports, *Licit*, 110-12). Adulterants cannot be the only factor because sudden deaths are reported among British addicts using pure heroin (Kaplan, *Hardest*, 130; the reports, however, may ignore that many British addicts supplement pure supplies with adulterated black market heroin), and no harm comes to colleagues of American victims who use the victim's supply. Safe sharing argues against the suspicion that police undercover agents have poisoned the supplies (King, *Drug*, 341-42). Heroin addicts are notorious polydrug abusers, however, taking assorted substances simultaneously. Little attention has been paid to possible interactions even though they might be potent, as demonstrated by the demise of someone who uses liquor to wash down a "safe" dose of sleeping pills. Another theory emphasizes the importance of setting, and argues that a routine dose can be lethal if the user takes it in an environment different from usual surroundings (Siegel et al., "Heroin," 436-37). Nearly all the deaths, however, occur among heroin addicts rather than occasional users. An addict takes the drug in so many different circumstances that there may be no "usual surroundings." Moreover, addicts who took massive amounts of morphine in clinical experiments certainly did so in surroundings that differed from street use. Edward Brecher searched for studies testing theories on the cause of sudden expiration following heroin injection. He found none (Brecher

and Consumer Reports, *Licit*, 108, 114). Twenty years later I looked for studies that may have appeared after Brecher's search. I found only two, both published in 1970 (Pickett, "Acute," 145-46; "Cerebral," 967). Given the frequency with which "heroin overdose" is decried as a terrible hazard, and given the number of persons dropping dead for no apparent reason, the paucity of research is remarkable. Perhaps residents of skid row are considered expendable, just as homosexual men were considered expendable when AIDS appeared among them first.

65. Pfeffer and Ruble, "Chronic," 665-72; Goodman and Gilman, *Pharmacological* 2nd ed., 242; Kolb, *Drug*, 104-5, 109, 120; Rounsaville et al., "Neuropsychological," 209-16; Cohen, "Urge, I," 213; Cohen, "Urge, II," 335-53; Craig, "Personality," 235-37.

66. Zinberg and Robertson, *Drugs*, 48.

67. Vaillant, "12-Year," 604-7.

68. "Without laboratory technics, even skilled clinicians cannot distinguish between patients maintained on methadone and patients who are drug free" (Jaffe, "Drug Addiction and Drug Abuse," in Goodman and Gilman, *Pharmacological* 6th ed., 547).

69. Daly, "[Letter]," 190; Ahlborn, "Heroine," 235; Morgan, *Yesterday's*, 28-29; Szasz, *Ceremonial*, 193; King, *Drug*, 17; Lennard et al., "[Letter]," 1078-79.

70. Ahlborn, "Heroine," 235; Rublowsky, *Stoned*, 130; Duster, *Legislation*, 8; Lennard et al., "[Letter]," 1078-79; Szasz, *Ceremonial*, 12; Taylor, Chambers, and Bowling, "Addiction," 33-34.

71. Spotts and Shontz, *Lifestyles* (National Institute on Drug Abuse), 562-63; Nadelmann, "Drug," 941.

72. Dr. William Stewart Halsted, whose opiate addiction has been mentioned, used cocaine in his earlier years. Grinspoon and Bakalar (*Cocaine*, 32) offer this example of writing that Halsted apparently did while using cocaine to heighten his intellect (Halsted, "Practical," 294):

> Neither indifferent as to which of how many possibilities may best explain, nor yet at a loss to comprehend, why surgeons have, and that so many, quite without discredit, could have exhibited scarcely any interest in what, as a local anaesthetic, had been supposed, if not declared, by most so very sure to prove, especially to them, attractive, still I do not think that this circumstance, or some sense of obligation to rescue fragmentary reputation for surgeons rather than the belief that an opportunity existed for assisting others to an appreciable extent, induced me, several months ago, to write on the subject in hand the greater part of a somewhat comprehensive paper, which poor health disinclined me to complete.

I personally observed the performance of a highly trained worker in a scientific profession who claimed to be using cocaine. The person's self-confidence swelled but, alas, was not accompanied by improved judgment. For example, the person often skipped writing down data and instead depended on memory—a memory that seemed to grow ever worse. Admittedly such a decline is not inevitable, but watching the descent of a personal acquaintance can leave a vivid impresison.

73. Siegel, *Intoxication*, 309-10; Bower, "Drugs," 393.

74. Siegel, *Intoxication*, 309-10; Bower, "Drugs," 393.

75. Siegel, *Intoxication*, 182-83.

76. Ibid., 309-10.

77. Siegel, "Cocaine," 321-22.

78. Smart, " 'Crack,' " 1316-17.

79. Van Dyke et al., "Cocaine," 271.

80. Van Dyke and Byck, "Cocaine," 128; Fischman and Schuster, "Cocaine," 243.

81. Van Dyke and Byck, "Cocaine," 139; Muntaner et al., "Placebo," 282; Daniel Lazare, "The Drug Trade Obeys the Laws of Commerce," *In These Times*, September 6-12, 1989, p. 3.

82. Brown and Middlefell, "Fifty-Five," 946.

83. Morley, "What," 12-13; "Attitude," 4, 40; Johnston, O'Malley, and Bachman, *Drug* (National Institute on Drug Abuse), 6, 39; Siegel, *Intoxication*, 309-10. See also Raymond, "Researchers," A10.

84. A laundry list of afflictions can be found in Allen, "Modes of Use, Precursors, and Indicators of Cocaine Abuse" in Allen, *Cocaine*, 17-19.

85. Grinspoon and Bakalar, *Cocaine*, 144.

86. Weil, *Natural*, 47.

87. Brown and Middlefell, "Fifty-Five," 946.

88. Siegel, *Intoxication*, 311.

89. Van Dyke and Byck, "Cocaine," 141.

90. Carr and Meyers, "Marijuana and Cocaine: The Process of Change in Drug Policy" in Drug Abuse Council, *Facts*, 184; Gosselin, Smith, and Hodge, *Clinical*, III-115. The Drug Abuse Warning Network collects data about drug-related deaths around the United States. DAWN does not pick up every fatality, and its statistical base changes from year to year, so it cannot be used to track the amount of drug use. But it does include big cities, and therefore gives a rough idea about the size of a problem. Although traces of cocaine were found in 604 bodies in 1984 (National Institute on Drug Abuse, *DAWN* (1984): 52), those traces do not mean that cocaine was a factor in a particular death, let alone the cause. Drug interactions, however, are a factor. For example, tricyclic antidepressants boost cocaine effects (Frank, Pommering, and Nitz, "Interactive," 1-4). If a fatality occurs, to which drug should it be ascribed? In 1986 cocaine was found in 1,092 bodies, but 81 percent of those corpses contained other drugs as well (National Institute on Drug Abuse, *DAWN* (1986): iv-v, 53). The population of the United States was about 240 million.

91. Carr and Meyers, "Marijuana and Cocaine: The Process of Change in Drug Policy," in Drug Abuse Council, *Facts*, 184-88; Newcomb, Bentler, and Fahy, "Cocaine," 1167.

92. Allen, "Modes of Use, Precursors, and Indicators of Cocaine Abuse," in Allen, *Cocaine*, 23-24.

93. "Users Tell of a Cocaine 'Honeymoon,' " *Kansas City Star*, May 9, 1989, pp. 1A, 4A.

94. Gawin and Kleber, "Abstinence," 107-13.

95. Kleber and Gawin, "In," 298.

96. Kleber, "Cocaine," 1364.

97. Gawin and Kleber, "Abstinence," 112.

98. Kleber and Gawin, "In," 298.

99. For skeptical authorities see chapter 6, note 138. A friendly treatment can be found in Jerome H. Jaffe, "Drug Addiction and Drug Abuse," in Goodman and Gilman, *Pharmacological* 7th ed., 554. Brower and Paredes report physical cocaine withdrawal symptoms such as muscle pain, chills, twitching, and tremors ("Cocaine," 297), but their report has not been embraced by the scientific community.

100. *Diagnostic,* 166-68.

101. Ibid., 179.

102. Ibid.

103. Kleber, "Epidemic," 1364.

104. Oswald, "Cocaine," 139.

105. Miller, Gold, and Millman, "Cocaine," 393.

106. Kleber, "Epidemic," 1364.

107. Ibid.; Gawin and Kleber, "Evolving," 129.

108. Cocaine abuse may cause unquestionable brain damage such as intracranial bleeding and aneurysms, although research that reports this fails to provide previous medical and drug use histories (Lowenstein et al., "Acute," 841-46), so we do not know brain condition before cocaine abuse began. Nonetheless, damage caused by a drug is not evidence of resonance or physical dependence.

109. Miller, Gold, and Millman, "Cocaine," 393.

110. Gawin and Kleber, "Evolving," 129.

111. Grinspoon and Bakalar, *Cocaine,* 183; Beaubrun, "Cocaine Update," in Allen, *Cocaine,* 169; Post and Rose, "Increasing," 731-32; Post and Kopanda, "Cocaine . . . Tolerance," 409-10; Post and Kopanda, "Cocaine . . . Psychosis," 627-34.

112. Fischman, "Acute," 677-82; Ambre et al., "Acute," 1-8. Some workers resolve the sensitization/tolerance contradiction by concluding that both occur, that sensitization develops for some effects and tolerance for others (Grabowski and Dworkin, "Cocaine," 1081).

113. Nadelmann, "Drug," 944; Graham et al., "Pregnancy," 143; Newcomb, Bentler, and Fahy, "Cocaine," 1167; Grabowski and Dworkin, "Cocaine," 1077.

114. Summarized in Smith, "Cocaine," 117.

115. Summarized in Erickson et al., *Steel,* 136-37.

116. Summarized in ibid., 54.

117. Ibid., 76, 118. Cocaine might be offered on social occasions, so even without a personal cache a user could still take a dose.

118. Kandel and Raveis, "Cessation," 109-16.

119. Siegel, "Changing Patterns of Cocaine Use: Longitudinal Observations, Consequences, and Treatment," in Grabowski, *Cocaine* (National Institute on Drug Abuse), 106-7.

120. Nadelmann, "Drug," 944.

121. Ibid. Tobacco smokers are generally considered to be compulsive users of nicotine, but not all nicotine addicts are compulsive users, and not all users are addicts. See Shiffman, "Tobacco," 539-47.

122. Murphy, Reinarman, and Waldorf, "11-Year," 427-36.

123. Craig Reinarman, quoted in Raymond, "Researchers," A10.

124. Grinspoon and Bakalar, *Cocaine*, 143. See also Wise, "Neural Mechanisms of the Reinforcing Action of Cocaine," in Grabowski, ed., *Cocaine* (National Institute on Drug Abuse), 27.

125. David F. Allen, "Modes of Use, Precursors, and Indicators of Cocaine Abuse," in Allen, *Cocaine*, 21.

126. Allen, "Cocaine Addiction: A Socio-Ethical Perspective," in ibid., 208.

127. Washton, "Cocaine: Drug Epidemic of the '80's," in ibid., 52.

128. A study of 169 single-vehicle fatalities revealed 0.6 percent of drivers with cocaine or a metabolite in the blood, but 66.9 percent with an alcohol level high enough to make them legally intoxicated—let alone the additional percentage that had alcohol at a lower level (Owens, McBay, and Cook, "Use," 372-79). Combining the cocaine and alcohol categories grossly inflates the apparent use of cocaine.

129. Washton, "Cocaine: Drug Epidemic of the '80's," in Allen, *Cocaine*, 55.

130. Weil, *Natural*, 74-75.

131. Weil, Zinberg, and Nelsen, "Clinical," 1234-42.

132. See, for example, Murray, "Marijuana's," 29, 40-41; Brandt and Doyle, "Concept," 559; Culver and King, "Neuropsychological," 707; Brill and Christie, "Marihuana," 713; Wert and Raulin, "Chronic: I," 605-28 and Wert and Raulin, "Chronic: II," 629-42. A detailed and less benign review of physical effects can be found in Bernstein, "Medical Consequences of Marihuana Use," in Mello, *Advances*, 255-82. The problems cited are, however, subject to the same qualifications found in other lists of illicit drug hazards. For example, pulmonary problems attributed to marijuana seem related more to the method of administration (smoking) than to the drug itself—like blaming heroin for hepatitis spread by dirty hypodermic needles. Some "potential hazards" are speculative extrapolations on the meaning of data. Such speculation is useful and responsible, but is not the same as proven fact. Bernstein rightly concludes (p. 279) that "major neurological signs and symptoms have not been associated with cannabis use." Studies that suggest otherwise have met heavy criticism. Jaffe ("Drug Addiction and Drug Abuse," in Goodman and Gilman, *Pharmacological* 7th ed., 560) finds "no evidence to suggest that any personality changes are due to irreversible organic brain damage." A general critique of marijuana hazard research is presented by Ungerleider and Andrysiak, "Bias," 1535-85. The effect of setting on research results is examined by Stark-Adamec, Adamec, and Phil, "Experimenter," 203.

133. A good anthology of classic reports is David Soloman, ed., *The Marihuana Papers* (Indianapolis: Bobbs-Merrill, 1966). The classics are *The Indian Hemp Drugs Commission Report* (summary volume reprinted in 1969 by Jefferson Press of Silver Springs, Md.); J. F. Siler et al., "Mariajuana Smoking in Panama," *Military Surgeon*

73 (1933): 269-80; and the LaGuardia Committee Report (reprinted in *The Marihuana Papers*). Later highly regarded investigations include the Wootton Report (Advisory Committee on Drug Dependence, *Cannabis* (London: HMSO, 1968); Commission of Inquiry into the Non-Medical Use of Drugs, *Le Dain Commission Interim Report* (Toronto, Canada: Addiction Research Foundation of Ontario, 1970); and National Commission on Marihuana and Drug Abuse, *Marihuana: A Signal of Misunderstanding* (Washington, D.C.: GPO, 1972, SuDoc Y3.M33/2:2MM33, plus appendix volumes).

134. Weil, *Natural*, 96; the placebo characterization is also found in research cited by Louria, *Overcoming*, 38. Murray ("Marijuana's," 29) reports, "Frequent users seemed more likely to respond to cues of familiar taste and smell (i.e., psychological factors) than to the THC content [marijuana's psychoactive chemical] of the cigarettes. Response variability seemed to be a function of users' expectations and their previous experience with marijuana."

135. Trivial effects are effects nonetheless and may be less trivial in special circumstances. For example, marijuana may be useful in treating glaucoma and epilepsy, and in overcoming nausea caused by cancer chemotherapy. Marijuana was once accepted for a variety of medical uses (see Walton, *Marihuana*, 151-57). Laboratory preparations of high potency delta-9-tetrahydrocannabinol (THC) isomer may produce more pronounced effects than marijuana does, just as freebase cocaine may produce stronger effects than coca leaves. Discussion of marijuana, however, generally pertains to natural plant leaves, and their THC content is far lower than refined laboratory preparations.

136. Plant, *Drugtakers*, 30, 147.

137. One culture's use of marijuana to stimulate boisterousness was documented in the 1970s (Jones, "Cannabis," 329-32), a time when marijuana was decried for producing passivity among American users. See also Dreher, *Working*, and Carter, *Cannabis*, for examples of marijuana use very different from that found in the United States. The passivity and amotivation ascribed to marijuana has not been detected in double blind study when sociocultural factors are controlled (Page, "Amotivational," 266).

138. Zinberg and Robertson, *Drugs*, 47; Onyango, "Cannabis," 419-23. Case studies can be found of persons exhibiting psychotic behavior whle using marijuana, but no cause/effect relationship is apparent; such individuals typically have a variety of problems that encourage strange behavior. Even some researchers who contend that marijuana causes psychosis admit that the psychosis ends when marijuana intoxication ends, for example Ghodse, "Cannabis," 473-78.

139. Weil, *Natural*, 87.

140. Kagel, Battalio, and Miles, "Marihuana," 373, 390.

141. Sutton, "Effects," 442. See also Crancer et al., "Comparison," 851-54; McBay and Owens, "Marijuana and Driving," in Harris, *Problems 1980* (National Institute on Drug Abuse), 258-61; Owens, McBay, and Cook, "Use," 378. Contrary findings come from Klonoff, "Marijuana," 317-24 and Murray, "Marijuana's," 34-37. Yet Murray also notes that subjects report a placebo as more powerful than marijuana (29).

142. Weil, *Natural*, 47.

143. Ibid. See also Brecher and Consumer Reports, *Licit*, 395; Trebach, *Great*, 81; Mikuriya, "Historical," 905.

144. Goode, *Drugs*, 56, 59 n. 1.

145. National Institute on Drug Abuse, *DAWN* (1984): 52 and (1986): 55.

146. House Ways and Means Committee, *Taxation*, 24.

147. Senate Judiciary Committee, *Illicit*, 16.

148. Crothers, *Morphinism*, 304.

149. Rowell and Rowell, *On*, 72-74.

150. Towns, "Injury," 770.

151. Zinberg and Robertson, *Drugs*, 41.

152. Plant, *Drugtakers*, 194.

153. Lipscomb, "Drug," 1168.

154. Kozel, DuPont, and Brown, "Narcotics," 446. Only 2 percent of non-addicts used heroin; almost the entire 68 percent used no heroin.

155. Dreher, *Working*, 198.

156. Cuskey, Klein, and Krasner, *Drug*, 194; Cohen, "Multiple," 27-55.

157. Johnston, *Drugs*, 203; Duster, *Legislation*, 47. By the mid-1960s the chief federal drug law enforcer admitted that the progression to heroin was unobserved among college youths (Duster, *Legislation*, 46).

158. Trebach, *Great*, 83.

159. *Cannabis*, Report by the Advisory Committee on Drug Dependence (London: HMSO, 1968), 12-13, as cited in Zinberg and Robertson, *Drugs*, 141.

160. Some research results suggest just the opposite, that using marijuana can prevent a person from using more dangerous drugs (Trebach, *Great*, 84; Zinberg and Robertson, *Drugs*, 49).

161. Allen, "Modes of Use, Precursors, and Indicators of Cocaine Abuse," in Allen, *Cocaine*, 23.

162. Johnson, "Cocaine: The American Experience," in ibid., 35.

163. A different theory dismisses pharmacology and depends instead on economics, holding that drug selling leads a marijuana user into drugs of greater danger (Single and Kandel, "The Role of Buying and Selling in Illicit Drug Use," in Trebach, *Drugs*, 118, 127). Causality is uncertain here as well, because drug dealing can be an easy way of financing expensive habits, easier than finding a higher paying job. Using and dealing have a natural association, like salt and pepper, but neither necessarily causes the other.

164. Levine and Ludwig, "LSD," 318. See also McWilliams and Tuttle, "Long," 341, 349.

165. Bercher, *Licit*, 335; Strassman, "Adverse," 579; Jaffe, "Drug Addiction and Drug Abuse," in Goodman and Gilman, *Pharmacological* 7th ed., 565. Such a bold statement dares refutation by a single example. In 1977 a report surfaced of a decomposing body found a month after death, in which traces of LSD were discovered (Griggs and Ward, "LSD," 172-73). The report's authors speculated that LSD might have been the fatal agent. The year 1985 saw what was touted as the "first reported case of fatal poisoning by LSD" (Fysh et al., "Fatal," 109). The person in question

died after taking LSD, and a coroner's enquiry ruled LSD as the cause. The journal report tells how the presence of LSD was detected in the corpse but gives no evidence for the coroner's conclusion. Indeed the article says, "No fatal levels of LSD in humans are given in the [scientific] literature" (ibid., 112). Death whle experiencing LSD intoxication is extraordinarily rare but, unlike coroners, the scientific investigators of such a death did not confuse temporal sequence (LSD ingestion followed by death) with cause and effect (Malleson, "Acute," 230). Even if a confirmed LSD fatality someday appears, the fact of LSD's safety would remain true enough, given the amount of use the drug has seen over a period of decades.

166. Weil, *Natural*, 47.

167. McGlothlin, Arnold, and Freedman, "Organicity," 704-9; Chandler and Hartman, "Lysergic," 298; Strassman, "Adverse," 580, 587-88. Evidence exists that subtle impairment of color vision may occur, but the studied group used illicit "LSD" that lacked laboratory confirmation of chemistry, and apparently no data exists on the group members' color vision before the unknown drug was consumed (Abraham, "Chronic," 518-19). LSD users have taken longer than non-users in performing the psychological Trail Marking Test (Brandt and Doyle, "Concept," 559) but nonetheless "performed within normal limits" (Culver and King, "Neuropsychological," 707), leading one pair of analysts to conclude, "Inference about possible organic dysfunction cannot be drawn from these findings" (ibid.), a conclusion supported by other workers as well (Kornblith, "Multiple," 530).

168. Peele, *Love*, 266.

169. McGlothlin, Sparkes, and Arnold, "Effect," 1483-87; Lubs and Ruddle, "Chromosomal," 495-98. See also Malleson, "Acute," 230; Jaffe, "Drug Addiction and Drug Abuse," in Goodman and Gilman, *Pharmacological* 7th ed., 565; Lenz and Feldmann, "Unilateral," 269; Long, "Does," 75-90; Shepard, "Teratogenic Drugs and Therapeutic Agents," in Shirkey, *Pediatric*, 103; Shepard, *Catalog*, p. 379, entry 1119. The McGlothlin, Sparkes, and Arnold study found ambiguous evidence that LSD users may have a higher spontaneous abortion rate than non-users, but the finding was intertwined with variables such as adulteration and medical versus nonmedical use.

170. Cohen, "Lysergic," 30-40. Masters and Houston report similar findings in their research (*Varieties*, 320 n. 23). Brecher and Consumer Reports (*Licit*, 360-61) summarize an unpublished British report with similar data. See also Chandler and Hartmen, "Lysergic," 298; Malleson, "Acute," 230; Jaffe, "Drug Addiction and Drug Abuse," in Goodman and Gilman, *Pharmacological* 7th ed., 564.

171. Cohen, "Lysergic," 33-34; Baker, "Use," 1202; Masters and Houston, *Varieties*, 320 n. 23; Brecher and Consumer Reports, *Licit*, 360-61. See also Chandler and Hartman, "Lysergic," 297; Malleson, "Acute," 229.

172. Brecher and Consumer Reports, *Licit*, 378; Weil, *Natural*, 61-62. From a physical standpoint, electroencephalograms made during flashbacks are normal (Blumenfeld, "Flashback," 41).

173. McGlothlin and Arnold, "LSD," 46. See also Strassman, "Adverse," 590; Abraham, "Visual," 888.

174. McGlothlin and Arnold, "LSD," 46. Brecher and Consumer Reports (*Licit*, 378) note that the Cohen study cited in these pages, conducted before LSD flashback received wide news media publicity, failed to yield a single flashback report among 5,000 LSD and mescaline users.

175. Weil, *Natural*, 96; Blumenfeld, "Flashback," 41; Yager, Crumptom, and Rubenstein, "Flashbacks," 860; Murray, "Marijuana's," 39-40; Stanton, Mintz, and Franklin, "Drug," 66. Some workers, however, are skeptical that marijuana flashbacks occur (Tennant and Groesbeck, "Psychiatric," 134; Brown and Stickgold, "Marijuana," 275-83.

176. McGlothlin and Arnold, "LSD," 49. Strassman, "Acute," 589; Naditch and Fenwick, "LSD," 352, 355, 357. The increase may not be linear (twice the LSD leading to twice the frequency of flashback) but may involve plateaus in which more use does not increase flashback frequency for a while (Abraham, "Visual," 888-89).

177. Naditch and Fenwick, "LSD," 358. See also Smith and Seymour, "Dream," 300.

178. McGlothlin and Arnold, "LSD," 43, 45; Jacobson and Zinberg, *Social*, 34.

179. McGlothin and Arnold, "LSD," 49; Jaffe, "Drug Addiction and Drug Abuse," in Goodman and Gilman, *Pharmacological* 7th ed., 564.

180. Brecher and Consumer Reports, *Licit*, 382-84; Griffiths, Bigelow, and Henningfield, "Similarities in Animal and Human Drug-Taking Behavior," in Mello, *Advances*, 15; Inciardi, *War*, 30-31; McGlothlin and Arnold, "LSD," 48-49; Jaffe, "Drug Addiction and Drug Abuse," in Goodman and Gilman, *Pharmacological* 7th ed., 565.

CHAPTER 2

1. A Georgia school teacher was fired because her *husband* used marijuana (*Kansas City Times*, Sept. 1, 1989, p. A2). Helmer (*Drugs*, 123) cites work that documents the reluctance of non-criminal middle class drug users to discuss their use.

2. Twenty-five pages of theories about heroin addiction can be found in Platt and Labate (*Heroin*, 99-125). And that is just for heroin.

3. Oswald, "Personal," 438; Kolb, *Drug*, 5 n. A study of hundreds of patients who received daily medical doses of heroin for months found none who developed the morbid craving associated with addiction even though some developed physical resonance (Twycross, "Clinical," 196-97). Similar studies involving thousands of patients are summarized in Melzack, "Tragedy," 30, 33.

4. Michael H. Beaubrun, "Cocaine Update," in Allen, *Cocaine*, 169.

5. "The underlying biomedical mechanism of addiction has yet to be found" (Marlott and Fromme, "Metaphors," 13).

6. Weil, *Natural*, 58. A plausible theory of physical mechanism holds that the more a drug is used, the faster it is metabolized, but such a theory fails to explain why many users do not increase their doses. Even proponents of the theory admit a psychological component in tolerance (Jaffe, "Drug Addiction and Drug Abuse," in Goodman and Gilman, *Pharmacological* 7th ed., 535-36).

7. Trebach, *Heroin*, 105; see also Twycross, "Clinical," 184-98.

8. Brown and Middlefell, "Fifty-Five," 946; see also Siegel, *Intoxication*, 309-10.

9. Bakalar and Grinspoon, *Drug*, 37; Weil, *Natural*, 59.

10. Weil, *Natural*, 58; Hinson and Siegel, "Nonpharmacological," 495-502; Twycross, "Clinical," 184-98; Melzack, "Tragedy," 30, 33. See also Zinberg and Lewis, "Narcotic," 992 and Zinberg, Harding, and Apsler, "What," 28 and Zinberg and Jacobson, "Natural," 38 for a case study of a morphine user who held the dose steady for at least a dozen years.

11. Andrew Weil reports that

all persons I met who were visibly dependent on drugs, whose lives were ruled by their habits, thought about drugs in a particular way. They were convinced that the experiences they enjoyed came in the joints of marijuana, tabs of acid, or shots of heroin, and they saw no other way of getting them. There is no doubt in my mind that drug dependence is essentially an error of thinking, not a pharmacological or biochemical phenomenon, even though it may be accompanied by changes in the physical body.

(Weil, *Natural*, 69. See also Hinson and Siegel, "Nonpharmacological," 495; Macrae, Scoles, and Shephard, "Contribution," 371-80.) A follow-up study of almost 12,000 persons who received opioids in medical settings found 4 drug abusers (Melzack, "Tragedy," 30). Another follow-up of 10,000 patients who steadily received opioids found 22 drug abusers afterwards, and all were abusers before receiving the medical opioids (ibid.). Yet another study of 38 patients who received opioids for up to 7 years had similar findings (ibid., 33). Addiction depends on the purpose for which a drug is used, not on the chemistry of a drug.

12. Chein et al., *Road*, 6, 237.

13. Grinspoon and Bakalar, *Cocaine*, 190.

14. Brecher and Consumer Reports, *Licit*, 13-14.

15. *Kansas City Star*, June 20, 1989, p. 6C. This advertisement, ironically entitled "Cocaine Lies," is from a series produced by "Partnership for a Drug-Free America," appearing in newspapers and magazines around the country.

16. Blachly, *Seduction*, 29-30.

17. Bakalar and Grinspoon, *Drug*, 40.

18. Falk, "The Place of Adjunctive Behavior in Drug Abuse Research," in Thompson and Johanson, *Behavioral* (National Institute on Drug Abuse), 272-73.

19. Grinspoon and Bakalar, "Adverse," 128.

20. The "Cocaine Lies" ad refers to "severe *physical* withdrawal symptoms commonly associated with heroin—delirium, muscle-cramps, and convulsions." Delirium and convulsions may indeed be commonly associated with heroin withdrawal in the public mind, but are almost unheard of medically. With the words "monkeys won't smoke tobacco or marijuana," the ad invalidates its implication that monkey experiments are totally applicable to humans. Moreover, the ad's claim about monkeys is incorrect—they will smoke tobacco (Siegel, *Intoxication*, 87-89), as will chimpanzees. Chimps will also smoke marijuana (ibid., 150-51).

Although we cannot be sure, references to a monkey who pressed a bar 12,800 times for cocaine probably refer to work done at the University of Michigan in the

1960s. Each monkey was restrained inside a cubicle measuring 36 inches by 30 inches by 26 inches, with a catheter surgically implanted in the monkey's jugular vein for drug delivery (Deneau, Yanagita, and Seevers, "Self," 32, 35). The experiment which produced 12,800 bar pressings was a "progressive ratio" exercise, meaning that the monkey was trained to double and redouble its work for the same reward. After teaching the monkey to press the cocaine bar 100 times for a reward, the number of pressings was doubled to 200, etc. (Yanagita, "Experimental," 57-64). In this experiment the choice was not between cocaine or food, but rather between cocaine or nothing. Such a test does not measure inherent craving for cocaine, but instead measures whether a monkey will work harder for cocaine than for other rewards offered in the same circumstances. In one 24-hour period the monkey pressed the bar 12,800 times for a cocaine dose. The monkey did not continually work that hard for cocaine for days on end. An important detail, normally omitted from citations of this experiment, was that the cubicle contained *two* bars to press, one hooked to the cocaine injection apparatus and one that was a dummy. This setup allows us to judge whether the monkey was pressing a bar for the reward, or just pressing any available bar out of boredom or some other reason. The smaller the difference in the number of times each bar was pressed, the smaller the likelihood that the monkey sought the reward. The researchers did not give comparative figures for the progressive ratio experiment, but "during periods of high [cocaine] drug intake all monkeys pressed the inactive lever as frequently as the active lever" (Deneau, Yanagita, and Seevers, "Self," 41).

21. Alexander Coambs, and Hadaway, "Effect," 175-178; Schenk, "Cocaine," 227-31.

22. Siegel, *Intoxication*, 176-78, 182-83.

23. Griffiths, Bigelow, and Henningfield, "Similarities in Animal and Human Drug-Taking Behavior," in Mello, *Advances*, 5-7.

24. Arntzen, "Psychological," 424-25; Rublowsky, *Stoned*, 88.

25. Brecher and Consumer Reports, *Licit*, 227 n.; Rublowsky, *Stoned*, 88.

26. Bellis, *Heroin*, 143.

27. Morgan, *Drugs*, 129; Zinberg and Robertson, *Drugs*, 60; Zinberg and Lewis, "Narcotic: Spectrum," 989-93; Isbell and Fraser, "Addiction," 355-57, 390; Kolb, *Drug*, 93-116; Lasagna, von Felsinger, and Beecher, "Drug-Induced," 1113-15.

28. Until the early twentieth century drug addiction was an upper and middle class phenomenon, but after muckrakers and law enforcement authorities targeted drug abuse, prevalence switched to lower classes. Because millions of personalities did not change, one might see the demographic shift as evidence against psychological addiction (Duster, *Legislation*, 156). Actually the shift illustrates the influence of setting on social customs, and tells us nothing about the mechanism of addiction.

29. Platt and Labate, *Heroin*, 192, 251; Rublowsky, *Stoned*, 88, 189-90.

30. Chein et al., *Road*, 14.

31. Vinar, "Dependence," 1190. Earlier examples are given by Crothers, *Morphinism*, 34-37.

32. Biernacki, *Pathways*, 25; Kolb, *Drug*, 44-45; Plant, *Drugtakers*, 140.

33. Quoted in Biernacki, *Pathways*, 127.

34. Morgan, *Drugs*, 133.

35. Grim examples can be found in O'Donnell, *Narcotics* (U.S. Public Health Service). Case 193 was "confined to a wheel chair in his home" and unable to roam in a search for narcotics even though "he still begged for drugs constantly" (ibid., 205). Case 183 was also confined to a wheelchair and remained abstinent from completion of his "cure" until his death. "His last words were a request for morphine" (ibid., 205).

36. Brecher and Consumer Reports, *Licit*, 13-14.

37. Chein et al., *Road*, 364; Blachly, *Seduction*, 37; Kolb, *Drug*, 83-84; Boyle and Brunswick, "What," 109.

38. Blachly, *Seduction*, 38, 43. Some Canadian addicts who emigrated to England for "legal heroin" apparently returned to their homeland because they missed the old hustle (Spear and Glatt, "Influence," 141-49).

39. Cuskey and Edington, "Drug Abuse as Self-Destructive Behavior," in Roberts, *Self*, 139.

40. Platt and Labate, *Heroin*, 107; Restak, *Mind*, 118; Schroeder, *Politics*, 76.

41. Kaplan, *Hardest*, 10, 43-46; Blachly, *Seduction*, 30; Childress, "Extinction of Conditioned Responses in Abstinent Cocaine or Opioid Users," in Harris, *Problems 1986* (National Institute on Drug Abuse), 189-95; Hinson and Siegel, "Nonpharmacological," 496-502; Stewart, De Wit, and Eikelboom, "role," 251-68.

42. Persistent craving may have more to do with conditioning than pharmacology. Behavior associated with drug abuse, such as violence, can also derive from psychological conditioning. See Falk, "The Place of Adjunctive Behavior in Drug Abuse Research," in Thompson and Johanson, *Behavioral* (National Institute on Drug Abuse), 276.

43. Bakalar and Grinspoon, *Drug*, 135; Hunt and Chambers, *Heroin*, 117; Kaplan, *Hardest*, 33-34; King, *Drug*, 234; Scher, "The Impact of the Drug Abuser on the Work Organization," in Scher, *Drug*, 11; Leader-Elliott, "Heroin," 136.

44. Chein et al., *Road*, 22-23, 159; Johnson et al., *Taking*, 2; Judson, *Heroin*, 80; Louria, *Overcoming*, 84; Schroeder, *Politics*, 72-73; Chein and Rosenfeld, "Juvenile," 54; Kandel, "Convergences in Prospective Longitudinal Surveys of Drug Use in Normal Populations," in Kandel, *Longitudinal*, 16. Someone who does not use heroin enough to develop resonance is not an addict. In the previous chapter we noted the fortitude and industriousness required to develop resonance, factors which in themselves argue that most heroin users would be chippers.

45. Hunt and Chambers, *Heroin*, 117; Powell, "Pilot," 586-94; Zinberg, "Nonaddictive Opiate Use," in Weissman and DuPont, *Criminal*, 5-11; Jacobson and Zinberg, *Social*, 15. Being "like anyone else" does not mean that all chippers are saintly. The chipper population has a spread of personal characteristics; some members may be Good Samaritans, others vicious thugs.

46. Erickson et al., *Steel*, 118.

47. Weil, *Natural*, 100-1.

48. Peele, *Love*, 40. See also Blum, "A Background History of Drugs," in Blum et al., *Society*, 10.

49. Blum and Blum, "A Cultural Case Study," in Blum et al., *Society*, 189.

50. Ibid., 227.

51. Szasz, *Ceremonial*, 9, 169.

52. Cultural bias can even be found in the drug abuse definition used by the World Health Organization (Zinberg, Harding, and Apsler, "What," 9, 19-26).

53. This is true around the world. See Viani et al., "Drug," 145-51 (Italy) and Winslow, "Drug," 531-40 (Denmark) and Comitas, "The Social Nexus of *Ganja* in Jamaica," in Rubin, *Cannabis*, 119-32. Dreher (*Working*, 200) notes, "It may not be accurate . . . to define a group in terms of its drug-using aspects alone. If persons convene primarily to smoke marihuana, why are such groupings often structured along age, class, occupational, or ethnic dimensions?" In the United States, Barrett and James-Cairns conclude, "Despite high levels of [marijuana] drug use, the most frequent reason for group participation was friendship, and diverse social activities occurred in the group." The "role of marijuana in the group appears to be secondary to the fulfillment of interpersonal needs" ("Social," 677, 687).

54. Blachly, *Seduction*, 39; Duster, *Legislation*, 66; Johnson, "cocaine: The American Experience." in Allen, *Cocaine*, 36; Washton, "Cocaine: Drug Epidemic of the '80's," in Allen *Cocaine*, 45; Helmer, *Drugs*, 148-49; Platt and Labate, *Heroin*, 147-48, 150-53, 165-69. Some findings reported in Platt and Labate demonstrate invalid variables. For example, when various researchers conclude that the intelligence of drug addicts is lower, higher, and the same as the general population, that means intelligence has nothing to do with addiction. "No single variable of personality or circumstances predicts who will become addicted" (Bakalar and Grinspoon, *Drug*, 43). The only thing that distinguishes drug addicts from the general population is drug addiction; just as the only thing that distinguishes blue-eyed people is eye color. Addicts and blue-eyed people are the same sort of persons. "Drug users in New York City may be very different from those in Miami, Chicago, or San Francisco. In fact, drug users and addicts may differ considerably in various locations within the same city" (Biernacki, *Pathways*, 194). If there is no specific user type, users are same as the general population. Investigators in England have made similar findings (Judson, *Heroin*, 78; Beckett and Lodge, "Aspects," 29-36). Some geographical areas have a higher rate of drug use than others, but the statistical ability to predict the level of drug use in a neighborhood is not the same as being able to predict which individuals use drugs.

55. Weil, *Natural*, 58. See also Platt and Labate, *Heroin*, 171; Biernacki, *Pathways*, 6, 36; Stephen Waldron statement and testimony, House Select Committee on Crime, *Improvement*, 287, 291; Platt and Labate, *Heroin*, 171; Craig Reinarman comments in Raymond, "Researchers," A6-A7, A10-A11.

56. O'Donnell, *Narcotics* (U.S. Public Health Service), 56, 60, 79-80, 94-98, 204, 211, 214, 217, 223-33, 241; Zinberg and Lewis, "Narcotics: Spectrum," 989; White House, *Proceedings*, 305; Hentoff, *Doctor*, 43-44; Cuskey, Klein, and Krasner, *Drug-Trip*, 94-96.

57. Morhous, "Drug," 189. Similar sanitarium demographics were reported 50 years earlier ("Report," 473).

58. Stephen Waldron statement and testimony, House Select Committee on Crime, *Improvement*, 287, 291.

59. Helmer (*Drugs*, 122, 124) dissents from the preceding portrait of middle and upper class use; he argues that such users are an insignificant curiosity.

60. Chein et al., *Road*, 127; Peele, *Love*, 35; Bellis, *Heroin*, 6, 8. This has been found by researchers in other countries also. See Dreher, *Working*, 199-200; Carter, *Cannabis*, 153.

61. Kaplan, *Hardest*, 57; Morhous, "Drug," 189-90; Stephen Waldron statement and testimony, House Select Committee on Crime, *Improvement*, 287, 291.

62. Weil, *Natural*, x, 10; Rublowsky, *Stoned*, 186; Bower, "Drugs," 392-93.

63. Rublowsky, *Stoned*, 186-87; Siegel, *Intoxication*, 40, 51-56, 61-73.

64. Köhler, *Mentality*, 314-15.

65. Chein et al., *Road*, 6.

66. Peele, *Love*, 87; Rublowsky, *Stoned*, 128.

67. Judson, *Heroin*, 143-44; Weil, *Natural*, 108; Peele, *Love*, 59, 67.

68. Zinberg, "Nonaddictive Opiate Use," in Weissman and DuPont, *Criminal*, 15; Jacobson and Zinberg, *Social* 48, 50, 60.

69. Peele, *Love*, 59, 67.

70. Weil, *Natural*, 108.

71. Bakalar and Grinspoon, *Drug*, 47; Erickson et al., *Steel*, 118; Jacobson and Zinberg, *Social*, 8; Zinberg, Harding, and Apsler, "What," 13, 28.

72. Chein et al., *Road*, 12, 151-52; Duster, *Legislation*, 73, 181, 184; Jacobson and Zinberg, *Social*, 35, 42, 62-63; Brown et al., "In," 635-645; Bailey, "Heroin," 315.

73. Chein et al., *Road*, 152.

74. Erickson et al., *Steel*, 81.

75. Zinberg and Robertson, *Drugs*, 79. The phenomenon is documented overseas as well. See Ulff-Møller, "Drug," 105-11. Peer pressure also works in the opposite direction (Tobler, "Meta-Analysis," 537-67). The overwhelming disapproval that adolescents express about illicit drugs is a factor in the declining use.

76. Hunt and Chambers, *Heroin*, 124.

77. "Spread of drug use is associated with human misery, not with any intrinsic contagiousness. . . . There was only one census tract (a few square blocks) in New York City where as many as 10 per cent of the late-teen-aged boys became involved . . . with narcotics in the course of a four-year period. . . . Even if we were to interpret all of the cases in the tract as due to contagion, the degree of contagion is obviously limited" (Chein et al., *Road*, 328-29). Even proponents of the contagion model admit the mildness of contagion (Hunt and Chambers, *Heroin*, 25-26). Even in England, land of "legal heroin," mere availability does not cause addiction to spread. One study of a provincial town found almost no change in the number of addicts over a two-year period (Hutchins et al., "Two-Year," 129-40). Moreover, just as heroin use spreads as favorable information about it spreads, use declines as unfavor-

able information increases (Boyle and Brunswick, "What," 127). Perceptions of the drug, rather than its mere availability, determine the amount of use.

78. Kaplan, *Hardest*, 27-28; Lindesmith, *Addict*, 133; Hunt and Chambers, *Heroin*, 25-26; Brown et al., "In," 638, 643.

79. Hunt and Chambers, *Heroin*, 3.

80. Bellis, *Heroin*, 24; Chein et al., *Road*, 12; Eldridge, *Narcotics*, 28-29, 109; Erickson et al., *Steel*, 81; Platt and Labate, *Heroin*, 180; Schur, *Narcotic*, 142.

81. Johnson et al., *Taking*, 62; Duster, *Legislation*, 180-81.

82. Kaplan, *Hardest*, 86 n.68; Morley, "What," 12.

83. Kaplan, *Hardest*, 26.

84. Duster, *Legislation*, 73, 180-81, 183; Kaplan, *Hardest*, 27-29; Morgan, *Yesterday's*, 26; Platt and Labate, *Heroin*, 180-81; Brotman and Suffet, "The Concept of Prevention and Its Limitations," in Weissman and DuPont, *Criminal*, 182; Blum, "Normal Drug use," in Blum et al., *Society*, 260; Chein and Rosenfeld, "Juvenile," 58; Single and Kandel, "The Role of Buying and Selling in Illicit Drug Use," in Trebach, *Drugs*, 118, 127; Kandel, Kessler, and Margulies, "Antecedents of Adolescent Initiation into Stages of Drug Use: A Developmental Analysis," in Kandel, *Longitudinal*, 87, 89; Cuskey, Klein, and Krasner, *Drug*, passim; Jacobson and Zinberg, *Social*, 64; De Alarcón, "Spread," 17-22; Plant, *Drugtakers*, 75-78; Glatt et al., *Drug*, 48, 51, 57, 65-66, 76-77, 87. As some of these references show, the role of friends is seen internationally and is not just an American phenomenon.

85. Aitken, "The role of the Criminal Law in the Control of Drugs," in Vallance, *State*, 59.

86. Erickson et al., *Steel*, 81, 117. See also Allen, "Modes of Use, Precursors, and Indicators of Cocaine Abuse," in Allen, *Cocaine*, 23.

87. Chein et al., *Road*, 12. Despite alarmist rhetoric, few young novices start using heroin while on school grounds (Chein and Rosenfeld, "Juvenile," 58).

88. Blum, "Drugs, Behavior, and Crime," in Blum et al., *Society*, 285; Allen, "Modes of Use, Precursors, and Indicators of Cocaine Abuse," in Allen, *Cocaine*, 23.

89. Blum, "A History of Tobacco," in Blum et al., *Society*, 92-93.

90. Finestone, "Narcotics," 75-76; Gay, Senay, and Newmeyer, "Pseudo," 241-47.

91. Chein et al., *Road*, 240, 328-29. See also discussion and references in chapter 6.

92. Bakalar and Grinspoon, *Drug*, 45; Chein et al., *Road*, 161-62, 240, 380; Judson, *Heroin*, 71; Jacobson and Zinberg, *Social*, 46; Gay, Senay and Newmeyer, "Pseudo," 241-47. Tom Wolfe's book *The Electric Kool-Aid Acid Test* (New York: Farrar, Straus, and Giroux, 1968) documents the "acid head" lifestyle. One person told me that reading the book evoked the realization, "That's how I want to live." The person than consciously sought out drugs in order to take up that lifestyle; drugs did not cause the behavior.

93. Peele, *Love*, 66.

94. Ibid., 64-65.

95. Ibid., 60. Hospitalized addicts "not uncommonly would ask for more controls—not fewer" over their behavior (Vaillant, "12-Year," 735).

96. Bakalar and Grinspoon, *Drug,* 46; Kaplan, *Hardest,* 50; Platt and Labate, *Heroin,* 102; Vallance, "Introduction: Some Problems Stated," in Vallance, *State,* 21.

97. Blachly, *Seduction,* 38; Inciardi, *War,* 25.

98. Chein et al., *Road,* 192. In the late 1980s, California authorities made parents legally responsible for their children's crimes (Clarence Page, "Outlawing Parental Irresponsibility Is Cruel Charade," *Kansas City Times,* May 11, 1989, p. A15). A Georgia school board fired a teacher for failing to prevent her husband's use of marijuana ("School Won't Rehire Teacher Found Innocent in Drug Case," *Kansas City Times,* Sept. 1, 1989, p. A2). Thus do government officials promote addiction, absolving citizens (offspring and husbands) of responsibility for their actions.

99. O'Donnell, *Narcotics* (U.S. Public Health Service), 217; Kolb, *Drug,* 45. Said William James, "Religiomania is the best cure for dipsomania" (quoted in Grinspoon and Bakalar, "Can," 397.

100. Blum, "On the Presence of Demons," in Blum et al., *Society,* 336.

101. Dews, "Behavioral Effects of Drugs," in Farber and Wilson, *Conflict,* 151.

102. Blum, "Drugs, Behavior, and Crime," in Blum et al., *Society,* 289.

103. Chein et al., *Road,* 106. A summary of Chein's findings in this regard can be found in Schur, *Narcotic,* 237.

104. Platt and Labate, *Heroin,* 162. Given certain demographic information, one can predict higher drug abuse rates for some segments of a population than for others (Schroeder, *Politics,* 82-83). This statistical truth, however, does not mean that a "drug abuse personality" exists.

105. Newman, "We'll Make Them an Offer They Can't Refuse" in Weissman and DuPont, *Criminal,* 168-69. Newman's observation is supported by a Chicago study that was unable to find any change in the rate of new heroin use despite the work of drug abuse programs (Hunt and Chambers, *Heroin,* 125).

106. Peele, *Love,* passim.

107. Ibid., 19.

108. Chein et al., *Road,* 139-40; Jamieson, Glanz, and MacGregor, *Dealing,* 57-66, 85-91; Dorn and South, *Helping,* 124-25.

109. Corman et al., "Rehabilitation," 575.

110. Quoted in Johnson et al., *Taking,* 166.

111. Hunt and Chambers, *Heroin,* 94.

112. Johnson et al., *Taking,* 178.

113. Peele, *Love,* 18.

114. Ibid., 169.

115. Both narcotics and stimulants, depending on mode of administration, may induce euphoria. Such an effect can be attractive, but it is unclear whether most users ever feel such an effect. Of those who do, it is unclear that any but a small minority of psychotic hedonists attempt to maintain a continual euphoric state. Euphoria may be of small significance in the development of most addictions.

116. Bakalar and Grinspoon, *Drug,* 44; Chein et al., *Road,* 125; Kaplan, *Hardest,* 49-50, 54; Lindesmith, *Addict,* 283-284; Peele, *Love,* 68-70; Zinberg and Robertson, *Drugs,* 211.

117. Zinberg and Robertson, *Drugs*, 65, Firestone, "Cats," 3-13; Johnston, *Drugs*, 213.

118. Zinberg and Robertson, *Drugs*, 42-43; Zinberg and Lewis, "Narcotic: Spectrum," 989-93.

119. Blum, "A Background History of Drugs," in Blum et al., *Society*, 9; Blum, "A History of Tobacco," in ibid., 94; Room, "Evaluating the Effect of Drinking Laws on Drinking," in Ewing and Rouse, *Drinking*, 288.

120. Quoted from Blachly, *Seduction*, 4.

121. Chein et al., *Road*, 155.

122. Duster, *Legislation*, 70, 180; Kaplan, *Hardest*, 30; Brotman and Suffet, "The Concept of Prevention and Its Limitations," in Weissman and DuPont, *Criminal*, 186. The cited findings are for narcotics users, but could probably be duplicated for tobacco smokers.

123. Blachly, *Seduction*, 3.

124. Johnson, *Taking*, 181-182; Platt and Labate, *Heroin*, 319. This is seen in foreign countries as well (Plant, "Young" 31-43; Davidson, Etienne, and Piesset, "Medico-Social," 9-32).

125. Pokorny, "Self Destruction and the Automobile," in Roberts, *Self-Destructive*, 133.

126. Marc Hertzman and Emile A. Bendit, "Alcoholism and Destructive Behavior," in Roberts, *Self-Destructive*, 180.

127. Pokorny, "Self Destruction and the Automobile," in Roberts, *Self-Destructive*, 130.

128. Ibid., 133. See also Donovan, Marlatt, and Salzberg, "Drinking," 397, 416.

129. Zinberg, "Nonaddictive Opiate Use," in Weissman and DuPont, *Criminal*, 15.

130. Szasz, *Ceremonial*, 110.

131. O'Donnell, *Narcotics* (U.S. Public Health Service), 60.

132. Hunt and Chambers, *Heroin*, 127n; Inciardi, *War*, 158; Johnson et al., *Taking*, 3; Platt and Labate, *Heroin*, 184; Restak, *Mind*, 118. Polydrug abuse is typical of addicts worldwide, not just the United States. See Pierce James, "Changing," 119-34; Smart, " 'Crack,' " 1316-17; Bean, "Social," 80-86; Gordon, "Patterns," 205-10; Plant, "Young," 31-43; Davidson, Etienne, and Piesset, "Medico-Social," 9-32; Szewczyk and Jähnig, "Problem," 89-91; Leader-Elliott, "Heroin," 137; Dorn and South, *Helping*, 78, 86; Jamieson, Glanz, and MacGregor, *Dealing*, 20, 70-71.

133. Johnson et al., *Taking*, 31, 37.

134. A 1959 survey of 2,324 California penitentiary inmates found that 29 percent were drunk when arrested, and 60 percent had been drinking before committing a bold crime (Kaplan, *Marijuana*, 268). Another study showed about 75 percent of felons arrested in the act or soon afterward had alcohol in their system; similar results are found in other studies (Shupe, "Alcohol," 661-64; Guze et al., "Psychiatric," 512-21; Whalen and Lyons, "Medical," 497-502; Selling, "Rôle," 289-91; Smith, "Cocaine-Alcohol," 118; Nadelmann, "Drug," 941). The phenomenon is cross-cultural and has even been observed in Japan (Takemitsu Hemmi, "How

We Have Handled the Problem of Drug Abuse in Japan," in Sjöqvist and Tottie, *Abuse,* 151) and in communist Europe (Szewczyk and Jähnig, "Problem," 89-91).

135. One social worker said, "Quite a few people phone up here and say, 'I've been taking these black pills, what are they?' " (Dorn and South, *Helping,* 123). In contrast, opiate chippers indicate keen interest in positive identification of an ingested substance, preferring a known drug from a medical source rather than an unknown substance marketed as street "heroin" (Jacobson and Zinberg, *Social,* 59).

136. Johnson et al., *Taking,* 181-82.

137. Judson, *Heroin,* 84.

138. Bakalar and Grinspoon, *Drug,* 55.

139. Einstein and Garitano, "Treating," 324-25. Participants in a rock music concert or a religious revival meeting may act strangely, but American society leaves them alone and does not consider them crazy. Nor is such conduct portrayed as evidence of a sick nation. Contrast the American attitude toward behavior of mourners at the funeral of Iran's Ayatollah Khomeini.

140. Quoted in King, *Drug,* 38.

141. Szasz, *Ceremonial,* 7.

142. Bakalar and Grinspoon, *Drug,* 43.

143. Robinson v. California, 270 U.S. 660, 667 (1962).

144. American Child Health Association, *Physical,* 81-84. A subsidiary finding was that clinics consistently recommended radical intervention more often than private practitioners did (pp. 88-92), a finding perhaps relevant to understanding drug abuse clinic routines.

145. Council, "Narcotics," 976-82; "Editorial," 962.

146. Bakalar and Grinspoon, *Drug,* 128.

147. Chein et al., *Road,* 327. Chein's argument addresses the issue even though it predates the methadone clinic boom.

148. Bakalar and Grinspoon, *Drug,* 94; Bellis, *Heroin,* 43-44; Eldridge, *Narcotics,* 157.

149. Bellis, *Heroin,* 43-44, 105; Brecher and Consumer Reports, *Licit,* 162; Platt and Labate, *Heroin,* 298; Taylor, Chambers, and Bowling, "Addiction," 29-30.

150. Bellis, *Heroin,* 44, 46; Kaplan, *Hardest,* 215.

151. Bellis, *Heroin,* 45; Platt and Labate, *Heroin,* 261, 290; Goodman and Gilman, *Pharmacological,* 272; Martin, "From Morphine Maintenance to Methadone Maintenance, 1919-1975: The History, Promise, and Problems of Narcotic Clinics in the United States," in Trebach, *Drugs,* 12.

152. Martin et al., "Methadone," 286-95; Bellis, *Heroin,* 45; Platt and Labate, *Heroin,* 261. Methadone even relieves pain (Trebach, *Heroin,* 105), a classic opiate effect.

153. Quoted in Taylor, Chambers, and Bowling, "Addiction," 33. See also Taylor, Bowling, and Mason, "Methadone Iatrogenesis During Narcotic Substitution Therapy," in Singh, Miller, and Lal, *Drug,* 221; Trebach, *Heroin,* 200.

154. Jaffe, "Drug Addiction and Drug Abuse," in Goodman and Gilman, *Pharmacological* 7th ed., 544-45; Duster, *Legislation,* 48; Everson and Segal, "Trends in Nar-

cotics Use and Treatment in Toronto," in Trebach, *Drugs*, 99-100; Judson, *Heroin*, 70; Vogel, Isbell, and Chapman, "Present," 1022.

155. Bellis, *Heroin*, 60-64; Salim Muwakkil, " 'The Fast Food of Drugs' Poisons the Inner-City," *In These Times*, Feb. 1-7, 1989, p. 3; Salim Muwakkil, "Drugs as a Life(style) and Death Issue," *In These Times*, Sept. 27-Oct. 3, 1989, p. 7; Senay, "Methadone," 183.

156. Ahlborn, "Heroine," 235; Daly, "[Letter]," 190; Taylor, Chambers, and Bowling, "Addiction," 33-34; Lennard et al., "[Letter]," 1078-79.

157. Eldridge, *Narcotics*, 157.

158. Brecher and Consumer Reports, *Licit*, 162.

159. Kaplan, *Hardest*, 213; Platt and LaBate, *Heroin*, 63; Trebach, "Introduction" in Trebach, *Drugs*, 4; Blaine and Renault, *Rx* (National Institute on Drug Abuse).

160. Bellis, *Heroin*, 168; Duster, *Legislation*, 205; Peele, *Love*, 74.

161. Berger and Schwegler, "Voluntary," 1047.

162. This analysis is given in Bellis, *Heroin*, 106, 108-11.

163. Jasbir M. Singh, Melbra Diane Singh, and Miller, "Behavior Patterns of Addicts on a Methadone Substitution Program as Indicated by Urine Analysis," in Singh, Miller, and Lal, *Drug*, 183-85

164. Taylor, Bowling, and Mason, "Methadone Iatrogenesis During Narcotic Substitution Therapy," in Singh, Miller, and Lal, *Drug*, 218-19.

165. This analysis was done in Bellis, *Heroin*, 112-14. In another type of statistical message, criminal activity during treatment is compared to the patient's entire lifetime—a much longer period. Or the patient's highest amount of criminality is compared, rather than the average amount. See Platt and Labate, *Heroin*, 301, and Bellis, *Heroin*, 124-25. Bellis even wonders if a criminal addict may simply switch from many petty offenses to fewer serious offenses, a gain in statistics but a loss in public safety (Bellis, *Heroin*, 124-25). In Texas a clinic official discouraged about patient crime rates mused, "Maybe our methadone in San Antonio is not as strong as that in New York City" (quoted in Phillipson, "Methadone Maintenance: Some Uses, Some Limitations, Some Dangers," in Singh, Miller, and Lal, *Drug*, 180.

166. Maddux and Bowden, "Critique," 440-46; Platt and Labate, *Heroin*, 287, 300-1.

167. This analysis is found in Brecher and Consumer Reports, *Licit*, 75-76.

168. Brecher and Consumer Reports, *Licit*, 73. Research even indicates that persons required to receive methadone maintenance are not always addicts, but become addicted to opiates through the regular doses of methadone. See Phillipson, "Methadone Maintenance: Some Uses, Some Limitations, Some Dangers," in Singh, Miller, and Lal, *Drug*, 181; Taylor, Bowling, and Mason, "Methadone Iatrogenesis During Narcotic Substitution Therapy," in ibid., 217; Senay, "Methadone," 184; Jacobson and Zinberg, *Social*, 13 n. 12; O'Brien, "Experimental," 539-40; Dobbs, "Methadone," 1539; Taylor, Chambers, and Bowling, "Addiction," 28; Gay, Senay, and Newmeyer, "Pseudo," 241-47; Alexander and Hadaway, "Opiate," 372.

169. Hunt and Chambers, *Heroin*, 87.

170. Brecher and Consumer Reports, *Licit*, 73.

171. Ibid.

172. Kolb, *Drug*, 129-30; Kittrie, *Right*, 253; Graham-Mulhall, "Experiences," 107.

173. Musto, *American*, 78, 282 n. 29.

174. Eldridge, *Narcotics*, 152.

175. Musto, *American*, 282 n. 29.

176. Platt and Labate, *Heroin*, 297.

177. Bakalar and Grinspoon, *Drug*, 57; National Institute on Drug Abuse, *Evaluation*, 9-25; Simpson, "National Treatment System Evaluation Based on the Drug Abuse Reporting Program (DARP) Followup Research," in Tims and Ludford, *Drug* (National Institute on Drug Abuse), 29-41; Waldorf and Biernacki, "Natural," 281-82, 285-86.

178. Duster, *Legislation*, 36; Kaplan, *Hardest*, 34-36.

179. Kaplan, *Hardest*, 162 n. 16, 177.

180. Corman et al., "Rehabilitation," 576.

181. Zinberg, "Nonaddictive Opiate Use," in Weissman and DuPont, *Criminal*, 19.

182. Kolb, *Drug*, 90; Morgan, *Drugs*, 68.

183. Blachly, *Seduction*, 30.

184. Platt and Labate, *Heroin*, 192.

185. Szasz, *Ceremonial*, 82.

186. King, *Drug*, 261.

187. Kolb, *Drug*, 127. See also Trebach, *Heroin*, 203.

188. Quoted in Chein et al., *Road*, 158.

189. Quoted in Biernacki, *Pathways*, 126.

190. Quoted in ibid., 176.

191. Oswald, "Personal," 438.

192. Bakalar and Grinspoon, *Drug*, 144; Bellis, *Heroin*, 210; Chein et al., *Road*, 22-23, 159; Judson, *Heroin*, 78; Kaplan, *Hardest*, 36-38; Louria, *Overcoming*, 84; Platt and Labate, *Heroin*, 159-61, 193; Schroeder, *Politics*, 82; Szasz, *Ceremonial*, 83; Trebach, "The Potential Impact of 'Legal' Heroin in America," in Trebach, *Drugs*, 167-68; Nadelmann, "Drug," 944; Biernacki, *Pathways*, 226-28. The youthful start of drug abuse has been seen in Britain also (Plant, *Drugtakers*, 63-64; Gordon, "Patterns," 205-10) and France (Davidson, Etienne, and Piesset, "Medico-Social," 9-32).

193. Stephen Waldron statement and testimony, U.S. House Select Committee on Crime, *Improvement*, 287, 290; Winick, "Epidemiology of Narcotics Use," in Wilner and Kassebaum, *Narcotics*, 8.

194. Charles Winick, "Epidemiology of Narcotics Use," in Wilner and Kassebaum, *Narcotics*, 8-9.

195. Stephen Waldron statement, U.S. House Select Committee on Crime, *Improvement*, 287.

196. Biernacki, *Pathways*, 226-28, 231.

197. Raveis and Kandel, "Changes," 607-11. The percentages are for males; the article's chart lacked female percentages.

198. Biernacki, *Pathways*, 95, 97, 99.

199. Quoted in Jacobson and Zinberg, *Social*, 53.

200. Peele, *Love*, 19. See also Graeven and Graeven ("Treated," 207-18) for the importance of strong family support.

201. Bellis, *Heroin*, 223.

202. Morgan, *Yesterday's*, 26-27; Crothers, *Morphinism*, 54-55.

203. Platt and Labate, *Heroin*, 327; Alvin M. Shuster, "G.I. Heroin Addiction in Vietnam," *New York Times*, May 16, 1971, pp. 1, 20; Gloria Emerson, "A Major in Vietnam Gives All He's Got to the War on Heroin," *New York Times*, Sept. 12, 1971, p. 2. See also Peter G. Bourne, "Issues in Addiction," in Bourne, *Addiction*, 11; Robins, *Vietnam* (Special Action Office for Drug Abuse Prevention), 29; Kaplan, *Hardest*, 114; King, *Drug*, 331-32.

204. Kaplan, *Hardest*, 37.

205. Kandel, "Convergences in Prospective Longitudinal Surveys of Drug Use in Normal Populations," in Kandel, *Longitudinal*, 15; Brecher and Consumer Reports, *Licit*, 188, 188 n.; King, *Drug*, 332-33; Swiller, "Drug Abuse Patterns and Demographic Correlates Among Military Psychiatric Patients," in Singh, Miller, and Lal, *Drug*, 229-31; Black, Owens, and Wolff, "Patterns," 420-23; Platt and Labate, *Heroin*, 327.

206. King, *Drug*, 332-33.

207. Robins, Helzer, and Davis, "Narcotic," 955.

208. Brecher and Consumer Reports, *Licit*, 39; King, *Drug*, 332; Sanders, "Doper's," 71-72; Ingraham, " 'The Nam,' " 118-19.

209. Cuskey and Edington, "Drug Abuse as Self-Destructive Behavior," in Roberts, *Self-Destructive*, 138; Robins, *Vietnam* (Special Action Office for Drug Abuse Prevention), 31-32; Sanders, "Doper's," 71-72.

210. Norman E. Zinberg, "G.I.'s and O.J.'s in Vietnam," *New York Times Magazine*, Dec. 5, 1971, pp. 122-23.

211. Robins and Helzer, "Drug," 44, 45; Robins, Helzer, and Davis, "Narcotic," 959; Robins, Davis, and Nurco, "How," 38-43; Kandel, "Convergences in Prospective Longitudinal Surveys of Drug Use in Normal Populations," in Kandel, *Longitudinal*, 15; Bourne, "Issues in Addiction," in Bourne, *Addiction*, 11; Bellis, *Heroin*, 25; Schroeder, *Politics*, 72.

212. Bakalar and Grinspoon, *Drug*, 58; Brecher and Consumer Reports, *Licit*, 39.

213. Quoted in Biernacki, *Pathways*, 52.

214. Ibid., 43-44.

215. Bellis, *Heroin*, 134; Platt and Labate, *Heroin*, 102; Wilner et al., "Heroin," 401.

216. Biernacki, *Pathways*, 161; Duster, *Legislation*, 209-11.

217. Trebach, *Great*, 110.

218. Biernacki, *Pathways*, 124-25; Judson, *Heroin*, 143-44; Kaplan, *Hardest*, 38; Schroeder, *Politics*, 72-73; Robins and Helzer, "Drug," 49; Jacobson and Zinberg, *Social*, 14.

219. Blachly, *Seduction*, 80. Such experience, Blachly notes, contradicts the theory of "equivalence of psychic energy, . . . that if one does not rid himself of tension by one vice, it will express itself by another" (p. 80).

220. Biernacki, *Pathways*, 161.

221. Ibid., 27, 99, 179; Robins, "The Interaction of Setting and Predisposition in

Explaining Novel Behavior: Drug Initiations Before, In, and After Vietnam," in Kandel, *Longitudinal,* 181. Indeed, avoiding the "junkie" label can be an important part of avoiding addiction in the first place (Blackwell, "Drifting," 219-35).

222. Biernacki, *Pathways,* 192-93.

CHAPTER 3

1. Blum, "Drugs, Behavior, and Crime," in Blum et al., *Society,* 289; Blum, "On the Presence of Demons," in ibid., 329.

2. Feldman, "PCP Use in Four Cities: An Overview," in Feldman, Agar, and Beschner, *Angel,* 30, 39-50; Blum, "Drugs, Behavior, and Crime," in Blum, *Society,* 289; Michael A. Fauman and Beverly J. Fauman, "The Psychiatric Aspects of Chronic Phencyclidine Use: A Study of Chronic PCP Users," in Petersen and Stillman, *PCP* (National Institute on Drug Abuse), 186; Marsella and Hicks, "Phenomenological Aspects of Phencyclidine Abuse Among Ethnic Groups in Hawaii," in ibid., 203, 205-6; Thombs, "Review," 327; Wish, "PCP and Crime: Just Another Illicit Drug?" in Clouet, *Phencyclidine* (National Institute on Drug Abuse), 179, 187. Because the worst drug abusers are polydrug abusers, we must also ask if the small minority of violent PCP individuals are simultaneously using other substances that affect behavior, either alone or through interactions. Chronic PCP abusers are notable for self-destruction: one study found that 24 percent had attempted suicide before using PCP, 36 percent had previously overdosed on other drugs, and 72 percent continued to use PCP after having bad experiences with it (Michael A. Fauman and Beverly J. Fauman, "The Psychiatric Aspects of Chronic Phencyclidine Use: A Study of Chronic PCP Users," in Petersen and Stillman, *PCP* [National Institute on Drug Abuse], 186, 193). A study of methadone and barbiturate overdose cases found that many "victims" took overdoses again and again (Ghodse, "Drug," 273-80). Hospital staffs encounter addicts who arrive unconscious, leave when they regain consciousness, buy and use more illicit drugs, and return by ambulance a few hours later (Mitchell and Rose, "Barbiturate," 1489-90). See also case studies in Jamieson, Glanz, and MacGregor, *Dealing,* 60, 65, 89-91.

3. Rublowsky, *Stoned,* 194-95.

4. Raymond, "Researchers," A11.

5. Bennett, quoted in King, *Drug,* 186.

6. Inciardi, *War,* 105.

7. The lack of impact is shown by the experience in Great Britain. Because crime is socially defined, comparing two jurisdictions having different laws and customs is treacherous. Nonetheless the British experience has relevance to the question at hand, because prisons in the United Kingdom contained only a minute percentage of the nation's drug addicts in the 1950s, when addicts were not harassed by authorities (Lindesmith, "British," 142; Schur, *Narcotic,* 138-39). If pharmacological properties of drugs caused people to assault and steal, a high percentage of Britain's addicts should have been found in jail.

8. Paul Wenske, "Demand for 'Crank' Fuels Illicit Rural Drug Industry," *Kansas City Times*, March 18, 1989, p. A23.

9. Ibid.; April D. McClellan, "White Flight to Drugs," *Kansas City Times*, March 29, 1989, p. A10.

10. Steve Kaut, "Addicts Drawn to Life of Crime to Support Drug Habits," *Kansas City Star*, Feb. 5, 1989, p. 1A.

11. Diuguid, "Garbage Thefts in Kansas City Undermine Recycling Project," *Kansas City Star*, June 21, 1989, Kansas City-Jackson County Star section, p. 3.

12. Eldridge, *Narcotics*, 69-70.

13. Ibid., 67 n. 39. Six years earlier Chicago police put the repeaters at 85 percent (John Dearham testimony, U.S. Senate Judiciary Committee Hearings, *Illicit*, 4252), and "narcotics" repeaters included marijuana smokers (Helmer, *Drugs*, 96).

14. Kandel, "Convergences in Prospective Longitudinal Surveys of Drug Use In Normal Populations," in Kandel, *Longitudinal*, 22, 27; Johnston, O'Malley, and Eveland, "Drugs and Delinquency: A Search for Causal Connections," in ibid., 147-49, 152, 155; Wiessman, "Understanding the Drugs and Crime Connection," in Weissman and DuPont, *Criminal*, 54; Blum, "Drugs, Behavior, and Crime," in Blum et al., *Society*, 288, 290; Trebach, "The Potential Impact of 'Legal' Heroin in America," in Trebach, *Drugs*, 167; Gerard and Kornetsky, "Adolescent," 472; Vaillant, "12-Year," 603-4, 608; Hill, Haertzen, and Glaser, "Personality," 137-38; Bakalar and Grinspoon, *Drug*, 60, 133. The phenomenon has been noted for decades: "Most of these people [habitual criminals] have become users of drugs *after* they had joined the ranks of the 'under world' " ("Report," *Proceedings Am. Pharm. Asn.*, 1903, p. 475). Foreign studies of criminal addicts have yielded the same conclusion (Pierce James and D'Orbán, "Patterns," 14; D'Orbán, "Heroin," 67-78; D'Orbán, "Female," 345-47; Bewley, "Maintenance," 597-611; Barnes and Noble, "Deprivation," 299-311; Friedman and Peer, "Drug Addiction Among Pimps and Prostitutes in Israel," in Shoham, *Israel*, 141-75; Brill and Hirose, "Rise," 179-94; Hemmi, "How We Have Handled the Problem of Drug Abuse in Japan," in Sjöqvist and Tottie, *Abuse*, 151; Leader-Elliott, "Heroin," 138-39; Marshall and Hendtlass, "Drugs," 237, 245; Dobinson and Ward, "Heroin," 257).

15. Kaplan, *Hardest*, 54-55. A study of California Civil Addict Program inmates (a population biased toward severe abusers) typically found their first arrests to occur 3½ to 4 years before their first narcotics use (McGlothlin, Anglin, and Wilson, "Narcotic," 298-99).

16. Inciardi, *War*, 159-60. Prostitution may have started after drug use began, but other crimes preceded prostitution.

17. Hammersley et al., "Relationship," 1029.

18. Kolb, *Drug*, 34. Statisticians attack such comparisons but, in this instance, Kolb's approach is useful because it is the approach used by many public policy makers, and he demonstrates that it does not yield the drugs-crime correlation that public officials glibly assert.

19. Kolb, *Drug*, 68-69.

20. Weissman, "Understanding the Drugs and Crime Connection," in Weissman

and DuPont, *Criminal,* 50; Johnston, *Drugs,* 213, 218; Hammersley et al., "Relationship," 1029-43.

21. Eldridge, *Narcotics,* 101.

22. Kaplan, *Hardest,* 55.

23. Goldman, "Heroin," 222-23.

24. Kaplan, *Hardest,* 199.

25. Cohen, "The Implications of Crack," in Allen, *Cocaine,* 28.

26. Authorities differ on how much cash a thief receives for stolen merchandise, but all agree that the amount is a fraction of the actual cash value. Kittrie says perhaps 20 percent or less (*Right,* 234); Cushman ("Methadone," 1772) says 35 percent; Bellis (*Heroin,* 202-3) says 10 percent to 20 percent; Scher (Scher, "The Impact of the Drug Abuser on the Work Organization," in *Drug,* 7) says 10 percent; a report done for the Bureau of Narcotics and Dangerous Drugs (McGlothlin et al., *Alternative* [U.S. Justice Dept.], 13) says 30 percent.

27. According to the Federal Bureau of Investigation, in 1988 the United States suffered a total financial loss from *all* thefts, burglary or otherwise, drug-related or not, of $12 billion (*Uniform Crime Reports,* 1988, p. 156).

28. Erickson et al., *Steel,* 117.

29. Ibid., 118.

30. King, *Drug,* 308.

31. Judson, *Heroin,* 134; Schroeder, *Politics,* 149.

32. *Uniform Crime Reports* 1970 (p. 117), 1971 (p. 113), 1972 (p. 117), 1973 (p. 120).

33. Inciardi, *War,* 122.

34. Heroin addict quoted in Kaplan, *Hardest,* 53. See also Johnson et al., *Taking,* 33, 47.

35. Chein et al., *Road,* 167-68.

36. Ibid., 15-16, 61-62, 64-65.

37. McGlothlin, Anglin, and Wilson, "Narcotic," 305-9.

38. Johnson et al., *Taking,* 55, 57.

39. Kaplan, *Hardest,* 56. See also Inciardi, *War,* 119; Nurco et al., "Criminality," 94-102; Leader-Elliott, "Heroin," 138-40; Dobinson and Ward, "Heroin," 257.

40. Judson, *Heroin,* 51; Lindesmith, *Addict,* 184-86; Zacune, "Comparison," 43-44, 46-47. These particular Canadian addicts, of course, had both the motivation and the means to emigrate to another country in hopes of changing their lives. Such a population is biased toward persons determined to succeed. Moreover, we apparently lack a control sample in Canada; possibly addicts simply grew older and wiser in England, developing stronger personalities and reduced criminality. Perhaps a different cultural environment allowed addicts to find new and lawful ways to express desires that Canadian mores had forced into illegal channels. Or maybe criminality declined in many addicts because cheap heroin reduced the number of income-producing crimes. The Canadian emigrant story raises intriguing questions.

41. McGlothlin, Anglin, and Wilson, *Evaluation* (National Institute on Drug Abuse), 73-74. These are "annualized" figures, meaning they are extrapolated from

incomes during months with particular levels of drug use. Those levels can vary in a year's time.

42. Johnson et al., *Taking,* 80.

43. Ibid.

44. Ibid., 5, 88-89. A criminal engages in crime, but only part of the person's behavior is criminal; the dichotomy by which a person is viewed as either a "criminal" or "noncriminal" is a legal artifact and distorts our understanding. Much of a criminal's behavior is law abiding.

45. Ibid., 99.

46. Stephen Waldron statement, House Select Committee on Crime, *Improvement,* 287.

47. Nurco et al., "Criminality," 96.

48. Weissman, "Understanding the Drugs and Crime Connection," in Weissman and DuPont, *Criminal,* 63.

49. McGlothlin, Anglin, and Wilson, *Evaluation* (National Institute on Drug Abuse), 74. This figure is for daily heroin users.

50. Weissman, "Understanding the Drugs and Crime Connection," in Weissman and DuPont, *Criminal,* 5.

51. Cushman, "Methadone," 1770.

52. Inciardi, *War,* 126-27. Similar results were found for non-narcotic drug users in Miami (Inciardi, *War,* 129).

53. Johnson et al., *Taking,* 76.

54. Platt and Labate, *Heroin,* 252.

55. Inciardi, *War,* 126-27.

56. Johnson et al., *Taking,* 115-18, 124-27.

57. See Lidz et al., "Heroin," 47; Bellis, *Heroin,* 202-3; O'Connor research, cited by Bakalar and Grinspoon, *Drug,* 142; Timmer, "Productivity," 383-96.

58. Johnson et al., *Taking,* 126.

59. Ibid.

60. Hawkins and Waller, "Critical," 693.

61. I gained that insight from Packer, *Limits,* 281.

62. Packer, *Limits,* 337-38.

63. Brecher and Consumer Reports, *Licit,* 419-20.

64. Ibid.

65. Hutto v. Davis, 454 U.S. 370 (1982); *New York Times,* Jan. 12, 1982, p. B15.

66. Bellis, *Heroin,* 181.

67. *Frontline,* "Who" transcript, 14.

68. Morley, "Great," 346.

69. Musto, *American,* 207-8.

70. Ibid.

71. Zinberg and Robertson, *Drugs,* 229-30.

72. King, *Drug,* 299.

73. Bellis, *Heroin,* 180. See also *Congressional Quarterly Weekly Report,* July 5, 1975, pp. 1427-30.

74. Trebach, *Great*, 343-44.

75. Ibid., 344. For example, see "Drug Agent Admits Acting as Cocaine Courier," *Kansas City Times*, Aug. 25, 1989, p. A5.

76. King, *Drug*, 324-25; Senate Report 1989 (82 Cong., 2 sess.), *Investigation*, 2, 12-16; Healy, "They."

77. *Knapp*, 91-115; Zinberg and Robertson, *Drugs*, 223. Kaplan (*Hardest*, 96-97) notes persuasive evidence of New York City police perjury in heroin cases dating from 1961. In that regard see also Barlow, "Patterns," 549-82; Younger, "Perjury," 596-97; People v. Berrios, 28 N.Y.2d 361, 321 N.Y.S.2d 884, 270 N.E.2d 709 (1971).

78. Manning and Redlinger, "Working Bases for Corruption: Organizational Ambiguities and Narcotics Law Enforcement," in Trebach, *Drugs*; Kaplan, *Hardest*, 174.

79. Quoted in Kirkpatrick, *Prosecution*, 39. The prosecutor was describing the attitude of colleagues, and indicated disapproval of that attitude.

80. Earl Warren, November 13, 1970, quoted in King, *Drug*, 324. Similar sentiments were expressed by the Nixon administration's first director of the Office of Drug Abuse Law Enforcement (Bellis, *Heroin*, 179-80).

81. King, *Drug*, 327.

82. Clark, *Fantastic*, 204.

83. President's Commission, *Cash*; *Frontline*, "Who" transcript, 24-26; *American Banker*, Feb. 14, 1985, p. 4 and Feb. 28, 1985, pp. 4, 8, 10, 12; *Business Week*, March 18, 1985, pp. 74-82; Roger Cohen, "Laundry Service: How the Mob Is Using Financial Institutions to Disguise Its Gains," *Wall Street Journal* (Eastern edition), March 12, 1985, pp. 1, 26; *World Press Review*, Nov. 1985, p. 58; John Yemma, "US Hot After Money Laundering," *Christian Science Monitor*, Oct. 18, 1985, p. 21; *Newsweek*, Sept. 23, 1985, p. 52; Tom Jackson, "Laundering Cash: Illicit Financial Wizardry," *Kansas City Times*, July 15, 1989, pp. A1, A8-A9; Morley, "Great," 343-44, 347.

84. Inciardi, *War*, 196.

85. *Frontline*, "Who" transcript, 18, 21.

86. Tom Jackson, "Laundering Cash: Illicit Financial Wizardry," *Kansas City Times*, July 15, 1989, pp. A8-A9; Tom Jackson, "Big Cash Purchase? Most Firms Say Ok," *Kansas City Times*, July 15, 1989, p. A8.

87. Bellis, *Heroin*, 195.

88. Ibid., 95.

89. Ibid., 195.

90. King, *Drugs*, 155. Bellis, *Heroin*, 181 notes well-known cases. Dozens of lesser known cases are noted in Kamisar, LaFave, and Israel, *Modern*, 36, 228, 250, 253, 268-69, 273, 280, 285, 292, 297-98, 300, 326, 329, 331-32, 335, 342, 344, 354-55, 372, 377, 392, 401, 405, 412, 484, 489, 520, 530, 533, 536-38, 844.

91. Turner, quoted in Trebach, *Great*, 237.

92. DuPont, Jr., in Trebach, *Great*, 236. See also p. 231.

93. Ibid., 242-43; Fritschi and Prescott, "Morphine," 116.

94. Trebach, *Great*, 235.

95. Senate Armed Services Committee, *Drug*, 5, 41-42, 134-36.

96. Sohn, "Analysis," 69, 72. See also Lewis et al., "Nalline," 169. Elliott et al. noted that when an individual receives a urine test and a pupil diameter test, the two different tests yield contradictory results in 50 percent of the cases ("Detection," 121, 125).

97. Gottheil, Caddy, and Austin, "Fallibility," 1036-38.

98. Hansen, Caudill, and Boone, "Crisis," 2382-83.

99. Melissa Berg, "Drug Testing in the Workplace," *Kansas City Times*, Sept. 8, 1989, p. A10.

100. Smith and Joseph, "EMIT Assays for Drugs of Abuse," in Deutsch, *Analytical*, 35-58.

101. Habig, "Time," 1682; Frings, White, and Battaglia, "Status," 1683.

102. Gottheil., Caddy, and Austin, "Fallibility," 1035-38; Hansen, Caudill, and Boone, "Crisis," 2382-83.

103. Habig, "Time," 1682; Burtis, "Answering," 891.

104. Frings, Battaglia, and White, "Status," 891-94.

105. Cone and Menchen, "Lack," 276-77; "Discussion," 111.

106. Bogema, Schwartz, and Godwin, "Evaluation," 272-73.

107. Simpson, Jarvie, and Heyworth, "Evaluation," 172, 177-79.

108. Ibid., 178-79.

109. Dextraze et al., "Comparison," 135-36.

110. Trebach, *Great*, 242-43.

111. Ibid., 235.

112. Arthur McBay, quoted in ibid., 234-35. See also McBay, "Problems," 39-40.

113. Hunt and Chambers, *Heroin*, 98-99.

114. Mike Tidwell, "Bennett's Lore on Drugs: The Myth of 'Lock 'Em Up and Throw Away the Keys,' " *In These Times*, July 5-18, 1989, p. 9; "Bennett Wants to Shift Drug War to Inner Cities," *Kansas City Times*, July 19, 1989, p. A8; Barbara Shelly and Kevin Murphy, "Casual Drug Use Criticized," *Kansas City Star*, Aug. 9, 1989, p. 1A; Wenske, "Bennett Gets Out the Anti-Drug Word," *Kansas City Times*, Aug. 10, 1989, p. A12; Dauner, " 'Users Create a Market and Set an Example,' " *Kansas City Times*, Sept. 19, 1989, p. B1.

115. Richard L. Berke, "Bennett Offers U.S. Battle Plan for War on Drugs," *Kansas City Times*, Aug. 2, 1989, pp. A1, A6; Jake Thompson, "Broad $7.9 Billion Strategy Targets Users and Suppliers," *Kansas City Times*, Sept. 6, 1989, p. A8; "Schools Told to Get Tough on Drug Use," *Kansas City Times*, Sept. 6, 1989, p. A10.

116. Editorial, *Kansas City Star*, July 25, 1989, p. 4A.

117. *New York Times*, March 21, 1989, p. A1 and March 22, 1989, p. A1; George F. Will, "U.S. Social Regression Is Without Precedent," *Kansas City Times*, April 10, 1989, p. A7.

118. Kittrie, *Right*, 249.

119. Ibid., 245.

120. California Welfare and Institutions Code 3200; Duster, *Legislation*, 134.

121. 28 U.S.C. Sec. 2903(d) (1982).

122. King, *Drug*, 156; Kittrie, *Right*, 257; *New York Times*, Nov. 14, 1967, p. 38.

123. I received that insight from Bakalar and Grinspoon, *Drug*, 50.

124. Duster, *Legislation*, 207-8, 213.

125. "More Drug Treatment Money Sought," *Kansas City Times*, Aug. 5, 1989, p. A3; Paul Wenske, "Bennett to Visit KC for a Firsthand Look at Fight Against Drugs," *Kansas City Times*, Aug. 8, 1989, p. A8.

126. Transcript in Kirkpatrick, *Prosecution*, 41-43.

127. Lester D. Volk, remarks, June 30, 1922, *Cong. Rec.*, 67 Cong., 2 sess., p. 9794; King, *Drug*, 59-60.

128. King, *Drug*, 61-63; Lindesmith, *Addict*, 256-57.

129. Fiedler, *Being*, 134-42, 164-77, 195-225, 247-55.

130. Examples in Zinberg and Robertson, *Drugs*, 172, 233-34.

131. Lester D. Volk, remarks, June 30, 1922, *Cong. Rec.*, 67 Cong., 2 sess., pp. 9794-95.

132. Kennett Love, "Report Questions Narcotics Policy," *New York Times*, April 30, 1961, p. 76; Schur, *Narcotic*, 181-82; Eldridge, *Narcotics*, 79; Lindesmith, *Addict*, 246, 249-51.

133. King, *Drug*, 85.

134. Trebach, *Great*, 187-89.

135. "Does 'Zero Tolerance' Go Overboard?" *Kansas City Times*, Dec. 3, 1988, p. A18.

136. Steve Kraske, "KC Police Are Getting a Free Ride," *Kansas City Star*, Sept. 19, 1988, pp. 1A, 5A.

137. Schroeder, *Politics*, 1.

138. Brecher and Consumer Reports, *Licit*, 419-20; Louria, *Overcoming*, 175-76.

139. Eldridge, *Narcotics*, 64.

140. U.S. v. Oviedo, 525 F.2d 881 (5th Cir. 1976).

141. Comprehensive Drug Control Act of 1989, sections 195.241, 195.242.

142. Chapter 195.020 RSMo. See prosecutor's manual (Law Enforcement Training Institute, *Missouri*, 61-62) for examples of how the law operates.

143. Zinberg and Robertson, *Drugs*, 172.

144. Platt and Labate, *Heroin*, 42.

145. Chapter 195.110 RSMo; Kirkpatrick, *Prosecution*, 9.

146. Bakalar and Grinspoon, *Drug*, 111.

147. Szasz, *Ceremonial*, 151.

148. Tom Jackman, "Letting Drug Sellers Off Easy," *Kansas City Times*, April 29, 1989, pp. A16-A17.

149. Bakalar and Grinspoon, *Drug*, 114.

150. Their atmosphere is captured in Kirkpatrick, *Prosecution*, 11-12, 17.

151. Grinspoon and Bakalar, *Cocaine*, 236-37; Schroeder, *Politics*, 53.

152. Kaplan, *Marijuana*, 9. See also Bakalar and Grinspoon, *Drug*, 110.

153. Albert Riederer, quoted in Edward M. Eveld, "Drug, Hazmat Taxes Approved," *Kansas City Times*, Nov. 8, 1989, p. A1.

154. Paul Wenske, "The War on Drugs: It's Costly, Complex and Largely Ineffec-
tive," *Kansas City Times*, May 15, 1989, pp. A1, A7; Jo Ann Kawell, "Just Say
'War,' " *In These Times*, April 12-18, 1989, p. 4; "Pentagon Boosts Aid to
Colombia," *Kansas City Times*, Sept. 1, 1989, p. A3; "Joint U.S.-Peruvian Team
Roots Out Three Jungle Labs.," *Kansas City Times*, Sept. 11, 1989, p. A5; "Drug Aid
to Colombia Doesn't Fit Need," *Kansas City Times*, Sept. 12, 1989, p. A6.

155. Marquis Shepherd, "Clay County Drug Squad Frittered Away Piles of
Cash," *Kansas City Times*, Dec. 3, 1988, p. A19.

CHAPTER 4

1. Rublowsky, *Stoned*, 123.

2. Schroeder, *Politics*, 29.

3. Washington, *Diaries*, 211, 213-15, 223-26, 236, 238.

4. For example, see James Madison to Thomas Jefferson, Aug. 20, 1784, in
Jefferson, *Papers*, 402.

5. Aaron and Musto, "Temperance and Prohibition in America: A Historical
Overview," in Moore and Gerstein, *Alcohol*, 136, 157, 164; Bakalar and Grinspoon,
Drug, 81; Jacobson and Zinberg, *Social*, 2.

6. *New York Times*, Dec. 30, 1877, p. 8, cols. 2-3; Crothers, *Morphinism*, 32;
Towns, "Peril," 580-88; Wholey, "Psychopathologic," 723-24; Graham-Mulhall,
"Experiences," 107. The process described in the twentieth-century articles also
operated in the previous century.

7. King, *Drug*, 16; Bettmann, *Good*, 143; Musto, *American*, 58.

8. Contemporary accounts include Oliver, "The Use and Abuse of Opium,"
Massachusetts State Board of Health, *Third Annual Report* (Boston: Wright and
Potter, State Printers, 1872), 162-77, reprinted in Morgan, *Yesterday's*, 49; *New York
Times*, Dec. 30, 1877, p. 8, col. 2; Beard, *American*; Crothers, *Morphinism*, 39.
Modern accounts include Lesy, *Wisconsin* and Bettmann, *Good*.

9. Eaton, "How," 665.

10. *New York Times*, Dec. 30, 1877, p. 8, col. 2; Crothers, *Morphinism*, 30, 44,
53-54; Blum, "A History of Opium," in Blum et al., *Society*, 54; Bellis, *Heroin*, 6, 8;
King, *Drug*, 18; Inciardi, *War*, 16; Schroeder, *Politics*, 78; Duster, *Legislation*, 3, 9, 12;
Rublowsky, *Stoned*, 130; Crothers, "Morphinism," 784-86; Morgan, *Drugs*, 14, 34,
39-40, 43; Morgan, *Yesterday's*, 14-15; "Opium," *Medical and Surgical Reporter*, 40,
Nolan, "Opium," 835; Hull, "The Opium Habit [in Iowa]," Iowa State Board of
Health, *Third Biennial Report* (Des Moines: George E. Roberts, 1885), 535-45,
reprinted in Morgan, *Yesterday's*, 40; Oliver, "The Use and Abuse of Opium,"
Massachusetts State Board of Health, *Third Annual Report* (Boston: Wright and
Potter, State Printers, 1872), 162-77 reprinted in Morgan, *Yesterday's*, 49; Earle,
"Opium," 442-46; Crothers, *Morphinism*, 44; "Report," *Proceedings Am. Pharm.
Asn.*, 472; Eberle, "Narcotics," 636. That demographic description is challenged by

Helmer (*Drugs*, 46), who contends that surveys often excluded lower class usage. Such users certainly existed. Less certain is the number of users from any class. Estimates vary so widely as to cast doubt on all of them.

Twentieth-century accounts claim that military doctors created the American opiate addiction problem through liberal injections of morphine to treat Civil War injuries, and say that morphine addiction was called "the soldiers' disease." Addiction demographics challenge that claim, as does the experience of war-torn European countries that saw wide medical use of morphine without a subsequent addiction problem matching that of the United States (Musto, *American*, 1-2). Moreover, apparently Civil War physicians most commonly sprinkled morphine on wounds rather than injecting it, and topical application would reduce the addiction potential. See Quinones, "Drug," 1007-20 and a somewhat different analysis in Courtwright, *Dark*, 54-56 for more details. An 1872 study on the rise of opiate addiction held the Civil War blameless, and talked instead of changing tastes in intoxicants—people switching from alcohol to opiates (Oliver, "The Use and Abuse of Opium," Massachusetts State Board of Health, *Third Annual Report* [Boston: Wright and Potter, State Printers, 1872], reprinted in Morgan, *Yesterday's*, 48-50. See also *New York Times*, Dec. 30, 1877, p. 8, col. 2). Morphine sales and the alcohol temperance movement rose together (Musto, *American*, 33). Opiates were more socially acceptable than alcohol (King, *Drug*, 17; Nolan, "Opium," 828) and were advocated as less harmful (Morgan, *Drugs*, 89). They also cost less than alcohol (King, *Drug*, 19). The very poorest users may have stolen to get money for drug purchases (Musto, *American*, 19-20; "Report," *Proceedings Am. Pharm. Asn.*, 475), but such crime was no more associated with drugs than with beer or food. Per capita opium import figures increased throughout the nineteenth century, with the Civil War marking no special change. No figures are ever cited to support claims that many Civil War soldiers were addicted. Lindesmith (*Addict*, 130) says that dysentery, not morphine addiction, was called the "soldiers' disease" at the time. Massive Civil War morphine addiction is a fable invented in the twentieth century.

11. Rublowsky, *Stoned*, 127; Isbell, "Historical Development of Attitudes Toward Opiate Addiction in the United States," in Farber and Wilson, *Conflict*, 156.

12. Grinspoon and Bakalar, *Cocaine*, 26; Kleber, "Introduction," 3; Siegel, *Intoxication*, 263-64; Siegel, "New Patterns of Cocaine Use: Changing Doses and Routes," in Kozel and Adams, *Cocaine* (National Institute on Drug Abuse), 205-7.

13. Morgan, *Drugs*, 19-22.

14. Schur, *Narcotic*, 45.

15. Inciardi, *War*, 96.

16. Nolan, "Opium," 835.

17. Quoted in "Opium," *Medical and Surgical Reporter*, 40.

18. Morgan, *Yesterday's*, 14-15.

19. Brecher and Consumer Reports, *Licit*, 6-7.

20. Musto, *American*, 22; Wright, quoted in Musto, *American*, 259 n.52. See also Street, "Patent," 1037-42. Purchases of non-opiate medicines rose; the decline was limited to opiates (Musto, *American*, 265 n.43).

21. As Szasz notes (*Ceremonial*, 76-77) opium was not considered harmful, otherwise its use would have been encouraged among the Chinese, just as alcohol was promoted among Native Americans. Measures designed to harass a particular minority are often disguised. Voter literacy laws and poll taxes said nothing about African-Americans, but the purpose was to deny them suffrage. Nightclubs have established dress and grooming codes banning hats and goatees, to exclude African-American males from the premises.

22. Samuel Gompers was prominent in the anti-Chinese agitation (Hill, "Anti-Oriental," 51-52).

23. Morgan, "The Legislation of Drug Law: Economic Crisis and Social Control," in Weissman and DuPont, *Criminal*, 36.

24. Quoted in ibid., 37. On p. 38 Morgan quotes a more explicit description from the Sacramento *Union:*

> Upon a matting-covered couch lay a handsome white girl in silk and laces, sucking poison from the same stem which an hour before was against the repulsive lips and yellow teeth of a celestial. She was just taking the last pipeful; the eyes were heavy, the will past resistance or offense. She glanced up lazily, but was too indifferent to replace the embroidered skirts over the rounded angles the disturbed drapery exposed.

25. "Report," *Proceedings Am. Pharm. Asn.*, 572.

26. The Philippine experience illustrated opium users' resistance to the label "sick." Ca. 1906 only 10 out of 12,700 registered users accepted a government cure offer (Musto, *American*, 261 n. 20). Normal users of drugs do not worry about their use (Blum, "Normal Drug Use," in Blum et al., *Society*, 268).

27. Taylor, *American*, vi; Musto, *American*, 30ff.

28. Wright, *Report*, S. Doc. 377, p. 50.

29. Musto, *American*, 43.

30. Taylor, *American*, 58-59, 59 n.29; Courtwright, *Dark*, 28-30. The atmosphere of fact-free agitation is illustrated by a drug firm's comments to Wright: "While there are no tangible figures on which to base an opinion, there certainly must be a foundation of fact underlying the widespread conviction that Morphinomania is on the increase" (Merck and Company to Hamilton Wright, Aug. 7, 1908, quoted in Morgan, *Drugs*, 100). Paradoxically, Wright said that opium smoking was no problem among military personnel in the Orient, a contention that would seem to allay concern about spread of the practice thousands of miles away in America (Wright, *Report*, S. Doc. 377, pp. 44, 50).

The best gauge of American narcotics and cocaine use in that period may be provided by military medical exams. The sample population is biased toward lower and middle class males in young adulthood, but the sample size is huge and the demographic characteristics broad enough. An oft-cited study using Army figures (Kolb and Du Mez, "Prevalence," 1181) says that 3,284 men, out of a total of 3.5 million examined, were rejected for drug addiction during the entire war (see also *World's Work* 49 (Nov. 1924): 17). In 1919 the New York City Parole Commission said that 80,000 conscripts were rejected for drug use nationwide during the war's first draft call-up (*New York Times*, April 15, 1919, p. 24). A Treasury Department report said thousands of conscripts showed drug addiction, as opposed to use (summarized in *New York Times*, Sept. 13, 1918, p. 10, col. 7), but a postwar War Department report declared that 1,488 addicts were detected nationwide in draft board exams (Love and Davenport, *Defects* (War Department), 359, 754-73). Shortly before the war an investigator studied the military prison population, where the rate for all sorts of deviancy would be higher than in the general population, and found that 4 percent or more of the prisoners had regularly used cocaine or opiates at some point during their lives (King, "Use," 273). From these numbers we cannot extrapolate a number for drug users in the general population, but we can conclude that drug use was neither prevalent nor unheard of; it was common enough that everyone may have known a user, but remained a minor feature of American life.

31. *New York Times*, April 2, 1918, p. 24, col. 1, and Aug. 20, 1918, p. 3, col. 5 and Editorial, Dec. 18, 1918, p. 14.

32. Musto, *American*, 310 n. 15.

33. Ibid., 300 n. 35.

34. Wright, *Report*, S. Doc. 377, p. 50.

35. Ibid.

36. Musto, *American*, 17.

37. "Report," *Proceedings Am. Pharm. Asn.* (1903), 472.

38. Christopher Koch testimony, House Ways and Means Committee, Hearings, *Importation*, 12.

39. Grinspoon and Bakalar, *Cocaine*, 38.

40. Platt and Labate, *Heroin*, 15.

41. Examples of that era's hysteria about African-Americans and cocaine are cited in Morgan, *Drugs*, 92-93 and Musto, *American*, 254 n. 15.

42. Wright, *Report*, S. Doc. 377, pp. 48-50.

43. Quoted in Musto, *American*, 255 n. 15.

44. One thinks of Wright when encountering passages such as this one, from *Chemist and Druggist* v. 77, Dec. 31, 1910, p. 44: "The Narcotic Evil has become so pronounced in the city of New Orleans, where there is a large Negro and Creole population, that the police have undertaken a vigorous campaign of prosecution. . . . It is just this condition of things which has developed a demand during the last few years for the enactment of the Federal law."

45. Green, "Psychoses," 702.

46. Morgan, *Drugs*, 34.

47. Musto, *American*, 98.

48. Helmer, *Drugs*, 83.

49. Ibid., 49-50.

50. Ibid., 51. Wright's own figures showed coca leaf imports declining from 1907 (ibid., 52).

51. Musto, *American*, 30-35.

52. Quoted in ibid., 267 n. 70.

53. Ibid., 265 n. 47.

54. Ibid., 50-51.

55. In practice the "Harrison Act" means the 1914 statute and a 1918 supplement.

56. Musto, *American*, 54-55.

57. Ibid., 66.

58. J. H. Gaines, *Cong. Rec.*, 60 Cong., 2 sess., Feb. 1, 1909, p. 1683.

59. Quoted in Musto, *American*, 267 n.72.

60. The same sequence appears in the origins of the Cold War (Miller, *Heritage*, 359, 362-63, 373), and prominent Cold Warriors also became prominent drug warriors. A later chapter will argue that the dovetailing was not coincidental.

61. Musto, *American*, 61, 273 n.25.

62. Ibid., 64.

63. Ibid., 64-65, 123; Platt and Labate, *Heroin*, 19.

64. Musto, *American*, 122.

65. Ibid.

66. Bailey, "Heroin," 315; Densten, "Drug," 748; Musto, *American*, 107; Morgan, *Drugs*, 109.

67. Musto, *American*, 126-128; Platt and Labate, *Heroin*, 19-20.

68. U.S. v. Jin Fuey Moy, 241 U.S. 394 (1916).

69. Ibid., 402.

70. 38 Stat. 786 (1915), Chapt. 1, sect. 2.

71. King, *Drug*, 40.

72. W. S. Webb and Jacob Goldman v. U.S., 249 U.S. 96 (1919).

73. Jin Fuey Moy v. U.S., 254 U.S. 189 (1920).

74. King, *Drug*, 42-43; Musto, *American*, 185; Platt and Labate, *Heroin*, 22.

75. U.S. v. Behrman, 258 U.S. 280 (1922).

76. Quoted in extension of remarks by Lester D. Volk, *Cong. Rec.*, 67 Cong., 2 sess., Jan. 13, 1922, Appendix p. 13341.

77. Council On Pharmacy and Chemistry, "What," 1220.

78. Extension of remarks by Lester D. Volk, *Cong. Rec.*, 67 Cong., 2 sess., Jan. 13, 1922, Appendix p. 13341. Volk's remarks note the repeated appearance of a small number of specific persons in assorted anti-drug agitations. He questioned whether their opinions reflected the consensus of the medical community. See also Volk's remarks of June 30, 1922, pp. 9789-90.

79. Musto, *American*, 309 n.7, 310 n.10.

80. Linder v. U.S., 268 U.S. 5 (1925).

81. Ibid., 22.

82. Quoted in Musto, *American*, 319 n.9.

83. U.S. v. Anthony, 15 F.Supp. 553, 557-58 (S.D. California, Central Division, 1936).

84. Extension of remarks by John M. Coffee, *Cong. Rec.*, 75 Cong., 3 sess., June 14, 1938, Appendix p. 2708.

85. Kolb, *Drug*, 154-55. For another case, see Melzack, "Tragedy," 33.

86. Anslinger and Oursler, *Murderers*, 169, 175-76, 181-82.

87. Lindesmith, *Addict*, 14-15.

88. Quoted in Straus, *Addicts*, 21.

89. Musto, *American*, 138, 152, 309 n. 5, 309 n. 6. Various studies show the vast majority of opiate users were white in the 1920s and 1930s (Winick, "Epidemiology of Narcotics Use," in Wilner and Kassebaum, *Narcotics*, 10, 12). Photographs of clinic operations show few clients who appear to be Hispanic or African-American.

90. Inciardi, *War*, 17.

91. Ibid., 99; Musto, *American*, 277 n.44, 322 n.33.

92. Quoted in Musto, *American*, 191. In 1924 Hobson incorrectly claimed "Heroin appeared in America only ten years ago" (quoted in *Literary Digest*, May 24, 1924, p. 32).

93. Musto, *American*, 112-13.

94. Lindesmith, *Addict*, 124; Duster, *Legislation*, 11-12; King, *Drug*, 18; Blair, "Relation," 284-96. Courtwright (*Dark*, 2-3, 114-15) sees the pattern beginning to shift ca. 1895 as state restrictions grew and medical use of opiates declined.

95. Bureau of Prisons, *Federal*, 336; National Commission on Law Observance and Enforcement, *Report*, H. Doc. 722, p. 58.

96. Bureau of Prisons, *Federal*, 336.

97. Kolb, "Let's," 54.

98. Schur, *Narcotic*, 57.

99. *Montana Standard*, January 27, 1929, quoted in Sloman, *Reefer*, 31.

100. Mabel Holdaway to James E. Murray, March 24, 1937, printed in House Ways and Means Committee, *Taxation*, 45.

101. Floyd K. Baskette to Bureau of Narcotics, Sept. 4, 1936, printed in House Ways and Means Committee, *Taxation*, 32.

102. Helmer, *Drugs*, 55.

103. Helmer, *Drugs*, 58-59.

104. Helmer, *Drugs*, 72; Weissman, "Drug Control Principles: Instrumentalism and Symbolism," in Weissman and DuPont, *Criminal*, 112.

105. Musto, *American*, 227; Sloman, *Reefer*, 58.

106. Schroeder, *Politics*, 31.

107. Quoted in Sloman, *Reefer*, 58-59.

108. Anslinger testimony, House Ways and Means Committee, *Taxation*, 24.

109. Anslinger testimony, Senate Judiciary Committee, *Illicit*, 16, 18.

110. "Federal," *Journal Am. Med. Asn.*, 1543-44.

111. Woodward testimony, House Ways and Means Committee, *Taxation*, 92.

112. *Newsweek*, Dec. 20, 1948, p. 42 and Nov. 20, 1950, pp. 57-58, and Jan. 29, 1951, pp. 23-24 and July 9, 1951, p. 23; *Life*, June 11, 1951, pp. 116-26; Lindesmith, *Addict*, viii. Solomon Kobrin describes the atmosphere in which sociologists labored when studying illicit drug use in the early 1950s (Bennett, *Oral*, 323 n. 26).

113. Senate Committee on the Judiciary, Subcommittee on Improvements in the Federal Criminal Code, 84 Cong., 1 sess., 1955.

114. Eldridge, *Narcotics*, 72. Admittedly such records measure law enforcement activity, not drug use, but they are the sort of records cited by public officials who determine drug policy.

115. Brecher and Consumer Reports, *Licit*, 58; King, *Drug*, 148-49.

116. Kolb, *Drug*, 157.

117. Ibid.

118. Ibid.

119. Lindesmith, "Dope," 229-30. Predominance of African-Americans among opiate addicts is not due to race alone; most African-Americans live in the South but most African-American addicts are from Los Angeles, Chicago, New York, and Washington, D.C. (Helmer, *Drugs*, 80, 83).

120. Jonah J. Goldstein in *New York Times*, March 5, 1955, p. 19.

121. Lindesmith, *Addict*, 90.

122. King, *Drug*, 93.

123. Lindesmith, *Addict*, 36-37.

124. Helmer, *Drugs*, 95-96.

125. John Gutknecht testimony, Senate Judiciary Committee, *Illicit*, 4295.

126. King, *Drug*, 279, 287-90.

127. Quoted in Bellis, *Heroin*, 23.

128. White House document from Epstein, "Krogh," 116.

129. Nixon, *Public*, Oct. 14, 1970, p. 844.

130. Sanders, "Addicts," 71.

131. Abelson, "Death," 1289.

132. Bellis, *Heroin*, 19.

133. Nixon, *Public*, June 18, 1971, p. 755 and Oct. 4, 1971, pp. 1019-20 and Jan.

134. King, *Drug*, 319.

135. Quoted in Kirkpatrick, *Prosecution*, 33.

136. Kirkpatrick, *Prosecution*, 29 n.

137. Epstein, *Agency*. Epstein's book is a partial antidote to drug crisis rhetoric of politicians.

138. Pepper statement, House Select Committee on Crime, *Narcotics*, 1. The spread of drug use into rural areas was also deplored in the 1980s. It is a perennial fear. Innovations, whether use of television or heroin, spread from larger cities to smaller ones (Hunt and Chambers, *Heroin*, 44-47). The appearance of particular drugs in small towns illustrates a well-known natural process and has nothing to do with corruption of Main Street values.

139. Bellis, *Heroin*, 71.

140. Carter, *Public*, Aug. 2, 1977. p. 1404 and Oct. 14, 1978, p. 1779.

141. Donald Elisburg, Assistant Secretary of Labor for Employment Standards, quoted in Philip Shabecoff, "Employers Told to Hire Alcoholics and Drug Abusers Able to Work," *New York Times*, July 6, 1977, p. A14, col. 1.

142. Quoted in Szasz, *Ceremonial*, 215-16. See also *New York Times*, Oct. 28, 1980, p. B1, col. 1.

143. Trebach, *Great*, 151.

144. Ibid., 170.

145. Ibid., 8; "National Security Peril Puts Military in War on Drugs Flow," *Kansas City Star*, Aug. 27, 1989, pp. 1A, 21A; "U.S. Troops Reportedly to Raze Drug Labs.," *Kansas City Times*, Feb. 8, 1989, p. A3; "A Real Drug War," *Kansas*

City Star, Aug. 13, 1989, p. 6A; "Pentagon Boosts Aid to Colombia," *Kansas City Times,* Sept. 1, 1989, p. A3; "Joint U.S.-Peruvian Team Roots Out Three Jungle Labs.," *Kansas City Times,* Sept. 11, 1989, p. A5.

146. Schroeder, *Politics,* 136.

147. "Narco-Terrorists," *In These Times,* Sept. 13-19, 1989, p. 4.

148. McConahay and Kirk, "Over There," *Mother Jones,* Feb./March 1989; Merrill Collett, "Colombia: Diary of a Dirty War," *In These Times,* Feb. 8-14, 1989, p. 22; Jo Ann Kawell, "Just Say 'War,' " *In These Times,* April 12-18, 1989, p. 4; "U.S. Lets Advisers Move Farther Afield in Latin Drug War," *Kansas City Times,* Sept. 11, 1989, pp. A1, A4; Michael Isikoff, "Secret Part of Bush Drug Program Sees Bigger Role for U.S. Military," *Washington Post* section of *Manchester Guardian Weekly,* Sept. 17, 1989, p. 17; Simon Tisdall, "A Prescription That Won't Cure the Disease," *Manchester Guardian Weekly,* Sept. 24, 1989, p. 9; Todd Steiner, "Drug War Victims: A Rain Forest, Restless Natives and U.S. Pot Smokers," *In These Times,* Sept. 20-26, 1989, pp. 4-5; "The War on Druguerillas," *In These Times,* Oct. 11-17, 1989, p. 5; Jo Ann Kawell, "Sending in Army Could Drag U.S. Into Morass," *In These Times,* Oct. 25-31, 1989, pp. 11, 22.

149. "Drug Aid to Colombia Doesn't Fit Need," *Kansas City Times,* Sept. 12, 1989, pp. A1, A6. A Peruvian police official noted that the Bush anti-drug effort in that country showed preference toward the military over the police and sought to inject the military into civilian law enforcement (Corinne Schmidt, "Aid to Latin American Military Is Not the Answer," *Washington Post* section of *Manchester Guardian Weekly,* Sept. 10, 1989, p. 17). Regardless of the effect on drugs, the Bush program had the effect of strengthening the military's influence in Latin American governments.

150. Bellis, *Heroin,* 86-87; McCoy, *Politics;* Prados, *Presidents',* 73, 75-76, 285-87; Sanders, "Doper's," 70; Jim Naureckas, "Drugs and the Contras: Washington Looks the Other Way," *In These Times,* April 26-May 2, 1989, p. 5; George Winslow, "Credibility a Casualty in the War on Drugs," *In These Times,* May 17-23, 1989, p. 19; Joel Bleifuss, "Turf Wars," *In These Times,* Oct. 4-10, 1989, pp. 4-5; Kathy Evans, "US Seeks Deal with Afghan Drug Baron," *Manchester Guardian Weekly,* Oct. 29, 1989, p. 9; McCoy, "The Politics of the Poppy in Indochina: A Comparative Study of Patron-Client Relations under French and American Administrations," in Simmons and Said, *Drugs,* 112-36; Robert Parry with Rod Nordland, "Guns for Drugs?" *Newsweek,* May 23, 1988, pp. 22-23; Stephen Kurkjian and Murray Waas, "Senate Panel to Delve into Latin Drug Ties," *Boston Globe,* April 4, 1988.

151. That question, which inspired this chapter's title, was asked by Zinberg and Robertson, *Drugs,* 57.

152. Claims are sometimes made that China eliminated opium and Japan eliminated amphetamines, but research for this book yielded no confirmation.

A National Academy of Science committee published a paper saying that the People's Republic of China ended all use and cultivation of opium in less than 4 years (Lowinger, "How the People's Republic of China Solved Their Drug Abuse Problem," in National, *Problems,* 431-42). But the paper also said that the average addiction cure in China, allegedly conducted in pleasant and humane conditions uncharacteristic of communist attitudes toward deviants, took only 12 days. Such a claim is inconsistent with experience of addiction treatment everywhere else, and raises questions about other claims regarding China's "success story." The same paper praised Communist China as a healthy society comprised of healthy individuals, a debatable assertion.

Accounts of Japan's "success" against amphetamines contain curiosities. The highly publicized standard story is that an outbreak of abuse beset Japan in the 1950s and was conquered by vigorous law enforcement. Certain details receive less publicity. For example, amphetamine use was introduced and encouraged by the Japanese government during World War II to increase military and business productivity (Brill and Hirose, "Rise," 179-94; Kato, "Epidemiological," 591-621; Hemmi, "How We Have Handled the Problem of Drug Abuse in Japan," in Sjöqvist and Tottie, *Abuse* [discussion], 161). After the war, drug companies were stuck with large amphetamine inventories no longer needed by the government, and the response was a vigorous advertising campaign (Hemmi, "How," in Sjöqvist and Tottie, *Abuse*, 148; Ishii and Motohashi, "Drug," 105-14) encouraging people to use more and more of a drug already surrounded by a patriotic aura and which provided more energy for workers laboring to rebuild Japan. The campaign succeeded. Japanese authorities suddenly declared the nation to be suffering from amphetamine abuse. Any reason for this change in attitude is unclear in standard accounts—perhaps the American occupation government promoted the change. Nor is the meaning of "abuse," "dependence," or "addiction," ever made clear, a confusion evidenced by figures given for the peak number of Japanese afflicted, ranging from 600,000 (Hemmi, "How," in Sjöqvist and Tottie, *Abuse* [discussion], 154) to 5 million (Kato, "Epidemiological," 591-621). Standard accounts all agree that strict enforcement of new laws against amphetamines reduced use to virtually zero. Less publicized is the fact that the laws prohibited manufacture and apparently coincided with exhaustion of pharmaceutical company overstock. Use ended when supplies did. The subsequent absence of a smuggling racket in the 1950s and 1960s raises a question about just how many million "addicts" ever existed. Japanese victory over drug abuse becomes even more problematical when one notes that the defeat of amphetamine use was accompanied by a rise in heroin use (Nagahama, "Review," 19-24; Brill and Hirose, "Rise," 179-94; Kato, "Epidemiological," 591-621; Ishii and Motohashi, "Drug," 105-14), that defeat of heroin in the 1960s was accompanied by an outbreak of lacquer thinner sniffing and abuse of analgesics and methaqualone—best known as Quaalude (Brill and Hirose, "Rise," 179-94; Kato, "Epidemiological," 591-621; Hemmi, "How," in Sjöqvist and Tottie, *Abuse* [discussion], 157-58), followed by a reappearance of stimulants (Ishii and Motohashi, "Drug," 105-14; Nakatani et al., "Methamphetamine," 1548-49). Are Japanese authorities chalking up victory against one drug after another, or is drug use in Japan following the pattern seen everywhere else, of one substance supplanting another as fashions change?

153. "Marijuana," *UCLA Law Review*, 1517 n. 14.

154. Kaplan, *Marijuana*, 29.

155. Grinspoon and Bakalar, *Cocaine*, 236-37.

156. Towell and Montney, *Directories*, 1044-45.

157. Ibid., 1045.

158. Barbara A. Washington, "Reaction Mixed on Bonds for Drug War," *Kansas City Star*, Aug. 11, 1989, p. 3A; Jerry Heaster, " 'Drug War Bonds' another Example of Weak Leadership," *Kansas City Star*, Aug. 13, 1989, p. 2F.

CHAPTER 5

1. "Total identity" is a term taken from Duster (*Legislation*, 68).

2. "Evil Other" is a term taken from Blum ("On the Presence of Demons," in Blum, *Society*, 338).

3. Duster, *Legislation*, 213.

4. The tactic is not unique to modern times or the United States. King James I of Great Britain opposed tobacco as a habit acquired from savages (American Indians). The Chinese imperial regime opposed opium as an import from European barbarians (Blum, "A Background History of Drugs," in Blum, *Society*, 12).

5. Musto, *American*, 300 n. 34 notes 1919 fears. In the 1950s federal Narcotics Commissioner Harry Anslinger claimed that Communist China promoted heroin in the United States (Anslinger testimony, Senate Judiciary Committee, *Communist*, 1-12; Anslinger testimony, Senate Judiciary Committee, *Scope*, 3611-25), and the Daniel Subcommittee agreed (Senate Committee on the Judiciary, *Report*, S. Rpt. 1440, pp. 3-4). The claim received more publicity than did facts that contradicted it (Fort, "A World View of Drugs," in Blum, *Society*, 234; Kolb, *Drug*, 144; McCoy, *Politics*, 145-48). "There are a very great many fine men on the Federal bench today, but there are just too many political touts and parlor pinks utterly incapable of understanding the danger of organized crime and organized subversion" (U.S. Rep. Burr P. Harrison, speaking of drug abuse, House Ways and Means Committee, *Control*, 56). The administration of California governor Ronald Reagan even said that "subversive elements" used drugs to cause rebellion among college students (quoted in Kaplan, *Marijuana*, 8). Communist origins of illicit drugs was a frequent theme among rightists in the 1980s. Germany were blamed for World War I heroin use; Japanese were blamed for World War II opium use (Vogel, Isbell, and Chapman, "Present," 1019; King, *Drug*, 215). Political implications of drugs are nothing new. In the 1600s, when Islamic regimes suspected that subversives met at coffee houses, harsh punishments were decreed for coffee drinkers (Blum, "A Background History of Drugs," in Blum, *Society*, 11-12).

6. Johnson, Petersen, and Wells, "Arrest Probabilities for Marijuana Users as Indicators of Selective Law Enforcement," in Weissman and DuPont, *Criminal*, 90; Zinberg and Robertson, *Drugs*, 233-34. This phenomenon has also been observed in Canada (Erickson, "Deterrence and Deviance: The Example of Cannabis Prohibition," in Trebach, *Drugs*, 135), and in Britain (Zinberg and Robertson, *Drugs*, 148-49).

7. Johnson, Petersen, and Wells, "Arrest Probabilities for Marijuiana Users as Indicators of Selective Law Enforcement," in Weissman and DuPont, *Criminal*, 90.

8. Youths, of course, are no more monolithic than any other broad demographic group. Many youths are content with the status quo, and not all who call for social change seek progressive reform. Illicit drug use may even be excused among such youths—for example, news media coverage of the 1988 election campaign largely ignored reports of Dan Quayle's college days' use of marijuana ("The 'Vice' President," *In These Times*, November 16-22, 1988, p. 5; "V.P. J.D.," *In These Times*, Sept. 20-26, 1989, p. 5), but we may be sure that similar reports about a progressive candidate would have been publicized as evidence of anti-Americanism. In this book the discussion of "youths" is limited to social progressives, as is much discussion of youths anywhere else.

9. The extreme level of hatred was illustrated by a 1969 survey in which 42 percent of parents were ready to notify a law officer if their children used illegal drugs (Zinberg and Robertson, *Drugs*, 29-30). It is one thing for a parent to call police if a son mugs somebody or a daughter parks a stolen car in the driveway. It is another thing to summon police if the child's conduct harms no one but the child.

10. Doe v. Renfrow, 475 F.Supp. 1012 (N.D. Ind. 1979); Doe v. Renfrow, 631 F.2d 91 (7th Cir. 1980); Doe v. Renfrow, 451 U.S. 1022 (certiorari denied). Facts stated by the 3 courts differ on the number of students found with contraband.

11. Trebach, *Great*, 230-31.

12. Michael Martinez, "Kansas School Defends Its Drug-Testing Proposal," *Kansas City Times*, May 13, 1989, pp. A1, A20.

13. *Washington Post*, Sept. 8, 1984, p. A16.

14. Zinberg and Weil, "Comparison," 122; Zinberg and Robertson, *Drugs*, 85.

15. For example, see the chapter "Three Governments that Fought the Future," in Miller, *Heritage*, 115-28.

16. Szasz, *Ceremonial*, 70; Gordon, *Hitler*, 171-73, 177, 187, 200, 206, 297; Stern, "Introduction," in Eschenburg et al., *Path*, xix.

17. The atmosphere of sales to the Jews' neighbors is captured in memoirs by Weiss, *Nazi*. The atmosphere at American auctions was captured by the *Frontline* "Who" television documentary.

18. Kittrie, *Right*, 229.

19. 1952 N.J. Laws 230, pp. 776-79.

20. Brecher and Consumer Reports, *Licit*, 419-20.

21. Paul Wenske, "Bennett Gets Out the Anti-Drug Word," *Kansas City Times*, Aug. 10, 1989, p. A12; Jake Thompson, "Bush Starts Promoting Drug Plan," *Kansas City Times*, Sept. 7, 1989, p. A15; Lewis W. Diuguid, "Local Soldiers in Drug War Find Hope in New Plan," *Kansas City Star*, Sept. 13, 1989, Kansas City-Jackson County Star section, p. 14.

22. Brecher and Consumer Reports, *Licit*, 59.

23. Oberia D. Dempsey, quoted in Will Lissner, "Harlem Leaders Weighing Plan For Camps to Restrain Addicts," *New York Times*, July 18, 1969, p. 36. See also John Sibley, "Forced Care for Addicts Is Approved by Assembly," *New York Times*, March 31, 1966, pp. 1, 28; and *New York Times*, Nov. 19, 1967,. section 4, p. E7.

24. Lawrence Sherman, quoted in Paul Wenske, "Anti-Drug Proposal Under Fire," *Kansas City Times*, Aug. 3, 1989, p. A20.

25. Joe Lambe, " 'Justice Without Jails,' " *Kansas City Star*, Jan. 29, 1990, p. 1A.

26. Trebach, *Great*, 130.

27. Melissa Berg, "Are Drug Users Fit Mothers?" *Kansas City Times*, Feb. 11, 1989, p. A19; Clarence Page, "Jail Is Wrong Way to Try to Deter Drug Use by Pregnant Women," *Kansas City Star*, May 23, 1989, p. 7A; "Cocaine Mother Gets Probation," *Kansas City Times*, Aug. 26, 1989, p. A6; David Goldstein, "Is Fight to Stamp Out Drugs Stomping on Civil Liberties?" *Kansas City Times*, Aug. 31, 1989, p. A1; LaCroix, "Birth," 585-88. Moss ("Separated," 38) notes a case where an infant was seized from a woman who smoked a marijuana cigarette during childbirth, a practice that an article in the *Journal of the American Medical Association* described as effective for easing childbirth without harm to woman or infant ("Effects," 1165). That medical article, however, appeared in 1930—before society declared marijuana users to be criminal perverts.

28. Schroeder, *Politics*, 54.

29. Drug Chief William Bennett declared, "Ask most Americans if they saw someone in the streets selling drugs to their kids, what they would feel morally justified in doing—tear them [dealers] limb from limb." He added, "It's not a moral problem. I used to teach ethics." ("Drug Chief Urges Death Penalties," *Kansas City Star*, June 16, 1989, p. 1A).

30. William Bennett interview, "This Week With David Brinkley," telecast by National Broadcasting Company network, Dec. 17, 1989.

31. "Narco-Terrorists," *In These Times*, Sept. 13-19, 1989, p. 4. See also Jim Naureckas, "CIA Pushes for Ambiguities in 'Accidental' Killing Law," *In These Times*, November 15-21, 1989, p. 3.

CHAPTER 6

1. Duster, *Legislation*, 244-45.

2. Blum, "On the Presence of Demons," in Blum, *Society*, 332-33.

3. Ibid., 335.

4. Packer, *Limits*, 65-66.

5. Blum, "A History of Opium," in Blum, *Society*, 49, 50n.

6. Taylor, *American*, 32.

7. Ibid., 42.

8. Bejerot, *Addiction*, 36-37.

9. Trebach, *Great*, 105.

10. Sylbing and Persoon, "Cannabis," 51, 58-59.

11. Nadelmann, "Drug," 944.

12. Van de Wijngaart, "What," 991.

13. Zerbetto, "Overview," 43-50.

14. Plant, *Drugtakers*, 45.

15. Stimson, *Heroin*, 73.

16. Zinberg and Robertson, *Drugs*, 139.

17. Kaplan, *Hardest*, 158; Zinberg and Robertson, *Drugs*, 127-29; Trebach, *Heroin*, 182-83; Trebach, *Great*, 305-6.

18. The accuracy of numbers on which that consensus is based is irrelevant to the present discussion, but long-standing skepticism exists about them (see Chein et al., *Road*, 372, for an early example). Reports from credible authorities vary greatly. Bakalar and Grinspoon (*Drug*, 94) say about 1,000 opiate addicts existed in Britain in the mid-1980s; Inciardi (*War*, 156) says 50,000 Britons were then addicted to heroin, let alone all opiates.

19. Dorn and South, *Helping*, 21, 31, 41-44, 60, 80, 85-86, 121-22; Jamieson, Glanz, and MacGregor, *Dealing*, 11, 57-66, 70, 77-79, 83-91, 94-95, 120; Plant, *Drugtakers*, 139.

20. Quoted in Judson, *Heroin*, 152.

21. Eldridge, *Narcotics*, 112; Hess, *Chasing*, 8-11, 93-94.

22. Adams, *Diary*, 128-30, 151-52, 190-92, 210-11, 214-15; Kobler, *Ardent*, 31.

23. Quoted in Kobler, *Ardent*, 33.

24. Bakalar and Grinspoon, *Drug*, 82; Rublowsky, *Stoned*, 70.

25. Aaron and Musto, "Temperance and Prohibition in America: A Historical Overview," in Moore and Gerstein, *Alcohol*, 162.

26. Ibid., 146. Reformers declared similar goals in other countries as well; see also, Bakalar and Grinspoon, *Drug*, 80 for an international context.

27. Amendment 18, U.S. Constitution.

28. Henry McElroy, quoted in Miller, *Truman*, 188.

29. Sinclair, *Era*, 410.

30. Warburton, "Prohibition and Economic Welfare," in *Annals* (1932), 93, 97; Aaron and Musto, "Temperance and Prohibition in America: A Historical Overview," in Moore and Gerstein, *Alcohol*, 164-65; Room, "Evaluating the Effect of Drinking Laws on Drinking," in Ewing and Rouse, *Drinking*, 287.

31. Or perhaps not. One statistical examination included this caveat: "As in any statistical study, these findings do not offer definitive proof of anything." (Cook, "The Effect of Liquor Taxes on Drinking, Cirrhosis, and Auto Accidents," in Moore and Gerstein, *Alcohol*, 273).

32. Warburton, *Economic*, 24.

33. Ibid., 108.

34. Ibid., 260.

35. Jellinek, "Recent," 9-10.

36. Aaron and Musto, "Temperance and Prohibition in America: A Historical Overview," in Moore and Gerstein, *Alcohol*, 159.

37. Bakalar and Grinspoon, *Drug*, 86, 105.

38. Warburton, *Economic*, 90, 213-14.

39. Emerson, "Prohibition and Mortality and Morbidity," in *Annals* (1932), 59-60.

40. Warburton, *Economic*, 262-63; Bakalar and Grinspoon, *Drug*, 86; Room, "Evaluating the Effect of Drinking Laws on Drinking," in Ewing and Rouse, *Drinking*, 287.

41. Jellinek, "Recent," 40. Because alcohol-related disease comes from years of abuse, disease statistics for the 1930s and 1940s may indicate 1920s behavior.

42. Aaron and Musto, "Temperance and Prohibition in America: A Historical Overview," in Moore and Gerstein, *Alcohol*, 165.

43. Warburton, *Economic*, 101-2.

44. Blum, "Mind Altering Drugs and Dangerous Drugs: Alcohol," President's Commission, *Drunkenness*, 40-41.

45. Warburton, *Economic*, 224-27, 263.

46. Landesco, "Prohibition and Crime," *Annals* (1932), 128; Aaron and Musto, "Temperance and Prohibition in America: A Historical Overview," in Moore and Gerstein, *Alcohol*, 166.

47. Warburton, *Economic*, 171.

48. Ibid., 263. Nor was Warburton able to measure an effect on worker productivity, industrial accidents, or automobile accidents (Warburton, "Prohibition and Economic Welfare," in *Annals* (1932), 94-97.

49. Sinclair, *Era*, 184.

50. Fosdick and Scott, *Toward*, 11; Kobler, *Ardent*, 272-82.

51. Sinclair, *Era*, 175.

52. Ibid., 187-88, 200-1; *New York Times*, Dec. 30, 1926, pp. 1-2 and Dec. 31, 1926, pp. 1-2.

53. Sinclair, *Era*, 188; Kobler, *Ardent*, 288-91; *New York Times*, Feb. 16, 1924, p. 1, col. 2 and Feb. 18, p. 10, col. 2 and Feb. 19, p. 1, col. 5 and Feb. 20, p. 4, col. 5 and Feb. 21, p. 17, col. 5 and Feb. 22, p. 2, col. 6 and Feb. 24, p. 21, col. 3 and Feb. 25, p. 5, col. 4 and Feb. 26, p. 3, col. 2 and March 9, sect. 2, p. 1, col. 7.

54. Sinclair, *Era*, 188.

55. National Commission on Law Observance and Enforcement, *Report*, H. Doc. 722, p. 58. This figure is for sentences exceeding one year.

56. Ibid.

57. Sinclair, *Era*, 190.

58. Kaplan, *Marijuana*, 358; Sinclair, *Era*, 193.

59. Chapman, "Drink," 108.

60. Fosdick and Scott, *Toward*, 15.

61. Scher, *Drug*, 12; DuPont, "The Future of Drug Abuse Prevention," in Weissman and DuPont, *Criminal*, 196-97.

62. Zinberg and Robertson, *Drugs*, 85.

63. Chein et al., *Road*, 339-40; Rublowsky, *Stoned*, 79-81, 207; Blum, "A Background History of Drugs," in Blum et al., *Society*, 11-12; idem, "A History of Tobacco," in ibid., 90-91; idem, "A History of Stimulants," in ibid., 100-101; Szasz, *Ceremonial*, 185-86.

64. Erickson et al., *Steel*, xvi, 85-88; Brown et al., "In," 639.

65. Erickson et al., *Steel*, 119.

66. Platt and Labate, *Heroin*, 191.

67. Weissman, "Understanding the Drugs and Crime Connection," in Weissman and DuPont, *Criminal*, 67.

68. Erickson et al., *Steel*, 120.

69. Jacobson and Zinberg, *Social*, 70; Johnston, O'Malley, and Bachman, *Drug* (National Institute on Drug Abuse), 143.

70. Jacobson and Zinberg, *Social*, 70.

71. Erickson et al., *Steel*, 113, 116.

72. Schroeder, *Politics*, 24.

73. Popham, Schmidt, and de Lint, "Government Control Measures to Prevent Hazardous Drinking," in Ewing and Rouse, *Drinking*, 240-47.

74. Popham, Schmidt, and de Lint, "Government Control Measures to Prevent Hazardous Drinking," in ibid., 248-53, 261.

75. Room, "Evaluating the Effect of Drinking Laws on Drinking," in ibid., 285.

76. Griffiths, Bigelow, and Henningfield, "Similarities in Animal and Human Drug-Taking Behavior," in Mello, *Advances*, 30.

77. Abelson et al., "Drug Experience, Attitudes and Related Behavior Among Adolescents and Adults," in National Commission on Marihuana and Drug Abuse, *Drug*, 501; Johnston, *Drugs*, 218-19; Carr and Meyers, "Marijuana and Cocaine: The Process of Change in Drug Policy," in Drug Abuse Council, *Facts*, 179.

78. Johnston, O'Malley, and Bachman, *Drugs* (National Institute on Drug Abuse), 138, 244.

79. "Drug Use Is Immoral, Poll Respondents Say," *Kansas City Star*, February 27, 1990, p. 1A, 10A.

80. Apsler, Brady, and Barker, "Reasons," 553, 556, 564.

81. Schroeder, *Politics*, 24.

82. Johnston, O'Malley, and Bachman, *Drug* (National Institute on Drug Abuse), 143-44.

83. Patricia G. Erickson, "Deterrence and Deviance: The Example of Cannabis Prohibition," in Trebach, *Drugs*, 149.

84. This theory is consistent with experiments summarized in Griffiths, Bigelow, and Henningfield, "Similarities in Animal and Human Drug-Taking Behavior," in Mello, *Advances*, 34-36. An alcohol intake experiment showed consumption to increase as price declined, but the amount of increase depended on amount of previous use—heavy drinkers boosted their intake much more than light users.

85. Loeb, "Relationship of State Law to Per Capita Drinking," in Ewing and Rouse, *Drinking*, 219-38.

86. Room, "Evaluating the Effect of Drinking Laws on Drinking," in ibid., 278.

87. Ravin v. State, 537 P.2d 494 (Alaska 1975).

88. Trebach, *Great*, 103.

89. Schroeder, *Politics*, 22.

90. Ibid., 24.

91. Carr and Meyers, "Marijuana and Cocaine: The Process of Change in Drug Policy" in Drug Abuse Council, *Facts*, 177-78; Bakalar and Grinspoon, *Drug*, 116. In an experiment that required subjects to smoke specified amounts of marijuana, subjects' complaints about excessive levels of consumption led the investigators to conclude that legalization need not increase marijuana use (Kagel, Battalio, and Miles, "Marijuana," 390).

92. Domestic Council Drug Abuse Task Force, *White*, 25.

93. White House, Drug Abuse Policy Office, *1984 National*, 19.

94. Eldridge, *Narcotics*, 74.

95. Smart, "Effects," 55-65.

96. Zacune, Mitcheson, and Malone, "Heroin," 557-70.

97. Single and Kandel, "The Role of Buying and Selling in Illicit Drug Use," in Trebach, *Drugs*, 118, 127.

98. Rublowsky, *Stoned*, 19-20, 48, 57; Jacobson and Zinberg, *Social*, 26-27.

99. Jacobson and Zinberg, *Social*, 2.

100. Ibid., 2 n.; Fort, "A World View of Drugs," in Blum et al., *Drugs*, 241; Rublowsky, *Stoned*, 72.

101. Becker, "History," 163-76.

102. Blum, "A Background History of Drugs," in Blum et al., *Society*, 10.

103. Kaplan, *Marijuana*, 334.

104. Fackelmann, "HIV," 172.

105. President George Bush, Sept. 5, 1989, quoted in *Kansas City Times*, Sept. 6, 1989, p. A8.

106. U.S. Rep. Stewart McKinney, mid-1980s, quoted in Trebach, *Great*, 168.

107. President Richard Nixon, in Nixon, *Public*, October 27, 1970, p. 948.

108. Louria, *Overcoming*, 12.

109. Governor Ronald Reagan of California, quoted in King, *Drug*, 342-43.

110. U.S. Attorney General John Mitchell, ca. 1969, quoted in King, *Drug*, 308.

111. President Lyndon Johnson, in Johnson, *Public*, July 14, 1965, p. 754.

112. Schur, *Narcotic*, 51.

113. *"True," Science Digest*, 34.

114. Walton, describing the New Orleans situation of 1926, *Marihuana*, 30-31.

115. Fossier, "Mariahuana," 249-50.

116. Kolb, *Drug*, 65, describing a 1924 case.

117. Richmond Hobson, quoted in *Literary Digest*, May 24, 1924, p. 32.

118. McGuire and Lichtenstein, "Drug," 189.

119. Lichtenstein, "Narcotic," 962.

120. Towns, "Peril," 585.

121. Wolff, "Necessity," 521-22.

122. Gompers and Gutstadt, *Some* (S. Doc. 137), 22.

123. Dr. Harris of Virginia City, Nevada, describing situation in 1870s, quoted in Kane, *Opium*, 3.

124. *New York Times*, July 29, 1877, p. 10, col. 6.

125. Morgan, *Yesterday's*, 15. See Morgan, *Drugs*, 37 for more citations of nineteenth-century sources.

126. Chein et al., *Road*, 367; Gerard and Kornetsky, "Adolescent," 457-86; Kandel, "Convergences in Prospective Longitudinal Surveys of Drug Use in Normal Populations," in Kandel, *Longitudinal*, 26. A Canadian study found that persons 17 years or older at their first marijuana use were less likely to continue using than persons who started at 16 or younger (Erickson, "Deterrence and Deviance: The Example of Cannabis Prohibition," in Trebach, *Drugs*, 145); the more deviant a person is, the earlier it shows up.

127. The phenomenon is not limited to the United States. In 1973, Dr. Peter Chapple said that 500,000 London schoolchildren had tried drugs, but the total enrollment was less than that (Plant, *Drugtakers*, 69, 69n).

128. Kolb, "Let's," 54.

129. Bellis, *Heroin*, 187.

130. National Institute on Drug Abuse, *DAWN* 1984, 71; Trebach, *Great*, 11. DAWN 1984 statistics for children covered ages 6 to 17.

131. National Institute on Drug Abuse, *DAWN* 1986, 56; U.S. Bureau of the Census, *Current*, 22; U.S. Bureau of the Census, *Statistical*, 73. Statistics for children covered ages 10 to 17. Total deaths from all causes in that age group were perhaps about 11,500 (a *very* rough figure calculated from death rates of 29 per 100,000 among persons aged 5-14 and 60 per 100,000 in ages 15-24).

132. Erickson et al., *Steel*, 59; Trebach, *Great*, 12-13, 69, 103, 105; *U.S. News and World Report*, Nov. 18, 1985, p. 16; Beschner, "Understanding Teenage Drug Use," in Beschner and Friedman, *Teen*, 2; White House, Drug Abuse Policy Office, *1984 National*, 19; Paul Wenske, "At Last, One Good Drug Study," *Kansas City Times*, March 1, 1989, pp. A1, A8; Jake Thompson and Paul Wenske, "Fewer People Using Illegal Drugs in U.S., Government Survey Says," *Kansas City Times*, Aug. 1, 1989, pp. A1, A10; Clark, "Drugs," 408; "Crackmire," 10; Johnston, O'Malley, and Bachman, *Drug* (National Institute on Drug Abuse). Although Republican presidents might like to credit their tough anti-drug policies for the decline, it began while Jimmy Carter was president.

133. Johnston, *Drugs*, 190-91.

134. Erickson, *Steel*, 47.

135. Quoted in Judson, *Heroin*, 121.

136. Finnegan, "Effects," 143; Finnegan, "Neonatal Abstinence Syndrome," in Nelson, ed., *Current*, 314.

137. Merker, Higgins, and Kinnard, "Assessing," 178.

138. For skepticism about cocaine resonance see Andrew E. Skodol, "Diagnostic Issues in Cocaine Abuse," in Spitz and Rosecan, *Cocaine*, 120; Teller and Devenyi, "Bromocriptine," 1197-1205; Burgen and Mitchell, *Gaddum's*, 76; Reynolds, *Martindale*, 914; Arena, *Poisoning*, 557. For outright rejection of cocaine resonance see *Drug*, 2078; Goth, *Medical*, 350; Brenda K. Colasanti, "Contemporary Drug Abuse," in Craig and Stitzel, *Modern*, 620; Frederick J. Goldstein and G. Victor Rossi, "Pharmacological Aspects of Drug Abuse," in Gennaro, *Remington's*, 1351; McEvoy, *American*, 1508; Kaye, *Handbook*, 272; Gosselin, Smith, and Hodge, *Clinical*, III 117.

139. Merker, Higgins, and Kinnard, "Assessing," 178.

140. Finnegan, "Neonatal Abstinence Syndrome," in Nelson, ed., *Current*, 315. For example, see Madden, Payne, and Miller, "Maternal," 209-11; Hadeed and Siegel, "Maternal," 205; Ryan, Ehrlich, and Finnegan, "Cocaine," 295-98.

141. Edelin et al., "Methadone," 400; Fulroth, Phillips, and Durand, "Perinatal," 906-7; Oro and Dixon, "Perinatal," 572.

142. Mitchell et al., "Ultrasonic," 1104, 1106.

143. Edelin et al., "Methadone," 399; Zelson, Lee, and Casalino, "Neonatal,"

1216, 1220; Pierson, Howard, and Kleber, "Sudden," 1733-34; Finnegan, "Effects," 143-44; Merker, Higgins, and Kinnard, "Assessing," 177. See also Olsen and Lees, "Ventilatory," 983-84; Finnegan and Reeser, "Incidence," 405.

144. Graham et al., "Pregnancy," 147.

145. Ibid., 143.

146. Edelin et al., "Methadone," 400-1, 403; Fulroth, Phillips, and Durand, "Perinatal," 908; Frank et al., "Cocaine," 890-92; Finnegan, "Neonatal Abstinence Syndrome," in Nelson, ed., Current, 315.

147. Mitchell et al., "Ultrasonic," 1108-9; Chasnoff et al., "Temporal," 1743; Frank et al., "Cocaine," 888, 894; Ryan, Ehrlich, and Finnegan, "Cocaine," 298; Oro and Dixon, "Perinatal," 576.

148. Weil, Natural, 30.

149. Trebach, Great, 75.

150. Quoted in ibid., 95.

151. Schur, Narcotic, 76.

152. Laurie, Drugs, 141.

153. Courtwright, Dark, 60.

154. Eldridge, Narcotics, 24; Khantzian, "Self-Medication," 1259.

155. Kolb, Drug, 11, 106; Trebach, Great, 92-93; Chein et al., Road, 358, 358 n.26; Wikler, Opiate, 57.

156. Kolb, Drug, 11, 47, 106.

157. Kolb, Drug, 97; Chein et al., Road, 228-29.

158. Cuskey and Edington, "Drug Abuse as Self-Destructive Behavior" in Roberts, Self-Destructive, 138; Sanders, "Doper's," 71-72.

159. Khantzian, "Self-Medication," 1259.

160. Brecher and Consumer Reports, Licit, 368; Rublowsky, Stoned, 159.

161. Godfrey, "LSD Therapy," in Catanzaro, Alcoholism, 237-52; Abramson, Use. Less hopeful appraisals of LSD in this context can be found in Smart et al., Lysergic and Ludwig, Levine, and Stark, LSD.

162. Ames, "Clinical," 976.

163. Chopra and Chopra, "Use," 13.

164. Comitas, "The Social Nexus of Ganja in Jamaica," in Rubin, Cannabis, 119-32; Jan Rocha, "Blood in the Rivers of Gold," Manchester Guardian Weekly, Dec. 10, 1989, p. 24; Dreher, Working, 133, 173, 175, 179-85, 197; Page, Carter, and De Frenkel, "Marihuana and Work: Users at School and on the Job," in Carter, Cannabis, 155-56.

165. Musto, American, 72.

166. Stanley, "Morphinism," 753.

167. Grinspoon and Bakalar, Cocaine, 99.

168. Simonton, "Increase," 556.

169. "Cocaine," British Medical Journal, 1729; see also Wright, Report, S. Doc. 377, p. 49.

170. Edward Marshall, " 'Uncle Sam Is the Worst Drug Fiend in the World,' " New York Times, March 12, 1911, sect. 5, p. 12; Morgan, Yesterday's, 4.

171. Siegel, *Intoxication*, 308-11.

172. Grinspoon and Bakalar, *Cocaine*, 99-100; Bakalar and Grinspoon, *Drug*, 126; Siegel, "New Patterns of Cocaine Use: Changing Doses and Routes," in Kozel and Adams, *Cocaine* (National Institute on Drug Abuse), 206. One hypothesis holds that top athletes face a greater danger of cocaine-induced death than the rest of us face (Giammarco, "Athlete," 412-14)—a sobering trade off for improved performance.

173. Grinspoon and Bakalar, *Cocaine*, 21; Szasz, *Ceremonial*, 192.

174. Louria, *Overcoming*, 33; Rublowsky, *Stoned*, 173; Blum, "A History of Stimulants," in Blum et al., *Society*, 108; Sanders, "Doper's," 72.

175. Brecher and Consumer Reports, *Licit*, 353.

176. Sapira, "Narcotic," 573-74.

177. Bejerot, *Addiction*, 33 (Table 2).

178. Ibid., 36-37; Kaplan, *Hardest*, 5.

179. Newman, "We'll Make Them an Offer They Can't Refuse," in Weissman and DuPont, *Criminal*, 168-69. See also Bakalar and Grinspoon, *Drug*, 139.

Sources Cited

BOOKS

Abramson, Harold A., ed. *The Use of LSD in Psychotherapy and Alcoholism.* Indianapolis: Bobbs-Merrill Company, 1967.

Adams, John. *Diary and Autobiography of John Adams.* Vol. 1. L. H. Butterfield, ed. Cambridge, Mass.: The Belknap Press of Harvard University Press, 1961.

Allen, David, ed. *The Cocaine Crisis.* New York: Plenum Press, 1987.

American Child Health Association. *Physical Defects: The Pathway to Correction.* New York: American Child Health Association, 1934.

Anslinger, Harry J., and Will Oursler. *The Murderers: The Story of the Narcotics Gangs.* New York: Farrar, Straus and Cudahy, 1961.

Arena, Jay M., ed. *Poisoning: Toxicology, Symptoms, Treatments.* 5th ed. Springfield, Ill.: Charles C. Thomas, 1986.

Bakalar, James B., and Lester Grinspoon. *Drug Control in a Free Society.* Cambridge: Cambridge University Press, 1984.

Beard, George M. *American Nervousness: Its Causes and Consequences, A Supplement to Nervous Exhaustion (Neurasthenia).* New York: G. P. Putnam's Sons, 1881.

Bejerot, Nils. *Addiction and Society.* Springfield, Ill.: Charles C. Thomas, 1970.

Bellis, David J. *Heroin and Politicians: The Failure of Public Policy to Control Addiction in America.* Westport, Conn.: Greenwood Press, 1981.

Bennett, James. *Oral History and Delinquency: The Rhetoric of Criminology.* Chicago: University of Chicago Press, 1981.

Beschner, George, and Alfred S. Friedman. *Teen Drug Use.* Lexington, Mass.: D.C. Heath and Company, 1986.

Bettmann, Otto L. *The Good Old Days—They Were Terrible!* New York: Random House, 1974.

Biernacki, Patrick. *Pathways from Heroin Addiction: Recovery without Treatment.*

Health, Society, and Policy series, ed. Sheryl Ruzek and Irving Kenneth Zola. Philadelphia: Temple University Press, 1986.

Blachly, Paul H. *Seduction: A Conceptual Model in the Drug Dependencies and Other Contagious Ills.* Springfield, Ill.: Charles C. Thomas, 1970.

Blum, Richard H., et al. *Society and Drugs: Drugs I: Social and Cultural Observations.* The Jossey-Bass Behavioral Science Series. San Francisco: Jossey-Bass, 1969.

————. *Students and Drugs: College and High School Observations.* The Jossey-Bass Behavioral Science Series and the Jossey-Bass Series in Higher Education (published jointly). San Francisco: Jossey-Bass, 1969.

Bourne, Peter G., ed. *Addiction.* New York: Academic Press, 1974.

Brecher, Edward M., and the Editors of Consumer Reports. *Licit and Illicit Drugs: The Consumers Union Report on Narcotics, Stimulants, Depressants, Inhalants, Hallucinogens, and Marijuana—Including Caffeine, Nicotine, and Alcohol.* Boston: Little, Brown and Company, 1972.

Burgen, A. S. V., and J. F. Mitchell. *Gaddum's Pharmacology.* 9th ed. Oxford: Oxford University Press, 1985.

Carter, William E., ed. *Cannabis in Costa Rica: A Study of Chronic Marihuana Use.* Philadelphia: Institute for the Study of Human Issues, 1980.

Catanzaro, Ronald J., ed. *Alcoholism: The Total Treatment Approach.* Springfield, Ill.: Charles C. Thomas, 1968.

Chein, Isidor, Donald L. Gerard, Robert S. Lee, and Eva Rosenfeld. *The Road to H: Narcotics, Delinquency, and Social Policy.* New York: Basic Books, 1964.

Clark, Janet [pseud.]. *The Fantastic Lodge: The Autobiography of a Girl Drug Addict.* Edited by Helen MacGill Hughes. Boston: Houghton Mifflin Company, 1961.

Courtwright, David T. *Dark Paradise: Opiate Addiction in America before 1940.* Cambridge: Harvard University Press, 1982.

Craig, Charles R., and Robert E. Stitzel, eds. *Modern Pharmacology.* 2d ed. Boston: Little, Brown and Company, 1986.

Crothers, T. D. *Morphinism and Narcomanias from Other Drugs.* Philadelphia: W. B. Saunders and Company, 1902.

Cuskey, Walter R., Arnold William Klein, and William Krasner. *Drug-Trip Abroad: American Drug-Refugees in Amsterdam and London.* Philadelphia: University of Pennsylvania Press, 1972.

Deutsch, Dale G., ed. *Analytical Aspects of Drug Testing.* Chemical Analysis, Vol. 100. A Wiley-Interscience Publication. New York: John Wiley & Sons, 1988.

Diagnostic and Statistical Manual of Mental Disorders. 3rd ed., rev. Washington, D.C.: American Psychiatric Association, 1987.

Dorn, Nicholas, and Nigel South. *Helping Drug Users: Social Work, Advice Giving, Referral and Training Services of Three London "Street Agencies."* Hants, England: Gower Publishing Company Limited, 1985.

Dreher, Melanie Creagan. *Working Men and Ganja: Marihuana Use in Rural Jamaica.* Philadelphia: Institute for the Study of Human Issues, 1982.

Drug Abuse Council. *The Facts about "Drug Abuse."* New York: The Free Press, 1980.

Drug Facts and Comparisons. 1990 ed. St. Louis: Facts and Comparisons, 1989.

Duster, Troy. *The Legislation of Morality: Law, Drugs, and Moral Judgment.* New York: The Free Press, 1970.

Eldridge, William Butler. *Narcotics and the Law: A Critique of the American Experiment in Narcotic Drug Control.* 2d ed., rev. Chicago: University of Chicago Press, 1967.

Epstein, Edward Jay. *Agency of Fear: Opiates and Political Power in America.* New York: G. P. Putnam's Sons, 1977.

Erickson, Patricia G., et al. *The Steel Drug: Cocaine in Perspective.* Lexington Books. Lexington, Mass.: D.C. Heath and Company, 1987.

Eschenburg, Theodor, et al. *The Path to Dictatorship. 1918-1933.* Translated by John Conway. Garden City, N.Y.: Doubleday & Company, 1966.

Ewing, John A., and Beatrice A. Rouse, eds. *Drinking: Alcohol in American Society— Issues and Current Research.* Chicago: Nelson-Hall, 1978.

Farber, Seymour M., and Roger H. L. Wilson, eds. *Conflict and Creativity: Part Two of Control of the Mind.* Man and Civilization. New York: McGraw-Hill, 1963.

Feldman, Harvey W., Michael H. Agar, and George M. Beschner, eds. *Angel Dust: An Ethnographic Study of PCP Users.* Lexington, Mass.: D.C. Heath and Company, 1979.

Fiedler, Leslie A. *Being Busted.* New York: Stein and Day, 1969.

Fosdick, Raymond B., and Albert L. Scott. *Toward Liquor Control.* New York: Harper & Brothers Publishers, 1933.

Gennaro, Alfonso R., ed. *Remington's Pharmaceutical Sciences.* 17th ed. Easton, Pa.: Mack Publishing, 1985.

Glatt, Max M., et al. *The Drug Scene in Great Britain: "Journey into Loneliness".* London: Edward Arnold Ltd., 1967.

Goode, Erich. *Drugs in American Society.* New York: Alfred A. Knopf, 1972.

Goodman, Louis S., and Alfred Gilman. *The Pharmacological Basis of Therapeutics.* 2d, 6th, and 7th eds. New York: The Macmillan Company, 1955, 1980, 1985.

Gordon, Sarah. *Hitler, Germans, and the "Jewish Question."* Princeton: Princeton University Press, 1984.

Gosselin, Robert E., Roger P. Smith, and Harold C. Hodge. *Clinical Toxicology of Commercial Products.* 5th ed. Baltimore: Williams & Wilkins, 1984.

Goth, Andres. *Medical Pharmacology: Principles and Conduct.* 11th ed. St. Louis: C.V. Mosby Company, 1984.

Grinspoon, Lester, and James B. Bakalar. *Cocaine: A Drug and Its Social Evolution.* New York: Basic Books, 1976.

Gusfield, Joseph R. *Symbolic Crusade: Status Politics and the American Temperance Movement.* Urbana, Ill.: University of Illinois Press, 1963.

Helmer, John. *Drugs and Minority Oppression.* New York: The Seabury Press, 1975.

Hentoff, Nat. *A Doctor Among the Addicts.* Chicago: Rand McNally, 1968.

Hess, Albert G. *Chasing the Dragon: A Report on Drug Addiction in Hong Kong.* New York: The Free Press, 1965.

Hunt, Leon Gibson, and Carl D. Chambers. *The Heroin Epidemics: A Study of Heroin Use in the United States, 1965-75*. Sociomedical Science Series. New York: Spectrum Publications, 1976.

Inciardi, James A. *The War on Drugs: Heroin, Cocaine, Crime, and Public Policy*. Palo Alto, Calif.: Mayfield Publishing Company, 1986.

Jacobson, Richard, and Norman E. Zinberg. *The Social Basis of Drug Abuse Prevention*. Special Studies Series, no. 5. Washington, D.C.: The Drug Abuse Council, 1975.

Jamieson, Anne, Alan Glanz, and Susanne MacGregor. *Dealing with Drug Misuse: Crisis Intervention in the City*. London: Tavistock Publications, 1984.

Jefferson, Thomas. *The Papers of Thomas Jefferson*. Vol. 7. Julian P. Boyd, ed. Princeton: Princeton University Press, 1953.

Johnson, Bruce D., et al. *Taking Care of Business: The Economics of Crime by Heroin Abusers*. Lexington, Mass.: D.C. Heath and Company, 1985.

Johnston, Lloyd. *Drugs and American Youth*. Ann Arbor, Mich.: Institute for Social Research, University of Michigan: 1973.

Judson, Horace Freeland. *Heroin Addiction in Britain: What Americans Can Learn from the English Experience*. New York: Harcourt Brace Jovanovich, 1973.

Kamisar, Yale, Wayne R. LaFave, and Jerold H. Israel. *Modern Criminal Procedure: Cases, Comments and Questions*. 5th ed. American Casebook Series. St. Paul, Minn.: West Publishing Co., 1980.

Kandel, Denise B., ed. *Longitudinal Research on Drug Use: Empirical Findings and Methodological Issues*. Washington, D.C.: Hemisphere Publishing Corporation, 1978.

Kane, H. H. *Opium-Smoking in America and China*. New York: G. P. Putnam's, 1882.

Kaplan, John. *The Hardest Drug: Heroin and Public Policy*. Studies in Crime and Justice. Chicago: University of Chicago Press, 1983.

_____. *Marijuana – The New Prohibition*. New York: The World Publishing Company, 1970.

Kaye, Sidney. *Handbook of Emergency Toxicology: A Guide for the Identification, Diagnosis, and Treatment of Poisoning*. 5th ed. Springfield, Ill.: Charles C. Thomas, 1988.

King, Rufus. *The Drug Hang-Up: America's Fifty Year Folly*. New York: W. W. Norton & Company, 1972.

Kirkpatrick, Thomas B., Jr. *Prosecution Perspectives on Drugs*. Washington, D.C.: The Drug Abuse Council, 1975.

Kittrie, Nicholas N. *The Right To Be Different: Deviance and Enforced Therapy*. Baltimore: The Johns Hopkins Press, 1971.

Knapp Commission Report on Police Corruption. New York: George Braziller, [1973?].

Kobler, John. *Ardent Spirits: The Rise and Fall of Prohibition*. New York: G. P. Putnam's Sons, 1973.

Köhler, Wolfgang. *The Mentality of Apes*. Translated by Ella Winter. International

Library of Psychology, Philosophy and Scientific Method. London: Routledge & Kegan Paul Ltd., 1927.

Kolb, Lawrence. *Drug Addiction: A Medical Problem.* Springfield, Ill.: Charles C. Thomas, 1962.

Laurie, Peter. *Drugs: Medical, Psychological, and Social Facts.* Baltimore: Penguin Books, 1969.

Law Enforcement Training Institute, School of Law, and Extension Division, University of Missouri—Columbia. *The Missouri Criminal Code: A Handbook for Law Enforcement Officers.* Extension Division Manual 121. Columbia, Missouri: University of Missouri, 1986.

Lesy, Michael. *Wisconsin Death Trip.* New York: Pantheon Books, 1973.

Lindesmith, Alfred R. *The Addict and the Law.* Bloomington: Indiana University Press, 1965.

Louria, Donald B. *Overcoming Drugs: A Program for Action.* New York: McGraw-Hill Book Company, 1971.

Ludwig, Arnold M., Jerome Levine, and Louis H. Stark. *LSD and Alcoholism: A Clinical Study of Treatment Efficacy.* Springfield, Ill.: Charles C. Thomas, 1970.

McCoy, Alfred W. *The Politics of Heroin in Southeast Asia.* With Cathleen B. Read and Leonard P. Adams II. New York: Harper & Row, 1972.

McEvoy, Gerald K., ed. *American Hospital Formulary Service Drug Information.* Bethesda, Md.: American Society of Hospital Pharmacists, 1989.

Masters, R.E.L., and Jean Houston. *The Varieties of Psychedelic Experience.* New York: Dell Publishing Co., 1966.

Mello, Nancy K., ed. *Advances in Substance Abuse: Behavioral and Biological Research: A Research Annual.* Vol. 1. Greenwich, Conn.: JAI Press, 1980.

Miller, Richard Lawrence. *Heritage of Fear: Illusion and Reality in the Cold War.* New York: Walker and Company, 1988.

———. *Truman: The Rise to Power.* New York: McGraw-Hill Book Company, 1986.

Moore, Mark H., and Dean R. Gerstein, eds. *Alcohol and Public Policy: Beyond the Shadow of Prohibition.* Washington, D.C.: National Academy Press, 1981.

Morgan, H. Wayne. *Drugs in America: A Social History, 1800-1980.* Syracuse, N.Y.: Syracuse University Press, 1981.

———, ed. *Yesterday's Addicts: American Society and Drug Abuse 1865-1920.* Norman: University of Oklahoma Press, 1974.

Musto, David F. *The American Disease: Origins of Narcotic Control.* New Haven: Yale University Press, 1973.

National Academy of Science. *Problems of Drug Dependence, 1972.* Proceeding of the 34th Annual Scientific Meeting. Committee on Problems of Drug Dependence. Washington, D.C.: National Academy of Science, 1972.

Nelson, Nicholas M., ed. *Current Therapy in Neonatal-Perinatal Medicine—2.* Philadelphia: B.C. Decker, 1990.

Packer, Herbert L. *The Limits of the Criminal Sanction.* Stanford: Stanford University Press, 1968.

Peele, Stanton. With Archie Brodsky. *Love and Addiction*. New York: Taplinger Publishing Company, 1975.

Plant, Martin A. *Drugtakers in an English Town*. London: Tavistock Publications, 1975.

Platt, Jerome J., and Christina Labate. *Heroin Addiction: Theory, Research, Treatment*. Wiley Series on Personality Processes. A Wiley Interscience Publication. New York: John Wiley & Sons, 1976.

Prados, John. *Presidents' Secret Wars: CIA and Pentagon Covert Operations Since World War II*. New York: William Morrow and Company, 1986.

Restak, Richard M. *The Mind*. New York: Bantam Books, 1988.

Reynolds, James E. F. *Martindale: The Extra Pharmacopoeia*. 28th ed. London: The Pharmaceutical Press, 1982.

Roberts, Albert R., ed. and comp. *Self-Destructive Behavior*. Springfield, Ill.: Charles C. Thomas, 1975.

Rowell, Earle Albert, and Robert Rowell. *On the Trail of Marihuana: The Weed of Madness*. Mountain View, Calif.: Pacific Press Publishing Association, 1939.

Rubin, Vera, ed. *Cannabis and Culture*. The Hague: Mouton Publishers, 1975.

Rublowsky, John. *The Stoned Age: A History of Drugs in America*. Capricorn Books. New York: G.P. Putnam's Sons, 1974.

Scher, Jordan M., ed. *Drug Abuse in Industry: Growing Corporate Dilemma*. Springfield, Ill.: Charles C. Thomas, 1973.

Schroeder, Richard C. *The Politics of Drugs: An American Dilemma*. 2d ed. Washington, D.C.: Congressional Quarterly Press, 1980.

Schur, Edwin M. *Narcotic Addiction in Britain and America: The Impact of Public Policy*. Bloomington: Indiana University Press, 1962.

Shepard, Thomas H. *Catalog of Teratogenic Agents*. 6th ed. Baltimore: Johns Hopkins University Press, 1989.

Shirkey, Harry C., ed. *Pediatric Therapy*. 6th ed. St. Louis: C.V. Mosby Company, 1980.

Shoham, S., ed. *Israel Studies in Criminology, I*. Tel Aviv: Goneh Press, 1970.

Siegel, Ronald K. *Intoxication: Life in Pursuit of Artificial Paradise*. New York: Dutton, 1989.

Simmons, Luiz R. S., and Abdul A. Said, eds. *Drugs, Politics, and Diplomacy: The International Connection*. International Yearbooks of Drug Addiction and Society, vol. 2. Beverly Hills, Calif.: Sage Publications, 1974.

Sinclair, Andrew. *Era of Excess: A Social History of the Prohibition Movement*. New York: Harper & Row, Publishers, 1964. (First published by Little, Brown in 1962 under the title *Prohibition: The Era of Excess*.)

Singh, Jasbir, M., Lyle Miller, and Harbans Lal, eds. *Drug Addiction: Clinical and Socio-Legal Aspects*. Vol. 2. Mount Kisco, N.Y.: Futura Publishing Company, 1972.

Sjöqvist, Folke, and Malcolm Tottie, eds. *Abuse of Central Stimulants*. New York: Raven Press, 1969.

Sloman, Larry. *Reefer Madness: The History of Marijuana in America*. Indianapolis: Bobbs-Merrill Company, 1979.

Smart, Reginald G., et al. *Lysergic Acid Diethylamide (LSD) in the Treatment of Alcoholism: An Investigation of Its Effects on Drinking, Behavior, Personality Structure, and Social Functioning.* Brookside Monograph of the Addiction Research Foundation, no. 6. Toronto: University of Toronto Press, 1967.

Spitz, Henry I., and Jeffrey S. Rosecan, eds. *Cocaine Abuse: New Directions in Treatment and Research.* New York: Brunner/Mazel, 1987.

Stimson, Gerry V. *Heroin and Behaviour: Diversity among Addicts Attending London Clinics.* New York: John Wiley & Sons, 1973.

Straus, Nathan, III, ed. *Addicts and Drug Abusers: Current Approaches to the Problem.* New York: Twayne Publishers, 1971.

Szasz, Thomas. *Ceremonial Chemistry: The Ritual Persecution of Drugs, Addicts, and Pushers.* Rev. ed. Holmes Beach, Fla.: Learning Publications, 1985.

Taylor, Arnold H. *American Diplomacy and the Narcotics Traffic, 1900-1939: A Study in International Humanitarian Reform.* Durham: Duke University Press, 1969.

Towell, Julie E., and Charles B. Montney, eds. *Directories in Print.* 7th ed. Detroit: Gale Research, 1990.

Trebach, Arnold S. *The Great Drug War And Radical Proposals That Could Make America Safe Again.* New York: Macmillan Publishing Company, 1987.

_____. *The Heroin Solution.* New Haven: Yale University Press, 1982.

_____, ed. *Drugs, Crime, and Politics.* New York: Praeger Publishers, 1978.

Vallance, Elizabeth, ed. *The State, Society and Self-Destruction.* Acton Society Studies, no. 4. London: George Allen & Unwin Ltd., 1975.

Walton, Robert P. *Marihuana: America's New Drug Problem.* Philadelphia: J. B. Lippincott Company, 1938.

Warburton, Clark. *The Economic Results of Prohibition.* Studies in History, Economics and Public Law, no. 379. New York: Columbia University Press, 1932. Reprint. New York: AMS Press, 1968.

Washington, George. *The Diaries of George Washington 1748-1799.* John C. Fitzpatrick, ed. Vol. 1, 1748-1770. Boston: Houghton Mifflin Company, 1925.

Weil, Andrew. *The Natural Mind: An Investigation of Drugs and the Higher Consciousness.* Rev. ed. Boston: Houghton Mifflin Company, 1986.

Weiss, Winfried. *A Nazi Childhood.* Santa Barbara, Calif.: Capra Press, 1983.

Weissman, James C., and Robert L. DuPont, eds. *Criminal Justice and Drugs: The Unresolved Connection.* Multi-Disciplinary Studies in the Law. Port Washington, N.Y.: Kennikat Press, 1982.

Wikler, Abraham. *Opiate Addiction: Psychological and Neurophysiological Aspects in Relation to Clinical Problems.* American Lectures in Neurology, edited by Charles D. Aring, American Lecture Series publication no. 161. Springfield, Ill.: Charles C. Thomas, 1953.

Wilner, Daniel M., and Gene G. Kassebaum, eds. *Narcotics.* University of California Medical Extension Series—Los Angeles. New York: McGraw-Hill Book Company, 1965.

Zinberg, Norman E., and John A. Robertson. *Drugs and the Public.* New York: Simon and Schuster, 1972.

UNITED STATES GOVERNMENT DOCUMENTS

Blaine, Jack D., and Pierre F. Renault, eds. *Rx: 3x/Week LAAM: Alternative to Methadone.* National Institute on Drug Abuse, Research Monograph no. 8., 1976. (SuDoc HE20.8216:8.)

Bureau of Prisons. *Federal Offenders 1940.* 1941. (SuDoc J16.1:1940.)

Carter, Jimmy. *Public Papers of the Presidents of the United States: Jimmy Carter, 1977-1981.* 9 vols. 1977-82.

Clouet, Doris H., ed. *Phencyclidine: An Update.* National Institute on Drug Abuse, Research Monograph Series, no. 64. 1986. (SuDoc HE20.8216:64.)

Domestic Council Drug Abuse Task Force. *White Paper on Drug Abuse.* 1975. (SuDoc PrEx15.2D84.)

Federal Bureau of Investigation. *Uniform Crime Reports* for 1970-73, 1988. (SuDoc J1.14/7:970-73, 988.)

Gompers, Samuel, and Herman Gutstadt. *Some Reasons for Chinese Exclusion. Meat vs. Rice. American Manhood Against Asiatic Coolieism. Which Shall Survive?* 57 Cong., 1 sess., 1902. S. Doc. 137.

Grabowski, John, ed. *Cocaine: Pharmacology, Effects, and Treatment of Abuse.* National Institute on Drug Abuse, Research Monograph no. 50. 1984. (SuDoc HE20.8216:50.)

Harris, Louis S., ed. *Problems of Drug Dependence, 1980: Proceedings of the 42nd Annual Scientific Meeting, The Committee on Problems of Drug Dependence, Inc.* National Institute on Drug Abuse, Research Monograph Series, no. 34. 1981. (SuDoc HE 20.8216:34.)

_____. ed. *Problems of Drug Dependence, 1986: Proceedings of the 48th Annual Scientific Meeting, The Committee on Problems of Drug Dependence, Inc.* National Institute on Drug Abuse, Research Monograph Series, no. 76. 1987. (SuDoc HE20.8216/5:986.)

Johnson, Lyndon B. *Public Papers of the Presidents of the United States: Lyndon B. Johnson, 1963-1969.* 10 vols. 1965-70.

Johnston, Lloyd D., Patrick M. O'Malley, and Jerald G. Bachman. *Drug Use, Drinking, and Smoking: National Survey Results from High School, College, and Young Adults Populations 1975-1988.* National Institute on Drug Abuse, DHHS Publication No. (ADM) 89-1638. 1989. (SuDoc HE20.8202:D83.)

Kozel, Nicholas J., and Edgar H. Adams, eds. *Cocaine Use in America: Epidemiologic and Clinical Perspectives.* National Institute on Drug Abuse, Research Monograph Series, no. 61. 1985. (SuDoc HE20.8216:61.)

Krasnegor, Norman A., ed. *Behavioral Tolerance: Research and Treatment Implications.* National Institute on Drug Abuse Research Monograph, no. 18. Department of Health, Education, and Welfare Publication No. (ADM) 78-551. 1978. (SUDoc HE20.8216:18.)

Love, Albert G., and Charles B. Davenport. *Defects Found in Drafted Men.* War Department, 1920. (Text citation is to War Dept. version, but document is also available as a Committee Print of the Senate Committee on Military Affairs, 66 Cong., 1 sess., 1919. SuDoc Y4.M59/2:D78/2.)

McGlothlin, William H., M. Douglas Anglin, and Bruce D. Wilson. *An Evaluation of the California Civil Addict Program.* National Institute on Drug Abuse, Services Research Monograph Series. 1977. (SUDoc HE20.8216:2-2:C12.)

McGlothlin, William H., et al. *Alternative Approaches to Opiate Addiction Control: Costs, Benefits, and Potential.* Bureau of Narcotics and Dangerous Drugs. U. S. Department of Justice. 1972. (SuDoc J24.14:7.)

National Commission on Law Observance and Enforcement (Wickersham Commission). *Report on the Enforcement of the Prohibition Laws of the United States.* 71 Cong., 3 sess., 1931. H. Doc. 722. (SuDoc Y3.N21/7:2.)

National Commission on Marihuana and Drug Abuse. *Drug Use in America: Problem in Perspective.* Vol. 1, appendix. 1973. (SuDoc Y3.M33/2:1/973/App./v.1.)

National Institute on Drug Abuse. Services Research Monograph Series. *Evaluation of Drug Abuse Treatments Based on First Year Followup.* Department of Health, Education, and Welfare Publication No. (ADM) 78-701. 1978. (SuDoc HE20.8216/2-2:T71/2.)

_____. Statistical Series. *Data from the Drug Abuse Warning Network (DAWN)* for 1984 and 1986. (SuDoc HE20.8212/11:984 and HE20.8212/11:986.)

Nixon, Richard M. *Public Papers of the Presidents of the United States: Richard Nixon, 1969-1974.* 6 vols. 1971-75.

O'Donnell, John A. *Narcotics Addicts in Kentucky.* U.S. Public Health Service Publication No. 1881. National Institute of Mental Health. 1969. (SuDoc FS2.22:N16/3.)

Petersen, Robert C., and Richard C. Stillman, eds. *PCP: Phencyclidine Abuse: An Appraisal.* National Institute on Drug Abuse, Research Monograph Series, no. 21. 1978. (SuDoc HE20.8216:21.)

President's Commission on Law Enforcement and the Administration of Justice. *Task Force Report: Drunkenness.* 1967. (SuDoc Pr36.8:L41/D84/2.)

_____. *Task Force Report: Narcotics and Drug Abuse.* 1967. (SuDoc Pr36.8:L41/N16.)

President's Commission on Organized Crime. *The Cash Connection: Organized Crime, Financial Institutions, and Money Laundering.* Interim Report to the President and the Attorney General. 1984. (SuDoc Pr40.8:C86/C26.)

Robins, Lee N. *The Vietnam Drug Abuser Returns.* Final Report. Special Action Office for Drug Abuse Prevention. 1974. (SuDoc PrEx20.9:A/2.)

Spotts, James V., and Franklin C. Shontz. *The Lifestyles of Nine American Cocaine Users: Trips to the Land of Cockaigne.* National Institute on Drug Abuse Research Issues Series, no. 16. 1976. (SuDoc HE20.8214:16.)

Thompson, Travis, and Chris E. Johanson, eds. *Behavioral Pharmacology of Human Drug Dependence.* National Institute on Drug Abuse Research Monograph, no. 37. 1981. (SuDoc HE20.8216:37.)

Tims, Frank M., and Jacqueline P. Ludford, eds. *Drug Abuse Treatment Evaluation: Strategies, Progress, and Prospects.* National Institute on Drug Abuse Research Monograph, no. 51. 1984. (SuDoc HE20.8216:51.)

U.S. Bureau of the Census. Series P-25, No. 1000. *Current Population Reports: Estimates of the Population of the United States, by Age, Sex, and Race: 1980 to 1986.* 1987. (SuDoc C3.186/7- 2:980-86.)

————. *Statistical Abstract of the United States 1988.* 1987. (SuDoc C3.134:988.)

U.S. Congress. House. Select Committee on Crime. Hearings. *The Improvement and Reform of Law Enforcement and Criminal Justice in the United States.* 91 Cong., 1 sess., 1969. (SuDoc Y4.C86/3:L41.)

————. House. Select Committee on Crime. Hearings. *Narcotics Research, Rehabilitation and Treatment.* 92 Cong., 1 sess., 1971. (SuDoc Y4.C86/3:92-1/pt.1.)

————. House. Committee on Ways and Means. Hearings. *Taxation of Marihuana.* 75 Cong., 1 sess., 1937. (SuDoc Y4.F49:M33.)

————. House. Committee on Ways and Means. Subcommittee. Hearings. *Control of Narcotics, Marihuana, and Barbiturates.* 82 Cong., 1 sess., 1951. (SuDoc Y4.W36:N16/3).

————House. Committee on Ways and Means. Hearings. *Importation and Use of Opium.* 61 Cong., 3 sess., Dec. 14, 1910. (SuDoc Y4.W36:Op3/3.)

————. Senate. Committee on Armed Services. Subcommittee on Drug Abuse in the Military. Hearings. *Drug Abuse in the Military.* 92 Cong., 2 sess., 1972. (SuDoc Y4.Ar5/3:D84/3.)

————. Senate. Committee on the District of Columbia. *Investigation of Crime and Law Enforcement in the District of Columbia.* 82 Cong., 2 sess., 1952. S. Rept. 1989.

————. Senate. Committee on the Judiciary. Subcommittee on Improvements in the Federal Criminal Code. Hearings. *Illicit Narcotics Traffic.* 84 Cong., 1 sess., 1955. (SuDoc Y4.J89/2:N16/1-10.)

————. Senate. Committee on the Judiciary. Subcommittee to Investigate the Administration of the Internal Security Act and Other Internal Security Laws. Hearings. *Communist China and Illicit Narcotics Traffic.* 84 Cong., 1 sess. 1955. (SuDoc Y4.J89/2:C44/2.)

————. Senate. Committee on the Judiciary. Subcommittee to Investigate the Internal Security Act and Other Internal Security Laws. Hearings. *Scope of Soviet Activity in the United States.* 85 Cong., 1 sess. 1957. (SuDoc Y4.J89/2:So8/4/pt. 55.)

————. Senate. Report of the Committee Appointed by the Philippine Commission. *Use of Opium and Traffic Therein.* 59 Cong., 1 sess., 1906. S. Doc. 265.

————. Senate. Committee on the Judiciary. Report, Containing a Summary of Preliminary Findings and Recommendations of the Subcommittee on Improvements in the Federal Criminal Code. *The Illicit Narcotics Traffic.* 84 Cong., 2 sess., 1956. S. Rpt. 1440.

White House. Drug Abuse Policy Office, Office of Policy Development. *1984 National Strategy for Prevention of Drug Abuse and Drug Trafficking.* 1984. (SuDoc PrEx24.2:St8/984.)

White House Conference on Narcotic and Drug Abuse. *Proceedings.* 1962. (SuDoc Y3.W58/5:2P94/962.)

Wright, Hamilton. *Report on the International Opium Commission and on The Opium Problem As Seen Within the United States and Its Possessions.* Published in *Opium Problem. Message from the President of the United States.* 61 Cong., 2 sess., 1910. S. Doc. 377.

JOURNALS AND PERIODICALS

Abelson, Philip H. "Death from Heroin." Editorial. *Science* 168 (1970): 1289.

Abraham, Henry David. "A Chronic Impairment of Colour Vision in Users of LSD." *British Journal of Psychiatry* 140 (1982): 518-19.

————. "Visual Phenomenology of the LSD Flashback." *Archives of General Psychiatry* 40 (1983): 888-89.

Ahlborn, Maurice B. "Heroine in the Morphine Habit." *New York Medical Journal* 74 (1901): 235.

Alexander, Bruce K., Robert B. Coambs, and Patricia F. Hadaway. "The Effect of Housing and Gender on Morphine Self-Administration in Rats." *Psychopharmacology* 58 (1978): 175-78.

Alexander, Bruce K., and Patricia F. Hadaway. "Opiate Addiction: The Case for an Adaptive Orientation." *Psychological Bulletin* 92 (1982): 367-81.

Ambre, John J., et al. "Acute Tolerance to Cocaine in Humans." *Clinical Pharmacology and Therapeutics* 44 (1988): 1-8.

Ames, Frances. "A Clinical and Metabolic Study of Acute Intoxication with *Cannabis Sativa* and its Role in the Model Psychoses." *Journal of Mental Science* 104 (1958): 976.

Annals of the American Academy of Political and Social Science 163 (1932): 59-60, 93-97, 128.

Apsler, Robert, Beverly Brady, and Pierce Barker. "Reasons for Not Using Licit and Illicit Drugs: The Role of Experience with Illicit Drugs." *Journal of Drug Issues* 9 (1979): 553, 556, 564.

Arntzen, F.I. "Some Psychological Aspects of Nicotinism." *American Journal of Psychology* 61 (1948): 424-25.

"Attitude Problem." *New Republic* 201 (October 9, 1989): 4, 40.

Bailey, Pearce. "The Heroin Habit." *New Republic* 6 (April 22, 1916): 314-16.

Baker, E.F.W. "The Use of Lysergic Acid Diethylamide (LSD) in Psychotherapy." *Canadian Medical Association Journal* 91 (1964): 1202.

Barlow, Sarah. "Patterns of Arrests for Misdemeanor Narcotics Possession: Manhattan Police Practices, 1960-62." *Criminal Law Bulletin* 4 (1968): 549-82.

Barnes, Gill G., and Peter Noble. "Deprivation and Drug Addiction: A Study of a Vulnerable Sub-Group." *British Journal of Social Work* 2 (1972): 299 311.

Barr, Gordon A. "Classical Conditioning, Decay and Extinction of Cocaine-Induced Hyperactivity and Stereotypy." *Life Sciences* 33 (1983): 1341, 1350.

Barrett, Carol J., and Diana James Cairns. "The Social Network in Marijuana-Using Groups." *International Journal of the Addictions* 15 (1980): 677-88.

Bean, Philip. "Social Aspects of Drug Abuse: A Study of London Drug Offenders." *Journal of Criminal Law, Criminology and Police Science* 62 (1971): 80-86.

Becker, Howard S. "History, Culture, and Subjective Experience: An Exploration of the Social Bases of Drug-Induced Experience." *Journal of Health and Social Behavior* 8 (1967): 163-76.

Beckett, H. Dale, and K. J. Lodge. "Aspects of Social Relationships in Heroin Addicts Admitted for Treatment." *Bulletin on Narcotics* 23, (no. 4, 1971): 29-36.

Berger, Herbert, and Michael J. Schwegler. "Voluntary Detoxification of Patients on Methadone Maintenance." *International Journal of the Addictions* 8 (1973): 1047.

Bewley, Thomas H. "Maintenance Treatment of Narcotic Addicts (Not British Nor a System, But Working Now)." *International Journal of the Addictions* 7 (1972): 597-611.

Black, Samuel, Kenneth L. Owens, and Ronald P. Wolff. "Patterns of Drug Use: A Study of 5,482 Subjects." *American Journal of Psychiatry* 127 (1970): 420-23.

Blackwell, Judith Stephenson. "Drifting, Controlling and Overcoming: Opiate Users Who Avoid Becoming Chronically Dependent." *Journal of Drug Issues* 13 (1983): 219-35.

Blair, Thomas S. "The Relation of Drug Addiction to Industry." *Journal of Industrial Hygiene* 1 (October 1919): 284-96.

Blumenfeld, Michael. "Flashback Phenomena in Basic Trainees Who Enter the Air Force." *Military Medicine* 136 (1971): 41.

Bogema, Stuart, Richard Schwartz, and Ira Godwin. "Evaluation of the Keystone Diagnostics Quik Test ™ Using Previously Screened Urine Specimens." *Journal of Analytical Toxicology* 12 (1988): 272-73.

Bower, Bruce, "Drugs of Choice." *Science News* 136 (1989): 392-93.

Boyle, John M., and Ann F. Brunswick. "What Happened in Harlem? Analysis of a Decline in Heroin Use Among a Generation Unit of Urban Black Youth." *Journal of Drug Issues* 10 (1980): 109-30.

Brandt, Jason, and Laurie F. Doyle. "Concept Attainment, Tracking, and Shifting in Adolescent Polydrug Abusers." *Journal of Nervous and Mental Disease* 171 (1983): 559.

Bridger, Wagner H., et al. "Classical Conditioning of Cocaine's Stimulating Effects." *Psychopharmacology Bulletin* 18 (1982): 213.

Brill, Henry, and Tetsuya Hirose. "The Rise and Fall of a Methamphetamine Epidemic: Japan 1944-55." *Seminars in Psychiatry* 1 (1969): 179-94.

Brill, Norman Q., and Richard L. Christie. "Marihuana Use and Psychosocial Adaptation: Follow-up Study of a Collegiate Population." *Archives of General Psychiatry* 31 (1974): 713.

Brower, Kirk J., and Alfonso Paredes. "Cocaine Withdrawal." *Archives of General Psychiatry* 44 (1987): 297.

Brown, Alan, and Arthur Stickgold. "Marijuana Flashback Phenomena." *Journal of Psychedelic Drugs* 8 (1976): 275-83.

Brown, Barry S., et al. "In Their Own Words: Addicts' Reasons for Initiating and Withdrawing from Heroin." *International Journal of the Addictions* 6 (1971): 635-45.

Brown, R., and R. Middlefell. "Fifty-Five Years of Cocaine Dependence." *British Journal of Addiction* 84 (1989): 946.

Burtis, Carl A. "Answering the Challenge." *Clinical Chemistry* 35 (1989): 891.

"Cerebral Edema Seen in Many 'Sudden Death' Heroin Victims." *Journal of the American Medical Association* 212 (1970): 967.

Chandler, Arthur L., and Mortimer A. Hartman. "Lysergic Acid Diethylamide (LSD-25) as a Facilitating Agent in Psychotherapy." *Archives of General Psychiatry* 2 (1960): 297-98.

Chapman, John Jay. "Drink and the Tyranny of Dogma." *Outlook* 136 (Jan. 16, 1924): 108.

Chasnoff, I. J., et al. "Temporal Patterns of Cocaine Use in Pregnancy. Perinatal Outcome." *Journal of the American Medical Association* 261 (1989): 1741-44.

Cheek, Frances E., Stephens Newell, and Milton Joffe, "Deceptions in the Illicit Drug Market." *Science* 167 (1970): 1276.

Chein, Isidor, and Eva Rosenfeld. "Juvenile Narcotics Use." *Law and Contemporary Problems* 22 (1957): 54, 58.

Childress, Anna Rose, A. Thomas McLellan, and Charles P. O'Brien. "Abstinent Opiate Abusers Exhibit Conditioned Craving, Conditioned Withdrawal and Reductions in Both through Extinction." *British Journal of Addiction* 81 (1986): 655-60.

Chopra, I. C., and R. N. Chopra. "The Use of the Cannabis Drugs in India." *Bulletin on Narcotics* 9 (January-March 1957): 13.

Clark, Ramsey. "Drugs, Lies & TV." *The Nation* 249 (1989): 408.

"The Cocaine Habit Among the Negroes." *British Medical Journal* (Nov. 29, 1902): 1719.

Cohen, Arie. "The 'Urge to Classify' the Narcotic Addict: A Review of Psychiatric Classification. I." *International Journal of the Addictions* 17 (1982): 213-25.

————. "The 'Urge to Classify' the Narcotic Addict: A Review of Psychiatric Classificaiton. II." *International Journal of the Addictions* 19 (1984): 335-53.

Cohen, Herman. "Multiple Drug Use Considered in the Light of the Stepping-Stone Hypothesis." *International Journal of the Addictions* 7 (1972): 27-55.

Cohen, Sidney. "Lysergic Acid Diethlyamide: Side Effects and Complications." *Journal of Nervous and Mental Disease* 130 (1960): 30-40.

Cone, Edward J., and Sandra L. Menchen. "Lack of Validity of the KDI Quik Test™ Drug Screen for Detection of Benzoylecgonine in Urine." *Journal of Analytical Toxicology* 11 (1987): 276-77.

Corman, A. G., et al. "Rehabilitation of Narcotic Addicts with Methadone: The Public Health Approach v. the Individual Perspective." *Contemporary Drug Problems* 2 (1973): 575-76.

Council on Mental Health and National Academy of Sciences—National Research Council's Committee on Drug Addiction and Narcotics. "Narcotics and Medical Practice: The Use of Narcotic Drugs in Medical Practice and the Medical Management of Narcotic Addicts." *Journal of the American Medical Association* 185 (1963): 976-82.

Council on Pharmacy and Chemistry. "What to Do with a Drug Addict." *Journal of the American Medical Association* 149 (1952): 1220.

"Crackmire," *New Republic* 201 (September 11, 1989): 10.

Craig, Robert J. "Personality Characteristics of Heroin Addicts: Review of Empirical Research 1976-1979." *International Journal of the Addictions* 17 (1982): 235-37.

Crancer, Alfred, Jr., et al. "Comparison of the Effects of Marihuana and Alcohol on

Simulated Driving Performance." *Science* 164 (1969): 851-54.

Crothers, T. D. "Morphinism among Physicians." *Medical Record* 56 (1899): 784-86.

Culver, Charles M., and Francis W. King. "Neuropsychological Assessment of Undergraduate Marihuana and LSD Users." *Archives of General Psychiatry* 31 (1974): 707.

Cushman, Paul. "Methadone Maintenance in Hard-Core Criminal Addicts: Economic Effects." *New York State Journal of Medicine* 71 (1971): 1770, 1772.

――――. "Narcotic Addiction and Crime." *Rhode Island Medical Journal* 57 (1974): 198.

Cutting, Windsor C. "Morphine Addiction for 62 Years." *Stanford Medical Bulletin* 1 (Aug. 1942): 39-41.

Daly, James R. L. "[Letter]." *Boston Medical and Surgical Journal* 142 (1900): 190.

Davidson, F., M. Etienne, and J. Piesset. "Medico-Social Survey of 662 Drug Users (April 1971-May 1972)." *Bulletin on Narcotics* 25 (no. 4, 1973): 9-32.

De Alarcón, R. "The Spread of Heroin Abuse in a Community." *Bulletin on Narcotics* 21 (no. 3, 1969): 17-22.

Deneau, Gerald, Tomoji Yanagita, and M. H. Seevers. "Self-Administration of Psychoactive Substances by the Monkey: A Measure of Psychological Dependence." *Psychopharmacologia* 16 (1969): 30-48.

Densten, J. C. "Drug Addiction and the Harrison Anti-Narcotic Act." *New York Medical Journal* 105 (1917): 748.

Dextraze, Paul, et al. "Comparison of Fluorescence Polarization Immunoassay, Enzyme Immunoassay, and Thin-Layer Chromatography for Urine Cannabinoid Screening. Effects of Analyte Adsorption and Vigorous Mixing of Specimen on Detectability." *Annals of Clinical and Laboratory Science* 19 (1989): 135-36.

"A Discussion of the KDI Quik Test™ Drug Screen." *Journal of Analytical Toxicology* 12 (1988): 111.

Dobbs, William H. "Methadone Treatment of Heroin Addicts." *Journal of the American Medical Association* 218 (1971): 1539.

Dobinson, Ian, and Pat Ward. "Heroin and Property Crime: An Australian Perspective." *Journal of Drug Issues* 16 (1986): 257.

Donovan, Dennis Michael, G. Alan Marlatt, and Philip M. Salzberg. "Drinking Behavior, Personality Factors and High-Risk Driving: A Review and Theoretical Formulation." *Journal of Studies on Alcohol* 44 (1983): 395-428.

D'Orbán, P. T. "Female Narcotic Addicts: A Follow-Up Study of Criminal and Addiction Careers." *British Medical Journal* no. 5888 (November 10, 1973): 345-47.

――――. "Heroin Dependence and Delinquency in Women—A Study of Heroin Addicts in Holloway Prison." *British Journal of Addiction* 65 (1970): 67-78.

Earle, Charles W. "The Opium Habit: A Statistical and Clinical Lecture." *Chicago Medical Review* 2 (1880): 442-46.

Eaton, Virgil G. "How the Opium Habit is Acquired." *Popular Science Monthly* 33 (September 1888): 665.

Eberle, Eug. G. "Narcotics and the Habitues." *Proceedings of the American Pharmaceutical Association* 50 (1902): 636.

Edelin, K. C., et al. "Methadone Maintenance in Pregnancy: Consequences to Care and Outcome." *Obstetrics and Gynecology* 71 (no. 3, pt. 1, 1988): 399-404.

"Editorial." *Journal of the American Medical Association* 185 (1963): 962.

"Effects of Alcohol and Cannabis During Labor." *Journal of the American Medical Association* 94 (1930): 1165.

Einstein, Stanley, and Warren Garitano. "Treating the Drug Abuser: Programs, Factors and Alternatives." *International Journal of the Addictions* 7 (1972): 324-25.

Elliott, H. W., et al. "Detection of Narcotic Use." *California Medicine* 109 (1968): 121, 125.

Engelsman, E. L. "Dutch Policy of the Management of Drug-Related Problems." *British Journal of Addiction* 84 (1989): 211-18.

Epstein, Edward Jay. "The Krogh File—The Politics of 'Law and Order.' " *The Public Interest* 39 (Spring 1975): 116.

Fackelmann, Kathy A. "HIV and IV Drug Abuse." *Science News* 135 (1989): 171.

"Federal Regulation of Medicinal Use of Cannabis." Editorial. *Journal of the American Medical Association* 108 (1937): 1543-44.

Finestone, Harold. "Cats, Kicks and Color." *Social Problems* 5 (July 1957): 3-13.

————. "Narcotics and Criminality." *Law and Contemporary Problems* 22 (1957): 75-76.

Finnegan, Loretta P. "The Effects of Narcotics and Alcohol on Pregnancy and the Newborn." *Annals of the New York Academy of Sciences* 362 (1981): 136-57.

Finnegan, Loretta P., and Dian S. Reeser. "The Incidence of Sudden Death in Infants Born to Women Maintained on Methadone." *Pediatric Research* 12 (1978): 405.

Fischman, Marian W. "Acute Tolerance Development to the Cardiovascular and Subjective Effects of Cocaine." *Journal of Pharmacology and Experimental Therapeutics* 235 (1985): 677-82.

Fischman, Marian W., and Charles R. Schuster. "Cocaine Self-Administration in Humans." *Federation Proceedings* 41 (1982): 243.

Fossier, A. E. "The Mariahuana Menace." *New Orleans Medical and Surgical Journal* 84 (1931): 249-50.

Frank, D. A., et al. "Cocaine Use During Pregnancy: Prevalence and Correlates." *Pediatrics* 82 (1988): 888-95.

Frank, Robert A., Thomas Pommering, and Douglas Nitz. "The Interactive Effects of Cocaine and Imipramine on Self-Stimulation Train-Duration Thresholds." *Pharmacology, Biochemistry and Behavior* 30 (1988): 1-4.

Fraser, H. F. "Tolerance and Physical Dependence on Opiates, Barbiturates, and Alcohol." *Annual Review of Medicine* 8 (1957): 427.

Frings, Christopher S., Danielle J. Battaglia, and Robert M. White. "Status of Drugs-of-Abuse Testing in Urine under Blind Conditions: An AACC Study." *Clinical Chemistry* 35 (1989): 891-94.

Frings, Christopher S., Robert M. White, and Danielle J. Battaglia. "Status of Drugs of-Abuse Testing in Urine: An AACC Study." *Clinical Chemistry* 33 (1987): 1683-86.

Fritschi, Giselher, and William R. Prescott, Jr. "Morphine Levels in Urine Subsequent to Poppy Seed Consumption." *Forensic Science International* 27 (1985): 116.

Fulroth, R., B. Phillips, and D. J. Durand. "Perinatal Outcome of Infants Exposed to Cocaine and/or Heroin in Utero." *American Journal of Diseases of Children* 143 (1989): 905-10.

Fysh, R. R., et al. "A Fatal Poisoning with LSD." *Forensic Science International* 28 (1985): 109-13.

Gawin, Frank H., and Herbert D. Kleber. "Abstinence Symptomatology and Psychiatric Diagnosis in Cocaine Abusers: Clinical Observations." *Archives of General Psychiatry* 43 (1986): 112.

————. "Evolving Conceptualizations of Cocaine Dependence." *Yale Journal of Biology and Medicine* 61 (1988): 129.

Gay, George R., Edward C. Senay, and John A. Newmeyer. "The Pseudo Junkie: Evolution of the Heroin Lifestyle in the Non-Addicted Individual." *Anesthesia and Analgesia—Current Researches* 53 (1974): 241-47.

Gerard, Donald L., and Conan Kornetsky. "Adolescent Opiate Addiction: A Study of Control and Addict Subjects." *Psychiatric Quarterly* 29 (1955): 457-86.

Ghodse, A. Hamid. "Cannabis Psychosis." *British Journal of Addiction* 81 (1986): 473-78.

————. "Drug Dependent Individuals Dealt with by London Casualty Departments." *British Journal of Psychiatry* 131 (1977): 273-80.

Giammarco, Rose A. "The Athlete, Cocaine, and Lactic Acidosis: A Hypothesis." *American Journal of the Medical Sciences* 294 (1987): 412-14.

Goldman, Fred. "Heroin and the Federal Strategy: A Policy in Search of Evidence." *Journal of Psychoactive Drugs* 13 (1981): 222-23.

Gordon, Alistair M. "Patterns of Delinquency in Drug Addiction." *British Journal of Psychiatry* 122 (1973): 205-10.

Gottheil, Edward, Glenn R. Caddy, and Deborah L. Austin. "Fallibility of Urine Drug Screens in Monitoring Methadone Programs." *Journal of the American Medical Association* 236 (1976): 1035-38.

Grabowski, John, and Steven I. Dworkin. "Cocaine: An Overview of Current Issues." *International Journal of the Addictions* 20 (1985): 1077, 1081.

Graeven, David B., and Kathleen A. Graeven. "Treated and Untreated Addicts: Factors Associated with Participation in Treatment and Cessation of Heroin Use." *Journal of Drug Issues* 13 (1983): 207-18.

Graham, K., et al. "Pregnancy Outcome Following First Trimester Exposure to Cocaine in Social Users in Toronto, Canada." *Veterinary and Human Toxicology* 31 (1989): 143-48.

Graham-Mulhall, Sara. "Experiences in Narcotic Drug Control in the State of New York." *New York Medical Journal* 113 (1921): 107.

Green, E. M. "Psychoses Among Negroes—A Comparative Study." *Journal of Nervous and Mental Disease* 41 (1914): 702.

Griggs, E. Allen, and Michael Ward. "LSD Toxicity: A Suspected Cause of Death." *Journal of the Kentucky Medical Association* 75 (1977): 172-73.

Grinspoon, Lester, and James B. Bakalar. "Adverse Effects of Cocaine: Selected Issues." *Annals of the New York Academy of Sciences* 362 (1981): 128.

_____. "Can Drugs Be Used to Enhance the Psychotherapeutic Process?" *American Journal of Psychotherapy* 40 (1986): 397-98.

Guze, Samuel B., et al. "Psychiatric Illness and Crime with Particular Reference to Alcoholism: A Study of 233 Criminals." *Journal of Nervous and Mental Disease* 134 (1962): 512-21.

Habig, Robert L. "It's Time to Take the Initiative" [Editorial], *Clinical Chemistry* 33 (1987): 1682.

Hadeed, A. J., and S. R. Siegel. "Maternal Cocaine Use During Pregnancy: Effect on the Newborn Infant." *Pediatrics* 84 (1989): 205-10.

Halsted, William S. "Practical Comments on the Use and Abuse of Cocaine; Suggested by Its Invariably Successful Employment in More Than a Thousand Minor Surgical Operations." *New York Medical Journal* 42 (1885): 294.

Hammersley, Richard, et al. "The Relationship Between Crime and Opioid Use." *British Journal of Addiction* 84 (1989): 1029-43.

Hansen, Hugh J., Samuel P. Caudill, and Joe Boone. "Crisis in Drug Testing: Results of CDC Blind Study." *Journal of the American Medical Association* 253 (1985): 2382-83.

Hawkins, E. R., and Willard Waller. "Critical Notes on the Cost of Crime." *Journal of the American Institute of Criminal Law and Criminology* 26 (1936): 693.

Healy, Paul F. "They Got the Goods on Washington's Cops." *Saturday Evening Post* 225 (Sept. 27, 1952).

Hill, Harris E., Charles A. Haertzen, and Robert Glazer. "Personality Characteristics of Narcotics Addicts as Indicated by the MMPI." *Journal of General Psychology* 62 (1960): 137-38.

Hill, Herbert. "Anti-Oriental Agitation and the Rise of Working-Class Racism." *Society* 10 (January-February 1973): 51-52.

Hinson, Riley E., and Shepard Siegel. "Nonpharmacological Bases of Drug Tolerance and Dependence." *Journal of Psychosomatic Research* 26 (1982): 495-503.

Hutchins, Laura, et al. "A Two-Year Follow-Up of a Cohort of Opiate Users from a Provincial Town." *British Journal of Addiction* 66 (1971): 129-40.

Ingraham, Larry H. " 'The Nam' and 'The World': Heroin Use by U.S. Army Enlisted Men Serving in Vietnam." *Psychiatry* 37 (May 1974): 118-19.

Isbell, Harris, and H. F. Fraser. "Addiction to Analgesics and Barbiturates." *Pharmacological Reviews* 2 (1950): 355-57, 390.

Ishii, Akio, and Nobuo Motohashi. "Drug Abuse in Japan." *Addictive Diseases* 3 (1977): 105-14.

Jellinek, E. M. "Recent Trends in Alcoholism and in Alcohol Consumption." *Quarterly Journal of Studies on Alcohol* 8 (June 1947): 9-10, 40.

Jones, A. D. "Cannabis and Alcohol Usage Among the Plateau Tonga: An Observational Report of the Effects of Cultural Expectation." *Psychological Record* 25 (1975): 329-32.

Kagel, John H., Raymond C. Battalio, and C. G. Miles. "Marihuana and Work Per-
    formance: Results from an Experiment." *Journal of Human Resources* 15
    (1980): 373, 390.

Kandel, Denise B., and Victoria H. Raveis. "Cessation of Illicit Drug Use in Young
    Adulthood." *Archives of General Psychiatry* 46 (1989): 109-16.

Kato, Masaaki. "An Epidemiological Analysis of the Fluctuation of Drug Dependence
    in Japan." *International Journal of the Addictions* 4 (1969): 591-621.

Khantzian, Edward J. "The Self-Medication Hypothesis of Addictive Disorders:
    Focus on Heroin and Cocaine Dependence." *American Journal of Psychiatry*
    142 (1985): 1259.

King, Edgar. "The Use of Habit-Forming Drugs (Cocaine, Opium & Its Deriva-
    tives) by Enlisted Men: A Report Based on the Work Done at the United
    States Disciplinary Barracks." *Military Surgeon* 39 (1916): 273.

Kleber, Herbert D. "Epidemic Cocaine Abuse: America's Present, Britain's Future?"
    British Journal of Addiction 83 (1988): 1364.

————. "Introduction: Cocaine Abuse: Historical, Epidemiological, and Psycho-
    logical Perspectives." *Journal of Clinical Psychiatry* 49 (February 1988 Supp.): 3.

Kleber, Herbert D., and Frank H. Gawin. "In Reply." *Archives of General
    Psychiatry* 44 (1987): 298.

Klonoff, Harry. "Marijuana and Driving in Real-Life Situations." *Science* 186
    (1974): 317-24.

Kolb, Lawrence. "Let's Stop This Narcotics Hysteria." *Saturday Evening Post* 229
    (July 28, 1956).

Kolb, Lawrence, and A. G. Du Mez. "Prevalence and Trend of Addiction in the
    United States and Factors Influencing It." *Public Health Reports* 39 (1924):
    1181.

Kornblith, Alice B. "Multiple Drug Abuse Involving Nonopiate, Nonalcoholic
    Substances. II. Physical Damage, Long-Term Psychological Effects and Treat-
    ment Approaches and Success." *International Journal of the Addictions* 16
    (1981): 530.

Kozel, Nicholas J., Robert L. DuPont, and Barry S. Brown. "Narcotics and Crime: A
    Study of Narcotic Involvement in an Offender Population." *International
    Journal of the Addictions* 7 (1972): 446.

Krippner, Stanley. "Drug Deceptions." *Science* 168 (1970): 654-55.

LaCroix, Susan. "Birth of a Bad Idea: Jailing Mothers for Drug Abuse." *The Nation*
    248 (1989): 585-88.

Lasagna, L., John M. von Felsinger, Henry K. Beecher. "Drug-Induced Mood
    Changes in Man." *Journal of the American Medical Association* 157 (1955):
    1113-19.

Leader-Elliott, Ian D. "Heroin in Australia: The Costs and Consequences of Prohibi-
    tion." *Journal of Drug Issues* 16 (1986): 136-40.

Lennard, Henry L., et al. "[Letter]." *Science* 179 (1973): 1078-79.

Lenz, Widukind, and Ursula Feldmann. "Unilateral and Asymmetric Limb Defects
    in Man: Delineation of the Femur-Fibula-Ulna Complex." *Birth Defects:
    Original Articles Series* 13 (1977): 269.

Levine, Jerome, and Arnold M. Ludwig. "The LSD Controversy." *Comprehensive Psychiatry* 5 (1964): 318.

Lewis, David C., and Norman E. Zinberg. "Narcotic Usage II. A Historical Perspective on a Difficult Medical Problem." *New England Journal of Medicine* 270 (1964): 1045-50.

Lewis, Virginia, et al. "Nalline and Urine Tests in Narcotics Detection: A Critical Overview," *International Journal of the Addictions* 8 (1973): 169.

Lichtenstein, Perry M. "Narcotic Addiction." *New York Medical Journal* 100 (1914): 962.

Lidz, Charles W., et al. "Heroin Maintenance and Heroin Control." *International Journal of the Addictions* 10 (1975): 47.

Light, Arthur B., and Edward B. Torrance. "Opium Addiction." *Archives of Internal Medicine* 44 (1929): 377-94.

Lindesmith, Alfred R. "The British System of Narcotics Control." *Law and Contemporary Problems* 22 (1957): 142.

_____. "Dope: Congress Encourages the Traffic." *The Nation* 184 (March 16, 1957): 229-30.

Lipscomb, Wendell R. "Drug Use in a Black Ghetto." *American Journal of Psychiatry* 127 (1971): 1168.

Long, Sally Y. "Does LSD Induce Chromosomal Damage and Malformations? A Review of the Literature." *Teratology* 6 (1972): 75-90.

Lowenstein, Daniel H., et al. "Acute Neurologic and Psychiatric Complications Associated with Cocaine Abuse." *American Journal of Medicine* 83 (1987): 841-46.

Lubs, H. A., and F. H. Ruddle. "Chromosomal Abnormalities in the Human Population: Estimation of Rates Based on New Haven Newborn Study." *Science* 169 (1970): 495-98.

McAuliffe, William E. "A Test of Wikler's Theory of Relapse: The Frequency of Relapse Due to Conditioned Withdrawal Sickness." *International Journal of the Addictions* 17 (1982): 19.

McBay, Arthur J. "Problems in Testing for Abused Drugs" [Letter]. *Journal of the American Medical Association* 255 (1986): 39-40.

McGlothlin, William H., M. Douglas Anglin, and Bruce D. Wilson. "Narcotic Addiction and Crime." *Criminology* 16 (1978): 298-309.

McGlothlin, William H., and David O. Arnold. "LSD Revisited—A Ten-Year Follow-Up of Medical LSD Use." *Archives of General Psychiatry* 24 (1971): 43-49.

McGlothlin, William H., David O. Arnold, and Daniel X. Freedman. "Organicity Measures Following Repeated LSD Ingestion." *Archives of General Psychiatry* 21 (1969): 704-9.

McGlothlin, William H., Robert S. Sparkes, and David O. Arnold. "Effect of LSD on Human Pregnancy." *Journal of the American Medical Association* 212 (1970): 1483-87.

McGuire, Frank A., and Perry M. Lichtenstein. "The Drug Habit." *Medical Record* 90 (1916): 185-91.

Macrae, James R., Michael T. Scoles, and Shephard Siegel. "The Contribution of
    Pavlovian Conditioning to Drug Tolerance and Dependence." *British Journal
    of Addiction* 82 (1987): 371-80.
McWilliams, Spencer A., and Renee J. Tuttle. "Long-Term Psychological Effects of
    LSD." *Psychological Bulletin* 79 (1973): 341-51.
Madden, J. D., T. F. Payne, and S. Miller. "Maternal Cocaine Abuse and Effect on
    the Newborn." *Pediatrics* 77 (1986): 209-11.
Maddux, James F., and Charles L. Bowden. "Critique of Success with Methadone
    Maintenance." *American Journal of Psychiatry* 129 (1972): 440-46.
Malleson, Nicolas. "Acute Adverse Reactions to LSD in Clinical and Experimental
    Use in the United Kingdom." *British Journal of Psychiatry* 118 (1971): 229-30.
"Marijuana Laws, An Empirical Study of Enforcement and Administration in
    Los Angeles County." *UCLA Law Review* 15 (1968): 1517 n.14.
Marlott, G. Alan, and Kim Fromme. "Metaphors for Addiction." *Journal of Drug
    Issues* 17 (1987): 13.
Marshall, Norma, and Jane Hendtlass, "Drugs & Prostitution." *Journal of Drug
    Issues* 16 (1986): 237, 245.
Martin, William R., et al. "Methadone—A Reevaluation." *Archives of General
    Psychiatry* 28 (1973): 286-95.
Melzack, Ronald. "The Tragedy of Needless Pain." *Scientific American* 262 (February
    1990): 27-33.
Merker, Lisa, Patricia Higgins, and Ellen Kinnard. "Assessing Narcotic Addiction
    in Neonates." *Pediatric Nursing* 11 (1985): 177-81.
Metzner, Ralph. "Reflections on LSD—Ten Years Later." *Journal of Psychedelic
    Drugs* 10 (1978): 139.
Mikuriya, Tod H. "Historical Aspects of Cannabis Sativa in Western Medicine,"
    New Physician 18 (1969): 905.
Miller, Norman S., Mark S. Gold, and Robert B. Millman. "Cocaine: General
    Characteristics, Abuse, and Addiction." *New York State Journal of Medicine* 89
    (1989): 393.
Mitchell, Bill, and Beryl Rose. "Barbiturate Abuse—A Growing Problem." *Nursing
    Times* 71 (1975): 1489-90.
Mitchell, M., et al. "Ultrasonic Growth Parameters in Fetuses of Mothers with
    Primary Addiction to Cocaine." *American Journal of Obstetrics and Gynecology*
    159 (1988): 1104-9.
Morhous, Eugene J. "Drug Addiction in Upper Economic Levels: A Study of 142
    Cases." *West Virginia Medical Journal* 49 (July 1953): 189-90.
Morley, Jefferson. "The Great American High: Contradictions of Cocaine Capital-
    ism." *The Nation* 249 (1989): 343-44, 346-47.
_____. "What Crack Is Like." *New Republic* 201 (October 2, 1989): 12-13.
Moss, Kay L. "Separated at Birth" [Letter]. *The Nation* 249 (1989): 38.
Muntaner, Carles, et al. "Placebo Responses to Cocaine Administration in Humans:
    Effects of Prior Administrations and Verbal Instructions." *Psychopharmacology*
    99 (1989): 282.
Murphy, Sheigla B., Craig Reinarman, and Dan Waldorf. "An 11-Year Follow-Up of

a Network of Cocaine Users." *British Journal of Addiction* 84 (1989): 427-36.

Murray, John B. "Marijuana's Effects on Human Cognitive Functions, Psychomotor Functions, and Personality." *Journal of General Psychology* 113 (1986): 23-55.

Musto, David F., and Manuel R. Ramos. "A Follow-Up Study of the New Haven Morphine Maintenance Clinic of 1920." *New England Journal of Medicine* 304 (1981): 1075-76.

Nadelmann, Ethan A. "Drug Prohibition in the United States: Costs, Consequences, and Alternatives." *Science* 245 (1989): 941, 943-44.

Naditch, Murray P., and Sheridan Fenwick. "LSD Flashbacks and Ego Functioning." *Journal of Abnormal Psychology* 86 (1977): 352-59.

Nagahama, Masamutsu. "A Review of Drug Abuse and Counter Measures in Japan Since World War II." *Bulletin on Narcotics* 20 (no. 3, 1968): 19-24.

Nakatani, Yoji, et al. "Methamphetamine Psychosis in Japan: A Survey." *British Journal of Addiction* 84 (1989): 1548-49.

Newcomb, Michael D., P. M. Bentler, and Bridget Fahy. "Cocaine Use and Psychopathology. Associations among Young Adults," *International Journal of the Addictions* 22 (1987): 1167.

Newmeyer, John, and Gregory Johnson. "Drug Emergencies in Crowds: An Analysis of 'Rock Medicine,' 1973-1977." *Journal of Drug Issues* 9 (1979): 242.

Nolan, D. W. "The Opium Habit." *Catholic World* 33 (1881): 828, 835.

Nurco, David N., et al. "The Criminality of Narcotic Addicts." *Journal of Nervous and Mental Disease* 173 (1985): 94-102.

O'Brien, C. P. "Experimental Analysis of Conditioning Factors in Human Narcotic Addiction." *Pharmacological Reviews* 27 (1975): 533-43.

Olsen, George D., and Martin H. Lees. "Ventilatory Response to Carbon Dioxide of Infants Following Chronic Prenatal Methadone Exposure." *Journal of Pediatrics* 96 (1980): 983-89.

Onyango, Richard S. "Cannabis Psychosis in Young Psychiatric Inpatients." *British Journal of Addiction* 81 (1986): 419-23.

"The Opium Habit," *Medical and Surgical Reporter* 38 (Jan. 12, 1878): 40.

Oro, A. S., and S. D. Dixon. "Perinatal Cocaine and Methamphetamine Exposure: Maternal and Neonatal Correlates." *Journal of Pediatrics* 111 (1987): 571-78.

Oswald, Ian. "Personal View." *British Medical Journal*, no. 5641 (February 15, 1969): 438.

Oswald, Lynn M. "Cocaine Addiction: The Hidden Dimension." *Archives of Psychiatric Nursing* 3 (1989): 139.

"Our American Letter." *Chemist and Druggist* 77 (Dec. 31, 1910): 44.

Owens, S. Michael, Arthur J. McBay, and Clarence E. Cook. "The Use of Marihuana, Ethanol, and Other Drugs among Drivers Killed in Single-Vehicle Crashes." *Journal of Forensic Sciences* 28 (1983): 372-79.

Page, J. Bryan. "The Amotivational Syndrome Hypothesis and the Costa Rica Study: Relationships between Methods and Results." *Journal of Psychoactive Drugs* 15 (1983): 266.

Pfeffer, A. Z., and Dorothy Cleek Ruble. "Chronic Psychoses and Addiction to Morphine." *Archives of Neurology and Psychiatry* 56 (1946): 665-72.

Phillips, G. T., M. Gossop, and B. Bradley. "The Influence of Psychological Factors on the Opiate Withdrawal Syndrome." *British Journal of Psychiatry* 149 (1986): 235-36.

Pickett, R. D. "Acute Toxicity of Heroin, Alone and in Combination with Cocaine or Quinine." *British Journal of Pharmacology* 40 (1970): 145-46.

Pierce James, I. "The Changing Pattern of Narcotic Addiction in Britain—1959 to 1969." *International Journal of the Addictions* 6 (1971): 119-34.

Pierce James, I., and P. T. d'Orbán. "Patterns of Delnquency Among British Heroin Addicts." *Bulletin on Narcotics* 22 (April-June 1970): 14.

Pierson, Paul S., Patricia Howard, and Herbert D. Kleber. "Sudden Deaths in Infants Born to Methadone-Maintained Addicts." *Journal of the American Medical Association* 220 (1972): 1733-34.

Plant, Martin A. "Young Drug and Alcohol Casualties Compared: Review of 100 Patients at a Scottish Psychiatric Hospital." *British Journal of Addiction* 71 (1976): 31-43.

Pope, Harrison G., Jr., Martin Ionescu-Pioggia, and Jonathan D. Cole. "Drug Use and Life-Style among College Undergraduates: Nine Years Later." *Archives of General Psychiatry* 38 (1981): 588-91.

Post, Robert M. "Drug-Environment Interaction: Context Dependency of Cocaine-Induced Behavioral Sensitization." *Life Sciences* 28 (1981): 755, 758-59.

Post, Robert M., and Richard T. Kopanda. "Cocaine, Kindling, and Psychosis." *American Journal of Psychiatry* 133 (1976): 627-34.

———. "Cocaine, Kindling, and Reverse Tolerance." *Lancet*, no. 7903 (February 15, 1975): 409-10.

Post, Robert M., and Harvey Rose. "Increasing Effects of Repetitive Cocaine Administration in the Rat." *Nature* 260 (1976): 731-32.

Powell, Douglas H. "A Pilot Study of Occasional Heroin Users." *Archives of General Psychiatry* 28 (1973): 586-94.

Quinones, Mark A. "Drug Abuse During the Civil War (1861-1865)." *International Journal of the Addictions* 10 (1975): 1007-20.

Raveis, Victoria H., and Denise B. Kandel. "Changes in Drug Behavior from the Middle to the Late Twenties: Initiation, Persistence, and Cessation of Use." *American Journal of Public Health* 77 (1987): 607-11.

Raymond, Chris. "Researchers Say Debate over Drug War and Legalization Is Tied to Americans' Cultural and Religious Values." *Chronicle of Higher Education* 36 (March 7, 1990): A6-A7, A10-A11.

"Report of Committee on Acquirement of the Drug Habit." *Proceedings of the American Pharmaceutical Association* 50 (1902): 572.

"Report of Committee on the Acquirement of Drug Habits." *Proceedings of the American Pharmaceutical Association* 51 (1903): 472-75.

Robins, Lee N., Darlene H. Davis, and David N. Nurco. "How Permanent Was Vietnam Drug Addiction?" *American Journal of Public Health* 64 (Suppl. 1974): 38-43.

Robins, Lee N., and John E. Helzer. "Drug Use Among Vietnam Veterans: Three

Years Later." *Medical World News* 16 (October 27, 1975): 44-49.

Robins, Lee N., John F. Helzer, and Darlene H. Davis. "Narcotic Use in Southeast Asia and Afterward: An Interview Study of 898 Vietnam Returnees." *Archives of General Psychiatry* 32 (1975): 955-61.

Rounsaville, Bruce J., et al. "Neuropsychological Functioning in Opiate Addicts." *Journal of Nervous and Mental Disease* 170 (1982): 209-16.

Ryan, L., S. Ehrlich, and L. Finnegan. "Cocaine Abuse in Pregnancy: Effects on the Fetus and Newborn." *Neurotoxicology and Teratology* 9 (1987): 295-98.

Sanders, Clinton R. "Doper's Wonderland: Functional Drug Use by Military Personnel in Vietnam." *Journal of Drug Issues* 3 (Winter 1973): 71-72.

Sanders, Marion K. "Addicts and Zealots: The Chaotic War Against Drug Abuse." *Harper's Magazine* 240 (June 1970): 71.

Sapira, Joseph D. "The Narcotic Addict as a Medical Patient." *American Journal of Medicine* 45 (1968): 573-74.

Schacter, Stanley, and Jerome E. Singer. "Cognitive, Social, and Physiological Determinants of Emotional State." *Psychological Review* 69 (1962): 379-99.

Schenk, Susan. "Cocaine Self-Administration in Rats Influenced by Environmental Conditions: Implications for the Etiology of Drug Abuse." *Neuroscience Letters* 81 (1987): 227-31.

Selling, Lowell S. "The Role of Alcoholism in the Commission of Sex Offenses." *Medical Record* 151 (1940): 289-91.

Senay, Edward C. "Methadone: Some Myths and Hypotheses." *Journal of Psychedelic Drugs* 4 (Winter 1971): 184.

Shiffman, Saul. "Tobacco 'Chippers'—Individual Differences in Tobacco Dependence." *Psychopharmacology* 97 (1989): 539-47.

Shupe, Lloyd M. "Alcohol and Crime: A Study of the Urine Alcohol Concentration Found in 882 Persons Arrested During or Immediately After the Commission of a Felony," *Journal of Criminal Law and Criminology* 44 (1954): 661-64.

Sideroff, Stephen I., and Murray E. Jarvik. "Conditioned Responses to a Videotape Showing Heroin-Related Stimuli." *International Journal of the Addictions* 15 (1980): 529-30, 534-35.

Siegel, Ronald K. "Cocaine Smoking." *Journal of Psychoactive Drugs* 14 (1982): 321-22.

Siegel, S., et al. "Heroin 'Overdose' Death: Contribution of Drug-Associated Environmental Cues." *Science* 216 (1982): 436-37.

Simonton, Thomas G. "The Increase of the Use of Cocaine Among the Laity in Pittsburg." *Philadelphia Medical Journal* 11 (1903): 556.

Simpson, D., D. R. Jarvie, and R. Heyworth. "An Evaluation of Six Methods for the Detection of Drugs of Abuse in Urine." *Annals of Clinical Biochemistry* 26 (1989): 172, 177-79.

Smart, Reginald G. " 'Crack' Cocaine Use In Canada: A New Epidemic?" *American Journal of Epidemiology* 127 (1988): 1316-17.

_____. "Effects of Legal Restraints on the Use of Drugs: A Review of Empirical Studies." *Bulletin on Narcotics* 28 (January-March 1976): 55-65.

Smith, David B., and Richard B. Seymour. "Dream Becomes Nightmare: Adverse

Reactions to LSD." *Journal of Psychoactive Drugs* 17 (1985): 300.

Smith, David E. "Cocaine-Alcohol Abuse: Epidemiological, Diagnostic and Treatment Considerations." *Journal of Psychoactive Drugs* 18 (April-June 1986): 117-18.

Smith, Gene M., and Henry K. Beecher. "Subjective Effects of Heroin and Morphine in Normal Subjects." *Journal of Pharmacology and Experimental Therapeutics* 136 (1962): 51-52.

Smith, Gene M., Charles W. Semke, and Henry K. Beecher. "Objective Evidence of Mental Effects of Heroin, Morphine and Placebo in Normal Subjects." *Journal of Pharmacology and Experimental Therapeutics* 136 (1962): 53, 58.

Sohn, David. "Analysis for Drugs of Abuse: The Validity of Reported Results in Relation to Performance Testing." *International Journal of the Addictions* 8 (1973): 69, 72.

Spear, H. B., and M. M. Glatt. "The Influence of Canadian Addicts on Heroin Addiction in the United Kingdom." *British Journal of Addiction* 66 (1971): 141-49.

Stanley, L. L. "Morphinism and Crime." *Journal of the American Institute of Criminal Law and Criminology* 8 (Jan. 1918): 753.

Stanton, M. Duncan, Jim Mintz, and Randall M. Franklin. "Drug Flashbacks. II. Some Additional Findings." *International Journal of the Addictions* 11 (1976): 66.

Stark-Adamec, Cannie, Robert E. Adamec, and R. O. Phil. "Experimenter Effects in Marihuana Research: A Note of Caution." *Psychological Reports* 51 (1982): 203.

Stewart, Jane, Harriet de Wit, and Roelof Eikelboom. "Role of Unconditioned and Conditioned Drug Effects in the Self-Administration of Opiates and Stimulants." *Psychological Review* 91 (1984): 251-68.

Strassman, Rick J. "Adverse Reactions to Psychedelic Drugs: A Review of the Literature." *Journal of Nervous and Mental Disease* 172 (1984): 577-95.

Street, John Phillips. "The Patent Medicine Situation." *American Journal of Public Health* 7 (1917): 1037-42.

Sutton, Lawrence R. "The Effects of Alcohol, Marihuana and Their Combination on Driving Ability." *Journal of Studies on Alcohol* 44 (1983): 438-45.

Sylbing, G., and J.M.G. Persoon. "Cannabis Use Among Youth in the Netherlands." *Bulletin on Narcotics* 37 (no. 4, 1985): 51, 58-59.

Szewczyk, Hans, and Heide-Ulrike Jahnig. "The Problem of Drug Misuse in the German Democratic Republic." *Journal of Drug Issues* 5 (1975): 89-91.

Taylor, W.J.R., C. D. Chambers, and Ch. E. Bowling. "Addiction and the Community (Narcotic Substitution Therapy)." *International Journal of Clinical Pharmacology, Therapy and Toxicology* 6 (1972): 29-38.

Teller, Douglas W., and Paul Devenyi. "Bromocriptine in Cocaine Withdrawal—Does It Work?" *International Journal of the Addictions* 23 (1988): 1197-1205.

Tennant, Forest S., and Jess Groesbeck. "Psychiatric Effects of Hashish." *Archives of General Psychiatry* 27 (1972): 134.

"They All Agree ____% of Viet G.I.s Are Addicts." *Medical World News*, September 3, 1971, pp. 15-17.

Thombs, Dennis L. "A Review of PCP Abuse Trends and Perceptions." *Public Health Reports* 104 (1989): 327.

Timmer, Doug. "The Productivity of Crime in the United States: Drugs and Capital Accumulation." *Journal of Drug Issues* 12 (1982): 383-96.

Tobler, Nancy S. "Meta-Analysis of 143 Adolescent Drug Prevention Programs: Quantitative Outcome Results of Program Participants Compared to a Control or Comparison Group." *Journal of Drug Issues* 16 (1986): 537-67.

Towns, Charles B. "The Injury of Tobacco and Its Relation to Other Drug Habits." *Century* 83 (1912): 770.

_____. "The Peril of the Drug Habit." *Century* 84 (1912): 585.

"*True* Drug Addicts." *Science Digest* 32 (Nov. 1952): 34.

Tu, Tsungming. "Statistical Studies on the Mortality Rates and the Causes of Death among the Opium Addicts in Formosa." *Bulletin on Narcotics* 3 (no. 2, 1951): 9-11.

Twycross, R. G. "Clinical Experience with Diamorphine in Advanced Malignant Disease." *International Journal of Clinical Pharmacology, Therapy and Toxicology* 9 (1974): 184-98.

Ulff-Møller, Boel. "Drug Use among Youth in Denmark in the Spring of 1968. Studies Among School Pupils and Other Young Persons Under Training." *Danish Medical Bulletin* 18 (no. 5, 1971): 105-11.

Ungerleider, J. Thomas, and Therese Andrysiak. "Bias and the Cannabis Researcher." *Journal of Clinical Pharmacology* 21 (1981): 153 S-158 S.

Vaillant, George E. "A 12-Year Follow-Up of New York Narcotic Addicts: III. Some Social and Psychiatric Characteristics." *Archives of General Psychiatry* 15 (1966): 603-8.

_____. "A 12-Year Follow-Up of New York Narcotic Addicts: I. The Relation of Treatment to Outcome." *American Journal of Psychiatry* 122 (1966): 727-36.

Van de Wijngaart, Govert F. "What Lessons from the Dutch Experience Can Be Applied?" *British Journal of Addiction* 84 (1989): 991.

Van Dyke, C., et al. "Cocaine and Lidocaine Have Similar Psychological Effects After Intranasal Application." *Life Sciences* 24 (1979): 271.

Van Dyke, Craig, and Robert Byck. "Cocaine." *Scientific American* 246 (March 1982): 128, 139, 141.

Viani, F., et al. "Drug Abuse in Adolescence: Some Remarks on Individual Psychopathology and Family Structure." *Acta Paedopsychiatrica* 42 (Oct. 1976): 145-51.

Vinar, Oldrich "Dependence on a Placebo. Case Report." *British Journal of Psychiatry* 115 (1969): 1190.

Vogel, Victor H., Harris Isbell, and Kenneth W. Chapman. "Present Status of Narcotic Addiction with Particular Reference to Medical Implications and Comparative Addiction Liability of the Newer and Older Analgesic Drugs."

Journal of the American Medical Association 138 (1948): 1019, 1022.

Waldorf, Dan, and Patrick Biernacki. "Natural Recovery from Heroin Addiction: A Review of the Incident Literature." *Journal of Drug Issues* 9 (1979): 281-82, 285-86.

Wallace, George B. "The Rehabilitation of the Drug Addict." *Journal of Educational Sociology* 4 (1931): 347.

Weil, Andrew T., Norman E. Zinberg, and Judith M. Nelsen. "Clinical and Psychological Effects of Marihuana in Man." *Science* 162 (1968): 1234-42.

Wert, Renee C., and Michael L. Raulin. "The Chronic Cerebral Effects of Cannabis Use. I. Methodological Issues and Neurological Findings." *International Journal of the Addictions* 21 (1986): 605-28.

––––––. "The Chronic Cerebral Effects of Cannabis Use. II. Psychological Findings and Conclusions." *International Journal of the Addictions* 21 (1986): 629-42.

Whalen, Robert P., and John J. A. Lyons., "Medical Problems of 500 Prisoners on Admission to a County Jail." *Public Health Reports* 77 (1962): 497-502.

Wholey, C. C. "Psychopathologic Phases Observable in Individuals Using Narcotic Drugs in Excess." *Pennsylvania Medical Journal* 16 (1913): 723-24.

Wilner, Daniel M., et al. "Heroin Use and Street Gangs." *Journal of Criminal Law, Criminology, and Police Science* 48 (1957): 401.

Winick, Charles. "Narcotics Addiction and Its Treatment." *Law and Contemporary Problems* 22 (1957): 13.

Winsløw, Jens J. B. "Drug Use and Social Integration." *International Journal of the Addictions* 9 (1974): 531-40.

Wolff, Gustave. "The Necessity of Legislation to Control the Sale of Narcotics." *Proceedings of the American Pharmaceutical Association* 51 (1903): 521-22.

Yager, Joel, Evelyn Crumpton, and Ralph Rubenstein. "Flashbacks among Soldiers Discharged as Unfit Who Abused More Than One Drug." *American Journal of Psychiatry* 140 (1983): 860.

Yanagita, T. "An Experimental Framework for Evaluation of Dependence Liability of Various Types of Drugs in Monkeys." *Bulletin on Narcotics* 25 (no. 4, 1973): 57-64.

Younger, Irving. "The Perjury Routine." *The Nation* 204 (May 8, 1967), 596-97.

Zacune, J. "A Comparison of Canadian Narcotic Addicts in Great Britain and Canada." *Bulletin On Narcotics* 23 (October-December 1971): 43-44, 46-47.

Zacune, J., Martin Mitcheson, and Sarah Malone. "Heroin Use in a Provincial Town—One Year Later." *International Journal of the Addictions* 4 (1969): 557-70.

Zelson, Carl, Sook Ja Lee, and Marie Casalino. "Neonatal Narcotic Addiction: Comparative Effects of Maternal Intake of Heroin and Methadone." *New England Journal of Medicine* 289 (1973): 1216-20.

Zerbetto, Riccardo. "An Overview on Drug Abuse in Italy." *Addictive Diseases* 3 (1977): 43-50.

Zinberg, Norman E., Wayne M. Harding, and Robert Apsler. "What is Drug Abuse?" *Journal of Drug Issues* 8 (1978): 9-35.

Zinberg, Norman E., and Richard C. Jacobson. "The Natural History of 'Chipping.' "
    American Journal of Psychiatry 133 (1976): 37-40.
Zinberg, Norman E., and D. C. Lewis. "Narcotic Usage: I. A Spectrum of a Difficult
    Medical Problem." *New England Journal of Medicine* 270 (1964): 989-93.
Zinberg, Norman E., and Andrew T. Weil. "A Comparison of Marijuana Users and
    Non-Users." *Nature* 226 (1970): 122.

ELECTRONIC MEDIA

Frontline. No. 706. "Who Profits from Drugs?" Produced by WGBH, Boston.
    Telecast on Public Broadcasting Service, February 21, 1989. Transcript and
    video recording.

Index

ABOUT THE AUTHOR

RICHARD LAWRENCE MILLER was trained as a broadcaster and historian, and resides in Kansas City, Missouri. Personal involvement in politics helped provide the richness of detail in Miller's book *Truman: The Rise to Power*. In *Heritage of Fear: Illusion and Reality in the Cold War* Miller established themes that he would draw upon while analyzing the drug war, particularly the importance of democracy as a tool to solve problems. Miller now brings together his mass communication talent, his scholarly discipline, and his Midwestern political savvy in *The Case for Legalizing Drugs*, continuing the celebration of democracy begun in his earlier works.